VOLUME 590

NOVEMBER 2003

THE ANNALS

of The American Academy of Political
and Social Science

ROBERT W. PEARSON, *Executive Editor*
ALAN W. HESTON, *Editor*

Rethinking Sustainable Development

Special Editor of this Volume

JUDE L. FERNANDO
University of Arizona

SAGE Publications Ⓢ Thousand Oaks · London · New Delhi

Origin and Purpose. The Academy was organized December 14, 1889, to promote the progress of political and social science, especially through publications and meetings. The Academy does not take sides in controverted questions, but seeks to gather and present reliable information to assist the public in forming an intelligent and accurate judgment.

Meetings. The Academy occasionally holds a meeting in the spring extending over two days.

Publications. THE ANNALS of The American Academy of Political and Social Science is the bimonthly publication of the Academy. Each issue contains articles on some prominent social or political problem, written at the invitation of the editors. Also, monographs are published from time to time, numbers of which are distributed to pertinent professional organizations. These volumes constitute important reference works on the topics with which they deal, and they are extensively cited by authorities throughout the United States and abroad. The papers presented at the meetings of the Academy are included in THE ANNALS.

Membership. Each member of the Academy receives THE ANNALS and may attend the meetings of the Academy. Membership is open only to individuals. Annual dues: $71.00 for the regular paperbound edition (clothbound, $108.00). For members outside the U.S.A., add $24.00 for shipping of your subscription. Members may also purchase single issues of THE ANNALS for $21.00 each (clothbound, $29.00). Student memberships are available for $49.00.

Subscriptions. THE ANNALS of The American Academy of Political and Social Science (ISSN 0002-7162) (J295) is published six times annually—in January, March, May, July, September, and November— by Sage Publications, 2455 Teller Road, Thousand Oaks, CA 91320. Telephone: (800) 818-SAGE (7243) and (805) 499-9774; FAX/Order line: (805) 499-0871. Copyright © 2003 by The American Academy of Political and Social Science. Institutions may subscribe to THE ANNALS at the annual rate: $454.00 (clothbound, $513.00). Add $24.00 per year for subscriptions outside the U.S.A. Institutional rates for single issues: $88.00 each (clothbound, $98.00).

Periodicals postage paid at Thousand Oaks, California, and at additional mailing offices.

Single issues of THE ANNALS may be obtained by individuals who are not members of the Academy for $33.00 each (clothbound, $46.00). Single issues of THE ANNALS have proven to be excellent supplementary texts for classroom use. Direct inquiries regarding adoptions to THE ANNALS c/o Sage Publications (address below).

All correspondence concerning membership in the Academy, dues renewals, inquiries about membership status, and/or purchase of single issues of THE ANNALS should be sent to THE ANNALS c/o Sage Publications, 2455 Teller Road, Thousand Oaks, CA 91320. Telephone: (800) 818-SAGE (7243) and (805) 499-9774; FAX/Order line: (805) 499-0871. *Please note that orders under $30 must be prepaid.* Sage affiliates in London and India will assist institutional subscribers abroad with regard to orders, claims, and inquiries for both subscriptions and single issues.

Printed on recycled, acid-free paper

THE ANNALS

Editorial Office: 3814 Walnut Street, Fels Institute for Government, University of Pennsylvania, Philadelphia, PA 19104-6197.

For information about membership° (individuals only) and subscriptions (institutions), address:
Sage Publications
2455 Teller Road
Thousand Oaks, CA 91320

Sage Production Staff: Scott F. Locklear, Matthew Adams, and Paul Doebler

From India and South Asia,
write to:
SAGE PUBLICATIONS INDIA Pvt Ltd
B-42 Panchsheel Enclave, P.O. Box 4109
New Delhi 110 017
INDIA

From Europe, the Middle East,
and Africa, write to:
SAGE PUBLICATIONS LTD
6 Bonhill Street
London EC2A 4PU
UNITED KINGDOM

°Please note that members of the Academy receive THE ANNALS with their membership.
International Standard Serial Number ISSN 0002-7162
International Standard Book Number ISBN 0-7619-2859-6 (Vol. 590, 2003 paper)
International Standard Book Number ISBN 0-7619-2860-X (Vol. 590, 2003 cloth)
Manufactured in the United States of America. First printing, November 2003.

The articles appearing in *The Annals* are abstracted or indexed in Academic Abstracts, Academic Search, America: History and Life, Asia Pacific Database, Book Review Index, CAB Abstracts Database, Central Asia: Abstracts & Index, Communication Abstracts, Corporate ResourceNET, Criminal Justice Abstracts, Current Citations Express, Current Contents: Social & Behavioral Sciences, e-JEL, EconLit, Expanded Academic Index, Guide to Social Science & Religion in Periodical Literature, Health Business FullTEXT, HealthSTAR FullTEXT, Historical Abstracts, International Bibliography of the Social Sciences, International Political Science Abstracts, ISI Basic Social Sciences Index, Journal of Economic Literature on CD, LEXIS-NEXIS, MasterFILE FullTEXT, Middle East: Abstracts & Index, North Africa: Abstracts & Index, PAIS International, Periodical Abstracts, Political Science Abstracts, Psychological Abstracts, PsycINFO, Sage Public Administration Abstracts, Social Science Source, Social Sciences Citation Index, Social Sciences Index Full Text, Social Services Abstracts, Social Work Abstracts, Sociological Abstracts, Southeast Asia: Abstracts & Index, Standard Periodical Directory (SPD), TOPICsearch, Wilson OmniFile V, and Wilson Social Sciences Index/Abstracts, and are available on microfilm from University Microfilms, Ann Arbor, Michigan.

Information about membership rates, institutional subscriptions, and back issue prices may be found on the facing page.

Advertising. Current rates and specifications may be obtained by writing to *The Annals* Advertising and Promotion Manager at the Thousand Oaks office (address above).

Claims. Claims for undelivered copies must be made no later than six months following month of publication. The publisher will supply missing copies when losses have been sustained in transit and when the reserve stock will permit.

Change of Address. Six weeks' advance notice must be given when notifying of change of address to ensure proper identification. Please specify name of journal. POSTMASTER: Send address changes to: *The Annals* of The American Academy of Political and Social Science, c/o Sage Publications, 2455 Teller Road, Thousand Oaks, CA 91320.

THE ANNALS

OF THE AMERICAN ACADEMY OF POLITICAL AND SOCIAL SCIENCE

Volume 590 November 2003

IN THIS ISSUE:

Rethinking Sustainable Development

Special Editors: JUDE L. FERNANDO

FORTHCOMING

Hope, Power, and Governance
Special Editor: VALERIE BRAITHWAITE
Volume 591, January 2004

Positive Youth Development
Special Editor: CHRISTOPHER PETERSON
Volume 592, March 2004

To Better Serve and Protect: Improving Police Practices
Special Editor: WESLEY G. SKOGAN
Volume 593, May 2004

Fieldwork Encounters and Ethnographic Discoveries
Special Editor: ELIJAH ANDERSON
Volume 594, July 2004

PREFACE

The Power of Unsustainable Development: What Is to Be Done?

By
JUDE L. FERNANDO

Regardless of the state of theory and practice in sustainable development, there is no doubt that an ethical/moral imperative exists to address socioeconomic inequality and degradation of the environment. To realize the goals of sustainable development, it must be liberated from its embeddedness in the ideology and institutional parameters of capitalism. This calls for a departure from the current reformist character of development theory and the practice and articulation of an alternative vision of political economy, as well as a politically strong commitment to realizing it. This endeavor should be global in scope: not in an attempt to create a homogeneous world order but rather to prevent social diversity from being reconfigured and disciplined according to the imperatives of capital. The state must play a pivotal role if social transformative efforts are to bear fruit and break through the impasse capitalism has imposed on realizing the goals of sustainable development.

Keywords: sustainable development; postdevelopmentalism; nongovernmental organizations; social justice

Sustainable, ecologically sound capitalist development is a contradiction in terms.
—David Pepper (quoted in Adams 1990, 139)

Capitalism triumphs when it becomes identified with the state, when it is the state.
—Fernando Braudel

Jude L. Fernando teaches political economy and sustainable development at the Department of Geography and Regional Development and the International College of the University of Arizona. His research focus is economic development and political economy, with a special emphasis on nonprofit organizations, environment, race, gender, and child labor, particularly in South Asia. He is currently completing a book titled Political Economy of NGOs: Modernizing Post-Modernity *(Pluto Press). He is also working on an edited volume on microcredit with Katherine Rankin to be published by Routledge.*

NOTE: This article is a result of a conference sponsored by the National Oceanic and Atmospheric Administration at the Office of Sustainable Development and Intergovernmental Affairs, U.S. Department of Commerce.

DOI: 10.1177/0002716203258283

Historically, development has shown a remarkable capacity to reinvent itself in response to challenges. These reinventions have led to significant shifts in the theory and practice of development, of which sustainable development is an important example. Although concern for sustainability entered the discourse of development in the early 1970s, the idea's official origins stem from Agenda 21, following the 1992 United Nations Conferences on Environment and Development in Rio De Janeiro, Brazil. Since then, the meaning of the term *sustainable development* has become broader and more integrative (see http://www.un.org/esa/sustdev.agenda21text.htm). It is concerned not only with environmental protection but also extends to social objectives such as equity, human rights, and social justice (Drummond and Marsden 1999, 19; Middleton and O'Keefe 2001; Haughton 1999). If one were to provide a generic definition, sustainable development can be said to be meeting the necessity of ensuring "a better quality of life for all, now, and into the future, in a just and equitable manner, while living within the limits of supporting ecosystems" (Agyeman, Bullard, and Evans 2002a, 2).

For many, sustainable development indicates a radical paradigm shift in development discourse and practice. The outcomes of existing practices of sustainable development and their future prospects, however, are disappointing. The very concept of sustainable development has become increasingly ambiguous and open to a wide range of interpretations and appropriations by a variety of interest groups. Now, there is growing concern as to whether sustainable development has reached an impasse both in theory and in practice. "Many analysts have come to regard it as an insubstantial and clichéd platitude unworthy of further interests or research, and perhaps even more significantly, theorizing of the idea seems to have reached something of an impasse" (Agyeman, Bullard, and Evans 2002a, 27). For O'Riordan (1987), sustainable development is an "inoperable concept" (p. 5)

Despite its failures, sustainable development is not a concept one can easily dismiss. At least, one cannot ignore its claims or the theoretical and methodological challenges it presents. To reject the concept is to tacitly accept unsustainability and is an admission of our failure to "address the key conceptual and methodological challenges which [sustainable development] presents" (Drummond and Marsden 1999, 2). It is crucial to understand the conditions and processes that produce unsustainable development—particularly how efforts toward sustainable development result in unsustainable outcomes. Today's challenge is to rethink current theory and practice in sustainable development, to claim a powerful political space for sustainable development so that it will be a realizable goal. Sustainable development has great potential as a "positive myth which [can] . . . bring together diverse and often competing causes" (Murphy and Bendell 1997, 2) capable of guiding the way to a sustainable relationship between humanity and the environment.

To claim a new and more powerful political space for sustainable development, it is necessary to provide a unified explanation for its current impasse both in practice and in theory. One strong unifying element may be found in terms of analyzing the practice of sustainable development within the context of capitalist development worldwide. This is not a random choice. More than ever, the social, political, and economic spheres of modern society are interconnected and interdependent through the mediation of capitalist forces and relations of production—no matter what claims are made to the contrary. Put somewhat differently, capitalism, as a unifying force, does not mean a disregard for diversity in social organization but "universal efforts" in configuring and disciplining diversity according to capital's own self-centered imperatives.

On one hand, as Timothy O'Riordan (1987) has noted, sustainable development will prove to be an "inoperable concept" because

> the contemporary world [is] dominated by the influence of capitalist forms on the alienation of humanity from the natural world. . . . It draws more from the environment than it returns yet does not pay for the loss of that environmental capital. (P. 13; Drummond and Marsden 1999, 18)

Consequently, "natural resources are systematically depleted in the accumulation drive by both private and multinational capital and the state. Ecological degradation in the South assumes emergency proportions through the mindless commitment to the economic growth strategy endemic to developed capitalism" (Redclift 1987, as quoted in Drummond and Marsden 1999, 18). On the other hand, currently, there exists no politically powerful alternative to capitalism. While capitalism may underpin the problems of sustainable development, as Dickens (1992, 7) noted, "the idea that the solution to these problems lie in the overthrow of capitalism, is outmoded" (see also Drummond and Marsden 1999, 18). The examples of sustainable development practices that directly contradict the interests of capitalism are rare, and the existing radical approaches "have hardly gained any political credibility, real scientific development, or for that matter widespread public support" (Drummond and Marsden 1999, 19).

The hegemony of capitalism has indeed provided many fruitful opportunities to rethink sustainable development. This is because the irreconcilable tension between the sustainability of capitalism and sustainable development has become far more visible than at any other time in its history. Hence, the need to engage directly with the capitalist forces and relations of production has become unavoidable as a fundamental prerequisite for the realization of sustainable development. Moreover, we also have a wealth of knowledge about the unsustainable development results from the former centrally planned socialist economies.

The following introduction is an attempt to create a broad-based awareness about the multifaceted issues and concerns faced by sustainable development both in theory and in practice. It attempts to bring together these challenges in such a way as to produce a coherent framework. It is hoped that this will, in turn, facilitate a comprehensive political program aimed at realizing the goals of sustainable development.

Prosperity, Poverty, and Insecurity

World population numbered 6.3 billion in the year 2000. Currently, it is growing at the rate of 77 million people per year. At the present rate, by 2050, total world population will be nearly 8.9 billion. The impact of this growth will be mainly concentrated in less developed countries that are least able to absorb large increases in population.

The world's urban population has grown from 30 percent in 1950 to an estimated 47 percent in 2000, and by the year 2050, it is likely to increase to around 53 percent. Large movements of people from rural to urban areas continue in most developing countries today, and large numbers of the urban poor live in slums and unplanned settlements (United Nations Development Program 1991, 26).

Presently, nearly 40 percent of the people in developing countries have an adult life expectancy of forty years (United Nations Development Program 1991, 26). In 2002, an estimated 800 million people were undernourished due to poverty, political instability, economic inefficiency, and social inequity. More than 1.3 billion live on less than U.S.$1 a day. Two billion more people in the world are only marginally better off. During the past decade—one that was theoretically committed to poverty reduction—the number of people living under conditions of actual poverty increased by 100 million. This occurred at a time when the world's income increased by an average of 2.5 percent annually. Forty percent of all Africans live below the poverty line. Women account for 70 percent of the world's poor, despite the fact that women grow 90 percent of the food for home consumption in developing countries.

Differences in income in the developed industrial countries increased greatly between the mid-1970s and the mid-1990s. The poorest 30 percent of the population in the countries examined received only 5 percent to 13 percent of the national income. Every fifth inhabitant of Germany (19.9 percent), every fourth U.S. citizen (25 percent), and more than a third of all British citizens (38.4 percent) experienced poverty at one time or another in the six-year control period.

The *United Nations Development Report* (United Nations Development Program 1991) noted that between 1960 and 1991, the richest 20 percent of the world population's share of the world income increased from 70 percent to 85 percent, while that of the poorest 80 percent declined from 2.3 percent to 1.4 percent. By 1991, more than 85 percent of the world's population received only 15 percent of the world's income, and the net incomes of the richest 358 people were equal to that of 40 percent of the world's population—or 2.3 billion people worldwide. Bill Gates's income alone is more than the aggregate income of 40 percent of Americans.

Contrary to claims that have been made about the end of labor or the end of the proletariat, the number of laborers worldwide has doubled since 1966 to 2.5 billion. According to the International Labor Organization, world unemployment in the year 2000 reached 180 million. After the telecommunication industry bubble burst, unemployment worldwide increased steeply, bringing it to the highest level ever recorded in the post–cold war period. Employment security in terms of contract duration, real wage increases, and compensation has seen a rapid decline and faces an uncertain future due to rapid withdrawal of the state from providing employment security and social welfare.

In 1980, nearly 70 percent of the world's labor force was sheltered from international competition by trade barriers, capital controls, and planned trade. By the year 2005, less than 10 percent of workers will be insulated from adverse changes in the world market. Despite the fact that women's participation in the workforce has increased from 33 percent in 1960 to 54 percent in 1999, working women are still concentrated in the informal sector, where work conditions are far more precarious than for most men. The worldwide assault on social security and safety networks, driven primarily by privatization policies, has created an environment in which millions of working people have no prospect of receiving support when they retire. For example, less than 15 percent of the world's population older than sixty-five years of age now receives any retirement income, according to *New Ideas about Old Age Security*, a book published recently by the World Bank (Stiglitz and Holzmann 2001).

According to the International Confederation of Free Trade Union (2001) annual survey of trade and union rights, during the 1990s labor unrest around the world increased to its highest levels since the end of the cold war. Unrest centered on protests over layoffs, austerity measures, and economic crises. In response, state-sponsored suppression of labor is on the rise. The report noted,

> 209 trade unionists killed or "disappeared," 50 percent more than last year's figure, about 8,500 arrested, 3,000 more injured, over 100,000 harassed and nearly 20,000 dismissed because of their trade union activities. . . . In 2000 trade unionists paid a heavy price for their commitment. But these figures are just the tip of the iceberg.

Contrary to the claims about the end of labor/end of the proletariat, labor once again is emerging as an important challenge to capital.

Despite a tremendous increase in production and improvements in transportation and storage facilities, the number of people facing crises of food security increased from 896 million in 2001 to 1 billion in 2002. In 1999, developing countries consumed less than they did ten years before while increasing their agricultural exports to developed countries. Even in the United States, 34 million people lack food security, and 12 million children live in households (7.4 percent of total households) in which people skip meals to make ends meet. One out of ten households lives with hunger or the risk of hunger. In many less developed countries, trade-induced crises of subsistence are a growing phenomenon. More food does not necessarily translate into less hunger.

Global poverty is mostly concentrated among children and women. Today, 800 million children live in poverty and suffer from chronic hunger. Five percent of 12 million child deaths are due to malnourishment. Worldwide, 11 million children die each year from diseases such as diarrhea, polio, measles, and tetanus, which are all preventable given clean water to drink, a proper diet, shelter, and immunizations. In many developed countries, up to 15 percent of children die before their fifth birthdays. This means that the world can expect that at least one in ten children will die in their early years.

In the United States, 25 percent of children live in poverty—that is one out of every four children. This number is double that of any other advanced capitalist economy, except one, Britain. In terms of poverty among the elderly, the rate in the United States is 20 percent, but in Britain it is even higher. In England, 24 percent of old people now live in poverty.

Women and children also are exposed to the highest risks from the environmental hazards of industrial production. In the United States, about 1.6 million women of childbearing age eat amounts of mercury-contaminated fish sufficient to risk damaging the brain development of their children. One million children in the United States have dangerously high levels of lead in their blood.

If current trends continue, by 2015 there will be 46 million children between the ages of six and eleven not attending school in the less developed countries—nearly 7 million more than today. They are, overwhelmingly, working children; children affected by disability, HIV/AIDS, or war; children from poor families or ethnic minorities; or children living in rural and remote areas. The plight of the children is perhaps the most disturbing outcome of the exploitation of the environment without considering the needs of the future.

Twenty percent of the world's population—mostly in developed countries—receives 85 percent of the world's income and accounts for 80 percent of consumption, producing two-thirds of all greenhouse gases and 90 percent of ozone-depleting chlorofluorocarbons. If the current global population lived at the same consumption level as the richest 20 percent, consumption of energy would increase ten times and minerals two hundred times. Despite population growth, per capita energy consumption in developing countries is still only one-quarter of that in the Organization for Economic Cooperation and Development countries. The 2 billion rural people who have no access to modern energy services currently use as little as one-twentieth of the energy consumed by even the poorest in industrialized countries.

Increased levels of consumption within both developed and developing countries are associated with increasing indebtedness worldwide. The ratio of consumer debt as a percentage of disposable income increased from 68 percent in 1980 to 97 percent in 1999 to 100 percent in 2000, which *Forbes Magazine* (6 March 2000) referred to as "unprecedented burden." The debt burden of families in the Third World—the ratio of total family debt service payments to total family income—increased from 12.7 percent in 1989 to 14.5 percent in 1998. Debt burden was the highest among those families earning less than $10,000 per year, and the next highest debt burden was those families earning between $25,000 and $49,999 per year. Personal bankruptcies increased from 330,000 in 1980 to 1.4 million in 1999 in the United States. The ever-increasing threat of bankruptcy prompted Congress to push for dramatic bankruptcy reforms, which according to the *Washington Post* (18 February 2000) was "clamping down on (bankruptcy) shelters that matter to poor debtors."

As of the year 2000, developing countries owed $2.5 trillion or 40 percent of their national incomes to the rest of the world. Emerging markets in eastern Europe and forty-two of the heavily indebted countries collectively owed only $175 billion. In 1999, poor countries paid a total of $382 billion to their creditors—more than $1 billion each day. In 1999, heavily indebted countries spent $8.9 billion in servicing debts. In some poorer countries in Africa, debt payments ran up to 90 percent of their export revenues. The amount of this transfer is more than thirteen times the amount of funds transferred from developed countries to developing countries.

Borrowing by rich countries far exceeds borrowing by poor countries. The increase in imports in the United States is not met by increases in exports but by running a trade deficit of around $450 billion a year. As a result, each American owes $7,333—compared to $500 for each citizen in developing countries. Although the United States is the largest debtor in the world, it is less affected by the full implications of the debt crisis because of the dollar's role as a global reserve currency. This means that the United States can fix the interest rates on its own borrowing. Through various means, developing countries are persuaded to lend to the United States because these countries hold dollar reserves in the form of U.S. treasury bills. Consequently, the United States pays only $20 billion per year for servicing its $2.2 trillion debt.

The hope of decline in military spending and overall decline in defense industries in the aftermath of the cold war was short lived. Military expenditure in the United States is on the rise, particularly since September 11, 2001. Defense contractors have repositioned themselves as an important sector of the economy in terms of government spending, national income, and employment. In 2002, military spending worldwide grew to $900 billion (782 billion euros). The average global expenditure on defense was 2.6 percent of world GDP and $137 per capita.

The U.S. military budget request for fiscal year 2000 was $343.2 billion, as compared to $288.8 billion in 2001, and accounts for 48 percent of total world military expenditure. Between 1999 and 2000, military expenditure in the United States increased by $6 billion. The fifteen major spenders accounted for more than three-quarters of world military spending. Five countries account for more than half. The United States alone accounts for 36 percent, followed by Russia with 6 percent and France, Japan, and the United Kingdom with about 5 percent each. The sixty-three countries in Africa and Latin America together accounted for 5 percent of world military spending in 2001. High-income countries also have the highest per capita military spending. Countries with the highest defense burden, as measured by the share of military expenditure as a percentage of GDP, are located in the Middle East and Africa.

Military expenditure in the Middle East, East Asia, South America, and Africa grew throughout the late 1990s. Between 1998 and 2001, these regions showed a more than 25 percent growth in military spending in real terms. The steepest rise in military expenditure was in Asia, Africa, and the Middle East. Collectively, in real terms, the increase is about 35 percent (Stockholm International Peace Research Institute 2001).

Competition between major defense producers has intensified since the end of the cold war, and production is significantly concentrated. In 2002, of the eleven largest defense companies, seven are owned by the United States, two are French, one is German, and one is British. In terms of revenue, among the American firms, Lockheed Martin increased from $15.7 billion in 1994 to $18.6 billion in 2000, Boeing from $4.7 billion in 1994 to $16.9 billion in 2000, Raytheon from $4.1 billion in 1994 to $10.1 billion in 2000, and Northrop from $6.4 billion in 1994 to $6.7 billion in 2000. In the United Kingdom, BAE Systems increased sales from $8.2 billion in 1994 to $14.4 billion in 2000. Thales of France increased its revenue from $4.1 billion in 1994 to $5.6 billion in 2000, while the Franco-German-Spanish firm EADS had revenues of $5.8 billion in 2000 (Stockholm International Peace Research Institute 2001).

[T]he current imprisonment of the discourse of sustainable development within the parameters of capitalist development is not a sufficient reason to be pessimistic about the future.

The world's poorest countries have been increasing their military spending at a rate far exceeding their spending on social development. For example, globally, Pakistan is ranked 6th in terms of the size of its armed forces. It ranks 26th in arms imports as a percentage of total imports, 127th in national literacy, and 95th in the percentage of its population with access to safe drinking water. The cost of servicing its military debt is $600 million per year, and it spends 15 percent of its export earnings for military purposes and debt servicing.

In the period from 1999 to 2000, fifty-six major conflicts took place in forty-four different locations. All but three conflicts were internal to the nation-states involved. Of the fourteen intrastate conflicts examined, ten spilled over to the neighboring states and involved the international community. These conflicts generated more than 3 million refugees and rendered many states politically and economically unstable. The issue of global security was further complicated by transnational terrorism after September 11, 2001. While the economic and social costs of terrorism and counterterrorism are a global concern, they fall disproportionately on the poor. Pakistan's expenditure for secret services is Rs 4 billion. The opportunity cost of a single Mirage 2000 fighter jet is equal to 8 million new primary schools and the annual cost of maintaining 30 million primary schools with three teachers per school. The opportunity cost of a tank equals the cost of immunizing 4 million children (Kardar 1999).

All these trends point to a growing worldwide sense of insecurity, fear, and instability arising from multiple socioeconomic and political sources. The issues surrounding the possibility of a sustainable alternative have become ever more complex, underlining an urgent need for serious rethinking of the current discourse on sustainable development. This rethinking is further complicated by the fact that we need to pursue it within the context of a rapidly globalizing capitalist economy. Despite the growing realization of these challenges, however, most current efforts in this regard continue to be reformist. Even those efforts touted as "radical" have often become counterproductive to realizing the goals of genuinely sustainable development. Nonetheless, the current imprisonment of the discourse of sustainable development within the parameters of capitalist development is not a sufficient reason to be pessimistic about the future.

To fall victim to such pessimism would be to subscribe to a vulgar materialist doctrine that was condemned even by Marx (1965): "If man is a product of material conditions, he can never emancipate from their impact. If the world is not of man's making, how can he change it?" (p. 58).

There are, for example, instances of what Bebbington (1997) has called "islands of sustainability" around the world where there are counterhegemonic intellectual and material practices closer to the ideal goals of sustainable development. To deny this would be to grossly misunderstand the reality of a capitalist system that is riddled with internal contradictions and constantly faced with challenges for its sustainability. Bebbington's examples illustrate the efforts by indigenous communities to "negotiate and influence dominant institutions" that marginalize them. Their efforts are helpful at least in terms of visualizing, implementing, and maintaining a social context within which the goals of sustainable development might be pursued.

Several limitations of the idea of islands of sustainability should be noted, however. First, they appear to be sustained by the very forces that are responsible for unsustainable development in a more global context. Bebbington (1997) argued, "What has made these cases [islands of sustainability] possible is market demand" (p. 195). In typical neoclassical economic fashion, he took market demand as given and did not engage with the political economy of market demand in its broader implications. In other words, Bebbington's notion of "islands" of sustainable development is predicated on artificially carving out a territorial space based on certain productive practices outside of the larger context of global political economy. Second, there is the problem of broad-based replicability of these localized practices. Third, there has been little work done either to find synergy between these scattered efforts or to find ways of establishing an institutional environment within which they might be sustained and replicated in a broader context. The following discussion presents one way to learn from such diverse islands of sustainability and islands of unsustainability, particularly in terms of their relationship to the larger capitalist economy, which simultaneously constrains and provides new opportunities for the world community to pursue sustainable development.

Disciplining Diversity

The idea of sustainability entered the discourse of development at the same time as what is known as the "postdevelopmentalist" turn in thinking on development generally. The rejection of the mainstream paradigm of development is rooted in a rejection of the Western project of modernity, which "has sought to subordinate, contain and assimilate the Third World as Other" (Slater 1993, 421) and, in the process, colonize the world with the Western dream of progress. As Arturo Escobar (a leading proponent of the postdevelopment school) has said, the reality of the Third World has been colonized by the discourse on development, and there is a need to construct a different reality (Escobar 1994; Esteva and Prakash 1998). Escobar argued that the discursive power of development is such that its opponents are forced to phrase their critiques in the very language that they oppose: another development, self-reliant development, participatory development, and so on. Sympathizers of this perspective make a persuasive argument for the abandonment of a universal paradigm for development and for the need to develop diverse, culturally sensitive paradigms of development.

This emphasis on diversity as opposed to universality was an important influence of the postdevelopmentalist school on the theory and practice of sustainable development. But many questions have come up, particularly in the present context, in which the diversity of sustainable development practices confronts the worldwide colonizing effect of capitalist accumulation. Does diversity mean that one cannot talk about sustainable development as a coherent phenomenon? If one simply celebrates and promotes diversity, how far can one progress in realizing the universal and relative goals of sustainable development? How is it possible to effectively use the diversity of social systems in sustainable development in the face of the increasing globalization of capital?

Several weaknesses of the postdevelopmentalist turn in development theory should be noted here. First, it has contributed toward much ambiguity in both the theory and practice of development. In fact, ambiguity is one of the defining characteristics of poststructuralism that provides an ideological basis for postdevelopmentalism. This is precisely where the main limitation of postdevelopmentalism lies. For Terry Eagleton (1992), this was an ethics issue, "more precisely, an embarrassment with political ethics," because

> equivocation and ambiguity are not always moral virtues; and there seems to be no doubt that such fine-spun obliquity on issues of central political importance has done much to disillusion those erstwhile enthusiasts for deconstruction who somewhat gullibly credited its promissory note to deliver some political goods. In its finely drawn distaste for categories, deconstruction is merely the mirror image of the banal liberal humanism it seeks to subvert. (P. 125)

The issue of ambiguity is further compounded by the postdevelopmentalist emphasis on relativism. This is once again an issue of ethics and morality, as it makes it difficult to assign any responsibility for (un)sustainable development to anybody in a meaningful way. It also contributes, in the name of cultural relativism, to shielding and legitimizing the actions of those who violate basic human rights. It provides much comfort for the academic and practitioner alike to be able to talk about radical sustainable development but not to have to take a clear position on it based on a set of values or to have to worry about the consistency (or lack thereof) between their work and their personal lifestyles. I am referring specifically here to highly paid "radical activist"–type academics, development practitioners, and consultants, particularly those who are financially thriving on the post–development/ cultural turn in the social sciences. Their type of activism is what Eagleton (1992) referred to as "commercial humanism." Quite simply, it is about the commodification of development, period.

The problem with such "bourgeois radicals" is that their scholarly and activist interventions in sustainable development are rooted in the very modernist ideology of progress they condemn. Their efforts are often limited to inventing a new language that does not present any significant challenge to the status quo they seek to transform and instead provides the social capital necessary for its popular legitimacy and political stability. Part of the reason for this, I believe, is the unwillingness among these academics to take risks and become unpopular by disturbing the status quo. We need to remind ourselves that "the truth that neither liberals nor post-structuralists seem able to countenance is that there are certain key political struggles that someone is going to have to win and someone will have to lose" (Eagleton 1992, 124).

Diversity in social practices is not a novel idea invented by the postdevelopmentalists. Examination of society from any one particular perspective will reveal diversity in terms of ways of life, standards of living, patterns of resource use, relations with the ecosystem, and social, political, and cultural forms. At the same time, diversity is not always a natural condition whose meaning is fixed in time and place. Instead, it is produced through a complex web of institutional relations operating interactively in local, national, and international domains. Hence, diversity ought to be understood in relational terms. This is especially unavoidable in the present context, in which the determinants and coordinates of diversity of social relations worldwide are increasingly determined by the global expansion of capitalist accumulation. This makes it inevitable that we think about sustainable development in terms of a universal project of social change under the conditions of capitalist accumulation. According to Georg Lukacs (1971),

> the category of totality does not to reduce its various elements to an undifferentiated uniformity, to identity. The apparent independence and autonomy which they posses in the capitalist system of production is an illusion only in so far as they are involved in a dynamic dialectical relationship with one another and can be thought of as the dynamic dialectical aspects of an equally dynamic and dialectical whole. (P. 13)

In real life, the reasoning behind this relational approach to totality makes sense, not because

> production, distribution, exchange and consumption are identical, but they are all members of one totality, different aspects of a unit. . . . Thus a definite form of production determines definite form of consumption, distribution and exchange as well as relations between these elements. . . . A mutual interaction takes place between these elements. This is the case with every organic body. (Marx 1904, 291)

Hence, the fundamental weakness of postdevelopmentalism is its failure to explain how the expansionary forces and relations of production in the capitalist system engage the plurality and diversity of social relations. Consequently, for the most part, current interventions in sustainable development, particularly those by the nongovernmental organizations (NGOs), obscure how their so-called socially and culturally sensitive sustainable development practices have become the means by which capitalist class relations are produced and consolidated in ways detrimental to the goals of sustainable development.

Under these circumstances, the rethinking of sustainable development ought to focus on several issues:

> How are all these diverse potentialities and possibilities controlled and disciplined to produce permanence, circular structures and systems that we encounter in that entity we call society? . . . How do the stabilities of a historically and geographically achieved social order get crystallized out from flux and fluidity of social processes? (Harvey 1996, 26)

How are correspondence rules established between different moments to guarantee the stability of a given social order? Who and where are the loci of social change? What are the implications of the answers to these questions for various practices of sustainable development, particularly those pursued by the NGOs? What these questions suggest is that fruitful rethinking of sustainable development should be predicated on a sound theory of social change—one that takes into account what it is and what it ought to be for a sustainable world order.

NGOs: Negotiating between Capital and Civil Society

NGOs deserve much of the credit for mainstreaming sustainable development and its achievements. Their performance, however, is now under critical scrutiny. The most serious accusation leveled at NGOs is that they contribute to the strengthening and legitimization of the same institutions and power relations that they purport to transform. As Finger and Chatterjee (1994) have noted,

> The non-governmental movement was co-opted to a process that ultimately worked against their interests. Most NGOs were invited in, indeed, sucked in by the lure of influ-

ence and by generous funding, to lend their support to the "Rio process"—fed into the green machine. (P. 79; see also Adams 1990, 140)

The current positioning of NGOs in sustainable development coincides with the withdrawal of the state from its conventional role in social development and its replacement by the private sector. It was widely believed that the NGOs were capable of effectively responding to the weaknesses of the state and the private sector. Contrary to expectations, investments by NGOs have by no means compensated for what society has lost due to the withdrawal of the state from social development, nor have they shielded social development from the negative consequences of private sector–led development. Instead, NGOs have evolved as institutions that discipline social order to function according to the dictates of neoliberal institutions. In this process, NGO activities have contributed toward the decapitation of the state in areas where it has historically performed well, particularly for the marginalized segments of the population.

During the past decade, differences between the organizational cultures of NGOs and for-profit organizations have become blurred. Their ability to mobilize voluntary material and nonmaterial contributions from broader society as well as from commercial enterprises has rapidly declined. Increasingly, one finds that both individual and corporate contributions are derived from the contributor's participation in the very institutions and power relations that require transformation to achieve the goal of sustainability.

Even more significant are the findings of current research that point to the failures of NGOs to transform the practices of the state in ways conducive to realizing the goals of sustainable development. Instead, the activities of NGOs have contributed toward the "domestication" and "centralization" of state power so that the state changes its role according to the dictates of capital. In fact, the neoliberal institutions that discipline state and society to function according to the imperatives of capital are appropriating the very language and practices of NGOs. For example, NGO criticisms of state practices with respect to development and NGO demands for strengthening of the role of civil society organizations in development have been exploited by neoliberal institutions to legitimize their pressures on the state to liberalize social development (Fernando forthcoming). NGOs have not compensated, however, for what society has lost due to the withdrawal of the state from social development. Instead, the vacuum was filled by the very liberal institutions that the NGOs had purported to transform to achieve the goal of sustainable development. In short, NGOs, the state, and for-profit organizations are partners in the neoliberal project of social change. The reason for this is that NGOs do not have a vision of a world order that is fundamentally different from the current one that is dominated by global capitalism. Consequently, there is hardly any difference between the role of slavery in feudal society and the role of NGOs in the "postmodern" phase of capitalist development.

Although the interdependence between the state, profit organizations, and NGOs continues to grow in ways that are counterproductive to the interests of sustainable development, the potential of NGOs to reemerge as a counterhegemonic force cannot be entirely discounted. This would occur only if and when a given society experienced a profound sense of alienation from the state-capital alliance and had no institutional means of expressing its concerns. NGOs in their current form, however, are unlikely to evolve as a counterhegemonic force. First, they do not present a coherent and politically potent counterhegemonic ideology or program capable of meeting the challenges of state and capital. Second, the NGO sector does not seriously engage with questions such as, What should be the ideal nature of the state in a sustainable world? What should be the nature of property rights and nature-society relations? What exchange relations are ideal for sustainable development? NGOs have not only bypassed these questions, but their interventions have effectively marginalized the institutions that might address these issues. Part of the reason for this is that NGOs are considered as legitimate institutions only as long as they function within the legal parameters of the state that provides them with official recognition. NGOs are therefore unlikely to evolve as a counterhegemonic force, unless there are fundamental changes in the material and social relations within which state power is embedded.

Overproduction and Scarcity

Excessive consumption by a minority of the world's population and increasing deprivation of basic subsistence for nearly a third of the world's population are widely contested topics in debates on sustainable development. Our current understanding of the relationship between overconsumption, underconsumption, and sustainable development, however, remains narrow and misleading. This is partly because our current studies are not concerned with the conditions under which the link between consumption and unsustainable development is produced. Instead, there is an overemphasis on the need to change the patterns of consumption through redistribution, "greening," and placing limits on unsustainable consumption. As Marx (1965) noted in *The German Ideology*,

> All revolutions until now have only shifted the internal distribution of productive relations, without changing this relationship itself; they have transferred control over means of production and property from one class to another, but have not transformed the nature of this control. (P. 83)

Underconsumption and overconsumption are two sides of the same coin. Or, to put it another way, underconsumption does not exist without overconsumption; rather, the former is the source of the latter. Such a relationship is a structural necessity for the self-realization of capital. Continuing expansion of consumption is necessary for the reproduction of capitalist accumulation. The progress of the modern global economy is predicated on the expansion of consumption rather than on the expansion of the productive capacity of the earth or of technology. Patterns of consumption, however, have to be profitable and must be produced under the conditions set by capital. Profit maximization is predicated on what economists refer to as scarcity of resources/production in relation to needs. Far from being a naturally given condition, scarcity is an institutionally produced condition, resulting from the capitalist system's need simultaneously to expand the desire for consumption and to limit actual consumption to those who can afford it. Basic economic questions such as what and how much to be produced and how production is distributed are determined not by the availability of natural resources or levels of technology but by the profitability of production. At the level of production, this means orienting production toward commodities that maximize exchange values as opposed to use values. This may even mean subsiding producers to abandon and limit the production of commodities essential for basic subsistence of millions in the population who are living below the poverty line. The basic logic of the system is to produce just the sufficient amount for those with the ability to pay, or "effective demand."

Creating effective demand is a contradictory process, and it is limited by the internal dynamic of the capitalist accumulation process itself.

> If there is to be profit, then the capitalist and the workers must produce more than what they consume. On the other hand, if there is to be accumulation, the capitalist class and its dependents cannot consume all of that surplus value. If the working class together with the capitalist class and its dependents cannot form an adequate market and buy all the commodities, then even though exploitation has taken place and surplus value has been extracted, that value cannot be realized. (Hardt and Negri 2000, 223)

The barriers to the continuing expansion of effective demand, and hence the barriers to the expansion of capitalist accumulation, increase as labor becomes more productive. As productivity expands, the number of workers with effective demand necessary to increase consumption becomes limited. The crisis of underconsumption is further worsened when production shifts from one national setting to another in response to increasing labor costs. As David Harvey (1996) noted,

> This theory of effective demand does not sit easily with the theory of overpopulation. For one thing, it appears illogical (if not obscene) to assert that the power to consume be withheld from the lower classes in society in the name of controlling the pressure of population on resources, while asserting via the theory of effective demand that upper classes should consume as much as possible. Within the advanced capitalist countries this obscenity is now rampant as we find "consumer confidence" (and the penchant for debt financing of consumption of the upper classes) depicted as fundamental to accumulation of capital, while all forms of welfare for the lowers classes are slashed because they are regarded as pernicious drains on growth. (P. 26)

This is not to dismiss entirely the natural limits of the productive capacity of the earth but rather to emphasize that the scarcity of resources in relation to basic needs is, to a large extent, a systemic one. Expansion of accumulation is predicated on continuous production of scarcity in two senses: first, in the creation of systemic shortages and, second, in the reallocation of resources only to commercially profitable products. Excessive consumption and inequitable consumption are two sides of the same coin; hence, maximization of capitalist profit and environmentally sustainable and equitable consumption cannot be achieved simultaneously. As James O'Connor (1998b) noted,

> Any particular shortage of commodity demand presupposes a given amount of surplus value produced or a given rate of exploitation. The greater the amount of surplus value produced or higher the rate of exploitation, the greater the difficulty of realizing surplus value in the market. (P. 162)

Hence, as Harvey (1996) observed, "What is then evident is that all debate about ecoscarcity, natural limits, overpopulation, and sustainability is a debate about the prevention of a particular social order rather than a debate about the preservation of nature per se" (p. 149). In such a social order, spatially differentiated resource

---

It is futile to talk about a social justice approach to sustainable development without being clear about what constitutes a just relation between nature and society, as well as a political will and a commitment to realize such a relationship.

---

scarcity is viewed purely in narrow physical and cultural terms, rather than as a systemic relation produced by the process of the accumulation of capital.

The continuity of capitalist accumulation depends on overcoming the crisis of underconsumption, rather than on increasing the productivity of labor. Yet the very policies used to overcome deficit consumption have proven to be short-term measures and have had irreversible consequences for sustainable development. The relentless expansion of debt-driven consumption has proven to be counterproductive in both economic and social terms. The displacement of production to locations that offer lower production costs increases unemployment at one location while decreasing it at another. Exploitation of labor and the environment is simply transported from one location to another. The other policy option is to gain direct control over natural resources and markets beyond national boundaries. The latter policy becomes even more aggressive as a capitalist system reaches the limit of its expansion within national boundaries. As Rosa Luxemburg (1968) noted, pursuit of capitalist profit forms the basis of imperialism characterized by pillage and theft that ransack the world, it procures its means of production from all corners and from all society. . . . It becomes necessary for capital progressively to dispose ever more fully of the whole globe, to acquire unlimited choice of means of production, with regard to both quantity and quality, so as to find productive employment for the surplus value it has realized. (Quoted in Hardt and Negri 2000, 225)

The compulsion for imperialist expansion is greater for countries with high standards of consumption that are heavily reliant on market forces and whose consumption is far distanced from the centers of production. One would expect that such pressures would be relatively less for poorer nations whose subsistence systems are still intact and where centers of production and consumption are located closer to each other. Moreover, poorer countries do not have as much political and military power to expand beyond their national boundaries, particularly into territories already controlled by richer countries. The poorer states due to their low bargaining power have been forced to make significant compromises in their quests for sustainable development just to achieve a competitive edge in the global economy. In fact, neoliberal institutions such as the World Trade Organization, the World Bank, and the International Monetary Fund are silent about the widespread protectionist policies implemented by developed countries to protect their environments and the welfare of citizens. Nonetheless, these institutions adopt harsh policies to force the poorer countries to liberalize their economies, despite the widespread evidence of unsustainable outcomes of economic liberalization. In this process, the state eventually emerges as an important actor because in the final analysis, it is responsible for addressing the multiple needs of the economy and society, that is, security, creating conditions for capitalist expansion, and the welfare of its own citizens.

Bringing Back the State

The role of the state is crucial to realizing the goals of sustainable development, even more so now than during the cold war period. Pressure on state actors to comply with the demands of sustainable development is likely to increase in the future. Under present politico-economic conditions, however, states confront a serious dilemma. On one hand, the state is committed to creating the political and social conditions necessary for capitalist development. As economic progress in their respective countries is predicated on their abilities to secure a competitive advantage in the global economy, states will be under enormous pressure to compromise the goals of sustainable development for the sake of economic growth. In this context, the primary responsibility of the state is to discipline the social order according to the imperatives of capital. On the other hand, the state will continue to be the primary agency responsible for sustainable development. Even the most radical sustainable development interventions will be channeled to the domains of the state. But under present conditions, the political and fiscal power of the state to respond positively to such demands is severely curtailed.

Since the Rio conference, states at large have adopted three policies to overcome this dilemma. The first is making national interests consistent with corporate interests, either by acquiring more power to discipline society to function according to the interests of capital or by using state power to ensure that the international consensus on sustainable development will not be harmful to national and corporate interests. The United States, for example, effectively dissociated itself from two principles in Agenda 21, which had been ratified by a majority of the member states of the United Nations. The U.S. delegation argued that development was not a right but a goal and rejected any "interpretation of the principle that suggested any form of international liability" (Adams 1996, 83).

The second policy pursued by states is to privilege national interests over global interests in securing the conditions for sustainable development. These policies have resulted in nationalizing the benefits of sustainable development and externalizing its costs, particularly to the poorer and politically weak communities and nations.

Third, states have been extremely successful in appropriating the language and practices of sustainable development and, in the process, co-opting and disciplining the multiplicity of institutions to function according to the interests of capital. Realization of sustainable development and the sustainability of capitalist accumulation are subjected to a common logic. These two processes are made interdependent, self-enforcing processes capable of achieving their respective equilibrium, and the responsibility of the state is simply to secure conditions for it.

As the distinction between state and capital continues to blur, the gap between the state and those who pursue sustainable development is likely to widen. This situation ought to be considered as an opportunity rather than an obstacle because it provides a much clearer space within which we could rethink the current role of the state in sustainable development. The challenge is not to abandon the state as irrelevant but to liberate its power from being determined by the dictates of capital. In the final analysis, it is the state that could shoulder responsibility for securing the conditions necessary for sustainable development.

Cultures of Insecurity and Violence

Many expected the world would become more peaceful with the end of the cold war and that democracy and economic prosperity would reign. These hopes were buttressed by the increasing commitment of states to a "free market" economy in which the freedom to participate in economic activities was supposed to bring about a sustainable democratic political culture. Such hopes were short lived. The post–cold war period has seen the rise of ethnic and nationalist tensions and the rise of the threat of transnational terrorism, coupled with the grim prospects of slow economic growth. For many, the post–cold war expectations of a prosperous and peaceful world order are rapidly giving way to insecurity and disorder.

From the perspective of sustainable development, the world community is confronted with two mutually reinforcing "cultures of insecurity." The first results from inequalities and uncertainties in the world economy. The second results from transnational terrorism and the ability of states to use deadly military power in external affairs far more easily than during the cold war. While the reasons for the latter cannot be entirely reduced to economic forces, nor can they be adequately explained outside the context of economic forces. Given the high potential for convergence of the two forms of fear and insecurity—with catastrophic economic and political consequences—security has evolved as a central concern of sustainable development. This has had some positive impact on current thinking about sustainable development, not only because it has broadened our understanding of sustainable development, but it also has forced us to come to terms with the fact that security concerns are not immune to the processes of capitalist development. Following the September 11 terrorist attacks on the United States, the United Nations Educational, Scientific, and Cultural Organization (2001) noted that it

> together with other actors of the international community is called upon to help to bring about conditions under which the peoples of the world, communities and indeed each individual may enjoy genuine human security. Poverty and conflict are prime causes that put human security at risk and endanger human dignity and social justice. Human security is inconceivable without sustainable development including environmental protection. Its attainment will require profound changes in people's and societies' attitudes and production, as well as enhanced cooperation.

Yet the evolving political and military responses to security issues do not offer much hope for realizing such a vision. First, there is the increasing corporatization of security measures and the subordination of security decisions of national concern to the interests of corporations. The privatization of the global arms industry and the priority given to parochial national interests over universal interests have completely ended post–cold war attempts to reduce the arms race and set limits on the proliferation of nuclear weapons. Second, the evolving global security regime is overdetermined by the distribution of military and economic capabilities between the states, rather than by the established international protocols of the United Nations. Developments after September 11 have shown that a minority of powerful states have acquired even greater powers than during the cold war period, not only to bypass the international protocols that govern the transnational state system but also to ignore the voices of their own citizens regarding their states' involvement in external affairs. Economic pressures resulting from the rapidly internationalizing capitalist economy have severely constrained the capabilities of states and transnational institutions to give priority to the concerns of sustainable development. Third, under the pretense of national security, both rich and poor states have acquired greater powers to implement policies detrimental to the interests of sustainable development. Global and national security is fast evolving as the domain within which many of the conditions of unsustainable development are reproduced and legitimized.

In this context, we find that neoliberal consensus and neo-Malthusian doctrines have gained even more power in the current discussion of sustainable development. A case study of Rwanda found that "environmental and population pressures had at most a limited, aggravating role" in causing the genocide there and criticized those who place excessive emphasis on such pressures as being too "simplistic"; rather, the study pointed out a more obvious causal relationship between "environmental scarcity and high levels of grievances, political instability, and the manipulation of ethnic identity" (Homer-Dixon 1998, as quoted in Peluso and Watts 2002, 57). The explanation of these roles highlights the impact of structural adjustments, the fall in coffee prices, and declining food production in creating "general economic malaise." Paul Collier's (1999) work found that "presence (not scarcity) increases the risk of civil conflict and, interestingly . . . ethnic and religious fractionalization substantially reduces the risk because it is harder to mobilize a large enough force for a successful rebellion" (quoted in Peluso and Watts 2002, 56). Consequently, the research on contemporary civil conflicts points out that "war has increasingly become continuation of economics by other means. War is not simply a breakdown in a particular system, but a way of creating an alternative system of profit, power and even protection" (Peluso and Watts 2002, 56).

While violence and conflict are context specific, they are embedded in larger systemic forces that operate interactively in local, national, and global domains. The fundamental problem with current interventions in antiterrorism, humanitarian assistance, conflict resolution, and peace building is that they are scattered and isolated, both from one another and from larger social, cultural, and economic contexts. In fact, one can argue that for the most part these interventions, by both states and NGOs, deliberately marginalize and suppress the economic impact of those forces that are fundamentally responsible for violence and conflict and thereby contribute toward further instability and disorder. To put it slightly differently, these interventions create a free space for global economic forces to expand and consolidate their positions by exploiting the existing conditions of fear, insecurity, and violence. For students of history, this trend has been continuing since the origins of the United Nations Universal Declaration of Human Rights, "which gives greater emphasis to civil and political rights rather than economic and social rights, prioritizes the interests of those closest to the processes of economic globalization rather than those on the periphery" (Evens 2001, 4). Creating conditions for a more fruitful reconciliation of social and economic rights with political and civil rights remains the most important challenge for those interested in sustainable development.

Sustainable Development as Social Justice

One of the most promising developments in the discourse of sustainable development in recent times is to approach sustainable development from the perspective of social justice. According to a recent anthology,

> This greater emphasis on equity as a desirable and a just social goal, is intimately linked to a recognition that, unless society strives for a greater level of social and economic equity,

both within and between nations, the long term objective of a more sustainable world is unlikely to be secured. (Agyeman, Bullard, and Evans 2002, 2)

A social justice–centered perspective provides many valuable contributions to our efforts in rethinking sustainable development. First, it makes the link between inequality, capitalism, and sustainable development more direct and concrete. In other words, it has brought the tensions between realization of sustainability of capitalism and sustainable development to the center of the discourse on sustainable development.

Second, the social justice perspective has brought existing strategies of sustainable development under critical scrutiny and given substance to a more integrative and dynamic approach to sustainable development. As Michael Heiman (1996) has noted, "If we settle for liberal procedural and distributional equity, relying upon negotiation, mitigation and fair-share allocation to address some sort of disproportional impact, we merely perpetuate the current production system that by its very structure is discriminatory and non-sustainable" (p. 120).

Third, current discussions of sustainable development from a social justice perspective seem to be moving in the direction of emphasizing the need for universal and transcendent theoretical and policy approaches to sustainable development. This is partly a response to the growing realization that problems of sustainable development "can no longer be dealt in isolation but must be placed in the context of global environmental change and the global economy" (Dovers and Handmer 1992, 42). James O'Connor (1998a) pointed out,

> Politically, this means that sooner or later, labor, feminist, urban, environmental, and other social movements need to combine into a single powerful democratic force—one that is both politically viable and also capable of radically reforming the economy, polity, and society. Individually, social movements are relatively powerless in the face of totalizing force of global capital. (P. 250)

Such a universal paradigm would "link environment and race, gender and social justice concerns into an explicit framework" (Taylor 2000, 34). As Richard Peet and Michael Watts have noted,

> Political ecology's conception of political economy appears fuzzy and diffuse. Their emphasis on plurality comes perilously close to voluntarism while their chains of explanation seem incapable of explaining how some factors become causes. Particularly striking is the fact that political ecology has very little politics in it. (Quoted in Commoner 1972, 32)

Fourth, an emphasis on equity as a necessary condition of sustainable development brings the tension between labor and capital to the center of sustainable development discourse. Such an emphasis on *class relations* (though the term has yet to be used as explicitly as it should be) is a noteworthy and welcome change because, for a long time, sustainable development movements were overdetermined by their emphasis on conservation, preservation, green production, and green consumption. This trend now seems to be changing:

Just as in the 1930s, when the labor movement was forced to change from craft to industrial unionism into an international conglomerate union, inclusive of women and all racial/ethnic people, just to keep pace with the restructuring of international capital. (Faber and McCarthy 2003, 61)

Moving forward with a social justice–centered paradigm of sustainable development requires first a utopian vision of a world order in which the relationship between the human world and the natural environment is structured differently from the one that underpins capitalist accumulation. Without such a counterhegemonic utopian vision, it is impossible to create the necessary conditions for sustainable development, what Barry Commoner (1972) called "social governance of the means of production—a radical democratization of all major political, social and economic institutions" (p. 27). It is futile to talk about a social justice approach to sustainable development without being clear about what constitutes a just relation between nature and society, as well as a political will and a commitment to realize such a relationship.

Second, the gigantic concentration of wealth and power in the hands of a few is a major threat to sustainable development. The challenge is not redistribution but the changing logic of production and social relations that produce inequality and difference. Hence, class relations should be at the center of such a utopian vision and the political strategies adopted to realize it. This is not because such an approach will automatically eradicate all other forms of inequality but to underscore the centrality of class relations to them. A class-centered approach is particularly useful in dealing with social inequities that are structured in the name of cultural relativism and demonstrating how sustainable development practices underpinned by nonclass identities and relations become arenas within which capitalist class relations are reproduced and legitimized.

Third, in the final analysis, any efforts toward sustainable development must entail radical reconfiguration of the power relations of society. As Nancy Leo Peluso and Michael Watts (2002) have observed,

Environmental resources—whether they are specifically land, plant, or nonrenewable resources such as diamonds—are implicated as part and parcel of social relations. This is not just identity politics (or group identity politics Hommer-Dixon invokes) but identity that constitute larger political frameworks of resource access and power. (P. 33)

While inequalities of power cannot be entirely reduced to material determinants in terms of ways they impinge on the goals of sustainable development, nor can they be adequately explained or transformed outside the context of the material world, in the present context, this calls for radical changes in the forces and relations of production that underpin capitalist accumulation. Such efforts are unlikely to bear sustainable results without the aggressive mediation of the state. Even more important is the need for radical reimagination of the nature of the state. The challenge is not simply to capture state power but to radically change the social bases of state power that are embedded in capitalist relations and forces of production. In the final analysis, the capacity of global communities to secure and maintain their diversity without compromising the goals of sustainable development lies in a strong state. Such a state system is unlikely to be realized unless there are global institutions to ensure their commitment and accountability to the universal goals of sustainable development.

Ultimately, our views about sustainable development are expressions of our positions on ethics, morality, and social justice and of our commitment to political strategies to realize them. It is imperative that we shift the debate on sustainable development toward the consideration of what ought to be the nature of a just world order and what types of forces and relations of production are ideal for its sustainability. A coherent and globally transcendent political ideology, and principles and strategies to organize and coordinate diverse efforts toward sustainable development, are essential to forge a broad-based political movement for sustainable development. In other words, I am suggesting we need a metanarrative of an alternative political economy that will directly counteract the hegemony exercised by capital in managing and disciplining social diversity in ways counterproductive to the goals of sustainable development. This must be considered in the most specific terms possible, and soon. Failure to do so will provide continuing opportunity for the reproduction of the socioeconomic forces that lead to unsustainable development.

Author Contributions

Julian Agyeman and Tom Evans's article examines the interconnectedness between environmental justice and sustainability and their practical application within an urban setting. They show how these concepts are now being translated into public policy and planning documents at the federal level as well as some states and localities. They argue that without a focus on justice and equity, sustainability will not have a lasting impact on quality of life. Their claims are based on the premise that practical, community-based initiatives to address environmental justice and sustainability concepts are the true test case for their theoretical compatibility.

David Satterthwaite's article examines the link between poverty and different categories of environmental hazards (biological pathogens and chemical pollutants in the air, water, soil, or food and physical hazards) and discusses which are most associated with poverty. It then considers the links between poverty and different forms of environmental degradation—including the high use of nonrenewable resources, degradation of renewable resources such as soil and fresh water, and high levels of biodegradable and nonbiodegradable waste generation. It suggests that there is little evidence of urban poverty being a significant contributor to environmental degradation in Africa, Asia, and Latin America but that there is strong evidence that urban environmental hazards are a major contributor to urban poverty. For most of the poor urban population, environmental hazards are among the main causes of ill health, injury, and premature death. This health burden can be greatly reduced by better environmental management. The article makes a strong case for the role of the state by examining consumption patterns of middle- and upper-income groups and by demonstrating the failure of governments to implement effective environmental policies. It highlights the extent to which good governance is at the core of poverty reduction and how meeting the environmental health needs of poorer groups need not imply greater environmental degradation.

Jude Fernando's article probes the question as to why well-intended interventions in sustainable development culminate in unsustainable results. Indigenous knowledge (IK) as currently used in NGO-mediated sustainable development projects plays an important role in connecting and subordinating diverse communities around the world to interests of neoliberal capitalist institutions. The results of the use of IK in sustainable development are yet another example of capitalism's capacity to discipline and manage development according to its own imperatives. IK, rather than being a means through which the goals of sustainable development could be realized, has become a means through which the diversity of knowledge systems is managed according to the expansionist needs of capital. In this process, NGOs play an important role as facilitators. Their language and practices such as "bottom-up development" and "empowerment of people" obscure the real interests of power relations that determine the current interests and outcomes of IK. Hence, liberating the radical potential of IK ought to be predicated on liberating the latter from its embeddedness in capitalist relations and forces of production. NGOs are highly unsuitable for this task because they can function as legal institutions only as long as they function within the institutional parameters of the state, which simply has become an instrument of capital.

Jim Glassman and Chris Sneddon examine the concept of urban sustainability within the context of two case studies from Thailand. Their article provides a critical analysis of how the decentralization of industrial growth and development of secondary urban centers, ostensibly to alleviate congestion and pollution in Bangkok, have been deployed in the context of urban primacy and uneven development in Thailand. They argue that these policies have helped induce some growth in the secondary cities in question, but in doing so, they have induced new problems of sustainability in the secondary cities and their surrounding rural areas without alleviating problems of sustainability in Bangkok. The kinds of policies the Thai state and its backers have advertised as suitable for encouraging decentralization and secondary urbanization are inappropriate to the goals of sustainability, urban or otherwise, and reflect the unwillingness or inability of the state to impose regulations that might procure greater sustainability at the expense of capital accumulation.

The article by Jorge Morello, Silvia Diana Matteucci, and Andrea Rodríguez explores the conflict between rural and urban development in the Pampa Ondulada, the eco-region in which the city of Buenos Aires is located, which is one of the world's richest and most productive agricultural areas. It describes the ecological changes brought by urban growth in peri-urban and rural areas, between 1869 and 1991, and the form that these have taken. The article emphasizes the absolute necessity of planning the expansion process of the urban agglomerations to secure conditions for sustainable urban development.

Amy K. Glasmeier and Tracey L. Farrigan focus on the sustainability issues in the Appalachian region, one of the poorest communities in the United States. The article raises several issues. To what extent can the rhetoric of sustainability be employed in areas where natural resource exploitation has rendered the environment despoiled and virtually unlivable? To what extent does the lived experience of a place shape the efficacy of policies that attempt to maintain and sustain the environment as part of development? Can notions of sustainability be used as a means of redistributing power and access to natural resources, or does the peculiar fate of a region, tied to massive natural resource extraction, eliminate such potential? The case study in the Appalachia region presents the peculiar fate of the region, tied as it has been to massive natural resource extraction, and reflects a landscape of uneven development. The maintenance of the environment is by default decided nonlocally, often by fiat. Despite living and working in areas with enormous natural resource wealth, residents often have only limited access to these resources. Recognizing the inability of conventional practice to resolve many of the development problems confronting communities in distress, a series of new policy initiatives is focusing on building sustainable community capacity from the ground up.

Simon Batterbury's article is concerned with the development of more effective, equitable, and sustainable forms of transportation within the context of "late capitalism." Its emphasis is on the institutional dimensions necessary to promote sustainable transportation thinking, by examining the political and activist coalitions that have attempted to address significant transportation problems in one of the densest transportation networks in the world—west London. It analyzes how citizens found ways to cooperate and work with progressive elements in mainstream planning and policy making. The article points out key lessons for forging and maintaining such environmentally based social networks, using the case of the promotion of cycling as a transport alternative. Environmental citizenship is crucial for the development of a sustainable transportation system. Such a system needs to be founded on social realities and conducted in mainstream political systems if it is to be effective in complex urban environments.

Philip F. Kelly's article, based on a case study of the rapidly urbanizing province of Cavite to the south of Manila, Philippines, shows how the patterns of land ownership have long been a source, and an outcome, of political power. It examines the process of land use conversion in two perspectives: first, in policy choices relating to the use of land that reflect a particular set of developmental priorities and, second, in the facilitation of conversion through the use of political power relations to circumvent regulations. The article shows the importance of power relations in creating conditions for sustainable development, particularly by analyzing the relationship between land ownership and political power.

Elaine Hartwick and Richard Peet explore some ideological means of reconciliation that appear to bridge the impassable divide between economic growth and environmental health. They also examine the displacement of political power from elected national governments toward international agreements and nonelected global governance institutions. By analyzing the process of neoliberal deflection by using the case of GATT and the World Trade Organization, they argue that environmental concern has been ideologically and institutionally incorporated into the global neoliberal hegemony of the late twentieth century. Consequently, the political pressures exerted by environmental movements have forced governments otherwise committed to neoliberal policies to find reconciliatory policy positions between two contradictory political imperatives—economic growth and environmental protection.

David Lewis examines the organizational culture of NGOs—a frequently neglected aspect of international development projects—and shows how it can contribute to a better understanding of the workings of projects in which different kinds of agency are brought together into collaborative operating relationships or partnerships. His focus is on the relationship between organizational culture and different forms of sustainability, particularly in relation to the work of NGOs working within such projects.

Joseph Devine draws on research from Bangladesh and questions the dominance of a narrow view of sustainability that rests predominantly on financial considerations. The push for financial sustainability has produced ambiguous results and, more important, has introduced a degree of uncertainty into the relationship NGOs maintain with their members. He shows that in the context of Bangladesh, an accurate notion of sustainability rests more on social and political than economic considerations. The challenge, however, is the fundamental tension that exists between social/political and economic considerations: the relentless pursuit of one may undermine efforts to establish the other.

Roger Magazine's article describes the practices of an NGO providing services for street children in Mexico City with an emphasis on the innovative capacities of these organizations. He shows that this NGO, because it is locally based, enjoys greater success in its attempts at innovation than organizations that are local branches of international NGOs and thus find their attempts at innovation hindered by responsibilities to a central authority. The logical contradictions between global and national leaders' projects do not inevitably result in conflict or cultural schizophrenia among national leaders. On the contrary, the juxtaposition of contradictory ideologies is a necessary but not sufficient condition for innovation. Second, this innovation can only succeed under particular organizational circumstances.

References

Adams, W. M. 1990. *Green development: Environment and sustainable development in the Third World.* New York: Routledge.

———. 1996. *Green development: Environment and sustainability in the South.* London: Routledge.

Agyeman, Julian, Robert D. Bullard, and Bob Evans. 2002a. Joined-up thinking: Bringing together sustainability, environmental justice and equity. In *Just sustainabilities: Development in an unequal world*, edited by Julian Agyeman, Robert D. Bullard, and Bob Evans. London: Earthscan.

———, eds. 2002b. *Just sustainabilities: Development in an unequal world.* London: Earthscan.

Bebbington, A. J. 1997. Social capital and rural intensification: Local organizations and islands of sustainability in the rural Andes? *Geographical Journal* 163 (2): 189-97.

Collier, Paul. 1999. Doing well out of war. Paper presented for the Conference on Economic Agenda in Civil Wars, London, April 26-27.

Commoner, Barry. 1972. *The closing circle: Confronting the environmental crisis*. London: Jonathan Cape.

Dickens, Peter. 1992. *Society and nature: Towards a green social theory*. London: Harvester.

Dovers, S., and J. Handmer. 1992. Uncertainty, sustainability and change. *Global Environmental Change* 24:262-76.

Drummond, Ian, and Terry Marsden. 1999. *The conditions of sustainability*. New York: Routledge.

Eagleton, Terry. 1992. Freedom and interpretation. In *Freedom and interpretation: The Oxford amnesty lectures*, edited by Barbara Johnson. New York: Basic Books.

Escobar, A. 1994. *Encountering development*. Princeton, NJ: Princeton University Press.

Esteva, Gustavo, and Madhu Suri Prakash. 1998. *Grassroots post-modernism: Remaking the soil of cultures*. New York: Palgrave Macmillan.

Evens, Tony. 2001. *The politics of human rights: A global perspective*. London: Pluto Press.

Faber, Daniel R., and Deborah McCarthy. 2003. Neoliberalism, globalization, and the struggle for ecological democracy. In *Just sustainabilities: Development in an unequal world*, edited by Julian Agyeman, Robert D. Bullard, and Bob Evans. London: Earthscan.

Fernando, Jude. Forthcoming. *Political economy of non-governmental organizations: Modernizing post-modernity*. London: Pluto.

Finger, Matthias, and Pratap Chatterjee. 1994. *The earth brokers: Power, politics and world development*. London: Routledge.

Hardt, Michael, and Antonio Negri. 2000. *Empire*. Cambridge, MA: Harvard University Press.

Harvey, David. 1996. *Justice, nature and geography of difference*. Cambridge, MA: Blackwell.

Haughton, G. 1999. Environmental justice and the sustainable city. *Journal of Planning Education and Research* 18 (3): 233-43.

Heiman, Michael. 1996. Race, waste, and class: New perspectives on environmental justice. *Antipode* 28:111-21.

Homer-Dixon, T. 1998. *Ecoviolence: Links among environment, population and security*. Lanham, MD: Rowman and Littlefield.

International Confederation of Free Trade Union. 2001. The International Confederation of Free Trade Union survey. Retrieved from http://www.ksworkbeat.org/Globalization/ICFTU_SURVEY_2001_/icftu_survey_2001_.html.

Kardar, Shaid Hafiz. 1999. War and peace economics. Paper presented in Karachi, Pakistan, January.

Lukacs, Georg. 1971. *History and class consciousness*. Delhi, India: Rupa and Company.

Luxemburg, Rosa. 1968. *The accumulation of capital*. Translated by Agnes Schwarzschild. New York: Monthly Review Press.

Marx, Karl. 1904. *A contribution to the critique of political economy*. Translated by N. I. Stone. London: Penguin.

———. 1965. *The German ideology*. London: Penguin.

Middleton, Neil, and Phil O'Keefe. 2001. *Redefining sustainable development*. London: Pluto.

Murphy, David F., and Jem Bendell. 1997. *In the company of partners: Businesses, environmental groups, and sustainable development post-Rio*. Bristol, UK: Policy Press.

O'Connor, James. 1998a. *Essays in ecological Marxism*. New York: Guilford.

———. 1998b. *Natural causes, essays in ecological Marxism*. London: Guilford.

O'Riordan, Timothy. 1987. The new environmentalism and sustainable development. *Science of the Total Environment* 108:5-15.

Peluso, Nancy Lee, and Michael Watts, eds. 2002. *Violent environments*. Ithaca, NY: Cornell University Press.

Redclift, Michael. 1987. *Sustainable development: Exploring the contradiction*. London: Methuen.

Slater, D. 1993. The geopolitical imagination and the enframing of development theory. *Transactions of the Institute of British Geographers* 18:419-37.

Stiglitz, Joseph E., and Robert Holzmann, eds. 2001. *New ideas about old age security: Toward sustainable pension systems in the 21st century*. Washington, DC: World Bank.

Stockholm International Peace Research Institute. 2001. Recent trends in military expenditure. Global military expenditure trend. Retrieved from http://projects.sipri.se/milex/mex_database1.html.

Taylor, D. E. 2000. The rise of the environmental justice paradigm: Injustice framing and the social construction of environmental discourses. *American Scientist* 43 (4): 508-80.

United Nations Development Program. 1991. *United Nations development report*. Oxford, UK: Oxford University Press.

United Nations Educational, Scientific, and Cultural Organization. 2001. Terrorism, human security and sustainable development. Retrieved from http://portal.unesco.org/en/en/ev.php@URL_ID=3932&URL_DO=DO_TOPIC&URL_SECTION=201.html.

Appendix
Additional References

Adams, W. M.. 2001. *Green development: Environmental and sustainability in the Third World*. New York: Routledge.

Agyeman, Julian, Robert D. Bullard, and Bob Evans, eds. 2003. *Just sustainabilities: Development in an unequal world*. London: Earthscan.

Alston, D. 1990. *We speak for ourselves: Social justice, race and environment*. Washington, DC: Panos Institute.

Bartelmus, P. 1994. *Environment, growth and development: The concepts and strategies of sustainability*. London: Routledge.

Beckerman, W. 1992. Economic growth and environment: Whose growth? Whose environment? *World Development* 20 (4): 481-96.

Bryant, B. 1995. *Environmental justice: Issues, policies, and solutions*. Washington, DC: Island Press.

Crush, J. 1995. *Power of development*. London: Routledge.

Environmental Audit Committee. 1999. *Second report: World trade and sustainable development: An agenda for the Seattle summit*. HC45. London: House of Commons.

Escobar, A. 1994. *Discourse and power of development: Michael Foucault and the relevance of his work to the Third World*. Princeton, NJ: Princeton University Press.

Esteva, G. 1987. Regenerating people's space. *Alternative* 10 (3): 125-52.

———. 1992. Development. In *The development dictionary: A guide to knowledge and power*, edited by W. Sachs. London: Zed Books.

Faber, D., and J. O'Connor. 1993. Capitalism and the crisis of environmentalism. In *Toxic struggles: The theory and practice of environmental justice*, edited by R. Hofricher. Philadelphia: New Society.

Fairclough, N. 1992. *Discourse and social change*. Cambridge, UK: Polity.

Field, R. 1998. Risk and justice: Capitalist production and the environment. In *The struggle for ecological democracy*, edited by D. Faber. New York: Guilford.

Galbraith, J. 2000. How the economists got it wrong. *American Prospect* 11 (7), 14 February.

Global Commons Institute. n.d. Equity for survival. Retrieved from http://www.gci.org.uk.

Godlewska, R., and G. Ledec. 1994. *Geography and the empire*. Oxford, UK: Blackwell.

Goldman, B. 1994. *Not just prosperity: Achieving sustainability with environmental justice*. Washington, DC: National Wildlife Federation Corporate Conservation Council.

Goodland, R., and G. Ledec. 1984. *Neoclassical economics and the principles of sustainable development*. Washington, DC: World Bank Environmental Affairs.

Gramsci, A. 1971. *Selections from prison notebooks*. London: Lawrence and Wishart.

Habermas, J. 1975. *Legitimization crisis*. Boston: Beacon.

Homer-Dixon, T. 1991. Environmental scarcity and violent conflict: Evidence from cases. *International Security* 19 (2): 76-116.

Manzur, L., ed. 1994. *Beyond the numbers: A reader in population, consumption and the environment*. Washington, DC: Island Press.

Myers, T. 1996. *Environmental basis of political stability*. Washington, DC: Island Press.

Peet, R., and Michael Watts. 1996. *Liberation ecologies: Environment, development, and social movements*. London: Routledge.

Ross, R., and K. Trachte. 1990. *Global capitalism: The new leviathan*. Albany: State University of New York Press.

Sachs, A. 1995. *Eco-justice: Linking human rights and the environment*. Worldwatch paper 127. Washington, DC: Worldwatch Institute.

Schutkin, W. 2000. *The land that could be: Environmentalism and democracy in the twenty-first century*. Cambridge, MA: MIT Press.

Weaver, J., and R. Means. 1996. *Defending Mother Earth: Native American perspectives on environmental justice*. New York: Orbis.

World Wildlife Fund. 2000. *Living planet report*. Gland, Switzerland: World Fund for Nature International.

Toward Just Sustainability in Urban Communities: Building Equity Rights with Sustainable Solutions

By
JULIAN AGYEMAN
and
TOM EVANS

Two concepts that provide new directions for public policy, environmental justice and sustainability, are both highly contested. Each has tremendous potential to effect long-lasting change. Despite the historically different origins of these two concepts and their attendant movements, there exists an area of theoretical compatibility between them. This conceptual overlap is a critical nexus for a broad social movement to create livable, sustainable communities for all people in the future. The goal of this article is to illustrate the nexus in the United States. The authors do this by presenting a range of local or regionally based practical models in five areas of common concern to both environmental justice and sustainability: land use planning, solid waste, toxic chemical use, residential energy use, and transportation. These models address both environmental justice principles while working toward greater sustainability in urbanized areas.

Keywords: environmental justice; sustainability; public policy; planning; transportation

Agreat deal has been written in the past few years about environmental justice, sustainability, and the putative compatibility of the

Julian Agyeman is an assistant professor of environmental policy and planning at Tufts University, Boston-Medford. His interests are in the relationship between environmental justice and sustainability, social learning for sustainability, education for sustainability, community involvement in local environmental and sustainability policy, and the development of sustainable communities. He is the founder and coeditor of the international journal Local Environment. *His book,* Just Sustainabilities: Development in an Unequal World *(2003, MIT Press), argues that social and environmental justice within and between nations should be an integral part of the policies and agreements that promote sustainable development.*

Tom Evans studied environmental biology at Macalester College and began a career in science and outdoor education. He returned to school to study local sustainability initiatives at the Urban and Environmental Policy and Planning Program of Tufts University. He completed his master of city planning at the University of California at Berkeley. He currently works for the San Francisco Redevelopment Agency.

DOI: 10.1177/0002716203256565

two concepts.[1] Environmental justice and sustainability concepts are now being translated into public policy statements at the federal level as well as at the level of some states and localities. This article explores the intersection of these concepts while focusing on their practical application within an urban setting. It is the premise of this article that community-based initiatives to address environmental justice and sustainability concepts are the true test case for their theoretical compatibility. After reviewing various individual projects from around the United States, the relevance of these efforts to the broader sustainability and environmental justice movement(s) will be discussed.

Sustainability and Environmental Justice in Theory

Agyeman (2000, 2001, 2002) and Agyeman, Bullard, and Evans (2002, 2003) have described the development of the concepts (and movements) of environmental justice and sustainability. It is not our intention to revisit these issues here. However, we must clarify our definitions. As with sustainability, there are many possible definitions of environmental justice. The Commonwealth of Massachusetts (2002) uses the following definition in its *Environmental Justice Policy*:

> *Environmental justice* is based on the principle that all people have a right to be protected from environmental pollution and to live in and enjoy a clean and healthful environment. Environmental justice is the equal protection and meaningful involvement of all people with respect to the development, implementation, and enforcement of environmental laws, regulations, and policies and the equitable distribution of environmental benefits.

This definition will inform the arguments made throughout this article. It has both procedural ("meaningful involvement of all people") and substantive ("right to live in and enjoy a clean and healthful environment") justice aspects.

The broad acceptance of sustainability as the overarching public policy goal (Agyeman and Evans 1995; Campbell 1996) does not mean that there is any one agreed-on definition of sustainability, although the definitions of the World Commission on Environment and Development (1987) and the International Union for the Conservation of Nature (1991) are most often quoted. Our working definition of *sustainability*, developed by Agyeman, Bullard, and Evans (2002), will be "the need to ensure a better quality of life for all, now and into the future, in a just and equitable manner, whilst living within the limits of supporting ecosystems" (p. 78). Neither the World Commission on Environment and Development (1987) nor the International Union for the Conservation of Nature (1991) definitions specifically mentions justice and equity, which we hold to be of pivotal importance in the move toward sustainable futures.

At a less pivotal but more practical level, there exists a nexus of theoretical compatibility between sustainability and environmental justice, including an emphasis on community-based decision making; on economic policies that account fiscally for social and environmental externalities; on reductions in all forms of pollution;

FIGURE 1
SIMPLE VENN DIAGRAM OF SUSTAINABLE DEVELOPMENT THEORY

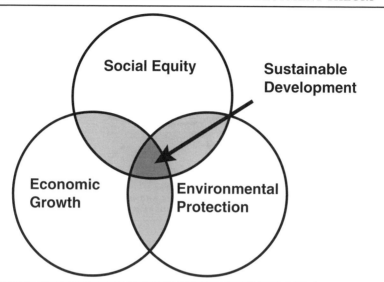

on building clean, livable communities for all people; and on an overall regard for the ecological integrity of the planet. A widely used Venn diagram illustrates the interdependent concepts of environmental protection, social equity, and economic growth (see Figure 1). Many regard this as the overarching visual representation of sustainability (O'Riordan 1999).

Others have looked at the model and the theories of environmental justice and sustainability to anticipate conflict(s) between their interests (Campbell 1996; Ruhl 1999; Dobson 1999, 2003) (see Figure 2). As an academic planner, Campbell (1996) identified these conflicts as "the property conflict" (between planning for economic growth and social justice), "the development conflict" (between planning for social justice and environmental protection), and "the resource conflict" (between planning for economic growth and environmental protection) (see Figure 2). He saw the planner's role as moving toward the center of the triangle, toward sustainable development ("green, profitable and fair").

Clearly, the interpretation of sustainability and environmental justice as a realm for collaboration or a source of conflict depends highly on the typology of sustainability[2] being described, the particular principles of environmental justice (see appendix) being emphasized (or which of Taylor's [2000] "six major thematic components"[3] are being emphasized), and the economic theories one supports. True sustainability with a full regard to environmental justice would be best reached by advancing sustainability ideals toward hard/strong sustainability or ecocentric theories while highlighting environmental justice theories that incorporate intergenerational, intragenerational, international, and interspecies equity,

FIGURE 2
SUSTAINABLE DEVELOPMENT AND ITS CONFLICTS

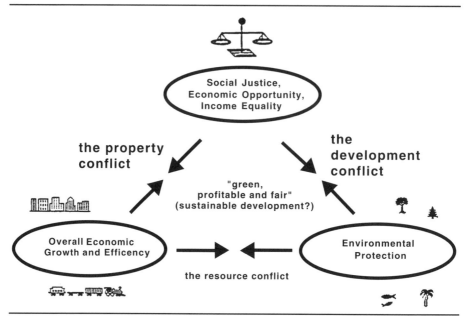

SOURCE: Campbell (1996).

and supporting economic reforms that value community economic development with redistributive values and policies.

Most sustainability and environmental justice advocates have a serious concern for the urban environment (Satterthwaite 1999). As the home for a growing percentage of the world's population, the cultural centers for many minority communities, and the consumer of large portions of the land's natural resources, cities represent a critical proving ground for both movements. Many cities across the United States, such as Seattle, Santa Monica, and Boston, have launched sustainability programs that often revolve around the identification and use of sustainability indicators that help chart progress toward or away from sustainability. Although many of these programs are well intentioned, declaring their definition and goals for sustainability, most fall short of addressing social justice and equity concerns as pivotal (Brugmann 1997; Yanarella 1999). Indeed, Portney (2003), in his study of what makes some cities take sustainability seriously, noted that "if equity issues are important conceptual components of sustainability, then sustainable cities initiatives in the US do not seem to take it very seriously" (p. 175).

Often, the sustainability measurements place a priority on economic sustainability and livability standards above all other factors. Lake (2000) identified Boston and Chattanooga in this category. On the other hand, in a study of sustainability projects in the largest U.S. cities, Warner (2002) found that few cities even acknowledged environmental justice as an aspect of sustainability. Forty websites were identified that deal with thirty-three cities of the seventy-seven cities with populations exceeding 200,000 in 1990. Of these, only five sites mentioned environmental justice as a substantive concern, and there was significant variation in the way that environmental justice was linked with sustainability in these few cases, from a few words to a full policy linkage with indicators (San Francisco). Similarly, the Environmental Law Institute (1999) analyzed 579 applications to the Environmental Protection Agency's 1996 Sustainable Development Challenge Grant Program. Fewer than 5 percent of applications had "equity" as a goal, and interestingly, fewer than 1 percent addressed "international responsibility."

Like Campbell (1996), we agree that "in the battle of big public ideas, sustainability has won: the task of the coming years is simply to work out the details, and to narrow the gap between its theory and practice" (p. 301). Whereas no one would claim that there is a chance of true sustainability or sustainable development in advanced industrial societies anytime soon, some practical policies for sustainable development that are being implemented to some extent in different parts of the world, including the United States, are the following:

- Ecotaxes, which shift the tax burden from good things like employment to bad things like pollution and excessive resource use.
- Elimination of agricultural and energy subsidies, which are environmentally damaging through their encouragement to overuse energy, fertilizer, pesticides, and irrigation water. Sustainable agriculture relies on the recycling of nutrients, natural pest control, labor intensivity, and reduced artificial usage.
- Local exchange trading schemes enable people to decide the local unit of currency and trade their skills in it. In time money schemes, the currency is the hours spent in volunteer activity, so that shopping for local elderly people becomes an alternative form of money.
- Affordable housing is being financed through community finance initiatives such as community development banks, corporations, and credit unions. Location-efficient mortgages, which reward certain locations (close to transit nodes), are being developed. Cooperatives and cohousing options are becoming increasingly popular.
- Recycling and renewable energy are being given greater prominence in some areas. Industrial ecology is showing how industrial systems can be made to mimic the closed cycle patterns of natural systems with materials reuse and minimal or zero waste.
- Efficient transportation systems, which replace energy-intensive automobile transport with high-speed trains, public transit, and greater use of bikes and walking, are being developed. City and suburban redesign through smart growth and new urbanism projects minimizes transportation needs through mixed-use developments. This creates a focus on access rather than mobility.
- Community-supported agriculture schemes, or community farms in Europe and food guilds in Japan, and farmer's markets are becoming increasingly popular in U.S. cities.

Following Campbell's (1996) point, the question now becomes, Can we achieve sustainable development and sustainable communities, as outlined in Table 1[4], by tweaking existing policies, which we are doing at present, or do we need a rethink: a paradigm shift away from our present market-driven, resource-intensive development paradigm (Milbrath's [1989] "Dominant Social Paradigm") to one in which society and social values come before economics (Milbrath's [1989] "New Environmental Paradigm")? The economy (i.e., the market) must become a tool to achieve policy goals as opposed to being the source of such goals. The market should be treated as a social institution, not as an objective entity; value-based political processes define goals, not global markets; economic activity is not an end in itself—it is valued only insofar as it contributes to the politically adopted goals of society (Levett 1997).

Economic activity is not an end in itself—it is valued only insofar as it contributes to the politically adopted goals of society.

The policy areas above (and those in Table 1) are valuable demonstrations of what we could achieve, and in certain cases and localities, are achieving, but they are still best practices, not ordinary or mainstream practices. And if we need a paradigm shift, will the New Environmental Paradigm alone deliver sustainable development? Taylor (2000) has argued that it is virtually devoid of an appreciation of social justice. Should the New Environmental Paradigm be combined with Taylor's (2000) Environmental Justice Paradigm to form a new, Just Sustainability Paradigm along the lines suggested by Agyeman, Bullard, and Evans (2003)?

Although Levett's (1997) "paradigm shift" (which is essential for true sustainability) may be as elusive as ever, there are numerous practical attempts to address the tensions (Campbell's [1996] "conflicts") between economic development, environmental protection, and social justice with innovative ideas, programs, and strategies that we detail below. These are resulting in more sustainable communities, not fully sustainable communities.

Sustainability and Environmental Justice in Practice

To investigate the applicability of environmental justice within sustainability formulations, or vice versa, a collection of ideas and programs has been assembled that provides proactive, balanced efforts to create sustainable urban development in U.S. cities. The objective of this section is to describe a sample of initiatives that illustrate the nexus of theoretical compatibility between sustainability and environmental justice, in practical programs and projects. The projects and organizations selected target different issues within the urban environment and may have alternative perspectives on the priorities, tensions, and conflicts between sustainability

TABLE 1

THE CHARACTERISTICS OF A SUSTAINABLE SOCIETY OR COMMUNITY

A sustainable community seeks to	
Protect and enhance the environment	Use energy, water, and other natural resources efficiently and with care
	Minimize waste; then reuse or recover it through recycling, composting, or energy recovery; and finally sustainably dispose of what is left
	Limit pollution to levels that do not damage natural systems
	Value and protect the diversity of nature
Meet social needs	Create or enhance places, spaces, and buildings that work well, wear well, and look well
	Make settlements human in scale or form
	Value and protect diversity and local distinctiveness and strengthen local community and cultural identity
	Protect human health and amenity through safe, clean, pleasant environments
	Emphasize health service prevention action as well as cure
	Ensure access to good food, water, housing, and fuel at reasonable cost
	Meet local needs locally wherever possible
	Maximize everyone's access to the skills and knowledge needed to play a full part in society
	Empower all sections of the community to participate in decision making, and consider the social and community impacts of decisions
Promote economic success	Create a vibrant local economy that gives access to satisfying and rewarding work without damaging the local, national, or global environment
	Value unpaid work
	Encourage necessary access to facilities, services, goods, and other people in ways that make less use of the car and minimize impacts on the environment
	Make opportunities for culture, leisure, and recreation readily available to all

SOURCE: Department of Environment, Transport and the Regions (1998).

and environmental justice. The importance, however, is that the ideas of sustainability and environmental justice are being applied in practice.

The avenues of implementation used at the community level are also varied, involving techniques ranging from street activism to private enterprise. Many initiatives are based on partnerships between community nonprofits, national nonprofits, local or federal governments, and/or private industries. This sample shows the involvement of various sectors of society in addressing sustainability and environmental justice principles.

Five "issue" categories of common concern to both environmental justice and sustainability are explored: land use planning, solid waste, toxic chemical use, residential energy use, and transportation. Most of the information about individual

programs was acquired initially over the Internet with some interviews with organization staff members. Although many of these organizations have been discussed
in articles, either academic or popular press, their websites were the most effective
source of recent information on the activities of community groups, activists, and
nonprofit organizations.

Land use planning

Historically, the primary tool of land use planning, zoning, has led to geographic
segregation of both people and land utility. Land use policy has led to the cumulative effects of environmental hazards' being shouldered within low-income and
minority communities (Bullard 1995). Planners concerned with sustainability
point out flaws in land use planning such as separation of uses and low-density
development, which have encouraged urban sprawl and auto dependent transportation (Beatley and Manning 1997; Newman and Kenworthy 1999). Recent movements in urban planning, however, have advocated for a change in the historical
land use planning to encourage more efficient land development, mixed-use and
mixed-income developments, and the reuse of former industrial sites (Duany,
Plater-Zyberk, and Speck 2000). In addition, procedural changes in the planning
process encourage greater community outreach and public participation in land
use decisions (Kelly and Becker 2000; American Planning Association 2000). Sustainable and just urban planning will require coordinated metropolitan/regional–
level regional planning in addition to crafting participatory approaches to comprehensive planning to prioritize existing community needs. In the meantime, community organizations are successfully developing tools to bridge the interests of
their residents and the municipal planning process.

Urban ecology. Urban Ecology in Oakland, California, is an organization
founded in 1975 that is engaged in two avenues toward promoting sustainability
and environmental justice principles in land use planning within the San Francisco
Bay Area. Its Community Design Program provides planning and design services
to low-income urban neighborhoods to assist them with community development.
It has developed a process to bring the services of city planners into communities to
engage in local needs assessments and community visioning. Urban Ecology helps
organizations facilitate the drafting of a community plan that addresses the immediate and long-term needs of the area and assists the local community organizations with implementation strategies. Although the needs of the community are
given first priority, Urban Ecology staff often promote ideas such as transit access,
pedestrian-friendly streetscapes, and affordable infill housing to help revitalize
neighborhoods with sustainability principles in mind (Urban Ecology 1996).
Urban Ecology's Sustainable Cities Program approaches municipal governments and community groups in cities in the midst of economic and population
growth to promote more sustainable development patterns. The suburbs at the
frontiers of urban sprawl are encouraged to adopt smart growth principles, which
allow for diverse housing options and alternative transportation infrastructure. Urban

Ecology advocates for infill development, affordable housing, transit-oriented development, reduced parking requirements, and mixed-use projects. It provides information to municipalities and citizen groups about private developers who have applied these principles in their projects. Urban Ecology also runs workshops for the public on how to review new projects and advocate for sustainable land development. In the Bay Area, the issues of urban sprawl, environment preservation, and social justice are deeply linked together, and groups such as Urban Ecology are working with many communities in pursuit of a more sustainable and equitable region (see http://www.urbanecology.org).

Solid waste management

Solid waste reduction is one of the keystone issues of the environmental movement. The most widely practiced strategy, recycling, is promoted as a municipal effort to reduce urban ecological footprints. At the same time, waste management

---

Up to 75 percent of an old structure can be reclaimed rather than demolished, and the materials can be sold at the ReUse Center.

---

facilities are one of the major issues confronted frequently by environmental justice groups. To communities overburdened with waste management facilities, new projects involving trash, whether they are transfer stations or recycling facilities, are usually not a welcomed land use. Sustainability advocates must use caution when proposing recycling industry facilities as community economic development opportunities for low-income areas. Waste can be an asset in local economic development, contributing to work opportunities, whereas some wastes, primarily toxic wastes, can be an assault on such communities (Ackerman and Mirza 2001). The goal of reducing waste generation and increasing recycling must be planned so the environmental and economic benefits are shared.

The Green Institute. The Phillips community is one of the most diverse neighborhoods in Minneapolis and has a long history of community activism. In the 1980s, the residents of Phillips organized a campaign to resist the construction of a garbage transfer station in their community. The city cleared twenty-eight homes for the ten-acre site, but the construction of the project was eventually halted by residents of the Phillips neighborhood. The People of Phillips neighborhood group then created the Green Institute (see http://www.greeninstitute.org) to create sustainable business enterprises on the now-vacant site in Phillips. The Green Institute is an entrepreneurial environmental organization creating jobs, improving the quality of life, and enhancing the urban environment in inner-city Minneapolis and now operates three revenue-generating ventures designed to combine green industry with local economic development. In 1995, the ReUse Center was developed to sell scavenged building and construction materials. The retail store reclaims materials from the local waste stream and sells them at low cost. The center offers living wages for employees and offers community classes on home improvement. In 1997, the Green Institute began its DeConstruction service to remove salvage materials from building or demolition sites. Through DeConstruction, up to 75 percent of an old structure can be reclaimed rather than demolished, and the materials can be sold at the ReUse Center. Most recently, the Phillips Eco-Enterprise Center, an award-winning business center built with green building technologies, was completed in 1999 on the site originally intended for the garbage transfer station. The Green Institute and their Phillips Eco-Enterprise Center are working to attract other environmentally conscious organizations and companies to continue their pursuit of sustainable economic development within the Phillips community (see http://www.greeninstitute.org).

Toxic chemical use

Four ideas have broadened the tools available to communities addressing the environmental justice and sustainability aspects of industrial operations. One is the "right to know" concept that requires full disclosure of chemical hazards to the community under the Emergency Planning and Community Right to Know Act (1986). This type of legislation is valuable as a small-scale industrial operation using hazardous materials has the opportunity to create large-scale public health and long-term ecological risks. The second tool is "toxic use reduction," aimed at redesigning industrial processes to use less hazardous substances and release less pollution into the air and water (Geiser 2001). Toxic use reduction allows for new production methods and application of new technology rather than requiring plant closures. This functions as a tool against the so-called jobs blackmail argument that industrial jobs in low-income communities will be sacrificed for environmental concerns. The third is the "precautionary principle,"[5] which argues that "where there are threats of serious or irreversible damage, lack of full scientific certainty should not be used as a reason for postponing measures to prevent environmental degradation" (Bergen Ministerial Declaration, cited in Raffensperger and Tickner 1999, 106). The sustainability and environmental justice movements would benefit from the creation of market demands that favor products generating fewer toxins and less solid waste at the end of the line, and from a regulatory system that enshrines the precautionary principle and promotes toxic use reduction. The fourth is "clean production," about which *Rachel's Environment and Health News* (Clean production 1999) says, "unlike 'pollution prevention' and 'recycling,' clean production asks fundamental questions about consumption: is a particular product even needed in the first place? And is it being produced in a way that promotes the goals of the community?" (p. 1). The first two tools are now well used in environmental justice and sustainability, but the other two, the precautionary principle and clean production, are still relatively new.

Toxic Use Reduction Institute (TURI). Based in Lowell, Massachusetts, home of the United States's first manufacturing corporation, TURI is a university and state office collaborative organization designed to decrease the quantity of toxic materials used and created by the state's industries. Based within the University of Massachusetts, Lowell's School of Engineering, TURI researchers consult with companies and community groups working to reduce toxic use. The goal is to help industries continue production and contribute to local economic health while cleaning up the environment in a state with a long history of polluting industrial practices. In addition, TURI funds and facilitates multiple public education programs regarding toxic chemical use.

One example of this was a two-day training workshop on clean production coorganized by the Lowell Center for Sustainable Production (a project of TURI), the Deep South Center for Environmental Justice at Xavier University, and the Clean Production Network. Here, theoretical linkages and practical coactivism were explored, led by trainers from both the environmental justice and the sustainability/clean-production fields. Sessions included tools for clean production, life-cycle assessment, design for environment, sustainable product design, policies and resources for clean production, extended producer responsibility, ecological taxes, product life-cycle labeling, applying clean production in campaigns, brownfield redevelopment, and developing a vision for clean production.

The institute was created to help the state's industries comply with the state's innovative Toxic Use Reduction Act passed in 1989. The institute functions as the state's clearinghouse of resources on toxic use reduction. TURI conducts research on toxic use reduction technology, trains certified toxic use reduction planners, and distributes grant funding to cities, towns, and community or environmental organizations. The grants are part of the Toxic Use Reduction Networking program that aims to develop model projects in Massachusetts's communities. Some examples of the programs include healthier cosmetology practices, safer food production in school cafeteria serves, integrated pest management programs, and household hazardous products education (see http://www.turi.org).

Residential energy use

Energy conservation in general is a win-win opportunity within the sustainability and environmental justice agendas. Cutting energy costs can provide economic assistance to low-income residents, particularly in northern regions. A reduction in demand for energy resources has a long-distance benefit to communities affected by their proximity to mining operations, power plants, and hazardous waste disposal facilities. However, the investment necessary to increase the environmental efficiency of existing homes and reduce the ecological impact of new home construction is often seen as incompatible with affordability goals. Cities often rely on the filtering principle to generate affordable house stock. Older, less energy-efficient homes become occupied by lower-income residents, while wealthier households purchase new houses. Older rented housing units create a particularly difficult area in energy-efficiency policy as the benefactor of home infrastructure improvements is not always the owner. Even as new green building technology improves household energy efficiency, the challenge to broad energy use reduction will be creating the economic opportunity for technology investment and retrofitting of old infrastructure.

National Center for Appropriate Technology (NCAT). NCAT (see http://www.ncat.org), established as a nonprofit corporation in 1976, works to find solutions to environmental or economic challenges that use local resources and assist society's most disadvantaged citizens. It has developed multiple programs to address energy use for low-income communities. With the assistance of the Department of Housing and Urban Development, NCAT created the Resource Efficient Multi-Family Housing Project to provide technical and financial strategies to owners and operators of apartment buildings. The goals of the project are to decrease utility costs, improve resident health, and conserve energy and water. Working with housing authorities, the project targets multifamily buildings in developing a comprehensive plan for energy and water use reduction.

NCAT also operates the Low-Income Home Energy Assistance Program as an information clearinghouse on residential energy conservation for those with the greatest energy cost burden and/or highest need. The program targets community groups, housing officials, energy providers, and low-income residents, providing information on conservation, energy self-sufficiency, and cooperative utility programs. The Low-Income Home Energy Assistance Program administers grants to help implement the goals of reducing the energy burden of households. Another similar NCAT project is the Affordable Sustainability Technical Assistance Program that works with Department of Housing and Urban Development grant programs. The goal is to incorporate green building designs into affordable housing projects. NCAT's other energy projects include statewide solar initiatives, low-income solar home demonstrations, and multiple energy-efficiency consulting plans with state and local housing authorities (http://www.ncat.org).

Transportation planning

Transportation justice has addressed a wide range of issues during the past century, including bus and rail segregation, highway development, transit design, toxic freight, airport expansion, and neighborhood street safety (Conservation Law Foundation 1998). Historically, large-scale highway projects have had a significant impact on minority and low-income neighborhoods while facilitating increased automobile use and emissions by wealthier suburban residents. Activists are continuing to work to gain equity within transportation systems, particularly urban transit. In many cities, the differentiation of transit quality between services for suburban commuters and those for urban residents is analogous to the segregation fought in the bus boycotts of the 1950s and the Freedom Riders campaign in the 1960s (Bullard and Johnson 1997). Many urban sustainability advocates point to transportation as the number-one issue to address in creating sustainable cities, and gradually, federal, state, and local transportation agencies have included nonautomotive modes as relevant parts of transportation systems (Newman and Kenworthy 1999).

Spanish Speaking Unity Council–Fruitvale Transit Village. In the 1960s, a state agency was created to develop a unifying transit system in the San Francisco region, called Bay Area Rapid Transit (BART). As a transit system, BART has had mixed results and has come under a great deal of criticism for its high cost and focus on serving suburban commuter transit. An element of this commuter system design is that most BART stations include large-surface parking lots.

If enough examples of sustainability and environmental justice initiatives can be created and networked, then perhaps this can galvanize a movement to reinvent the definition of progress.

When plans were announced for an expanded parking facility at the Fruitvale station in Oakland to serve driving commuters from outside the predominantly Latino neighborhood, the Fruitvale community responded with frustration. The Spanish Speaking Unity Council (see http://www.unitycouncil.org), a community development corporation for the Fruitvale neighborhood, developed an alternative plan for transit-oriented development around the BART station. Through multiple community meetings and design charrettes with assistance from the University of California at Berkeley, the community created a plan for a transit village at the location of the parking facility. Through rounds of negotiation, the Unity Council was able to convince BART and the city of Oakland to endorse their transit village plan, designed around pedestrian access to BART, retail development, and transit-oriented housing.

The mixed-use development uses ten acres of BART-owned surface parking and an additional fifteen surrounding acres. The master plan includes affordable housing, a senior center, a community health center, day care facilities, street-level retail shops, and a hidden parking garage. The design incorporates streetscape elements and architecture that reflect the Latino heritage of the community. The Transit Village is the core of a neighborhood revitalization plan that also includes homeowners' programs and local business improvement workshops to help existing residents benefit from new development. The community-based plan for a neighborhood center next to a transit station is an example of how innovations in transportation and land use planning can meet the goals of community development and urban sustainability (see http://www.unitycouncil.org; Shutkin 2000).

Conclusions: From Policy to Practice

The projects in this article represent a small sample of the practical initiatives in the United States, which illustrate the nexus of theoretical compatibility between sustainability and environmental justice. In this emerging field, some tentative conclusions can be made. In the area of land use planning, the essential theme appears to be the empowerment of community members into decision making with local governments and developers. This approximates to procedural justice. This (relatively) successful pattern has not always been followed within urban transportation offices; thus, a more direct and activist approach to transportation equity has been called for in some cities such as Los Angeles and Boston. For toxic and solid waste reduction, collaboration with industries and regulatory bodies as well as enterprising activities by organizations such as NCAT and TURI have led to the application of innovative ideas. The challenge of residential sustainable energy remains creating the link between consumers and available technology in conservation and renewables.

The existence of these examples is not an endorsement of the current economic or social paradigm, a soft/weak sustainability or technocentric model, or a growth-dependent plan for equity. In fact, the requirements of nonprofit or government intervention to create business partnerships, the need for community activism to gain participation in governmental planning, or the reliance on subsidized services for many of these programs highlights the failures of the current system. Some may argue that such programs have proven to be economically unsustainable due to this dependence on grants or other pilot project funding. These limitations can also be seen as a reflection on the challenges ahead for the environmental justice and sustainability movements and, more especially, for those who want to see greater practical linkages between the two. Until government policies and subsidies encouraging unsustainable activities are removed, and negative environmental and social externalities can be accurately accounted for in fiscal terms, our market economy is going to require that these alternative programs gain out-of-the-loop support. These programs are attempting to address social and ecological concerns within an unsustainable and unjust economic system.

While this research focused on five issue areas—land use planning, transportation, residential energy use, solid waste, and toxic use reduction—there exists a range of other areas to be explored for emerging sustainability and environmental justice models. Issue areas worth additional research might include water pollution affecting drinking water, fishing areas, and waterways; open space, habitat preservation, and recreation facilities in urban areas; brownfield cleanup and redevelopment in formerly industrial areas; and sustainable agriculture, small-scale farming, and community food security.

Just as no community in the United States (or the world) meets all the characteristics of a sustainable community as defined by the British Department of Environment, Transport and the Regions (1998) highlighted in Table 1, the initiatives described in this article represent only a small step toward sustainability, or meeting those criteria. However, each program has had a significant impact within its community. More important, the programs show that people can come together to apply relevant ideas toward improving conditions within the community. This has not gone unnoticed in public policy circles. The Environmental Protection Agency, as well as national environmental groups, is relearning the power of community-level activism, or civic environmentalism. This is the idea that

> members of a particular geographic and political community should engage in planning and organizing activities to ensure a future that is environmentally healthy and economically and socially vibrant at the local and regional levels. It is based on the notion that environmental quality and economic and social health are mutually constitutive. (Shutkin 2000, 14)[6]

Both the environmental justice movement and sustainability organizers are increasingly making this perspective a priority, leading to what Schlosberg (1999) called "cooperative endeavors," such as that between the Lowell Center for Sustainable Production (a project of TURI), the Deep South Center for Environmental Justice at Xavier University, and the Clean Production Network. To borrow a metaphor from the antinuclear campaign, the challenge is to convert the one-hundredth monkey so that a small group applying good ideas sparks society's collective awareness (Keyes 1984). If enough examples of sustainability and environmental justice initiatives can be created and networked, then perhaps this can galvanize a movement to reinvent the definition of progress.

Appendix
Principles of Environmental Justice

1. Environmental justice affirms the sacredness of Mother Earth, ecological unity and the interdependence of all species, and the right to be free from ecological destruction.
2. Environmental justice demands that public policy be based on mutual respect and justice for all peoples, free from any form of discrimination or bias.
3. Environmental justice mandates the right to ethical, balanced, and responsible uses of land and renewable resources in the interest of a sustainable planet for humans and other living things.

4. Environmental justice calls for universal protection from nuclear testing and the extraction, production, and disposal of toxic/hazardous wastes and poisons, which threaten the fundamental right to clean air, land, water, and food.

5. Environmental justice affirms the fundamental right to political, economic, cultural, and environmental self-determination of all peoples.

6. Environmental justice demands the cessation of the production of all toxins, hazardous wastes, and radioactive materials and demands that all past and current producers be held strictly accountable to the people for detoxification and the containment at the point of production.

7. Environmental justice demands the right to participate as equal partners at every level of decision making including needs assessment, planning, implementation, enforcement, and evaluation.

8. Environmental justice affirms the right of all workers to a safe and healthy work environment, without being forced to choose between an unsafe livelihood and unemployment. It also affirms the right of those who work at home to be free from environmental hazards.

9. Environmental justice protects the right of victims of environmental injustice to receive full compensation and reparations for damages as well as quality health care.

10. Environmental justice considers governmental acts of environmental injustice a violation of international law, the Universal Declaration on Human Rights, and the United Nations Convention on Genocide.

11. Environmental justice must recognize a special legal and natural relationship of native peoples to the U.S. government through treaties, agreements, compacts, and covenants affirming sovereignty and self-determination.

12. Environmental justice affirms the need for urban and rural ecological policies to clean up and rebuild our cities and rural areas in balance with nature, honoring the cultural integrity of all our communities, and providing fair access for all to the full range of resources.

13. Environmental justice calls for the strict enforcement of principles of informed consent and a halt to the testing of experimental reproductive and medical procedures and vaccinations on people of color.

14. Environmental justice opposes the destructive operations of multinational corporations.

15. Environmental justice opposes military occupation; repression; and exploitation of lands, peoples, cultures, and other life forms.

16. Environmental justice calls for the education of present and future generations, which emphasizes social and environmental issues, based on our experience and an appreciation of our diverse cultural perspectives.

17. Environmental justice requires that we, as individuals, make personal and consumer choices to consume as little of Mother Earth's resources and to produce as little waste as possible and make the conscious decision to challenge and reprioritize our lifestyles to ensure the health of the natural world for present and future generations.

Notes

1. Some authors such as Dobson (1999, 2003) take a separatist and traditional environmentalist view. They argue that the concepts of, and movements for, sustainability and environmental justice will come into conflict because of the environmental justice movement's primary focus on the issue of social equity, whereas the focus of environmental sustainability (as he calls it) is on green issues.

2. A descriptive typology within the sustainability discourse is that of "strong/hard" sustainability versus "weak/soft" sustainability (Jacobs 1992). Hard or strong sustainability, which equates with ecocentrism, implies that renewable resources must not be used faster than they can regenerate, that is, that (critical) natural capital must not be spent—we must live off the income produced by the capital. Soft or weak sustainability, which equates with technocentrism, accepts that certain resources may be depleted as long as others can substitute for them over time. Natural capital can be used up as long as it is converted into manufactured capital of equal value. One problem with weak sustainability is the difficulty in assigning monetary value to natural materials and services. In addition, it does not take into account the fact that manufactured goods and services cannot replace all resources. Strong sustainability thus maintains that there are certain ecological functions or services the environment provides that cannot be replaced by technological fixes.

3. Taylor (2000) argued that the Principles of Environmental Justice "show a well developed ideological framework that explicitly links ecological concerns with labor and social justice concerns" (p. 538). She continued, "The Principles contain six major thematic components that deal with (a) ecological principles; (b) justice and environmental rights; (c) autonomy/self determination; (d) corporate-community relations; (e) policy, politics and economic processes; (f) social movement building" (p. 539). She further argued that "environmental justice is grounded in ecocentric principles akin to those espoused by Muir" (p. 539). In addition, she argued that the environmental justice paradigm "is the first paradigm to link environment and race, class, gender, and social justice concerns in an explicit framework" (p. 42).

4. Table 1, developed by the then–Local Government Management Board in Great Britain in 1994, presents the characteristics of an ideal sustainable community that espouses these environmental, social, and economic goals. These characteristics and goals are remarkably similar to those Elements of a Sustainable Community, which were developed by the Board of the Institute for Sustainable Communities in Vermont and subsequently utilized by the President's Council on Sustainable Development (1997) in its task force report *Sustainable Communities*.

5. The Board of Supervisors of the city of San Francisco voted eight to two to adopt the precautionary principle as city policy in June 2003.

6. See Agyeman and Angus (2003) for a broader discussion of civic environmentalism.

References

Ackerman, F., and S. Mirza. 2001. Waste in the inner city: Asset or assault? *Local Environment* 6 (2): 113-20.

Agyeman, J. 2000. *Environmental justice: From the margins to the mainstream?* London: Town and Country Planning Association.

———. 2001. Ethnic minorities in Britain: Short change, systematic indifference and sustainable development. *Journal of Environmental Policy and Planning* 3 (1): 15-30.

———. 2002. Constructing environmental (in)justice: Transatlantic tales. *Environmental Politics* 11 (3): 31-53.

Agyeman, J., and B. Angus. 2003. The role of civic environmentalism in the pursuit of sustainable communities. *Journal of Environmental Planning and Management* 46 (3): 345-63.

Agyeman, J., R. Bullard, and B. Evans. 2002. Exploring the nexus: Bringing together sustainability, environmental justice and equity. *Space and Polity* 6 (1): 77-90.

———, eds. 2003. *Just sustainabilities: Development in an unequal world*. Cambridge, MA: MIT Press.

Agyeman, J., and B. Evans. 1995. Sustainability and democracy: Community participation in local agenda 21. *Local Government Policy Making* 22 (2): 35-40.

American Planning Association. 2000. *Policy guide on planning for sustainability*. Washington, DC: American Planning Association.

Beatley, T., and K. Manning. 1997. *The ecology of place*. Washington, DC: Island Press.

Brugmann, J. 1997. Is there a method in our measurement? The use of indicators in local sustainable devel-
    opment planning. *Local Environment* 2 (1): 59-81.
Bullard, R. 1995. Residential segregation and urban quality of life. In *Environmental justice—Issues, poli-
    cies, and solutions*, edited by Bunyan Bryant. Washington, DC: Island Press.
Bullard, R., and S. Johnson, eds. 1997. *Just transportation*. Gabriola Island, Canada: Island Press.
Campbell, S. 1996. Green cities, growing cities, just cities? Urban planning and the contradictions of sustain-
    able development. *Journal of the American Planning Association* 62 (3): 296-312.
Clean production. Part 1. 1999. *Rachel's Environment and Health News*, 13 May.
Commonwealth of Massachusetts. 2002. *Environmental justice policy*. Boston: State House.
Conservation Law Foundation. 1998. *City routes, city rights: Building livable neighborhoods and environ-
    mental justice by fixing transportation*. Boston: Conservation Law Foundation.
Department of Environment, Transport and the Regions. 1998. *Sustainable local communities for the 21st
    century*. London: Department of Environment, Transport and the Regions.
Dobson, A. 1999. *Justice and the environment: Conceptions of environmental sustainability and dimensions
    of social justice*. Oxford, UK: Oxford University Press.
———. 2003. Social justice and environmental sustainability: Ne'er the twain shall meet? In *Just
    sustainabilities: Development in an unequal world*, edited by Julian Agyeman, Robert D. Bullard, and
    Bob Evans, 83-95. Cambridge, MA: MIT Press.
Duany, A., E. Plater-Zyberk, and J. Speck. 2000. *Suburban nation: The rise of sprawl and decline of the Amer-
    ican dream*. New York: North Point Press.
Environmental Law Institute. 1999. *Sustainability in practice*. Washington, DC: Environmental Law
    Institute.
Geiser, K. 2001. *Materials matter: Toward a sustainable materials policy*. Cambridge, MA: MIT Press.
International Union for the Conservation of Nature. 1991. *Caring for the earth*. Gland, Switzerland: Interna-
    tional Union for the Conservation of Nature.
Jacobs, M. 1992. *The green economy: Environment, sustainable development and the politics of the future*.
    London: Pluto.
Kelly, D., and B. Becker. 2000. *Community planning: An introduction to the comprehensive plan*. Washing-
    ton, DC: Island Press.
Keyes, K. 1984. *The hundredth monkey*. Coos Bay, OR: Vision Books.
Lake, R. W. 2000. Contradictions at the local scale: Local implementation of local agenda 21 in the USA. In
    Consuming cities, edited by Nicholas Low, Brendan Gleeson, Ingemar Elander, and Rolf Lidskog, 70-90.
    London: Routledge.
Levett, R. 1997. Tools, techniques and processes for municipal environmental management. *Local Environ-
    ment* 2 (2): 189-202.
Milbrath, L. 1989. *Envisioning a sustainable society: Learning our way out*. Albany: State University of New
    York Press.
Newman, P., and J. Kenworthy. 1999. *Sustainability and cities: Overcoming automobile dependence*. Wash-
    ington, DC: Island Press.
O'Riordan, T. 1999. *Planning for sustainable development*. Tomorrow series. London: Town and Country
    Planning Association.
Portney, K. E. 2003. *Taking sustainable cities seriously*. Cambridge, MA: MIT Press.
President's Council on Sustainable Development. 1997. *Sustainable Communities Task Force report*. Wash-
    ington, DC: Government Printing Office.
Raffensperger, C., and J. Tickner, eds. 1999. *Protecting public health and the environment: Implementing the
    precautionary principle*. Washington, DC: Island Press.
Ruhl. 1999. The co-evolution of sustainable development and environmental justice: Cooperation, then com-
    petition, then conflict. *Duke Environmental Law and Policy Forum* 9:161.
Satterthwaite, D. 1999. *Earthscan reader in sustainable cities*. London: Earthscan.
Schlosberg, D. 1999. *Environmental justice and the new pluralism: The challenge of difference for environ-
    mentalism*. Oxford, UK: Oxford University Press.
Shutkin, W. 2000. *The land that could be: Environmentalism and democracy in the twenty-first century*.
    Cambridge, MA: MIT Press.

Taylor, D. 2000. The rise of the environmental justice paradigm. *American Behavioral Scientist* 43 (1): 508-80.

Urban Ecology. 1996. *Blueprint for a sustainable Bay Area.* Oakland, CA: Mobius Press.

Warner, K. 2002. Linking local sustainability initiatives with environmental justice. *Local Environment* 7 (1): 35-47.

World Commission on Environment and Development. 1987. *Our common future.* Oxford, UK: Oxford University Press.

Yanarella, E. J. 1999. Local sustainability programmes in comparative perspective: Canada and the USA. *Local Environment* 4 (2): 209-24.

NGOs and Production of Indigenous Knowledge under the Condition of Postmodernity

By
JUDE L. FERNANDO

Indigenous knowledge (IK), experienced in development, is a product of a set of institutions often external to where they are located. The results of the use of IK in sustainable development are another example of capitalism's capacity to configure development according to its own imperatives. Rather than being an instrument of sustainable development, IK has become a means through which the diversity of knowledge systems and the embedded cultures in which they exist are disciplined and managed according to capital's need to expand. The collaborative role played by the nongovernmental organizations (NGOs) in this process is obscured by their use of the seductive language of empowerment of marginalized social groups. NGOs' interventions run counter to the interests of the people they claim to serve. The challenge to work towards an alternative institutional environment that could liberate the use of IK from being determined by the ideology and institutions of capitalism.

Keywords: indigenous knowledge; NGOs; capitalism; power; inequality; sustainable development

A defining characteristic of the history of development is the periodic conceptual and policy innovations that become its central focus for a period until a new one emerges. By doing so, it has been able to reinvent itself in the face of the challenges it faces, without fundamentally changing its basic ideological and institutional underpinnings. These periodic shifts are due to several factors: (1) the reconfiguration of the meanings and priorities of development and the means of realizing them in the light of the past shortcomings and failures of development, (2)

Jude L. Fernando teaches political economy and sustainable development at the Department of Geography and Regional Development and the International College of the University of Arizona. His research focus is economic development and political economy, with a special emphasis on nonprofit organizations, environment, race, gender, and child labor, particularly in South Asia. He is currently completing a book titled Political Economy of NGOs: Modernizing Post-Modernity *(Pluto Press). He is also working on an edited volume on micro-credit with Katherine Rankin to be published by Routledge.*

DOI: 10.1177/0002716203258374

the discovery of a vital area of development that had been previously neglected, (3) the emergence of an area/field from the practices of development, and (4) an interest arising from the academic pursuit of knowledge about development and competition between development practitioners for the legitimacy of their respective endeavors.

The current positioning of indigenous knowledge (IK) in the discourse of sustainable development is arguably a result of the constellation of all these factors. Perhaps, similar to what was expected from the feminist interventions in development via the compelling need to assign priority consideration to gender, IK promises to bring about a radical change in the theory and practice of development and, in the process, help development to overcome its current impasse. Apart from calls by the indigenous communities to protect their environments from the onslaught of development, IK offers a framework of ideas, guidelines, and institutional foundations that can offer entry points into alternative ways of thinking about sustainable development.

The term local . . . *is relative and its boundary with the universal is dynamic.*

Similar to other innovative changes in post–World War II development paradigms, IK has also become an essential component of the many different approaches to sustainable development by different interest groups. For those who still function within the mainstream paradigms of development, IK is an important source of overcoming the limitations and failures of development. For the adherents of the postdevelopment school, IK is an important source of imagining and realizing alternative paradigms of development. For the culturalists, IK is an invaluable source of politics of difference/politics of identity. For multinational corporations concerned with sustainable development, IK is a highly promising area of investment, a way of making their investments socially responsible. IK has evolved as a means of legitimizing as well as resisting mainstream development. The political power of IK lies in its amenability to such different projects—all claiming their aim is to work toward sustainable development.

This article explores the relationship between the mobilizations of IK by nongovernmental organizations (NGOs) within the context of the expansion of capitalism worldwide. In other words, it probes the implications of the diverse mobilizations of IK in sustainable development by NGOs in the current phase of capitalist accumulation. The focus of NGOs and capitalist accumulation are not random choices. The NGOs are reputed to represent the diversity of IK systems and claim to have been at the forefront of the movements that brought IK to the center of the discourse on sustainable development. "Radical" NGOs strive to shield IK and their cultural environments from the negative impacts of the current global political economy. Although the NGOs are an ideologically and operationally diverse group of organizations, they do not function in a vacuum but are embedded in the institutional structures of the wider economy. Recent studies have shown, however, that NGOs tend to legitimize the very practices that they seek to transform (Fernando forthcoming). At the same time, IK-related issues have become politically controversial, and many of these issues remain unresolved.

One of the main obstacles to understanding the impact of NGOs in sustainable development is the scant attention given to the interface between NGO interventions in IK systems and the expansion of capitalism worldwide. Very little is known about how NGO attempts at using IK to empower local communities produce results that are detrimental not only to the communities concerned but also to the wider society. A good deal of knowledge exists concerning the negative results of projects but not about the processes through which they occur and the institutions and power relations embedded in them. To fill this void, this article examines the impact of IK use by NGOs on the institutional and power relations of the current capitalist economy and their implications for the stated goals of sustainable development. The emphasis of this analysis is on the processes through which the NGOs seek to realize their goals of sustainable development, rather than the final outcomes of their projects. The ethnography of the following analysis is primarily based on the actor-oriented research methods used by Norman Long and his associates (Long and Long 1998; Long 2001; Long and Arce 1999).

Definition of IK

The meaning of IK is ambiguous, yet to dismiss the matter would be a serious error, given the many things said and done in its name with far-reaching consequences for the world's quest for sustainable development. Generally, IK is considered a body of knowledge associated with a fixed territorial space for a considerably long period of time. Such systems of knowledge are informal, experiential, and uncodified compared to the knowledge systems associated with the Western sciences.

IK is unique to a community, culture, or society; is the basis for local-level decision making in agriculture, health, natural resource management, and other activities; is embedded in community practices, institutions, relationships, and rituals; and as such is a powerful tool to create sustainable change, particularly in resource-poor rural communities. The scattered nature of IK systems raises two important issues. First,

> if indigenous knowledge is inherently scattered and local in character, and gains its vitality from being deeply implicated in peoples' lives, then attempts to essentialize, isolate,

archive, and transfer such knowledge can only seem contradictory. If Western sciences are to be condemned for being non-responsive to local demands, and divorced from people's lives, then centralized storage and management of indigenous knowledge lays itself to the same criticism. (Agrawal, 1995a)

Second, from a methodological point of view, "the ultimate irony of the attempts to valorize indigenous knowledge may lie in the willingness to adopt the methods and instruments of Western science" (Agrawal 1995a; 1995b, 4). In other words, "the validation of the indigenous knowledge is by means of scientific criteria" (Agrawal 1995a; 1995b, 4).

Competing definitions of IK tell one more about what IK is not rather than what it is. The binary opposition between IK and scientific knowledge/Western knowledge is an institutionally produced one, rather than a naturally given condition. Systematic empirical and comparative studies on IK versus scientific knowledge systems suggest that apart from the epistemological and methodological similarities between the two systems of knowledge, historically complex forms of interconnectedness have existed between them through exchange, communications, and learning, which result in their mutual transformation (Agrawal 1995a, 1995b). A long-held assumption is that scientific knowledge, in search of universal validity, is divorced from the social, political, and economic contexts in which it is produced and implemented. As Arun Agrawal pointed out, this is an untenable position because the "so-called technical solutions are as anchored in a specific milieu as any other system of knowledge" (Agrawal 1995a; 1995b, 36). Many have observed that scientists work in a context characterized by "multiplicity, and heterogeneity of space"; hence, science needs to be viewed as practice and culture (Agrawal 1995a, 429).

To explore the implications of IK for sustainable development, it makes more sense to view such knowledge as produced by a specific set of intellectual and institutional practices. The process of the production of IK involves a number of phases: identification, particularization, validation, and generalization followed by dissemination and utilization. These processes represent the interests and power of a broad spectrum of institutions. They in many ways have undermined stated goals of using IK in sustainable development. For example, the creation of databases tends to undermine the goals of mobilizing IK for development. What happens in this process is "the elimination of that very difference that the advocates of indigenous knowledge seek to build and defend" (Geertz 1991, 129). The very process, in turn, submits IK to the power of science. The "creation of a spatial and temporal distance between IK and scientific knowledge through the scientific method undermines the very characteristic of IK that 'render it indigenous' " (Geertz 1991, 129). Through the databases, the external actors and whatever controls local communities had over their environments are taken away and make IK legally open to interventions. Through the production of IK in a specific form within the discourse of development, "the commensuration between the indigenous and the scientific is established, in other words, by denying culturally produced ways of experiencing time, ways of sharing and experiencing time that underpinned the initial awareness of specific indigenous knowledge" (Geertz 1991, 132).

IK, as opposed to scientific knowledge, is considered local in terms of its origin and applicability to local communities. The term *local*, however, is an ambiguous concept. It is relative and its boundary with the universal is dynamic. As Clifford Geertz pointed out, "in the solar system, the earth is local; in the galaxy, the solar system is local; and in the universe the galaxy is local." Within transnational institutions, the state is local; within states, the region is local; within the region, the community is local; and within the community, the family is local, and so on. What is local knowledge is construed in relation to its exterior. Thus,

> the opposition, if we must have one (and I am not persuaded that an opposition—another opposition—is what we need or ought to want rather than a shifting focus of particularity), is not one between local and universal knowledge, but between one sort of local knowledge (say, neurology) and another (say, ethnography). As all politics, however inconsequential, is local, so is all understanding, however ambitious. No one knows everything, because there is no everything to know.... Let us then try to avoid any radical dichotomy between local and universal knowledge. Little is purely local, less is truly universal. (Geertz 1991, 132)

The binary between IK and universal knowledge systems exists through negotiations between them, rather than as a given mechanical opposition. "The Universal contained in the particular just as particular contained in the universal" (Geertz 1991, 132).

It is difficult to maintain that a particular system of knowledge of an individual, community, nation, or transnational group is pure and authentic in terms of its origins, content, and methods of practical use. The epistemic origins of scientific and folk knowledge are hidden and unclear. Hybridity rather than difference is more the norm than the exception of IK systems. For example, Michael R. Dove's (2002) study on the use of rubber in Asia and South America has shown that such practices are a "mix of hybridity, mistranslation, and incommensurability" (p. 356). Hybridization has a history of centuries where knowledge systems of distant localities have been contacting, communicating, and learning from each other. As globalization engulfs the world, there will be fewer and fewer areas where the term *indigenous knowledge* is applicable in any meaningful way.

I am not suggesting that within the context of globalization, every local knowledge system is becoming hybridized as it is stripped of its local roots, but even those systems that struggle to protect their localities by resisting globalization cannot be understood outside the determinants of globalization. The point here is that any meaningful understanding of the indigenous cannot be excluded from the reference to a wider context. In fact, the current interest in IK is largely a result of a force external to where they are located. Therefore, instead of striving to arrive at a clear, precise definition, it would be far more productive to view IK as a social phenomenon produced within a specific social, economic, and political context and, thereafter, proceed to analyze the relevance of such meanings and the institutional and power relations embedded in them for achieving the goals of sustainable development.

Production of IK in this article is viewed as a process mediated by many institutions with diverse ideological and operational orientations. Institutions that concern us here are the ones interested in sustainable development. Their central argument is that if development is to be sustainable, it must be embedded in the local knowledge systems. This article intends to understand the processes through which IK is used in development. The study is conducted from the perspective of NGOs. The analysis is based on a study of one NGO in two project settings in Sri Lanka.[1] The emphasis is on the systematic analysis of the process, beginning with initial motives for investing in IK to project evaluation. The assumption is that in this process, NGOs come into contact with numerous institutions that do not necessarily share the same ideological and operations orientations as the NGOs. The outcomes of NGOs in these projects are determined by the interactions with these institutions. By examining the interactions between NGOs and the other institutions involved in the projects, this article seeks to explain how and why IK is mobilized in the discourse of development and to arrive at a better explanation for the consequences of such practices for development.

NGOs and IK

The local organization examined in the study is a partner of foreign NGOs. The latter was also the main donor of the local NGO, which took the initial interest in investing in IK-related projects in Sri Lanka. However, during formal and informal conversations with me, the foreign NGO made an extra effort to emphasize that they are responding to the needs of the people and are not interested in following "top-down" models of development. Indeed, I was seduced to believe that they are trying to initiate a new counterhegemonic revolutionary process of development from the grass roots. The survival of the foreign NGO, too, was based on recruiting NGOs from the Third World for the development of IK systems, with an emphasis on poverty alleviation and the protection of local cultures. Similar to the local NGOs, the interest of the donor agency coincided with two important trends in the field of development. First, increased funding was available due to worldwide interest in the protection of indigenous rights and the controversies over intellectual property rights. Second, unless organizations are willing to engage in funding-friendly areas such as IK, they are faced with the threat of closure. In addition, the NGO faced ongoing pressure to expand into new areas or increase the volume of their projects, rather than simply continue to invest in the same project.

Prior to the fact-finding mission, the foreign NGO had several meetings with their donor organizations in the West, for example, the European Union and other Western governments. The outcomes of these meetings were not available to the public. Whatever was available was simply what is widely known in development circles; that is, they stressed the importance of providing assistance to those projects that are more likely to safeguard the interests of local communities.

After arriving at an understanding of financial assistance between these foreign NGOs and their donors, the former proceeded to make initial contact with the local NGOs through a local academic with a reputation as an NGO consultant. His participation was widely used by the donors as evidence of listening to the voices of the local people. The consultant/academic maintained close relations with the NGOs in various capacities. Later discovery revealed that negotiations between the academic and the local NGO selected for the project occurred well before the

The increasing need for cash, partly driven by the need to service debt, has led to commercialization of local systems of survival and placed them under the control of local businesses and other external actors, thereby strengthening the existing systems of power relations that the NGOs purport to transform.

academic prepared the report to the donors. Part of the reason was that this academic had previously worked as a consultant to the NGO. These initial negotiations were also influenced by the local and national political authorities that have an interest in making use of NGO funding to their respective electorates.

The international NGO provided the consultant/academic with detailed guidelines as to the expectations of the report and how it should be prepared. The consultant/academic prepared the project without visiting the villages that he selected and was not familiar with the local languages or lifestyles of the villages. Two university students did survey some villages; however, it turned out that these villages were not the ones subsequently selected. The consultancy report was not available to the public because it was an internal document. The local communities actually chosen did not have any knowledge about the report or the identity of the consultant/academic. Until the implementation stage, the local communities were not aware of the detailed information about the interest of the NGO. Within the villages, there was absolutely no dialogue on IK as it was within and between the NGOs during the initial stages of the project. In fact, among the villagers, there was no habit of separating IK from other forms of knowledge systems, but they were more than willing to accept hybrid systems depending on their day-to-day needs. Even after months of participating in the projects, the NGO language of IK was quite alien to the villagers. What the villages knew was simply that another aid agency was coming into the village as a response to a request made by the member of Parliament for the area. Subsequently, several villagers made visits to the member of Parliament's office and its local representatives to secure assistance from the NGO.

The donor agency, however, stipulated certain contradictory conditions to determine the eligibility of the local villages for funding. These conditions were the nonnegotiable guidelines for writing the consultant report. On one hand, the projects required the involvement of the local population and clear policies to protect local culture. The projects had to use IK systems and technologies. However, the guidelines did not clarify the meaning of IK. On the other hand, while empowerment of the local populations and their diverse cultures was a stated goal, measurement was in terms of increased levels of income. The self-sufficiency of the borrowers was measured simply in terms of the level of their dependence on state welfare and the ability to develop entrepreneurial skills to profitably participate in the market economy.

The need to develop entrepreneurial skills to meet the demands of global markets was an important guideline given to the field officers who were in charge of loans. In this sense, what could be legitimately included as IK-based livelihood strategies were those transformable into commodities for the world market. The main policy instruments of commodification of local systems of production were micro-finance and "expert" assistance from the marketing and agro-industry professionals external to the local environments. Far more than the NGO field officers, these professionals were very familiar with the language of sustainable development, although they were ultimately accountable to the for-profit corporations.

While the NGO aid was intended to target the poorest groups, whose traditional lifestyles were based on local systems of knowledge, they did not receive first preference in the disbursement of loans because of the detailed/rigid criterion used by the NGO field officers to decide the credit worthiness of the borrowers. At this point, those who were not eligible for loans solicited those with capital and political influence to be the guarantors of the loans. The conditions of the guarantee agreement were that they would mortgage their land (if they had land) with the guarantor, invest the NGO funds entirely for the development of products determined by the NGO in the mortgaged land or the land owned by the guarantor, and sell the product to the guarantor. This is a common outcome when projects to promote IK are tied to micro-finance—where the local elites, as a result of the local power networks, automatically become the managers of the credit and IK-based production systems. Subsequently, high rates of loan default led to more land becoming concentrated in the hands of fewer people and/or entities and a larger number of recipients of aid were forced to turn to wage labor.

While empowerment was defined by NGOs as a change of power relations, there were no clear indicators to measure such impacts of IK-centered projects. This lapse points to another contradiction in the donor mission. On one hand, the organization seeks to change power relations, but there was no clarity as to what relations of power, their transformation, and sustainability. On the other hand, it seeks to protect local cultures, transforming them being viewed as a highly undesirable goal—it was not "politically correct" for an outside agency to do so. Such a position differs from that of the villagers about the local cultures. While they admired their cultural environment, they were also very clear about the need to change unequal and highly oppressive relations of power in them. They were not as fascinated with IK as the NGOs and the donors were. For the villagers, some of their local systems were of no help in improving their standards of living and could not be profitable because of the influx of cheap imports and the spread of market-driven consumerism in their communities. Many pointed out that they have lost control over IK due to the increasing debt burden and that landlessness had forced them to become wage laborers. In the final analysis, the increasing need for cash, partly driven by the need to service debt, has led to the commercialization of local systems of survival and placed them under the control of local businesses and other external actors, thereby strengthening the existing systems of power relations that the NGOs purport to transform.

The fear of foreign corporations taking control over their resources was a widespread concern among the villagers. These sentiments were politicized by both "radical" political parties—the Sinhala Urumaya (Sinhalese Heritage Party) and the Marxist-Leninist Janatha Vimukthi Peramuna (the People's Liberation Front). They provided the villagers and me with detailed information on the intrusion of multinational corporations into the area that took control of plants and species that hitherto were not marketable and how local populations lost control over their own environments and cultures. They also pointed out that large sums of money as aid and the promise of a better income fooled the people, and with the interventions of NGOs, local elites, and the corporations, these foreign agents had consolidated their hold over the locals' livelihoods based on traditional systems of knowledge. Ensuing protests fueled the anti-NGO sentiments and extremist nationalistic politics that prevail at the national level.

Such destructive potential for exploitation of IK for political opportunism was not, however, a part of the donor and NGO deliberations at local, national, or international levels. In fact, the NGO field officers were asked to "keep out of politics." The calculation of the political risks taken by the NGOs in a given project was determined by the time frame given by their donors for the implementation and evaluation of the project, which, in turn, is often tied to the fiscal policies of the donor country. It can also be argued that the imposition of highly romanticized "spaces of indigenous knowledge" constructed by the NGOs on the local communities not only forecloses the possibility of them to resist the inequalities internal and external to their communities but also generates social capital for extremist political groups that derived their ideological bases from tradition and culture.

Following negotiations between the donors and the NGOs, the latter proceeded to select villages eligible for assistance. Interestingly, the selection of these local communities was based on the recommendations and requests made by politicians and government departments. At times, NGOs contacted these authorities seeking areas for projects as a way of gaining national recognition. Generally, the local community was not directly involved in the selecting and planning of the project, particularly selecting the intended beneficiaries. They were simply beneficiaries of loans on the request made by their local political representatives. Villagers were well aware of the discriminatory practices used by the local power structures in disbursing NGO aid. They were unwilling to challenge the local power relations because from their perspective, NGOs are temporary and highly unreliable actors in their localities that provide simply one source of their overall income.

The imposition of highly romanticized "spaces of indigenous knowledge" constructed by the NGOs on the local communities not only forecloses the possibility of them to resist against the inequalities internal and external to their communities but also generates social capital for extremist political groups who derived their ideological bases from tradition and culture.

The time frame for selecting the village and beginning the project was set by the fiscal imperatives of the donor agencies, which were in turn determined by the legal structures of the governments of their respective countries. Generally, there was a rush to start the project after donors approved the funds. After selecting the villages for projects, the field officers visit the village and first meet with local religious leaders and the newly emerging business class, who in many cases were sons and relatives of the old landed elites. In fact, in this case, the chief religious leader of the area was a landlord, and the leadership of his establishment circulated within the family to retain the control of the land within the family.

After negotiating with the local power elites, NGOs, as a "custom," organize a series of public meetings. These meetings include traditional ritual and cultural practices that provide meaning and legitimacy for the same power relations that are oppressive to the marginalized segment of the local community. While these public meetings are usually well attended by representatives from different political factions and their supporters, those with close relations with the ruling party at a national level and the religious establishment tend to dominate the discussions. In the case at hand, despite the presence of the local NGO and their foreign partner, the content of the speeches at the meetings was about how the governing political party was fulfilling their election promises, particularly helping the poor. There was absolutely no mention about IK. These meetings received widespread coverage by the national media and were used as advertising material by the NGO for the purpose of fund-raising.

There were significant differences between what was said at the meetings and what was said to me by donors and the NGOs about their projects, as well as by the officers before they visited the village. At the level of the donor and NGO, the project was all about empowerment, protecting the indigenous cultures, and poverty alleviation. As one moves down the ladder of institutional hierarchy to the local level, the goals of the project are reduced to the simple increase of income levels of the poor. In other words, the main burden of the project was how to transform the production systems based on IK into commodities profitable in the world market through micro-credit.

The villagers did not perceive the NGOs as saviors of their traditional knowledge and cultures but as organizations with foreign money. For them, these organizations were simply another source of income. During the final stages of planning the project, NGOs spend most of their time with their key contact persons, who happen to be the village elite. Through these elites, a small group or village committee was formed to implement the project. Selection of beneficiaries was not based on the factors determining the protection of IK; rather, beneficiaries were handpicked by the village elites based on patron-cliental relationships that would create an enabling environment for the commercialization of local production systems. At this stage, politicians from the local to the national level were heavily involved. Interestingly, none of these leaders mentioned anything about IK. Instead, they spoke about the use of funds in commercially viable ways: they recommended that funds be invested in the cultivation of plants that had export value. They boasted about how foreigners like their local products, and it is their patriotic duty to promote them in the international markets. For some in the villages, emphasis on income generation through the commodification of IK was an interesting shift in the NGO projects, which in the past emphasized improving their basic subsistence, education, and health care. According to one villager, the NGO had told them,

> We want to help you to invest in areas where there is a steady income. These days, foreigners like local medicinal plants, herbs, and cut flowers. They want these to be cultivated according to traditional knowledge. Unlike those days, the foreigners value our traditional products. So we are here to help you.

Through the patron-cliental networks, a larger portion of the NGO funds was filtered into the hands of the landed elites through existing dependency networks. As these products became profitable in the marketplace, the conversion of more and more land, once used for cultivation of subsistence crops, was converted for cultivation of such commercial crops. Those small farmers who were not making ends meet either sold or mortgaged their land to the large landowners and subsequently became daily wage laborers on their own land. Another reason for the transfer of land was increasing debt and lack of capital to finance the projects. In many cases, NGO funds were supplemented by funds from the village moneylenders and landlords; in many cases, they even happened to be the same people who bought their produce.

Months after implementation of the project, the NGO carried out extensive surveys to explore the potential of indigenous resources and knowledge. The locals were told that the purpose of the survey was to protect their local resources and cultures. Some were told that making local resources yield profits would, in the long run, be a more effective and reliable way of saving their local cultures from destruction by external forces than conventional approaches, such as relying on aid and political protection from governments and private organizations. At the same time, this provides them with a more reliable and less environmentally destructive source of funds to meet basic needs, such as medicine, education, and other services, than either government aid or engaging in environmentally destructive activities. There was no evidence that the information gathered by the survey was used in the projects at the local level. At this stage, it appeared that a wide gulf spanned between the reasons for the survey and how it was used. Later, it was evident that the survey was a project within a project of global proportions, the motives of which could have far more negative consequences for the local communities.

The survey results were systematically classified into different categories based on their export income-earning potential. Some knowledge systems and productive practices were deliberately devalued and ignored by the survey—even if they are important for people's subsistence and local culture—and locals who associated with them were not selected as worthy of NGO assistance. Then the information was entered into a database available to the public. All the records were held in English, and the local communities were neither aware of them nor had access to them. According to NGO officers, the researchers in the universities of the developed countries now have access to these databases to develop hybrid varieties of the indigenous plants and seeds. The multinational corporations sponsored the research and retained complete control over the research findings. Evidence from many parts of the world shows how corporations have used governments of the developed industrialized countries and the World Trade Organization to claim property rights over the traditional plants when they were modified by corporate-funded research in the universities in the Western countries (Correa 2000; Brush and Stabinsky 1996; Ryan 1998; Perelman 2002). On several occasions, local academics participated in the research projects as consultants and were given research fellowships in Western universities. In some cases, the graduate students from developing countries were also awarded research scholarships to work on IK-related research projects in the Western universities. The findings of these research projects were kept in absolute secrecy within these universities and could be disseminated to the public only after the approval of their funding agencies, which often included multinational corporations.

As the NGO began providing financial and technical assistance to people, private investors had already completed negotiations with the local buyers of their plants. I later found that the methods of cultivation, processing, and marketing that the people expressed during the meetings were the result of negotiations between local buyers, who were closely connected with the local elites, and the outside private investors. Planned obstructions were placed on the local communities to prevent them from directly dealing with alternative buyers who compete with the local ones. Generally, the NGO does not provide all the necessary types of assistance

---

As the demand for IK-based products increases, the local communities are forced to increase productivity, either by using methods external to their traditional environments or increasing the size of land under cultivation by encroaching the land hitherto used for subsistence cultivation.

---

such as finance and marketing necessary to make IK projects profitable. Local communities are expected to rely on other sources. As a result, within a matter of one year, the participants in this case study became fully dependent on local elites who function as the intermediaries for foreign companies. The company set the price unilaterally and dictated how much or little it would buy. The most common ways of controlling the prices were through increasing the aid dependence and the financial and social networks within localities.

The volume of production output was regulated by external corporations so the producers are not expected to produce more than what is required by the corporations or to sell to other corporations that might offer them a better price. This meant that the locals were in fact denied the freedom to fully participate in the market economy—a stated ideological goal of capitalists. As the demand for IK-based products increases, the local communities are forced to increase productivity, either by using methods external to their traditional production environments or increasing the size of land under cultivation by encroaching the land hitherto used for subsistence cultivation. Some of these methods even included use of chemicals, fertilizers, and the knowledge of the experts from foreign countries. The villagers simply had no choice but to meet the deadlines set by the corporations. Farmers therefore had to put the demands of the foreign countries above other options, such as cultivation of crops for subsistence and other crops that would have yielded them higher profits in the marketplace. These pressures were worsened by the increasing debt repayment obligations.

Although NGOs emphasize participatory development and community-based development as ends of their interventions, the existing local social networks and power relations managed the financial assistance packages provided by the NGO. With the increasing competition for capital and market share, now the local communities have even less incentive to use IK-related productive activities for the collective benefit of the community and the environment.

The rhetoric of IK is used by these companies as a means of free advertising for the multinational companies that market their products as produced by the indigenous communities and with their traditional systems of knowledge. Such advertising is aimed toward an increasing number of socially conscious/green consumers in the Western markets and has a number of negative consequences. First, it connects the local communities with transnational capital or creates the space for the transnational capital to manage local knowledge according to the imperatives of the neoliberal trade regime. The ways in which the NGOs carve out autonomous spaces for the IK-based production systems also enable the corporations to bypass the difficulties they faced with national governments and social movements that are struggling against the transnational corporations' colonization of IK systems. Second, as the local communities become dependent on transactions with corporations, the NGOs disappear from the scene, noting that the project is now self-sufficient.

At the same time, the state and the local community organizations have become powerless to intervene on behalf of the villages when they faced server exploitation by these corporations. In fact, the state is under pressure to manage conflicts between the local populations and the corporations so that the latter continue to invest in the area. In the face of growing powers of the corporations, it is not only the local communities but also the state and the NGOs that have lost whatever autonomy and control they had in the local environments.

Indigenous Property Rights versus Capitalist Property Rights

Generally, in many parts of the developing world, IK systems are associated with a culturally determined diversity of property rights regimes. One of the important guidelines given to the consultant academic was to provide detailed information about the local systems of property rights. The concern of the donor NGO was about the potential conflict between the ways in which the NGOs intend to use IK and the local systems of property rights. The NGO was not concerned with transforming all systems of noncapitalist property rights into capitalist property rights but with ways to configure and manage the former to produce the same outcomes as the latter. At this point, there was some concern among the NGOs about the local power relations. The NGOs were more interested in working with the local landed elites and the business communities through their local patron-cliental relations, as long as they could provide the conditions for making IK-based products profitable. From the perspective of the NGOs, managing the local conflicts by the locals was safe and good for the sustainability of the projects.

The NGO-mediated attempts to reconcile the diverse local property rights with standardized global property rights have had a number of consequences. First, the multinational corporations have been able to secure the indirect control of diverse property rights regimes through patent rights, extension of credit, technical advice, and marketing assistance for the development of management of IK systems. Second, instead of completely redefining the diverse systems of property rights, the neoliberal institutions are able to discipline the diversity according to the imperatives of the market economy.

Local property rights regimes are also transformed through the shift of production from subsistence crops to IK-based so-called exotic products for the external markets. The most fertile land is used for the IK-based production for the external market, in which the wealthiest members of the community own such land either directly or through mortgage agreements. With the introduction of IK-based production, people need capital and marketing networks; ownership of these is indirectly transferred to the wealthy landowners and investors. As a result, the original owners of IK are deprived of their ownership rights to their land and the knowledge systems that made land productive. Instead, now they have become debt-ridden wage laborers on their own land. The micro-finance schemes have in fact intensified these forms of deprivation and dependency as the high repayment rates are based on the active assistance provided by the wealthy landowners and moneylenders.

The complex process of configuring and disciplining culturally determined diverse systems of property rights performs the same functions as the private property rights in a capitalist economy. Such creative efforts in turn help the resolution of both crisis of accumulation and crisis of legitimacy internal to the outward expansion of capital. Such process is no different to what Edward Said (1979) referred to as "imperial dynamic"—resembling the ways in which the colonial powers appropriated and exploited their colonies for centuries.

One of the main reasons for such a predicament is that NGOs and social movements that are involved in protecting the private property rights of the indigenous communities have neither a concept of property rights that is fundamentally different from the private property of the neoliberal economy nor strategies to undermine the subsumption of noncapitalist property regimes by the capitalist property rights regimes.

Conclusions

The analysis above demonstrates how the use of IK by the NGOs configures institutional and power relations that are located far removed from the primary centers of capital and are configured and disciplined according to the imperatives of global capitalism in ways contrary to the goals of sustainable development. It also demonstrates the remarkable creative powers of capital to achieve its ends by not only destroying and homogenizing diverse systems of knowledge but also disciplining and managing their diversity according to its own imperative.

NGO criticisms of the state and the transnational corporations and their insistence on the need to promote development practices in ways relevant to the interests of local cultures provide a much broader space and more seductive ways of connecting local communities with the centers of capital. In other words, at best, NGOs generate social capital necessary for the colonization of local communities by transnational capital. As Arun Agrawal (1996), a pioneer in research on IK systems, has noted,

> I believe indigenous peoples are caught on the horns of a dilemma that arises from the spreading interest in their knowledge and culture. Without control over their intellectual products, their knowledge stands to be expropriated without any material benefits reaching them. But even with intellectual property, and even if some capture significant material gains, their cultures will inevitably be radically transformed. I will not be misunderstood! My point is not that indigenous knowledge and peoples have not undergone change historically. It is, rather, that current attempts to exploit indigenous knowledge are a threat that has no historical parallel. While a principled stand by powerful government actors might help protect indigenous knowledge and peoples by opening options where future changes will take place in response to their decisions, the likelihood of such stances by governments is rather low. Ultimately, perhaps, we may have to come to terms with the conclusion that the "indigenous" cannot survive as long as interest in it endures on the part of powerful economic and political actors, and indigenous peoples do not organize and unite in the defense of their own knowledge and livelihoods.

In the final analysis, the use of IK in sustainable development is about directly engaging with the powers of neoliberal capitalist institutions. The present challenge is to create an institutional environment to prevent the commodification of IK systems in ways detrimental to the ideal goals of sustainable development. Some of the essential prerequisites of imaging such a counterhegemonic institutional environment are articulation of property rights regimes and systems as well as production and exchange that are not determined by the imperative systems of capitalism but by what Barry Commoner (1972) referred to as "social governance of the means of production—a radical democratization of all major political, social and economic institutions" (p. 27).

Note

1. The names of the informants of the nongovernmental organization, officers of the nongovernmental organization, and the villagers are not mentioned in this article at their request.

References

Agrawal, A. 1995a. Dismantling the divide between indigenous and scientific knowledge. *Development and Change* 26:413-39.
———. 1995b. Indigenous knowledge and scientific knowledge: Some critical comments. *Indigenous Knowledge and Development Monitor* 33 (3): 3-6.

———. 1996. How not to keep your cake nor get to eat it: "Intellectual property rights and indigenous knowl-
    edge resources." Retrieved from http://www.yvwiiusdinvnohii.net/articles/arun.htm.
Brush, Stephen B., and Doreen Stabinsky, eds. 1996. *Valuing local knowledge: Indigenous people and intel-
    lectual property rights*. Washington, DC: Island Press.
Commoner, Barry. 1972. *The closing circle: Confronting the environmental crisis*. London: Jonathan Cape.
Correa, Carlos Maria. 2000. *Intellectual property rights, the WTO and developing countries: The Trips
    Agreement and policy options*. London: Zed Books.
Dove, Michael R. 2002. Hybrid histories and indigenous knowledge among Asian rubber smallholders. *Inter-
    national Social Science Journal* 173:349-59.
Fernando, Jude L. Forthcoming. *Political economy of NGOs: Modernizing post-modernity*. London: Pluto
    Press.
Geertz, C. 1991. Local knowledge and its limits. *Yale Journal of Criticism* 5 (2): 129-35.
Long, Ann, and Norman Long, eds. 1998. *The battlefields of knowledge: The interlocking of theory and prac-
    tice in social research and development*. New York: Routledge.
Long, Norman. 2001. *Development sociology: Actor perspectives*. New York: Routledge.
Long, Norman, and Alberto Arce, eds. 1999. *Anthropology, development and modernities: Exploring dis-
    courses, counter-tendencies and violence*. New York: Routledge.
Perelman, Michael. 2002. *Steal this idea: Intellectual property rights and the corporate confiscation of cre-
    ativity*. New York: Palgrave Macmillan.
Ryan, Michael P. 1998. *Knowledge diplomacy: Global competition and the politics of intellectual property*.
    Washington, DC: Brookings Institution.
Said, Edward. 1979. *Orientalism*. New York: Random House.

Appendix
Additional References

Agrawal, A. 1993. Mobility and cooperation among nomadic shepherds: The case of the Raikas. *Human Ecol-
    ogy* 21 (3): 261-79.
———. 1999. On power of indigenous knowledge. In *Culture and spiritual values of biodiversity*, edited by
    D. A. Possy, 1777-80. Nairobi: United Nations Environment Programme.
Altieri, M. 1989. Rethinking crop genetic resource conservation: A view from the south. *Conservation Biol-
    ogy* 3 (1): 77-79.
Banuri, T., and F. Apffel-Marglin, eds. 1993. *Who will save the forests? Knowledge, power and environmental
    destruction*. London: Zed Books.
Barnes, B., and D. Bloor. 1982. Relativism, rationalism and the sociology of knowledge. In *Rationality and
    relativism*, edited by M. Hollis and S. Lukes, 1-20. Oxford, UK: Basil Blackwell.
Bates, R. 1981. *Markets and states in tropical Africa: The political basis of agrarian policies*. Berkeley: Uni-
    versity of California Press.
———, ed. 1988. *Toward a political economy of development: A rational choice perspective*. Berkeley: Uni-
    versity of California Press.
Black, J. 1993. Development jujitsu: Looking on the bright side. *Studies in Comparative International Devel-
    opment* 28 (1): 71-79.
Brokensha, D., D. Warren, and O. Werner, eds. 1980. *Indigenous knowledge systems and development*.
    Lanham, MD: University Press of America.
Brush, S. 1980. Potato taxonomies in Andean agriculture. In *Indigenous knowledge systems and develop-
    ment*, edited by D. Brokensha, D. Warren, and O. Werner, 37-47. Lanham, MD: University Press of
    America.
Chambers, R. 1980. *Understanding professionals: Small farmers and scientists*. IADS occasional paper. New
    York: International Agricultural Development Service.
Chambers, R., R. Pacey, and L. Thrupp, eds. 1989. *Farmer first: Farmer innovation and agricultural
    research*. London: Intermediate Technology Publications.

Compton, J. 1989. The integration of research and extension. In *The transformation of international agricultural research and development*, edited by J. L. Compton, 113-36. Boulder, CO: Lynne Rienner.

Conklin, H. 1957. *Hanunoo agriculture, a report on an integral system of shifting cultivation in the Philippines*. Forestry development paper 12. Rome: FAO.

Dei, G. 1993. Sustainable development in the African context: Revisiting some theoretical and methodological issues. *African Development* 18 (2): 97-110.

Dirks, N., G. Eley, and S. Ortner. 1994. Introduction. In *Culture-power-history: A reader in contemporary social theory*, edited by N. Dirks, G. Eley, and S. Ortner, 3-45. Princeton, NJ: Princeton University Press.

Evans-Pritchard, E. 1936. *Witchcraft, oracles and magic among the Azande*. Oxford, UK: Oxford University Press.

Falk, D. 1990. The theory of integrated conservation strategies for biological conservation. In *Ecosystem management: Rare species and significant habitats*, proceedings of the 15th Natural Areas Conference, edited by R. Mitchell, C. Sheviak, and D. Leopold, 5-10. Albany: New York State Museum.

Feyerabend, P. [1975] 1993. *Against method*. London: Verso.

Geertz, C. 1983. *Local knowledge: Further essays in interpretive anthropology*. New York: Basic Books.

Gupta, A. 1992. *Building upon people's ecological knowledge: Framework for studying culturally embedded CPR institutions*. Ahmedabad: Indian Institute of Management, Center for Management in Agriculture.

Hamilton, M. 1994. *Ex situ* conservation of wild plant species: Time to reassess the genetic assumptions and implications of seed banks. *Conservation Biology* 8 (1): 39-49.

Hobart, M., ed. 1993. *An anthropological critique of development: The growth of ignorance*. London: Routledge.

Horton, R. 1970. African traditional thought and western science. In *Rationality*, edited by B. Wilson, 131-71. Oxford, UK: Basil Blackwell.

Howes, M., and R. Chambers. 1980. Indigenous technical knowledge: Analysis, implications and issues. In *Indigenous knowledge systems and development*, edited by D. Brokensha, D. Warren, and O. Werner, 329-40. Lanham, MD: University Press of America.

Knorr Cetina, K. 1981. *The manufacture of knowledge: An essay on the constructivist and contextual nature of sciences*. Oxford, UK: Pergamon.

Kuhn, T. 1962. *The structure of scientific revolutions*. Chicago: University of Chicago Press.

Kulka, T. 1977. How far does anything go? Comments on Feyerabend's epistemological anarchism. *Philosophy of the Social Sciences* 7:277-87.

Latour, B., and S. Woolgar. 1979. *Laboratory life: The social construction of scientific facts*. Beverly Hills, CA: Sage.

Levi-Strauss, C. [1962] 1963. *Totemism*. Boston: Beacon.

———. 1966. *The savage mind*. Chicago: University of Chicago Press.

———. [1955] 1992. *Tristes tropiques*. New York: Penguin.

Massaquoi, J. 1993. Salt from silt in Sierra Leone. In *Tinker, tiller, technical change*, edited by M. Gamser, H. Appleton, and N. Carter, 48-63. London: Intermediate Technology Publications.

Nader, L. 1996. Anthropological inquiry into boundaries, power, and knowledge. In *Naked science: Anthropological inquiry into boundaries, power and knowledge*, edited by L. Nader, 1-25. New York: Routledge.

Posey, D. A. 1996. Indigenous knowledge, bio-diversity, and international rights: Learning about forest from the Kayapo Indians of the Brazilian Amazon. *Commonwealth Forestry Review* 76:53-60.

Posey, D. A., and G. Dutfield. 1996. *Beyond intellectual property: Toward traditional resource rights for indigenous people and local communities*. Ottawa, Canada: International Development Research Center.

Thrupp, L. 1989. Legitimatizing local knowledge: "Scientized packages" or empowerment for Third World people. In *Indigenous knowledge systems: Implications for agriculture and international development*, edited by D. M. Warren, J. Slikkerveer, and S. Titilola, 138-53. Ames: Iowa State University, Technology and Social Change Program.

Warner, K. 1991. *Shifting cultivators: Local technical knowledge and local resource management in the humid tropics*. Community forestry note 8. Rome: Food and Agriculture Organization.

Warren, D. M. 1989. Linking scientific and indigenous agricultural systems. In *The transformation of international agricultural research and development*, edited by J. L. Compton, 153-70. Boulder, CO: Lynne Rienner.

———. 1990. *Using indigenous knowledge in agricultural development*. World Bank discussion paper 127. Washington, DC: World Bank.

Warren, D. M., L. J. Slikkerveer, and S. Titilola, eds. 1991. *Indigenous knowledge systems: Implications for agriculture and international development*. Studies in technology and social change no. 11. Ames: Iowa State University, Technology and Social Change Program.

Watts, M. 1993. Development I: Power, knowledge and discursive practice. *Progress in Human Geography* 17 (2): 257-72.

World Bank. 2002. *Sub-Saharan Africa—Indigenous knowledge program*. Washington, DC: World Bank.

Zeven, A. 1988. Landraces: A review of definitions and classifications. *Euphytica* 104:127-39.

The Links between Poverty and the Environment in Urban Areas of Africa, Asia, and Latin America

By
DAVID SATTERTHWAITE

This article suggests that there is little evidence of urban poverty being a significant contributor to environmental degradation but strong evidence that urban environmental hazards are major contributors to urban poverty. The article considers the link between poverty and different categories of environmental hazards (biological pathogens, chemical pollutants, and physical hazards). It then considers the links between poverty and high use of nonrenewable resources, degradation of renewable resources such as soil and fresh water, and high levels of biodegradable and nonbiodegradable waste generation. This shows how environmental degradation is more associated with the consumption patterns of middle- and upper-income groups and the failure of governments to implement effective environmental policies than with urban poverty. The article also highlights how good governance is at the core of poverty reduction and how meeting the environmental health needs of poorer groups need not imply greater environmental degradation.

Keywords: urban poverty; environmental health; environmental degradation

The need to understand and act on poverty-environment linkages in urban areas becomes all the more imperative as urban populations (and the number living in poverty) grow and as the contribution of urban-based production and urban consumption to environmental degradation increases. By 2000, approximately two-fifths of Africa's and Asia's population and three-quarters of Latin America's population lived in urban areas (United Nations 2002). The trend is toward increasingly urbanized societies in most countries as most new investment is

David Satterthwaite is a senior fellow at the International Institute for Environment and Development in London, where he has worked since 1974. Trained as a development planner, he also has a doctorate in social policy from the London School of Economics. This article is a summary of a longer paper prepared in 1999 for the United Nations Development Programme and is modified to incorporate new material and references. It also draws on the author's work with Jorge E. Hardoy, Diana Mitlin, and Gordon McGranahan.

DOI: 10.1177/0002716203257095

urban based; as the Brundtland Commission's report *Our Common Future* remarked, "the future will be predominantly urban and the most immediate environmental concerns of most people will be urban ones" (World Commission on Environment and Development 1987, 255).

Africa, Asia, and Latin America also have nearly three-quarters of the world's urban population and most of the world's largest and fastest-growing cities. How these urban centers perform in terms of resource use and waste generation has very large implications for sustainable development within their regions and globally. But in these regions, increasing urbanization levels have also been characterized by growing numbers of people living in poverty. More than 600 million urban dwellers live in shelters and neighborhoods where their lives and health are continually threatened because of poor quality, overcrowded housing, and inadequate provision of safe water supplies, sanitation, drainage, and garbage collection (Cairncross, Hardoy, and Satterthwaite 1990; World Health Organization [WHO] 1992). Most of this population lives in squatter settlements or illegal subdivisions where the housing is makeshift and largely constructed of temporary materials or in tenements or cheap boarding houses with high levels of overcrowding (Hardoy and Satterthwaite 1989; United Nations Centre for Human Settlements [UNCHS] 1996). Typically, the inhabitants face multiple deprivations—inadequate food intakes; large health burdens from the illnesses and injuries associated with very poor-quality homes and inadequate water, sanitation, and garbage collection; inadequacies in public transport; difficulties in getting health care and affording medicines; difficulties (and often high costs) of keeping children at school; long hours worked; and the often dangerous working conditions. Many face a constant risk of violence and are threatened with eviction. Many are particularly vulnerable to extreme weather—to flooding because they live on floodplains or beside rivers, to landslides for those living on slopes. Of course, the scale and relative importance of these vary from person to person and place to place, but large sections of the urban population in virtually all low- and middle-income nations face a mix of these deprivations (Hardoy, Mitlin, and Satterthwaite 2001; UN-Habitat 2003).

It is often assumed that urban poverty is linked to environmental degradation or even that it is a major cause of environmental degradation (see World Commission on Environment and Development 1987; Clarke 1999). This article describes how this is not so. Indeed, the key relationship between environmental degradation and urban development is in regard to the consumption patterns of nonpoor urban groups (especially high-income groups) and the urban-based production and distribution systems that serve them. Ironically, at a continental or global level, high levels of urban poverty in Africa, Asia, and Latin America (which also means low levels of consumption, resource use, and waste generation) have helped to keep down environmental degradation.

A more precise understanding of the links between urban poverty and the environment is needed because this can provide the basis for combining improved environmental management with poverty reduction. Faulty diagnoses of the links between poverty and environmental degradation have led to inappropriate, ineffective, and often antipoor policies. If urban poverty and, by implication, the poor are seen as the cause of environmental degradation, policies to inhibit the move-ment of the poor to urban areas may be seen as a logical policy response. A failure to recognize the contribution of middle- and upper-income groups to environmen-tal degradation also implies a failure to put in place the environmental frameworks that are needed to keep down environmental degradation.

By seeking a summary that covers more than 1.5 billion people, this article fails to do justice to the great diversity between urban centers, as each has its own par-ticular range of environmental problems. The relative importance of such prob-lems varies, influenced both by the capacity and competence of local authorities and by local economic, social, and ecological factors. This makes it difficult to make accurate generalizations or specific recommendations, except that each urban cen-ter has to have locally determined environmental policies and priorities within which low-income groups have a major influence.

The Scale and Nature of Urban Poverty

The scale and depth of absolute poverty in urban areas of Africa, Asia, and Latin America have long been underestimated for two reasons. The first is that estimates are based only on income levels or consumption levels and take no account of other deprivations such as very poor housing conditions and lack of basic services. The second is that the income-based poverty lines used to make these estimates are set too low in relation to the costs of basic needs in most urban centers (Wratten 1995; Satterthwaite 1995; UNCHS 1996).

Absolute poverty in an urban context usually involves eight interrelated sets of deprivations:

1. Inadequate income (and thus inadequate consumption of necessities including food) and often problems of indebtedness, with debt repayments significantly reducing the income available for necessities.
2. Inadequate, unstable, or risky asset base (nonmaterial and material including educational attainment and housing) for individuals, households, or communities. Different assets have different roles—for instance, some are important for generating or maintaining income, some are important for helping low-income people cope with economic stresses or shocks, and some are important for limiting environmental hazards that can have seri-ous health and economic costs.
3. Inadequate shelter: typically poor quality and overcrowded and often insecure (because of no protection from eviction by landlords or landowners).
4. Inadequate provision of public infrastructure (piped water, sanitation, drainage, roads, footpaths, etc.).
5. Inadequate provision of basic services such as day care and schools, health care, emer-gency services, public transport, communications, and law enforcement.
6. Limited or no safety net to ensure basic consumption can be maintained when income falls and to ensure access to shelter and health care when these can no longer be paid for.
7. Inadequate protection of poorer groups' rights through the operation of the law: includ-ing laws and regulations regarding civil and political rights, occupational health and safety, pollution control, environmental health, protection from violence and other crimes, and protection from discrimination and exploitation.

8. Poorer groups' voicelessness and powerlessness within political systems and bureaucratic structures, leading to little or no possibility of receiving entitlements; of organizing, making demands, and getting a fair response; and of receiving support for developing their own initiatives. Also, no means of ensuring accountability from aid agencies, nongovernmental organizations (NGOs), public agencies, and private utilities and being able to participate in the definition and implementation of their urban poverty programs (Mitlin and Satterthwaite 2003).

It is difficult for those who think of urban poverty as inadequate income or inadequate consumption to accept this broader view, and it is difficult to incorporate some of the above aspects into quantitative measurements. But the need for this broader conception of urban poverty is now widely accepted (Wratten 1995; UNCHS 1996; World Bank 2001).

This widening in the definition of urban poverty is also central to understanding the environmental problems associated with poverty because the environmental problems that low-income groups face are often more related to inadequate provision of infrastructure and services, lack of any rule of law, discrimination, and lack of political influence than to a lack of income. A growing number of case studies show how the deprivations associated with low income can be much reduced without increasing incomes through improving infrastructure and services or through political changes, which allowed low-income groups to negotiate more support (Mitlin and Satterthwaite 2003).

The Range of Environmental Problems in Urban Areas

The distinction between environmental hazard and environmental degradation

At the core of most misunderstandings about the link between poverty and environment is the confusion between environmental hazards and environmental degradation. In most urban centers in Africa, Asia, and Latin America, a high proportion of the poor (however defined) face very serious environmental hazards in their homes and their surrounds and in their workplaces. Such hazards impose large burdens on such groups in terms of ill health, injury, and premature death. These health burdens are a major cause or contributor to poverty. But most of these environmental hazards are not causing environmental degradation. For instance, the inadequacies in provision for piped water, sanitation, and drainage in most low-income neighborhoods often mean very serious problems with insect-borne diseases such as malaria or dengue fever or filariasis and with diseases associated with a lack of water for washing such as trachoma, but these do not degrade any environmental resource.

The scale and range of environmental problems

Urban areas concentrate a wide range of environmental problems. Urban-based production and consumption also create environmental impacts outside city boundaries, including the region around the city, more distant ecosystems, and planetary systems. For some of these environmental problems, there is no association with poverty. For some, there is a strong association but little or no causal relationship. For some, there is both a strong association and a strong causal relationship—although this is generally through environmental problems causing or contributing to poverty rather than poverty contributing to environmental problems.

Ironically, at a continental or global level, high levels of urban poverty in Africa, Asia, and Latin America (which also means low levels of consumption, resource use, and waste generation) have helped to keep down environmental degradation.

Many of the most serious diseases in urban areas in Latin America, Asia, and Africa are environmental because they are transmitted through air, water, soil, food—or through insect or animal vectors. It is also through environmental modification that most such diseases can be prevented or controlled. Many diseases and disease vectors thrive when provision for water, sanitation, drainage, garbage collection, and health care is inadequate. As a result, urban centers can become among the most health-threatening of all human environments: disease-causing agents and disease vectors multiply; the large concentration of people living in close proximity to each other increases the risk of disease transmission; and health care systems become unable to respond rapidly and effectively (WHO 1999).

Water-related diseases are major contributors to the health burdens suffered by most urban poor households (WHO 1992; Cairncross and Feachem 1993). At any one time, close to half of the urban population is suffering from one or more of the main diseases associated with inadequate provision for water and sanitation (WHO 1999). Improved water and sanitation can bring great benefits in terms of improved health, reduced expenditures (on water vendors and on treatment from diseases), and much reduced physical effort, especially for those who have to collect and carry water from standpipes or other sources far from their shelters (UN-Habitat 2003).

Airborne infections are among the world's leading causes of death (and easily prevented death). For many, their transmission is aided by overcrowding and inadequate ventilation. While improving housing and other environmental conditions can reduce their incidence (and by reducing other diseases also strengthen people's defenses against these), medical interventions such as immunization or rapid treatment are more important for reducing their health impact.

Diseases spread by water-related insect vectors are among the most pressing environmental problems in many cities. These include malaria, which in many cities or poor peripheral city districts is one of the main causes of illness and death (WHO 1999). The vectors for malaria (*Anopheles* mosquitoes) breed in standing water, so good drainage is an important part of malaria control. The diseases spread by *Aedes* mosquitoes (dengue, dengue haemorrhagic fever, and yellow fever) are serious health problems in many cities; pots, small tanks, and cisterns used for storing water in houses lacking regular piped supplies can provide breeding habitats for these mosquitoes (WHO 1999). So too can small pools of clean water within residential areas in, for instance, discarded tin cans and rubber tires (Cairncross and Feachem 1993). Reliable piped water supplies (so households do not need to store water) and good garbage collection can greatly reduce the risk of diseases spread by *Aedes* mosquitoes.

There are also the health problems associated with garbage. It is common for 30 to 50 percent of the solid wastes generated in an urban area not to be collected; usually, the lower-income areas have the least adequate collection service (Cointreau 1982; UNCHS 1996). So wastes accumulate in open spaces and streets, clogging drains and attracting disease vectors and pests (rats, mosquitoes, flies). Inadequate collection also has wider environmental impacts as uncollected wastes are generally washed into water bodies, adding considerably to water pollution and blocking drains.

Urbanization can create foci for disease vectors and new ecological niches for animals that harbor a disease agent or vector—for instance, through the expansion of built-up areas, the construction of water reservoirs and drains, or the failure to remove human excreta, garbage, or wastewater (WHO 1992). Without good environmental and public health policies, it is difficult to control infectious diseases as societies urbanize, as population movements increase (including those across international borders), and as disease-causing agents develop resistance to public health measures or adapt to changing ecological circumstances in ways that increase the risks of infection for human populations.

A recent review of provision for water and sanitation suggests that at least 680 million urban dwellers in Africa, Asia, and Latin America lack adequate provision for water and at least 850 million lack adequate sanitation (UN-Habitat 2003). Earlier estimates had suggested that deficiencies in urban areas were less serious, but this was because of inappropriate criteria used to define what is adequate in terms of health benefits, convenience, and cost (UN-Habitat 2003; Hardoy, Mitlin, and

Satterthwaite 2001). Approximately 100 million urban dwellers defecate in the open or into waste materials ("wrap and throw") because they have no toilets in their homes and public provision is too inadequate, too distant, or too expensive (UN-Habitat 2003; Hardoy, Mitlin, and Satterthwaite 2001).

For chemical hazards, their scale and severity in urban areas generally increases rapidly with industrialization and with the growth in road traffic. While controlling infectious diseases centers on provision of infrastructure and services (whether through public, private, NGO, or community provision), reducing chemical hazards is largely achieved by regulating the activities of enterprises. A great range of chemical pollutants that are common in urban areas affect human health. Controlling occupational exposure is particularly important, from large factories down to small, backstreet workshops.

One of the most serious chemical hazards is indoor air pollution from smoke or fumes from open fires or inefficient stoves and inadequate attention to venting (WHO 1992). This is especially so when coal or biomass fuels are used as domestic fuels. These problems are generally concentrated among lower-income households, as people shift to cleaner, safer fuels when incomes rise. High levels of indoor air pollution can cause inflammation of the respiratory tract, which in turn reduces resistance to acute respiratory infections, while these infections in turn enhance susceptibility to the inflammatory effects of smoke and fumes. There are also many other health problems associated with high levels of indoor air pollution (WHO 1992).

As cities become larger, more industrialized, and wealthier, their need for more effective control of emissions from industries and motor vehicles grows. Worldwide, more than 1.5 billion urban dwellers are exposed to levels of ambient air pollution above the recommended maximum levels, and this causes an estimated 400,000 additional deaths each year (WHO 1999). If industrial pollution has been reduced, it is usually motor vehicle emissions that become the main source of urban air pollution.

Physical hazards are generally among the most significant causes of injury or premature death among low-income populations. Their health impact is often underestimated, as many environmental diagnoses overlook them. Accidents in the home are among the most common causes of injury and premature death, and the impacts are particularly serious in cities where a high proportion of the population live in accommodations with three or more persons to each room in shelters made from temporary (and inflammable) materials and with open fires or stoves used for cooking and (where needed) heating. In such circumstances, it is almost impossible to protect occupants (especially young children) from burns and scalds.

There are three other areas where physical hazards need reducing. The first is for traffic management, which minimizes the risk of motor vehicle accidents and which protects pedestrians and cyclists from motor vehicles. Deaths and injuries from motor vehicle accidents have become an increasingly significant component of all premature deaths and injuries in many cities, especially those where infectious and parasitic diseases and their underlying causes have been successfully addressed. The larger and wealthier cities in Asia and Latin America also have ratios of road vehicles to persons that are comparable to many European cities. Even where there are fewer road vehicles, road accidents are often a particular problem because the number of fatalities and serious injuries per road vehicle is much higher than in high-income countries (UNCHS 1996). The second is the need to reduce accidents in the workplace—and in most urban areas, there is an urgent need for measures to promote healthy and safe working practices and to penalize employers who contravene them. The third area is ensuring adequate provision of safe and stimulating play for children and recreation for the entire city population, especially in the poorest residential areas where homes have little interior and surrounding space for this.

The environmental problems that low-income groups face are often more related to inadequate provision of infrastructure and services, lack of any rule of law, discrimination, and lack of political influence than to a lack of income.

Disasters are considered to be exceptional events that suddenly result in large numbers of people killed or injured or large economic losses. As such, they are distinguished from the environmental hazards discussed above. This distinction has its limitations. For instance, far more urban dwellers die of easily prevented illnesses arising from environmental hazards in their food, water, or air than from disasters, yet the death toll from disasters gets more media attention.

Cyclones, high winds, and storms have probably caused more deaths in urban areas than other disasters in recent decades. Earthquakes have caused many of the biggest urban disasters. Floods affect many more people than cyclones and earthquakes but kill fewer people. Landslides, fires, epidemics, and industrial accidents are among the other urban disasters that need attention. Global warming will increase the frequency and severity of many disasters in urban areas. For instance, the rise in sea level will increase the risk of flooding for many port cities, will also disrupt sewers and drains, and may bring seawater intrusion into freshwater aquifers. Changes in rainfall regimes may reduce the availability of freshwater resources or bring increased risk of floods.

Increasingly, urban authorities recognize the need to integrate disaster prevention within environmental hazard prevention. Most disasters have natural triggers that cannot be prevented, but their impact can generally be greatly reduced by understanding who within the city population is vulnerable and acting to reduce this vulnerability before the disaster occurs. There are also important overlaps between the culture of prevention for everyday hazards and that for disasters. For instance, risks from flooding are much reduced for cities with good drainage and garbage collection systems.

The Interaction between Poverty and Environmental Risk

Poverty as a risk factor

The economic underpinning of the environmental risks described above becomes evident when comparing the risks faced by lower-income groups with those faced by higher-income groups. Most case studies on infectious and parasitic diseases and morbidity and mortality show that these mostly affect low-income groups—be they children; adults in crowded, unhygienic conditions; or workers in particular occupations (Bradley et al. 1991). The same is true for most chemical pollutants and physical hazards (Hardoy, Mitlin, and Satterthwaite 2001). Higher-income groups have better-quality homes and generally less dangerous jobs and work in occupations where occupational hazards are minimized.

Low income is a risk factor not only for exposure to environmental hazards but also for possibilities of rapid and effective treatment because of the lack of health care services in illegal settlements, tenement districts, or other areas where low-income groups are concentrated. Many children in low-income districts die of diseases that are easily prevented or cured.

Once one begins to examine what causes people's vulnerability to environmental hazards, the interaction between environmental hazards and social, economic, political, and demographic factors becomes clearer (Stephens and Harpham 1992). Virtually all environmental health problems in urban areas have a social, economic, or political underpinning in that social, economic, or political factors strongly influence who is most at risk and who cannot obtain the needed treatment and support when illness or injury occur. To give but one example, the high incidence of diseases associated with contaminated food and water in most poor urban communities is an environmental problem in the sense that the disease-causing agents infect humans through ingesting water or food—but it can also be judged to be a political problem because nearly all governments and aid agencies have the capacity to greatly reduce current levels of morbidity and mortality by improved provision of water, sanitation, and drainage. It can also be judged as a social or economic problem in that it is lower-income groups' limited means to pay for accommodation that usually underlies their poor housing conditions. This makes it difficult to isolate the impact of environmental factors on people's health problems as distinct from other factors.

To a large extent, capacity to obtain good-quality housing defines the scale of the environmental hazards present in the housing and living environment, including whether there is safe, sufficient water supplies; sanitation; garbage collection; and drainage. This in turn depends on income levels, assets, extent of access to credit, and political influence (as in, for instance, the possibility of negotiating access to land). Thus, the environmental hazards described above arise from a combination of five factors:

- low incomes;
- the refusal (or inability) of government to intervene to guarantee those with limited incomes access to shelters that are not so dangerous or to the resources that allow them to build safe, adequate-quality housing themselves;
- the refusal (or inability) of government to ensure that all urban dwellers receive some basic level of provision for water, sanitation, drainage, and garbage collection;
- the refusal (or inability) of government to provide the community-based health care and emergency services that can do so much to prevent illness or injury and to limit its impact; and
- the low priority given by most development assistance agencies to working with urban authorities to ensure low-income urban dwellers have adequate provision for water, sanitation, drainage, health care, and garbage collection (Hardoy, Mitlin, and Satterthwaite 2001; Satterthwaite 2001).

If individuals or households find minimum standard accommodation too costly, they have to make certain sacrifices in the accommodation they choose to bring down the price. They usually make sacrifices in environmental quality. Although this means health risks and much inconvenience, these are less important for their survival than, for instance, purchase of food, keeping children at school, or close proximity to income-earning opportunities. Ironically, dangerous or polluted land sites often serve poorer groups well, as these are the only sites well located in regard to income-earning opportunities on which they have some possibility of living (illegally) because the environmental hazards make them unattractive to other potential users.

Among those with low incomes, the scale and nature of environmental hazards to which they are exposed differ considerably, as does the severity of the illness or injury to which these contribute. For instance, certain occupations and certain settlements have particularly high levels of environmental risk. Particular groups face extreme difficulties getting access to water and washing and bathing facilities—such as pavement dwellers or those who sleep in open spaces, parks, and graveyards. There are also significant intrahousehold differentials in environmental hazards and in health burdens within most low-income areas (see, e.g., Pryer 1993). These differentials are also related to age, sex, and gender. Infants and children are at higher risk from many environmental hazards than most other age groups—because of weak body defenses, susceptibility to particular chemicals, and for younger children, inadequate or no understanding of how to avoid hazards. Women are more vulnerable than men to many environmental hazards, some because of biological differences and some because of the particular social and economic roles that women have, determined by social, economic, and political structures. Women are generally far more severely affected than men by over-crowded housing, the use of smoky fuels for cooking, and inadequate provision for water, sanitation, and health care (and also schools and nurseries) because they take most responsibility for looking after infants and children, caring for sick family members, and managing the household (Moser 1985; Songsore and McGranahan 1998). The elderly, those with physical disabilities, and those groups that face discrimination in obtaining access to environmental services (e.g., particular ethnic groups or immigrant groups) are also more vulnerable to particular hazards.

The Interaction between Poverty and Environmental Degradation in Urban Areas

City expansion and environmental degradation

As cities grow, they transform natural landscapes both within and around them. The expansion of cities means that land surfaces are reshaped; valleys and swamps filled; large volumes of clay, sand, gravel, and crushed rock extracted and moved; and water sources tapped—and rivers and streams channeled. In the absence of effective land-use management, this has serious ecological impacts such as the loss of agricultural land and of sites with valuable ecological functions (Douglas 1983).

The environmental impacts of solid, liquid, and airborne pollutants and wastes can be transferred to the surrounding region. Problems include the damage of fisheries by untreated liquid wastes, land and groundwater pollution from inadequately designed and managed solid waste dumps, and acid precipitation in the areas surrounding many of the larger and more industrial cities. Most solid wastes that are collected within cities are deposited in open dumps, which can give rise to many problems including the contamination of ground and surface water, methane generation, and air pollution from uncontrolled burning. Many industrial and institutional wastes are categorized as hazardous because of the special care needed to ensure they are isolated from contact with humans and the natural environment. In most urban centers, there is inadequate provision to monitor their production, collection, treatment, and disposal. Businesses generally have large incentives to avoid meeting official standards and little risk in doing so (Hardoy, Mitlin, and Satterthwaite 2001).

In regard to water, many cities have outgrown the capacity of their locality to provide fresh water or have overused or mismanaged local sources so these are no longer available. In many coastal cities, local aquifers have been overpumped, resulting in saltwater intrusion. Increasingly, distant and costly water sources have to be used, to the detriment of the regions from which these are drawn (Hardoy, Mitlin, and Satterthwaite 2001; UN-Habitat 2003).

There are also the impacts on more distant ecosystems. The demands that larger and wealthier cities concentrate for food, fuel, and raw materials may be increasingly met by imports from distant ecosystems. However, this generally means a transfer of costs to people and ecosystems in other regions or countries (Wackernagel and Rees 1995; McGranahan et al. 2001).

Other cost transfers are into the future. Emissions of carbon dioxide (the main greenhouse gas) are high in most prosperous cities and may continue to rise because of increasing private automobile use. This transfers costs to the future through the human and ecological costs of atmospheric warming. The generation of hazardous nonbiodegradable wastes (including radioactive wastes and those whose rising concentrations within particular ecosystems or the whole biosphere has worrying ecological implications) also transfers costs to the future. So are current levels of consumption for agricultural and forest products where the soils and forests are being destroyed or degraded and biodiversity reduced.

The link between wealth and environmental degradation in urban areas has become obscured because the ecological damage caused by the production of goods and services used by high-income groups is increasingly in ecosystems far away from where the high-income groups live or transferred to global systems. Thus, a wealthy city can achieve very high-quality environments within the city and its surrounds because all the pollution-intensive, energy-intensive goods (or goods whose production implies deforestation and soil erosion) can be imported from distant places.

Environmental degradation and poverty

There are four different kinds of environmental degradation associated with urban development: the first is high use or waste of nonrenewable resources—including the consumption of fossil fuels. There is little association between this and poverty since most poor urban dwellers have very low consumption levels for nonrenewable resources. Most of the houses in which they live (and often build for themselves) make widespread use of recycled or reclaimed materials and little use of cement and other materials with a high-energy input. Such households have too few capital goods to represent much of a draw on the world's finite reserves of metals and other nonrenewable resources. Most low-income groups rely on public transport (or travel by foot or bicycle), which ensures low averages for oil consumption per person. Low-income households on average have low levels of electricity consumption, not only because those who are connected use less but also because a high proportion of households have no electricity supply.

The second is high use of the renewable resources for which there are finite limits—for instance, fresh water, soil, and forests. Poor urban dwellers generally have much lower levels of consumption for renewable resources than middle- and upper-income groups. For instance, poor urban dwellers have much lower levels of consumption for fresh water (although this is due more to inconvenient and/or expensive supplies than to need or choice) (UN-Habitat 2003). They occupy much less land per person than middle- and upper-income groups. For instance, in Nairobi, the informal and illegal settlements that house more than half the city's population occupy less than 6 percent of the land area used for residential purposes (Alder 1995). Urban sprawl, which often means paving over very high-quality agricultural land, is far more the result of the residential preferences of middle- and upper-income groups, new commercial and industrial developments, and city-transport programs dominated by highway construction than of land occupation by low-income groups.

There are examples of low-income populations contributing to the degradation of some renewable resources such as low-income settlements developed in water-sheds—but this is not so much a problem of poor groups' causing degradation as a problem caused by the failure of urban authorities to ensure that they have access to other residential sites.

Low income is a risk factor not only for exposure to environmental hazards but also for possibilities of rapid and effective treatment because of the lack of health care services.

A third kind of environmental degradation associated with urban areas is high levels of biodegradable waste generation, which overtax the capacities of renew-able sinks (e.g., the capacity of a river to break down biodegradable wastes without ecological degradation). Low-income groups usually generate much lower levels per person than middle- and upper-income groups and thus contribute much less to the environmental degradation caused by the dumping of untreated wastes into water bodies and poorly managed waste dumps. In fact, the urban poor generally have a very positive role from an ecological perspective, as they are the main reclaimers, reusers, and recyclers of wastes from industries, workshops, and wealthier households. Some small-scale urban enterprises that can cause serious local environmental problems, such as the contamination of local water sources. But these enterprises' contribution to citywide pollution problems relative to other groups is usually very small. In addition, it is difficult to ascribe the pollution caused by small-scale enterprises to the urban poor when many such enterprises are owned by middle- or upper-income groups.

The fourth kind of environmental degradation associated with urban areas is high levels of generation of nonbiodegradable wastes/emissions that overtax the (finite) capacity of local and global sinks to absorb or dilute them without adverse effects (e.g., the use of persistent pesticides and the generation of greenhouse gases and stratospheric ozone-depleting chemicals). Low-income groups gener-ally contribute very little to their generation either directly (through the fuels they use and goods they consume) or indirectly (through the environmental costs created by the fabrication of the goods they use). For instance, in regard to green-house gas emissions, low-income groups usually generate much lower levels per person than middle- and upper-income groups because their use of fossil fuels or of goods or services with high fossil-fuel inputs is much lower. The only exception may be in urban areas where there is a need for space heating for parts of the year and a proportion of the urban poor use biomass fuels or coal in inefficient stoves or fires. This may result in these households' having above-average per capita contributions to carbon dioxide emissions (and also to urban air pollution), but these are exceptional cases, and in general, the consumption patterns of low-income groups imply much lower greenhouse gas emissions per person than those of middle- and upper-income groups.

Linking environmental action with poverty reduction in urban areas

Table 1 points to some of the environmental actions that can help reduce poverty.

There are also important possible synergies between well-managed services and long-term environmental goals. For instance, high-quality public transport, good traffic management (including appropriate provision for pedestrians and cyclists), land use management that encourages public-transport-oriented city expansion, and controls or disincentives on excessive private automobile use can bring important benefits to low-income groups as it keeps down the time and money costs of getting to work or to services. These also reduce fossil fuel use (and thus greenhouse gas emissions). Similarly, recognition of the importance of urban agriculture for the livelihoods of many low-income households in many urban centers can lead to policies that support low-income groups' access to land and enhance the ecological advantages of increased local production (Smit, Ratta, and Nasr 1996). Improved provision for water supply and sanitation can be done within a framework that recognizes potential freshwater shortages—for instance, through water tariffs, which ensure the price per liter rises with per-capita consumption, or community sewer systems that reduce the volume of water needed and have local treatment systems that allow the nutrients in the wastewater to be used for fish farming or crops (Smit, Ratta, and Nasr 1996; Gaye and Diallo 1997).

Environmental problems but political solutions? The role of good urban governance

It may be misleading to refer to many of the most pressing urban environmental problems as "environmental" because they arise not from some particular shortage of an environmental resource (e.g., land or fresh water) but from economic or political factors that prevent poorer groups from obtaining them or from organizing to demand them. The very inadequate access to fresh water that so many of the

TABLE 1

EXAMPLES OF HOW ENVIRONMENTAL ACTIONS
CAN HELP REDUCE POVERTY

Environmental Actions	Direct Effects	Other Effects
Improved provision for water and sanitation	Can bring a very large drop in health burdens from water-related infectious and parasitic diseases and some vector-borne diseases and also in premature death (especially for infants and young children)	For income earners, *increased income* from less time off work from illness or from nursing sick family members and less expenditure on medicines and health care • *Better nutrition* (e.g., less food lost to diarrhea and intestinal worms) • *Less time and physical effort* needed in collecting water • *Lower overall costs* for those who, prior to improved supplies, had to rely on expensive water vendors
Less crowded, better quality housing through supporting low-income groups to build, develop, or buy less crowded, better quality housing	Can bring a large drop in household accidents and remove the necessity for low-income groups to occupy land sites at high risk from floods, landslides, or other hazards. Can also help reduce indoor air pollution	*Lower risk* for low-income groups to lose their homes and other capital assets to accidental fires or disasters *Secure, stimulating indoor space* is an enormous benefit for children's physical, mental, and social development
Improved provision for storm and surface water drainage	Reduced flooding and reduced possibilities for disease vectors breeding bring major health benefits (flooding often spreads excreta everywhere)	Lowered risk of floods that can damage or destroy housing, which is often low-income households' main capital asset and also where they store other assets
Avoidance of hazardous land sites for settlements	Reduces number of people at risk from floods, landslides, or other hazards. The damage or destruction of housing and other assets from floods or landslides can be the shock that pushes low-income households into absolute poverty	Sites within cities that may be hazardous for settlements are often well suited to parks or wildlife reserves and may also be well suited to helping in flood protection and groundwater recharge
Promotion of cleaner household fuels	Reductions in respiratory and other health problems through reduced indoor and outdoor air pollution	Reduced contribution of household stoves to city air pollution

(continued)

TABLE 1 (continued)

Environmental Actions	Direct Effects	Other Effects
Improved provision for solid waste management	Removes garbage from open sites and ditches. Reduces risk of many animal and insect disease vectors and stops garbage blocking drains	Reduces time and physical effort for previously unserved households. Considerable employment opportunities in well-managed solid waste collection system where recycling, reuse, and reclamation are promoted
Support for community action to improve local environment	If well managed, many low-cost ways to reduce environmental hazards and improve environmental quality in informal settlements	Employment creation; minimum incomes help households avoid poverty. Can reduce sense of social exclusion
Support for more participatory plans	Low-income groups with more possibilities of influencing city authorities' priorities on environmental policy and investment	Precedents set in participatory Local Agenda 21s and other action plans can lead to low-income groups' getting greater influence in other sectors
Improved public transport	Cheap, good-quality public transport keeps down time and money costs for income earners getting to and from work; also enhances access to services	Can reduce air pollution and its health impacts. Can reduce the disadvantages of living in peripheral locations and help keep down house prices

urban poor face is a serious environmental problem for them, but rarely is its cause environmental; in most cities, it is not a shortage of freshwater resources but governments' refusal to give a higher priority to water supply and the competent organizational structure its supply, maintenance, and expansion require (Hardoy, Mitlin, and Satterthwaite 2001; UN-Habitat 2003). In some cities, there are serious constraints on expanding freshwater supplies, because the size of the city and its production base have grown to exceed the capacity of local resources to supply fresh water on a sustainable basis—but even here, providing adequate supplies to poorer groups often requires less water than could be saved by better maintenance of the existing system (e.g., reducing leaks) and more realistic charges for the largest industrial water users. For land, most cities or metropolitan areas have sufficient unused or underused land sites within the built-up area to accommodate most if not all of the low-income households currently living in very overcrowded conditions. Perhaps not surprisingly, one article discussing the linkages between poverty and the urban environment in Asia was subtitled "Access, Empowerment, and Community-Based Management" (Douglass 1992). Ensuring that low-income groups and their community organizations can obtain access to safe land sites and municipal services is central to an improved urban environment.

A failure of governance underlies most environmental problems—failures to control industrial pollution and occupational exposure, to promote environmental health, to ensure that city dwellers have the basic infrastructure and services essential for health and a decent living environment, to plan in advance to ensure sufficient land is available for housing developments for low-income groups, and to implement preventive measures, to avoid urban sprawl. For many countries, this can be partly explained by the national economy's weakness; effective local governance is particularly difficult without a stable and reasonably prosperous economy.

Remedying this failure of governance within cities and city-districts and addressing the underlying causes should be central to any urban environmental agenda. This may not parallel the contemporary urban agenda in Europe and North America—although it parallels the urban agenda there 100 to 150 years ago when public provision of infrastructure and services and public control of pollution and occupational health hazards were as inadequate as they are today in most of Africa, Asia, and Latin America. In effect, most cities in these regions still need the environmental health revolution that most European and North American cities underwent in the last decades of the nineteenth century and first few decades of the twentieth century, as well as action on the environmental concerns first raised in the 1960s and 1970s. Strengthening the capacity of city and municipal governments to address the lack of sanitation, drains, piped water supplies, garbage collection, and health services is also generally a precondition for building the institutional capacity to address air and water pollution, protect natural resources, and reduce greenhouse gas emissions.

Amid the widespread failure of national, provincial/state, and city governments to give sufficient attention to the environmental health needs of lower-income groups are many examples of innovation. Most fall into two categories. The first is the innovation shown by particular city authorities in developing and implementing their own local agendas as in Ilo in Peru and Manizales in Colombia (Vélasquez 1998; López Follegatti 1999). Another case is Porto Alegre in Brazil: its high-quality environment, high life expectancy, and model of governance with participatory budgeting is much admired (Menegat 2002). The second is the innovation shown by local NGOs working with organizations of the urban poor—sometimes working with government, sometimes working in the absence of government—for instance, the sewer and drain construction and health and other programs of the Orangi Pilot Project in Karachi and other cities in Pakistan (Hasan 1997) and the innovation among NGOs, community organizations, and small-scale private-sector entrepreneurs in improving provision for water and sanitation among the urban poor at a lower cost and with better cost recovery than conventional utilities (UN-Habitat 2003; Burra and Patel 2002). There are also the various examples of where urban poor organizations and federations have negotiated more appropriate government responses for improving housing and basic services—as in the work of Mahila Milan, the National Slum Dwellers Federations, and SPARC in various Indian cities (Patel and Mitlin 2001) and in the case of the South African Homeless People's Federation (Baumann, Bolnick, and Mitlin 2001). There are also important innovations at the national level—for instance, the work of the Community

Organizations Development Institute in Thailand in supporting a great range of community-level improvements to housing, basic services, and environmental management (Boonyabancha 2003) and the PRODEL program in Nicaragua, which supports municipal infrastructure improvements, housing improvement, and micro-finance for enterprise development with city authorities, NGOs, and community organizations (Stein 2001).

Amid the widespread failure of national, provincial/state, and city governments to give sufficient attention to the environmental health needs of lower-income groups are many examples of innovation.

Thus, precedents and pointers show the potential for more effective links between poverty reduction and environmental management. But these need democratic, accountable, effective, and innovative urban authorities—and the national frameworks that allow them to develop. Such national frameworks must also encourage environmental policies that not only address environmental health problems within urban areas but also limit the transfer of environmental costs to people and ecosystems beyond these boundaries.

This in turn requires international agencies that are able and willing to support this. But most international agencies give a very low priority to improving provision for water supply, sanitation, drainage, garbage collection, and health care in urban centers (Satterthwaite 2001). International agencies also need to go beyond more projects: what is needed is not so much more projects but more partnerships, which strengthens the capacity of urban authorities to develop appropriate responses. But the governments of many countries will not permit international agencies to work with local authorities—or the local authorities are too weak or too rooted in unaccountable clientelist political structures to be effective. Here, international agencies need to develop new channels to support community initiatives directly. The recent trend of some bilateral agencies withdrawing support from countries with undemocratic or ineffective governments is understandable, but this also penalizes the low-income groups within these countries. An example of such an innovation is channeling support to low-income groups directly through local funds for community initiatives (Satterthwaite 2002). This kind of support need not undermine good governance; indeed, many community-level initiatives that began independent of government later came to influence government actions in ways that brought many benefits for low-income groups.

References

Alder, Graham. 1995. Tackling poverty in Nairobi's informal settlements: Developing an institutional strategy. *Environment and Urbanization* 7 (2): 85-107.

Baumann, Ted, Joel Bolnick, and Diana Mitlin. 2001. The age of cities and organizations of the urban poor: The work of the South African Homeless People's Federation and the People's Dialogue on Land and Shelter. IIED working paper 2 on poverty reduction in urban areas, International Institute for Environment and Development, London.

Boonyabancha, Somsook. 2003. A decade of change: From the Urban Community Development Office (UCDO) to the Community Organizations Development Institute (CODI) in Thailand. Poverty Reduction in Urban Areas working paper 12, International Institute for Environment and Development, London.

Bradley, David, Carolyn Stephens, Sandy Cairncross, and Trudy Harpham. 1991. *A review of environmental health impacts in developing country cities*, Urban Management Program discussion paper no. 6, World Bank, UNDP, and UN (Habitat), Washington, DC.

Burra, Sundar, and Sheela Patel. 2002. Community toilets in Pune and other Indian Cities. *PLA Notes* 44:43-45.

Cairncross, Sandy, and Richard G. Feachem. 1993. *Environmental health engineering in the tropics: An introductory text.* 2d ed. Chichester, UK: Wiley.

Cairncross, Sandy, Jorge E. Hardoy, and David Satterthwaite. 1990. The urban context. In *The poor die young: Housing and health in Third World cities*, edited by Jorge E. Hardoy, Sandy Cairncross, and David Satterthwaite, 1-24. London: Earthscan.

Clarke, Robin, ed. 1999. *Global environmental outlook 2000.* London: Earthscan.

Cointreau, Sandra. 1982. *Environmental management of urban solid waste in developing countries.* Urban Development technical paper no. 5. Washington, DC: World Bank.

Douglas, Ian. 1983. *The urban environment.* London: Edward Arnold.

Douglass, Mike. 1992. The political economy of urban poverty and environmental management in Asia: Access, empowerment and community-based alternatives. *Environment and Urbanization* 4 (2): 9-32.

Gaye, Malick, and Fodé Diallo. 1997. Community participation in the management of the urban environment in Rufisque (Senegal). *Environment and Urbanization* 9 (1): 9-29.

Hardoy, Jorge E., Diana Mitlin, and David Satterthwaite. 2001. *Environmental problems in cities of Africa, Asia and Latin America.* London: Earthscan.

Hardoy, Jorge E., and David Satterthwaite. 1989. *Squatter citizen: Life in the urban Third World.* London: Earthscan.

Hasan, Arif. 1997. *Working with government: The story of OPP's collaboration with state agencies for replicating its Low Cost Sanitation Programme.* Karachi, Pakistan: City Press.

López Follegatti, Jose Luis. 1999. Ilo: A city in transformation. *Environment and Urbanization* 11 (2): 181-202.

McGranahan, Gordon, Pedro Jacobi, Jacob Songsore, Charles Surjadi, and Marianne Kjellén. 2001. *The citizens at risk: From urban sanitation to sustainable cities.* London: Earthscan.

Menegat, Rualdo. 2002. Participatory democracy and sustainable development: Integrated urban environmental management in Porto Alegre, Brazil. *Environment and Urbanization* 14 (2): 181-206.

Mitlin, Diana, and David Satterthwaite, eds. 2003. *Responding to squatter citizens: The role of local governments and civil society in reducing urban poverty.* London: Earthscan.

Moser, Caroline O. N. 1985. Housing policy and women: Towards a gender aware approach. DPU Gender and Planning working paper no. 7, University College, London.

Patel, Sheela, and Diana Mitlin. 2001. The work of SPARC and its partners Mahila Milan and the National Slum Dwellers Federation in India. IIED working paper 5 on urban poverty reduction, International Institute for Environment and Development, London.

Pryer, Jane. 1993. The impact of adult ill-health on household income and nutrition in Khulna, Bangladesh. *Environment and Urbanization* 5 (2): 35-49.

Satterthwaite, David. 1995. The underestimation of poverty and its health consequences. *Third World Planning Review* 17 (4): iii-xii.

———. 2001. Reducing urban poverty: Constraints on the effectiveness of aid agencies and development banks and some suggestions for change. *Environment and Urbanization* 13 (1): 137-57.

———. 2002. Local funds and their potential to allow donor agencies to support community development and poverty reduction. *Environment and Urbanization* 14 (1): 179-88.

Smit, Jac, Annu Ratta, and Joe Nasr. 1996. *Urban agriculture: Food, jobs and sustainable cities*. Publication series for Habitat II, vol. 1. New York: UNDP.

Songsore, Jacob, and Gordon McGranahan. 1998. The political economy of household environmental management: Gender, environment and epidemiology in the Greater Accra Metropolitan Area. *World Development* 26 (3): 395-412.

Stein, Alfredo. 2001. Participation and sustainability in social projects: The experience of the Local Development Programme (PRODEL) in Nicaragua. IIED working paper 3 on poverty reduction in urban areas, International Institute for Environment and Development, London.

Stephens, Carolyn, and Trudy Harpham. 1992. *The measurement of health in household environmental studies in urban areas of developing countries: Factors to be considered in the design of surveys*. London: London School of Hygiene and Tropical Medicine.

UN-Habitat. 2003. *Water and sanitation in the world's cities: Local action for global goals*. London: Earthscan.

United Nations. 2002. *World urbanization prospects: The 2001 revision: Data tables and highlights*. ESA/P/WP/173. New York: Population Division, Department of Economic and Social Affairs, United Nations Secretariat.

United Nations Centre for Human Settlements (UNCHS) (Habitat). 1996. *An urbanizing world: Global report on human settlements, 1996*. Oxford, UK: Oxford University Press.

Vélasquez, Luz Stella. 1998. Agenda 21: A form of joint environmental management in Manizales, Colombia. *Environment and Urbanization* 10 (2): 9-36.

Wackernagel, Mathis, and William Rees. 1995. *Our ecological footprint: Reducing human impact on the earth*. Gabriola, Canada: New Society.

World Bank. 2001. *World development report 2000/2001: Attacking poverty*. Oxford, UK: Oxford University Press.

World Commission on Environment and Development. 1987. *Our common future*. Oxford, UK: Oxford University Press.

World Health Organization (WHO). 1992. *Our planet, our health*. Report of the WHO Commission on Health and Environment. Geneva: World Health Organization.

———. 1999. Creating healthy cities in the 21st century. In *The Earthscan reader on sustainable cities*, edited by David Satterthwaite. London: Earthscan.

Wratten, Ellen. 1995. Conceptualizing urban poverty. *Environment and Urbanization* 7 (1): 11-36.

Chiang Mai and Khon Kaen as Growth Poles: Regional Industrial Development in Thailand and Its Implications for Urban Sustainability

By
JIM GLASSMAN
and
CHRIS SNEDDON

This article examines the concept of urban sustainability within the context of two case studies from Thailand. The Thai state, under the auspices of its development planning agencies, identified the secondary cities of Chiang Mai and Khon Kaen as growth poles in the 1970s. As such, both cities were perceived as engines of regional development in their respective regions of North and Northeast Thailand. The authors critically examine how the strategies of decentralization of industrial growth and development of secondary urban centers, ostensibly to alleviate congestion and pollution in Bangkok, have been deployed in the context of urban primacy and uneven development in Thailand. They argue that these policies have helped induce some growth in the secondary cities in question but that in doing so, they have induced new problems of sustainability in the secondary cities and their surrounding rural areas without alleviating problems of sustainability in Bangkok.

Keywords: urban sustainability; Thailand; growth pole; regional development

Primate cities in the Third World are by now almost reflexively associated with the image of enormous environmental problems. Symptomatic of this association, the question of whether recent patterns of Third World urban growth are sustainable has attracted much scholarly attention in recent years (Olpadwala and Goldsmith 1992; Atkinson 1994; Gilbert 1994; Drakakis-Smith 1995, 1996, 1997; Pugh

Jim Glassman is an assistant professor in the Department of Geography at the University of British Columbia. His interests are in political economy of development, with a special emphasis on the role of the state in the development of the Southeast Asian and Northeast Asian newly developing countries. He has traveled extensively and conducted research in Thailand since 1995.

Chris Sneddon is an assistant professor in the Environmental Studies Program and the Department of Geography at Dartmouth College. His interests revolve around the political ecology of water and development, the politics of sustainability, transnational river basins, and scale and social theory. He has lived, worked, and traveled throughout Southeast Asia since 1988.

DOI: 10.1177/0002716203257075

2000; Devuyst 2001; Lo and Marcotullio 2001; Evans 2002b). While no definitive conclusions emerge from this literature, there is clearly a broad consensus that environmental problems are one of the most pressing issues connected with urban growth and will continue to be so into the future.

The question of whether a given pattern of urban growth is sustainable is, however, a vexed one—perhaps most fundamentally because there is no solid agreement on precisely how to define the notion of sustainability (Sneddon 2000). In this article, we will not rectify this problem, but we will of necessity work with a very basic conception of sustainability as a backdrop to our analysis. Following David Drakakis-Smith (1995), we define sustainability in an urban context as a development pattern that (1) satisfies the requirement for equity, social justice, and human rights; (2) meets basic human needs; (3) allows social and ethnic self-determination; (4) promotes environmental awareness and integrity; and (5) promotes awareness of interlinkages between various living beings across both space and time (p. 664). In this vein, movement toward sustainability within cities also implies a means of "reducing the transfer of environmental costs to other people, other ecosystems or into the future" (Satterthwaite 1997, 1669). We identify sustainability in these terms to emphasize that sustainable outcomes necessarily require fulfilling social and biophysical demands simultaneously. We also recognize the inherently political character of asserting and implementing this vision of urban sustainability (Evans 2002a).

Our purpose here, however, is not to defend a particular notion of sustainability but to analyze how one particular approach to the problem of sustainable Third World urbanization—namely, the push to decentralize industrial growth and to develop secondary urban centers to alleviate congestion and pollution in primate cities—has been deployed in Thailand. The Thai case is interesting to examine for a wide variety of reasons, including the fact that the country's economy has, until recently, been one of the World Bank's star performers (World Bank 1993). Moreover, the Thai case is especially instructive because it illustrates the conundrums attending attempts to promote greater urban sustainability through approaches that refuse to discipline capital and instead rely on incentives for investors. Our suggestion is that such approaches would appear—insofar as the Thai case is representative—to fundamentally give away the game at the outset by privileging growth and maintenance of class privilege over other socioecological objectives.

We develop the argument by examining the specific case of Thai state policies designed to promote secondary urban centers and decentralization of the manufacturing industry. Focusing on Chiang Mai and Khon Kaen—two cities that are among the major urban centers of the North and Northeast regions, respectively (see Figure 1)—we show that these policies have helped induce some growth in the secondary cities in question but in doing so have induced new problems of sustainability in these cities and their surrounding rural areas without alleviating problems of sustainability in Bangkok. Our conclusion is that the kinds of policies the Thai state and its backers have advertised as suitable for encouraging manufacturing decentralization and secondary urbanization are inappropriate to the goals of sustainability and in fact reflect the unwillingness or inability of the state to

FIGURE 1

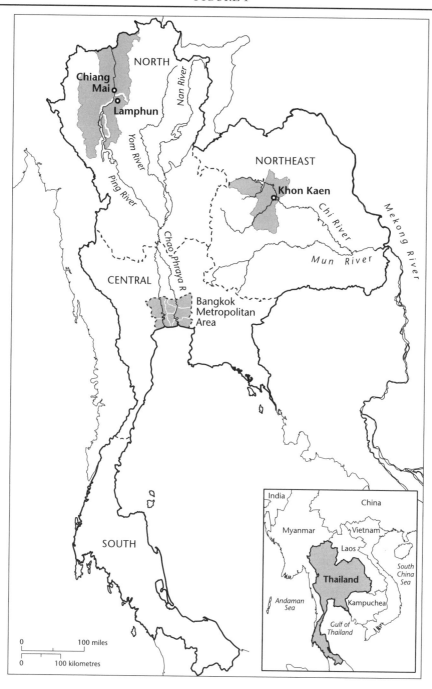

impose regulations that might procure greater sustainability at the expense of capital accumulation.

In the first section of the article, we provide a brief outline of the socioeconomic and environmental problems connected with Bangkok primacy and the kinds of policies that have been implemented to alleviate these. In the second section, we show how these policies have been implemented through the promotion of manufacturing development in the vicinity of Chiang Mai City. In the third section, we show how these policies, and associated efforts at rural industrialization, have been implemented through attempts to build the city of Khon Kaen into a major hub for its surrounding agrarian region in the Northeast. In the concluding section, we argue in more detail why the Thai state's policies, although helping to foment some desired urban-industrial growth in these regions, have been unsuccessful in stemming the tide of environmental deterioration in Bangkok while they have increased environmental problems and problems of social inequity in secondary urban centers.

Uneven Development in Thailand

Some authors have quipped that Thailand is less an industrializing country than Bangkok is an industrializing city (Hussey 1993, 19). Such a view is backed by the statistics on Bangkok's functional primacy. In 1960, for example, Bangkok contained 8.1 percent of the country's inhabitants and 23.8 of its gross domestic product; by 2000, it had increased its share to 10.4 percent of the population and 35.2 percent of the gross domestic product. Equally tellingly, the share of Bangkok and its surrounding five provinces (the Bangkok Metropolitan Region) in national manufacturing value added was 72 percent in 1981, declining somewhat to 57 percent in 1999. Moreover, most of the decline in the Bangkok Metropolitan Region's manufacturing primacy during these years is attributable to a deconcentration of some manufacturing activity to the nearby provinces of the surrounding Central Region. Indeed, between 1981 and 2000, the Central Region and the Bangkok Metropolitan Region combined consistently maintained nearly 90 percent of national manufacturing value added and increased their combined share of the gross domestic product from 64 to 71 percent, in spite of having only one-third of the national population (National Statistical Office of Thailand 1978-1995, 1990, 2000; National Economic and Social Development Board of Thailand [NESDB] 1981-2000).

Such a regionally skewed distribution of economic activities inevitably contributes to Thailand's high and rising national income disparities (Medhi 1996; Kakwani and Medhi 1996). It also creates enormous problems of urban pollution and congestion in Bangkok. For example, Bangkok's notoriously inadequate urban road network is clogged by some 2 million cars (approximately 50 percent of the national total), which move at an average pace of 1 to 2 kilometers per hour during the peak of rush hour and contribute 70 percent of Bangkok's air pollution—including levels of suspended particulate matter that are frequently between 200 and 400 times the recommended levels of the World Health Organization and carbon monoxide levels that are 50 percent higher than World Health Organization standards (Pendakur 1993, 56). In the late 1990s, levels of suspended particulate matter were measured at 330 micrograms per cubic meter, the highest level for any city in Asia other than Jakarta (Asia's best cities 1999, 46).

While Bangkok's roads and air are degraded by inadequately regulated automotive traffic, its water has been contaminated by unregulated dumping of pollutants by both households and industry. The lower Chao Phraya River, which runs through Bangkok, has levels of dissolved oxygen concentration, biochemical oxygen demand, and coliform bacteria that are all subpar in relation to Department of

---

Such approaches would appear—insofar as the Thai case is representative—to fundamentally give away the game at the outset by privileging growth and maintenance of class privilege over other socioecological objectives.

Health standards. There is concern that if sewage and wastewater treatment systems are not installed soon, the river could become anaerobic (Anuchat and Ross 1992, 22). Meanwhile, industries in the Bangkok area were already producing 40,000 to 60,000 tons of hazardous waste annually by the late 1980s and disposed of effluents containing 12 tons of heavy metals every year, with the consensus being that many did so in disregard of regulations on toxic waste disposal, which are not effectively enforced (Anuchat and Ross 1992, 23). During the economic boom at the end of the 1980s, the percentage of industries producing hazardous wastes increased from 25 percent to almost 60 percent, raising substantially the risks to human and animal health in the Bangkok area (Rajesh 1995).

These problems of urban primacy and pollution clearly suggest that Bangkok's pace and style of development is likely to be ecologically unsustainable, a view reinforced by the already very significant problems posed by annual flooding, which is exacerbated by subsidence from excessive withdrawals of groundwater under areas of massive construction (Ross and Suwattana 1995, 279-80; Ross 1997, 148-49). Yet despite these warning indicators, many of which have been evident for decades, growth has continued to cluster in the Bangkok region, and state policies have seemingly done very little to counter this.

Bangkok's primacy has very deep historical roots and thus would not be easy to redress through any simple sets of state policies (Dixon and Parnwell 1991). Even so, the Thai state has not only done very little to counter Bangkok's dominance but in fact done much to abet it (Dixon 1996; Sauwalak 2001). Perhaps most significantly, the state and its international backers have allowed and even encouraged lending policies that consolidate Bangkok's control over the rest of the country while taking few active measures to spread credit to disadvantaged regions. Nor has the state implemented any policies attempting to force relocation of firms to areas outside of the capital—as, for example, was attempted with some success by the South Korean state (Rondinelli 1991, 795; Markusen, Lee, and DiGiovanni 1999).

The Thai state's failure to discipline financial capital in any serious fashion, combined with its more general lack of strong statist controls on industry, has meant that where it has attempted promotion of manufacturing decentralization, its ability to do this is based largely on a series of policies attracting investment to given up-country locations by lowering production costs. Three major policies are particularly important in this regard: (1) the offer of regionally based investment incentives, such as tax write-offs, by the Board of Investment (BoI); (2) the development of productive infrastructure in the provinces through both general state expenditures on transportation and communications and through the Industrial Estate Authority of Thailand's development of provincial industrial estates; and (3) the maintenance by the Ministry of Labor's Wage Commission of a graded minimum wage structure, keeping provincial and nonurban wages lower than those in Bangkok or provincial urban centers.

These policies have been implemented within the overarching five-year development plans of the NESDB. The NESDB has given lip service for many years to the importance of improving rural incomes and decreasing the disparities between Bangkok and the rest of the country. Decentralization of industry has been argued for on the grounds that it can relieve Bangkok's congestion and pollution while reducing the income gap between the capital city and the rest of the country (Medhi, Tinakorn, and Suphachalasai 1992, 216-17; Parnwell 1992, 53; Parnwell and Suranart 1996, 161; Sauwalak 2001, 367).[1] Environmental benefits have been expected to be indirect in that movement of manufacturing investment to the periphery will not by itself cure Bangkok's congestion and pollution problems but will, rather, slow the rates of growth in Bangkok and thus buy the state more time for implementing environmental clean-up policies. The Third National Economic and Social Development Plan (1972-1976) called for urban-industrial decentralization through encouragement of industrial relocation. The plan designated nine provincial growth poles, including Chiang Mai and Khon Kaen, which were to serve as the loci of the strategy. Implementation began under the Fourth Plan (1977-1981) (Medhi, Tinakorn, and Suphachalasai 1992, 217; Parnwell 1992, 55).

It can be argued that NESDB plans may have less effect than advertised—even on government policies, let alone on capitalist investment behavior—because the most the NESDB can do is to mandate certain priorities on the part of ministries. It is not clear that it can enforce performance standards. Perhaps more significantly, however, the nature of the plans the NESDB develops is heavily influenced not only by the training of its officials but by the nature of the groups with whom it confers and collaborates in developing the plans. For the most part, this has meant that planning is driven by the needs of major investment groups that can offer the NESDB something in return for its own promises of infrastructure expenditure (personal interview, September 1996). As Michael Parnwell (1992) put it, planning has been growth first in orientation and has relied on "the same kinds of urban-industrial centered, top-down strategies which were responsible for enhancing the uneven pattern of development in the first place" (p. 56).

As Jonathan Rigg (2003) noted, the attraction of this kind of approach to planners like those in Thailand is that it seems to promise the prospects of improving certain social conditions without requiring the redistribution of wealth or other impositions on investors (p. 231). Yet these very constraints on the forms of industrial decentralization planning have had significant negative consequences for the Thai state's stated sustainability objectives. From the late 1980s into the 1990s, the combination of BoI incentives, industrial estate development, and lower provincial minimum wages did succeed in attracting new industrial development projects to Thailand's up-country regions. But the effects of this success were not so much to improve the prospects for meeting sustainability goals in Bangkok as to weaken them in Thailand's secondary cities. We demonstrate this through a brief examination of industrial decentralization in Chiang Mai and Khon Kaen.

Manufacturing Development in the Chiang Mai Region

In spite of Chiang Mai's long history as an urban center and a regional trade hub, manufacturing in the Chiang Mai area before the 1980s remained rudimentary, overwhelmingly small scale, and centered largely in agriculture. This industrial profile began to change from the mid-1980s, in part because of the development of the Northern Region Industrial Estate (NRIE), located on 1,788 rai (286 ha) of land in Lamphun Province, 23 kilometers south of Chiang Mai City and part of the broader Chiang Mai metropolitan area. The idea of the NRIE was first broached in the 1970s, construction was begun in April 1983, and the facility was completed in March 1985 (Thongnoi 1983; NRIE 1997).

The estate's location, along the Chiang Mai–Lampang superhighway, is strategic in multiple ways (Manat, Kerdphibul, and Leesuwan 1992, 12; Industrial Estate Authority of Thailand 1995/1996; NRIE 1997). First, the general location of the NRIE, in a region cooler than Bangkok, makes it more attractive to electronics manufacturers, who can reduce necessary temperature control costs by locating in a less hot and humid area (personal interview, October 1996). Second, the location in a specific area with a nearby urban center and a large labor force ensures—or so the factories have hoped—an adequate labor supply (personal interview, October 1996). Third, the combination of being located near Chiang Mai City and being located outside of it allows companies to simultaneously take advantage of urban amenities, including skilled workers trained by local universities and technical schools and the lower official minimum wages for nonurban areas. Fourth, the most significant specific advantage of being close to Chiang Mai City is the ease of access to Chiang Mai international airport, which can be reached by truck in about thirty minutes (various NRIE factory managers, personal interviews, October 1996-May 1997). Fifth, the specific location within Lamphun Province is close to required water supplies (Manat, Kerdphibul, and Leesuwan 1992, 10). Finally, because of its distance from Bangkok, specified industries in the Chiang Mai–Lamphun area are eligible for the maximum BoI incentives.

As land prices, wages, and other costs of production rose in Bangkok during the economic boom that began in 1987-1988, investors began to look for alternative production sites. In this context, the Thai state's investment in the NRIE began to pay off, and by 1991, at least eighty-six units of land were sold (Manat, Kerdphibul, and Leesuwan 1992, 12). As of February 1997, ninety-two units, representing more than 90 percent of all units available, had been sold, and sixty-two of the factories slated for these plots were in operation while another nineteen were under construction (NRIE 1997). Overall, as of 1995, NRIE was estimated to have received 19,925 million baht worth of investment and to be employing 22,000 persons (NRIE 1997). Electronics and machinery firms, most of them Japanese owned, were responsible for the greatest amount of invested capital and employment—probably more than 90 percent of capital and 60 percent of employment.[2] Thus, the NRIE has become a significant outpost of foreign investment in higher-technology export industries.

The NRIE has been successful in helping spur manufacturing growth within Lamphun Province and is part of a broader expansion of manufacturing in the Chiang Mai area. Between 1981 and 1996, for example, combined manufacturing value added in Chiang Mai and Lamphun Provinces increased from 1.7 million baht to 18.9 million baht, rising from less than 1 percent to nearly 2 percent of the national total (NESDB 1981-1996). In this sense, state policies promoting manufacturing decentralization to Northern Thailand can be said to have been successful, even if they have not yet led to the North's catching up with Bangkok economically. Yet if manufacturing decentralization policies are supposed to lead to more than just manufacturing growth outside of Bangkok—for example, if they are supposed to lead to greater sustainability—then they have clearly not been successful in the Chiang Mai case. Indeed, rapid economic growth has increased economic inequality and environmental damage within the North without substantially lessening national income disparities or environmental problems within Bangkok.

First of all, decentralization of industrial growth has contributed to the creation of Bangkok-like problems in Chiang Mai and Lamphun, including more air and water pollution, traffic congestion and related fatalities, and more pesticide runoff and other problems related to chemical-intensive agriculture (Satien 1992). A Chiang Mai–Lamphun planning study by the NESDB shows that the Chiang Mai metropolitan area produced more than 57,000 cubic meters of wastewater per day in 1995 and estimated that this total would rise to more than 70,000 cubic meters per day by 2005. Lamphun City produced 13,000 cubic meters of wastewater per day in 1995 and is predicted to produce 16,000 in 2005. Neither city has treatment facilities for this water. Chiang Mai produced 231 tons of garbage per day in 1995 and is predicted to produce 281 tons per day in 2005, while Lamphun produced 52 tons per day in 1995 and will produce 65 tons per day in 2005 (NESDB 1996, 43-46). Disposal facilities are inadequate, particularly in Chiang Mai, where much garbage has been stored illegally—including in places such as the graveyards of nearby villages. Indeed, the garbage disposal problem has reached the point where opponents of the Chiang Mai mayor were able to use it to force her out of office during 1998 (Busaba in tears 1998).

Rapid economic growth has increased economic inequality and environmental damage within the North without substantially lessening national income disparities or environmental problems within Bangkok.

Meanwhile, increased numbers of factories and automobiles are producing rapidly rising burdens of air pollution—a problem exacerbated by Chiang Mai–Lamphun's location within a valley, surrounded by mountains. Growing automotive traffic and inadequate development of either transportation infrastructure or public transportation have rendered Chiang Mai's roadways badly congested and noxious. Measurements of air quality along major transportation routes have registered high levels of carbon monoxide, nitrous oxides, sulfur dioxide, suspended particulate matter, and lead (NESDB 1996, 47). For Chiang Mai City as a whole, levels of suspended particulate matter reached seventy micrograms per cubic meter by the late 1990s, comparable to the levels in much larger and more industrialized cities such as Hong Kong and Seoul (Asia's best cities 1999, 46).

Since a goal of the manufacturing decentralization project has been to raise wages in up-country regions, it is fair to observe that such wage growth has clearly occurred in the North, with manufacturing wages rising from 1,178 baht per month in 1983 to 2,046 baht in 1996 (in constant 1988 prices)—along with the Northeast, the fastest increase in the country. However, it is also important to note that manufacturing wages in the North have been rising far less rapidly than manufacturing labor productivity. Thus, between 1983 and 1999, the wage index for workers in the North rose from 84 to 145 (1988 = 100), but labor productivity (output per worker) rose far more—from 61 to 229 (National Statistical Office of Thailand 1983-1999; NESDB 1983-1999). Such disparities between the growth of wages and total output have contributed to increasing economic disparities within the region as well as locally (Medhi 1996).

Weak wage growth relative to labor productivity growth is a major indicator of the weakness of labor organizations in the North: as of 1998, there were no labor unions in Chiang Mai or Lamphun Provinces (Department of Labor Protection and Welfare 1998). Such weakness is not a historical accident and has in fact been central to the state's promotion of capitalist development in the North. Indeed, the state's resources for regulating wages, work conditions, and the local environment in the North are—by design, it appears—quite weak.

We can see this by briefly examining the organization responsible for regulating the workplace environment, the Ministry of Labor and Social Welfare. The ministry's Department of Labor has inadequate personnel to monitor up-country factories. For example, there are only eight factory inspectors in the Chiang Mai Department of Labor, and the head of the department says that a minimum of fifty would be needed to adequately cover all the establishments in the province (personal interview, February 1997).[3] The absence of labor unions in the North interacts with such weaknesses in the Thai state regulatory apparatus, since even under the best of conditions, factory inspectors cannot hope to adequately cover establishments if there are not workers reporting or protesting conditions—and in the absence of unions, such behavior by workers is unlikely (personal interviews, February-March 1997).

Within this broad context of limited regulatory capacity, the NRIE factories have not necessarily been the worst offenders of labor rights, but their record has not been good. Beginning in 1993, for example, a number of workers at NRIE electronics firms began to die from unexplained causes, which involved headaches, inflamed stomachs, and vomiting. The exact number of workers who died is uncertain, but by 1994, the total may have reached as high as twenty-three (Forsyth 1994, 35; Theobald 1995, 18).[4] The causes of the deaths have not been definitively determined, but both local nongovernmental organizations and health officials believe that they were probably the result of sustained exposure to heavy metals such as lead. This was a particularly salient problem for young women working long hours in the electronics factories, who were suffering sustained exposures to chemicals by working overtime to make bonus pay (Forsyth 1994, 36).

While some improvements in these working conditions seem to have occurred since 1995—in part because of public outcry over the environmental and worker health effects of the NRIE—these events indicate the severe sustainability problems that attend rapid industrial growth in Chiang Mai–Lamphun. The picture that emerges from the case of manufacturing development in Northern Thailand, then, is of the expansion of advanced capitalist accumulation strategies to a region that is so far ill prepared to regulate the activities or deal with the human and environmental consequences.

Khon Kaen as Growth Pole

One of the notable omissions in discussions of regional development and growth pole strategies applied to Khon Kaen and the Northeast region of Thailand is the lack of attention given to the ecological implications of different urban and urban-focused regional planning strategies. While previous work has addressed shortcomings in the government's agricultural production strategies aimed at the Northeast (Dixon 1977), the politically driven nature of regional development (Somrudee 1991), and the flaws in regional industrialization policies and practice (Walton 1996; Parnwell and Suranart 1996), there has been little examination of the links between the Thai state's efforts to promote regional cities in the Northeast and the ecological impacts of these efforts on the targeted urban areas and their rural hinterlands.

In the remainder of this section, we want to draw attention to this lacuna by addressing the environmental consequences of Khon Kaen's recent growth from two angles. The first looks at a specific industrial operation, Phoenix Pulp and Paper Company; its role in industrial development in Khon Kaen; and the socioecological impacts accruing to the factory. The second angle focuses on environmental concerns within Khon Kaen Municipality related to water. In both instances, we argue that the role of the state—and its contradictory functions as development promoter and environmental manager—has been a critical contributor to what are arguably unsustainable processes.

In stark contrast to Chiang Mai, which has for centuries been a city of cultural and political-economic significance in the historical trajectories of Siam and Thailand, the emergence of Khon Kaen as a regional city was overseen and directed almost entirely by government planners as part of an overarching regional development initiative begun in the 1960s.[5] Located in Northeast Thailand, which by income levels and other measures of social welfare is the country's poorest region,[6] the municipality of Khon Kaen was until this time essentially a large village of several thousand inhabitants. Throughout the 1960s, the state focused development efforts (primarily road and irrigation system construction) in the region on rural areas due to concern over insurgency in the countryside, led by the Communist Party of Thailand. In the logic of this "development as counterinsurgency" campaign, the emphasis was decidedly not on "long-term efforts to alleviate the poverty of the rural population" but on "short-term, piecemeal attempts to win the people's loyalty" (Somrudee 1991, 194).[7]

Throughout the 1970s and subsequent decades, Khon Kaen materialized as the centerpiece of the government's turn toward a growth pole strategy in the Northeast. As outlined in official state planning documents, the city was to be promoted as a locale suitable for industrial development, which would, theoretically, deflect rural-urban migration from the Northeast to Bangkok by absorbing nonfarm labor. As highlighted earlier, the NESDB's Fourth Plan (1977-1981) encouraged decentralization through regional development and laid out several financial and monetary incentives for provincial industrial development (Walton 1996, 113-14).[8]

Regional development through the promotion of Khon Kaen as growth pole was intimately linked to state activities in the area of rural development. Despite the overwhelmingly agricultural character of the region, rural industrialization has long been a primary aim of development planning in the Northeast, as highlighted in a series of "regional" reports from the past three decades (Committee for Development of the Northeast 1961; Louis Berger, Inc. 1972; Biwater 1987). These reports—commissioned by state agencies and carried out by international consulting firms—point out the Northeast's potential in terms of agroprocessing industries and recommend an export-oriented strategy of industrial development as the most likely path toward economic growth. We turn now to a representative example of this strategy in the Northeast, the Phoenix Pulp and Paper factory, and its socioecological impacts.

Rural industrialization in the Northeast: The case of Phoenix Pulp and Paper

While industrialization in Thailand during the period of the economy's rapid growth from the 1970s to the 1990s was generally founded on the manufacturing sector, industrialization in the Northeast has followed a somewhat different path. The Northeast is the least industrialized region in the country, leading one set of authors to conclude that one's "lasting impression is of a largely unindustrialised, and certainly underindustrialised, regional economy" (Parnwell and Suranart 1996, 166). The industrial structure of the region clarifies the degree to which industry depends on the agricultural base. More than "four-fifths of industrial enterprise in the North-East consists of rice-milling, and much of the remainder is also based on the processing of agricultural and other primary produce" (Parnwell and Suranart 1996, 167). Non-resource-dependent industries in the region have been very few. Part of this can be explained by the labor market, which is tied to agriculture. There is a pronounced seasonal demand for labor due to the agricultural character of the region. In the off season, silk weaving, village handicrafts, and similar activities pick up the slack for some laborers. However, many migrate to Bangkok and other regions in search of nonfarm and farm labor opportunities (Walton 1996, 118).

John Walton (1996, 117) cited the Phoenix Pulp and Paper Mill (henceforth "Phoenix") as a "notable exception" in the failure of the province to attract private investment despite heavy public-sector investment in infrastructure and government administration and educational services. However, we argue that the limited success of the Phoenix plant as an exemplar of the type of industrial venture that state regional development policy is designed to attract is drawn into question by the deleterious socioecological consequences of the mill. In addition, the Thai state's encouragement of Phoenix to build a plant in Khon Kaen Province was part and parcel of the state's wider growth pole/regional development strategy.

In the late 1970s, Phoenix Pulp and Paper Company selected a site for its plant in the province of Khon Kaen on the right bank of the Nam Phong (literally, "River

Phong") approximately forty kilometers northwest of Khon Kaen municipality (the provincial capital). The company chose this location on the basis of the then-plentiful supply of *kenaf* (a grass-like plant whose fiber is useful in gunny sack and pulp production) in the immediate vicinity. Other locational factors in the company's decision to construct a plant in Khon Kaen included easy access to sufficient water (a crucial input in the production process and a medium of by-product disposal),[9] availability of cheap power, and accessibility of land for purchase (OIC et al. 1975). The nearness of Khon Kaen Municipality, which had achieved considerable growth by the 1970s as a result of the state's regional development program and

---

[T]he greatest beneficiaries of Khon Kaen's growth have not been members of the rural populace who were the planners' ostensible targets but rather urban middle-class in-migrants (lecturers, bureaucrats, businesspeople) . . . and . . . Bangkok banks.

---

growth pole strategy, was perceived by company officials as another locational advantage. In the words of the feasibility study for the creation of Phoenix, "Sufficient land is available for the construction of the factory as well as a housing colony. The provincial headquarters at Khon Kaen are only 35 km away where all facilities such as schools, shops, hospitals, etc. are available." Thus, the siting of the Phoenix plant along the Nam Phong was clearly part of the state's broader program of regional development, with Khon Kaen as the targeted growth pole.

The Thai state, largely under the auspices of BoI, took an extraordinarily active role in courting the financiers of Phoenix—a Thai, Indian, and Austrian joint venture—to move to the Nam Phong basin in the province of Khon Kaen. In September 1975, the Thai BoI issued a notification to the Phoenix Pulp and Paper Co., Ltd., giving preliminary approval for the construction of a large pulp mill somewhere in the country. This document also outlined the incentives and benefits available to Phoenix, under current Thai investment policy, based in part on plant location.[10] These special incentives offered by the Thai government included land purchasing rights (normally not extended to firms with non-Thai majority ownership), allowance of "skilled alien technicians" (non-Thai labor), an import duty exemption on imported equipment, exemption from income tax on net profit for the project's first five years of operation, and an additional 50 percent exemption from income tax during the second five years (OIC et al. 1975, 23-25). The proposed location of the plant, within the province of Khon Kaen, ensured the tax holiday because BoI had previously declared Khon Kaen an "investment promotion zone" (OIC et al. 1975, 242) in line with its status as a growth pole and regional city.[11] In a letter to Phoenix executives, BoI's secretary-general stressed that "the investment incentives granted by the BoI for the venture reflect the great importance which we attach to this project in terms of its potential contribution to the industrial development of our country" (OIC et al. 1975, 6).

A local Thai businessman played a decisive role in raising enough capital to proceed with the project following incorporation of the company in 1975. Phoenix's original Thai and foreign partners tapped Somboon Nandhabiwat, then-president of a medium-scale bank, to chair Phoenix and supervise financing efforts. Somboon was able to use his considerable political clout to convince business leaders that the pulp mill was an important "national project."[12] By August 1979, all sixteen Thai commercial banks agreed to provide credits and credit guarantees for the pulp plant, and construction moved forward. Phoenix also secured the support of the Ministry of Agriculture and Agricultural Cooperatives, whose minister noted the "national interest" aspects of the project and ensured "early implementation" (OIC et al. 1975, 5).

On establishment of the plant in 1982, Phoenix received full BoI privileges, such as reductions in business and corporate income taxes for a set period and expenditures on electricity, water supplies, and other infrastructure as deductibles (Walton 1996, 114-17). Despite the pulp mill's exceptional nature as a prime example of rural industrialization in the Northeast, Phoenix's economic and performance quality of management has been highly variable. The sizable financial losses of the company in the 1980s, associated with getting the pulp production lines up and running, had to be offset by subsidies from the government. While posting a pretax profit of nearly Bt1,074 million (U.S.$42.92 million) in 1995, the company faced heavy losses in 1996 and again in 2001 (Phoenix hit by drop in pulp price 2001). Wrangling over control of the company reached a fevered pitch in the late 1990s, when majority shareholder, European Overseas Development Corporation, accused a prominent minority stockholder (Globex Corporation) of manipulating Thai politicians to support a hostile takeover bid. In April 1998, the Stock Exchange of Thailand called for an investigation into alleged "financial irregularities, conflicts of interest and a lack of transparency by management" (Nantawan 1998).

Yet Phoenix's political-economic turmoil has been overshadowed by its environmental performance. Since an initial incident in April 1992, throughout the 1990s, Phoenix was repeatedly charged with polluting the Nam Phong and, time and again, ordered to halt production by the provincial governor, the Department of Industrial Works, the Pollution Control Department, or a combination of state agencies (Sneddon 2002, 733-35). Officials from the Department of Industrial Works allowed the plant to reopen in June 1992 following promises from plant management that they would strive to improve the quality of the treated wastewater they were releasing into Huay Chote, a small swamp adjacent to the Nam Phong that served as Phoenix's main repository of treated effluent (Kunsiri 1992). This cycle of closing down the plant, typically following the deaths of thousands of fish in the river, and then allowing production to gear up again was repeated in 1994, 1996, 1997, and 1998. Residents of villages near the plant most directly affected by the release of effluents have effectively argued for compensation from Phoenix for contaminated rice fields and fish ponds and called for stricter government regulations on water pollution, but Phoenix has effectively deflected such criticism by denying fault and insisting that environmental externalities are a small price to pay for the economic benefits brought by rural industrialization. While the government has advocated a Nam Phong Action Plan to restore the degraded river by bringing together the various agencies, Phoenix, and communities, peoples' organizations and nongovernmental organizations working in the Nam Phong have been frustrated by state agencies' continued delays and inaction with regard to preventing the pollution incidents (Sneddon 2002).

In addition, the threat of dioxins and other highly toxic compounds in the effluent from the Phoenix plant has heightened concerns within Khon Kaen Municipality over the impacts of the pulp mill on urban sustainability. Controversy over the presence of dioxins in Phoenix's effluent erupted in June 1992 after a laboratory in France found exceedingly high levels in the Nam Phong's water. This prompted the president of Khon Kaen University, Wanchai Wattanasap, to demand the Nam Phong be classified a "pollution control zone" under the 1992 Enhancement and Conservation of National Environmental Quality Act, a move that would effectively halt all industrial development along the river. Dr. Wanchai also raised the specter of dioxins emitted by the Phoenix plant directly contaminating urban water supplies, noting that "local waterworks authorities have never even examined the tap water [for Khon Kaen Municipality] to see if it is tainted with dioxins" (University study links 1993). Khon Kaen withdraws water for domestic consumption directly from a primary irrigation canal—fed by the Nam Phong—some twenty-five kilometers upstream of where the river passes by the city.

Khon Kaen's urban environment

The experiences of Khon Kaen as a growth pole during the past three decades led Somrudee Nicrowattanayingyong (1991) to conclude that "no provincial town in Thailand has ever experienced the central government's urban development planning for as long a period of time as Khon Kaen" (pp. 18-19). Despite this attention, Khon Kaen has largely failed to achieve the development goals set by planners. Part of the logic of the growth pole strategy was to slow the flow of people to Bangkok and thus relieve some of the negative social and ecological impacts of large numbers of people. In fact, the "town's [Khon Kaen's] experience has not mitigated, but accelerated, Northeastern rural migration to Bangkok (and to other big cities)" (Somrudee 1991, 25).[13] Furthermore, the greatest beneficiaries of Khon Kaen's growth have not been members of the rural populace who were the planners' ostensible targets but rather urban middle-class in-migrants (lecturers, bureaucrats, businesspeople) who have been able to take advantage of the service-oriented opportunities in the growing city and, in a very real sense, Bangkok banks that directed savings from other parts of the region to Khon Kaen and were able to take advantage of the increased level of business transactions filtering through Khon Kaen (Somrudee 1991, 249-54).

Despite the apparent failure of Khon Kaen to spur rural and industrial development in any meaningful way, its evolution into a regional city has been accompanied by most of the problems afflicting large cities throughout the Third World. The municipality itself covers forty-six square kilometers with a population of 142,313 in 1996, although the actual figure may be double due to the presence of unregistered migrants. Despite being the first provincial center in Thailand to have a town plan (Sternstein 1977, 106), the rapid growth of the city has generated several problems, particularly concerning public services such as electricity, piped water, garbage collection, and road construction and repair. However, the most serious environmental problems—both currently and in the future—revolve around water supply, wastewater treatment, and the community wastewater drainage system. A dilemma confronting all of Khon Kaen's residents, the environmental problems related to water affect different social groups within the city's boundary in unlike ways.

A recent survey of city residents undertaken by researchers at Khon Kaen University (Tuntuwanit et al. 1996), initiated as part of citywide project to involve residents in "community environmental management," attempted to identify the most critical environmental concerns of city residents. The researchers surveyed residents from six areas, two each of suburban, center, and low-income (slum) communities. Results showed that during the rainy season, the principal problem involves the town's drainage system and flooding. In the dry season, residents cite the amount of piped water as the most significant environmental issue (Tuntuwanit et al. 1996, 14).

The city maintains one main drainage canal, which is frequently clogged with garbage from tertiary sewers associated with residences and businesses. The canal runs through the city in a broad arch from the southwest to the northeast, emptying into series of gravity-style treatment ponds. Judging from measurements taken two decades ago, the amount of dissolved oxygen in the waterway is at or near zero, and urban residents have long been aware of the dangerous levels of fecal coliform bacteria in the water from human and animal waste being delivered to the canal (Danaisak 1976). Residents of low-income communities in the survey cited the utter lack of wastewater ditches, problems associated with living in the topograhically lowest section of the city (e.g., collection of flood waters), and the high levels of oil from gas stations and car garages as their most pressing concerns (Somrudee 1991, 15-17).

These low-income communities experience these water problems more intensely than other neighborhoods. Because of their legal status (they theoretically do not exist in the eyes of local authorities), a large majority of residents (85 to 92 percent) in both of the two communities surveyed receive no piped water service from the city and have difficult access or no access at all to the city drainage system. In spite of the lack of access to public services, and "even though members of low-income communities earn less . . . they pay higher prices for provided utilities" (Tuntuwanit et al. 1996, 12). For example, most city residents pay Bt100 to Bt200 (U.S.$4 to U.S.$8) per month for piped water, while those few slum residents who do receive water pay Bt330 to Bt450 (U.S.$13.20 to U.S.$18) per month.

How did this situation come about? The Khon Kaen city plan was completed in 1975, but since then, city authorities have shown little inclination for urban environmental planning or management. In the early 1980s, the Urban Development Office (of the Ministry of Interior) mobilized improvements in road, sanitary, and water supply systems in Khon Kaen (Somrudee 1991, 196). Plans for a modern wastewater treatment plant have been on the books since the early 1970s, but a series of oxidation ponds, Bung Thung Sang, have served as a wastewater treatment system since the mid-1970s (Danaisak 1976, 26). Ground was broken for a new plant in 1994, but a series of administrative delays and financial shortfalls have resulted in little substantial progress. Khon Kaen's wastewater treatment history is a lesson in urban planning failure and the lack of investment in environmental services by the state.

The cases of Phoenix, on one hand, and Khon Kaen's urban environment, on the other, demonstrate the dilemmas of socioecological sustainability that have so often accompanied state efforts to stimulate rapid economic development in the Third World. The pollution incidents associated with Phoenix, aside from their degrading effects on local ecosystems, have ignited local social movements that fundamentally question the state's preference for industrial development and transformation of the region's socioecological systems. Indeed, the Thai state mobilized every possible political-economic incentive to encourage Phoenix to construct and implement a plant in the Khon Kaen area in the name of rural industrialization and rural development. The idea of Khon Kaen as growth pole was part of this same overarching regional development strategy and thus must share a good deal of the blame for creating the political, economic, and social conditions that have contributed to the city's deteriorating urban environment. In both instances, the negative ecological impacts of economic development activities are distributed unequally with the rural and urban poor receiving the brunt of the consequences.

Conclusion: Decentralization Policies and Sustainability

Given the enormous amount of literature on Bangkok's social justice and ecological sustainability problems, we need do little here to substantiate the argument that the Thai state's decentralization policies have been unsuccessful as a means for reducing either social inequality or environmental problems in Bangkok. All of the problems connected with Bangkok's primacy, discussed earlier, have grown worse throughout the period in which the Thai state has been promoting (with at least limited success) industrial growth in up-country areas such as Chiang Mai and Khon Kaen. At the same time, as we have shown, the decentralization policies—insofar as they have had some success—have actually added new layers of concern over urban sustainability. Decentralization of economic and manufacturing growth has not satisfied the criteria of sustainability suggested by Drakakis-Smith (1997)—particularly his first, third, and fourth criteria—either in Bangkok or in Thailand's major secondary cities.

We will conclude by briefly suggesting why such an outcome should by no means be surprising. Our argument is that the policies we have discussed do not in fact have sustainability goals as their major purpose—and this is less because of whatever technical or ideological orientations might be ascribed to them than because of their class basis. The Thai state is tightly integrated with both leading domestic and international capitalists, something that has been true of it for more than a century (Hewison 1989; Suehiro 1989; Anek 1992; Chaiyan 1994). This fusion of power and purpose between capital and state has meant—especially in the context of the post–World War II cold war in Southeast Asia—that state policies have emphasized strongly capital-friendly and growth-oriented patterns of development. This has in turn affected the nature of rural development programs and regional planning. Indeed, Bangkok's relationship with regions such as the North and Northeast have been heavily marked by the project of exercising social control to undermine Leftist political movements and bring these regions more fully within the circuits of international capitalist accumulation processes centered in Bangkok (London 1985; Chairat 1988; Somrudee 1991; Chaiyan 1994).

The manufacturing decentralization policies outlined here are, in this sense, of a piece with the earlier counterinsurgency policies carried out by the Thai state from the 1960s into the 1980s: the goal in both cases was not to bring equal benefits to all Thais but to bring peripheral regions more fully into the industrial capitalist accumulation project. Insofar as sustainability goals are tacked onto this agenda, it is in the hope that some headway can be made in mitigating ecological and social justice problems without having to confront distributional issues. Decentralization strategies, therefore, are unlikely to result in greater social equality or environmental protection without the presence of strong social movements that can impose on capital and the state various redistributive and regulatory practices. Yet the project of the Thai state and its international backers has regularly involved attempting to undermine such social movements (Girling 1981; Morell and Chai-anan 1981; Turton 1987; Bowie 1997). The success of the state in doing this has enabled rapid capital accumulation precisely on the basis of inequitable distribution and ineffective regulation of capital.

Against this backdrop, what is in our view more important at this point than spinning more new schemes for urban sustainability in Thailand is discussing the conditions under which marginalized social groups might be able to claim more power and begin the process of social, political, and economic restructuring that would be a necessary (although not sufficient) condition for greater sustainability (cf. Douglass and Zoghlin 1994). While we make no bets about the prospects of this occurring, we note that such a task is neither irrelevant nor otherworldly since recently there has been not only increased popular struggle in Thailand but also renewed attempts to bring together a powerful national social movement composed of villagers, urban workers, environmentalists, and other marginalized groups, especially under the umbrella of the Assembly of the Poor (Baker 2000; Glassman 2002). While it cannot be said at this point whether such a social movement can succeed in the project of reconstituting Thai society, it is on the basis of such a social movement that policies for greater sustainability might have some chance of succeeding.

Notes

1. More general arguments for the virtues of decentralization and secondary urban center growth are put forward by Rondinelli (1991). For a more skeptical view of the virtues of promoting decentralization and non-Bangkok-centric growth, see Ayal (1992).

2. Precise figures are impossible to obtain from Industrial Estate Authority of Thailand publications since not all individual companies list the amounts of invested capital, and the Industrial Estate Authority of Thailand's listing of Northern Region Industrial Estate companies for 1995-1996 actually shows higher levels of invested capital in the electronics sector alone than what is registered in the Northern Region Industrial Estate's summary of all investment for 1995. Nonetheless, by extrapolating from the figures given in Industrial Estate Authority of Thailand (1995/1996), as we have done here, one can get a roughly accurate picture of the relative magnitudes.

3. There were officially 6,000 establishments in Chiang Mai as of 1997, but it is estimated that with various illegal and unregistered operations, the actual number was more like 10,000. The staff can at most inspect 100 factories per month.

4. The deaths were reported in a number of stories in the Thai English-language press throughout 1994. See, for example, "The Cause of Death" (1994), Sombat (1994a, 1994b), Atiya and Sombat (1994), Nantiya (1994), and Kamol (1994).

5. In the Northeast Development Plan, released to coincide with the First National Economic Development Plan, the government offered its rationale for selecting Khon Kaen as the "first development center" of the Northeast region. Reasons included Khon Kaen's fairly large population, its central location, pending completion of the Nam Phong Project and its supply of cheap electricity, its agricultural development potential (especially in terms of supplying raw materials for nascent industries), and the presence of rock salt as a basis for chemical industries (Committee for Development of the Northeast 1961, 2-3).

6. The Northeast region covers 168,900 square kilometers with a population, as of 1993, of 20.2 million (34.6 percent of the country) (Walton 1996, 116). Historically, Northeast Thailand has been considered culturally, and to some degree politically, separate from the rest of Thailand. In addition, it is physically differentiated from the rest of the country by its location on two plateaus that drain to the Mekong River.

7. By the end of the 1960s, the Northeast "had commanded a high priority on the planning agenda and had received unprecedented attention from international aid donors" (Phisit 1972, 46). The Northeast Economic Development was formalized in 1968 with a committee comprising key ministers and cabinet members and an advisory group set up under the technical assistance program of the U.S. Government (Phisit 1972, 52). The general aims of U.S. involvement (through the United States Operation Mission, the precursor to United States Agency for International Development) were fairly clear:

> The basic objective of the United States Operation Mission (USOM) assistance from 1965 to 1970 was to increase the resources available in northeastern Thailand, on the assumption that the provision of such resources would slow the spread of communist influence. (Somrudee 1991, 81)

8. In reality, decentralization of the planning process in Thailand has meant "local planners being able to choose from a 'menu' of projects offered by central authorities" with little legitimate input coming from local entities (Walton 1996, 110).

9. The plant is located on the banks of the Nam Phong ("River Phong"). The Nam Phong was the site of the Nam Phong Multipurpose Project undertaken in the 1960s for hydroelectric generation, irrigation development, and flood alleviation (Ruangdej 1987). Construction of the Ubolratana Dam in 1966 effectively regulated the flow of the Nam Phong, creating hydrologic conditions satisfactory for water-dependent industries such as pulp operations. The Phoenix plant is located approximately fifteen kilometers downstream of the dam.

10. Only projects constructed outside the Bangkok region were eligible for incentives.

11. Phoenix's interest in constructing a large-capacity pulp plant was clear. Investment analyses projected an average return on equity capital invested in the project of 32.2 percent and an average gross return on total capital of 17.3 percent to be realized in an estimated six years from the onset of production (OIC et al. 1975, 243-45).

12. Somboon was a close friend of then–Prime Minister Kriengsak Chamanant. Information on Somboon's role in the early phases of Phoenix comes from an undated pamphlet, "Biography of Somboon Nandhabiwat" (n.d.), published by Phoenix as a memorial following his death in 1995.

13. Khon Kaen serves as a kind of testing ground for skills, behaviors, and experiences necessary for Bangkok. Because transportation links between big cities in Thailand are much better than among secondary towns and rural areas, and as a result of other factors, the growth of Khon Kaen may actually be facilitating movement to Bangkok (Somrudee 1991, 230-32).

References

Anek, Laothamatas. 1992. *Business associations and the new political economy of Thailand: From bureaucratic polity to liberal corporatism.* Boulder, CO: Westview and Institute for Southeast Asian Studies.

Anuchat, Poungsomlee, and Helen Ross. 1992. *Impacts of modernisation and urbanisation in Bangkok: An integrative ecological and biosocial study.* Bangkok, Thailand: Institute for Population and Social Research, Mahidol University.

Asia's best cities. 1999. *Asiaweek*, 17 December.

Atiya, Achakulwisut, and Raksakul Sombat. 1994. The human price of development. *Bangkok Post*, 28 April.

Atkinson, Adrian. 1994. Introduction: The contribution of cities to sustainability. *Third World Planning Review* 16 (2): 97-101.

Ayal, Eliezar. 1992. Thailand's development: The role of Bangkok. *Pacific Affairs* 65 (3): 353-67.

Baker, Chris. 2000. Thailand's assembly of the poor: Background, drama, reaction. *South East Asia Research* 8 (1): 5-29.

Busaba in tears as she steps down as Chiang Mai mayor. 1998. *Bangkok Post*, 29 September.

Biography of Somboon Nandhabiwat. n.d. Khon Kaen, Thailand: Phoenix.

Biwater. 1987. *Investigation and preparation of a water resource development programme for North East Thailand, final report: Water resources.* Bangkok: Kingdom of Thailand.

Bowie, Katherine. 1997. *Rituals of national loyalty: An anthropology of the state and the village scout movement in Thailand.* Berkeley: University of California Press.

The cause of death. 1994. *Bangkok Post*, 24 February.

Chairat, Charoensin-o-larn. 1988. *Understanding postwar reformism in Thailand: A reinterpretation of rural development.* Bangkok, Thailand: Editions Duang Kamol.

Chaiyan, Rajchagool. 1994. *The rise and fall of the Thai absolute monarchy: Foundations of the modern Thai state from feudalism to peripheral capitalism.* Bangkok, Thailand: White Lotus.

Committee for Development of the Northeast. 1961. *The northeast development plan 1962-1966.* Bangkok, Thailand: Planning Office, National Economic Development Board, Office of the Prime Minister

Danaisak, Panyawai. 1976. *Water pollution and industry in Khon Kaen.* Project report no. I76-4. Khon Kaen, Thailand: Department of Industrial Engineering, Faculty of Engineering, Khon Kaen University.

Department of Labor Protection and Welfare (of Thailand). 1998. *Yearbook of labor statistics.* Bangkok, Thailand: Department of Labor Protection and Welfare.

Devuyst, Dmitri, ed. 2001. *How green is the city? Sustainability assessment and the management of urban environments.* New York: Columbia University Press.

Dixon, Chris. 1977. Development, regional disparity and planning: The experience of Northeast Thailand. *Journal of Southeast Asian Studies* 8 (2): 210-23.

———. 1996. Thailand's rapid economic growth: Causes, sustainability and lessons. In *Uneven development in Thailand*, edited by M. Parnwell. Aldershot, UK: Avebury.

Dixon, Chris, and Michael Parnwell. 1991. Thailand: The legacy of non-colonial development in South-East Asia. In *Colonialism and development in the contemporary world*, edited by M. Dixon and M. Heffernan. London: Mansell.

Douglass, Mike, and Malia Zoghlin. 1994. Sustaining cities at the grassroots: Livelihood, environment and social networks in Suan Phlu, Bangkok. *Third World Planning Review* 16 (2): 171-200.

Drakakis-Smith, David. 1995. Third World cities: Sustainable urban development I. *Urban Studies* 32 (4/5): 659-77.

———. 1996. Third World cities: Sustainable urban development II—Population, labour and poverty. *Urban Studies* 33 (4/5): 673-701.

———. 1997. Third World cities: Sustainable urban development III. *Urban Studies* 34 (5/6): 797-823.

Evans, Peter. 2002a. Introduction: Looking for agents of urban livability in a globalized political economy. In *Livable cities? Urban struggles for livelihood and sustainability*, edited by P. Evans. Berkeley: University of California Press.

———, ed. 2002b. *Livable cities? Urban struggles for livelihood and sustainability*. Berkeley: University of California Press.

Forsyth, Tim. 1994. Shut up or shut down: How a Thai medical agency was closed after it questioned worker safety at a factory owned by Thailand's largest employer. *Asia Inc* (April): 30-37.

Gilbert, Alan. 1994. Third World cities: Poverty, unemployment, gender roles and the environment during a time of restructuring. *Urban Studies* 31 (4/5): 605-33.

Girling, John. 1981. *Thailand: Society and politics*. Ithaca, NY: Cornell University Press.

Glassman, Jim. 2002. From Seattle (and Ubon) to Bangkok: The scales of resistance to corporate globalization. *Environment and Planning D: Society and Space* 20 (5): 513-33.

Hewison, Kevin. 1989. *Bankers and bureaucrats: Capital and the role of the state in Thailand*. New Haven, CT: Yale Center for International and Area Studies.

Hussey, Antonia. 1993. Rapid industrialization in Thailand. *Geographical Review* 83 (1): 14-28.

Industrial Estate Authority of Thailand. 1995/1996. *Factories in industrial estates, 1995/1996*. Bangkok, Thailand: Industrial Estate Authority of Thailand.

Kakwani, Nanak, and Krongkaew Medhi. 1996. Big reduction in "poverty." *Bangkok Post*, Economic Review Year-End 1996, pp. 21-23.

Kamol, Sukin. 1994. Mystery deaths plague workers. *The Nation* (Bangkok), 1 May.

Kunsiri, Kokilakanit. 1992. Phoenix "controls" waste water. *The Nation* (Bangkok), 27 June, p. B8.

Lo, Fu-chen, and Peter Marcotullio, eds. 2001. *Globalization and the sustainability of cities in the Asia Pacific region*. Tokyo: UN University Press.

London, Bruce. 1985. Thai city–hinterland relationships in an international context: Development as social control in Northern Thailand. In *Urbanization in the world economy*, edited by M. Timberlake. Orlando, FL: Academic Press.

Louis Berger, Inc. (Development Economics Group). 1972. *Northeast Thailand economic development study, final report, volume I: Recommended development budget and foreign assistance projects 1972-1976*. Bangkok, Thailand: NEDB.

Manat, Suwan, Udom Kerdphibul, and Chukiat Leesuwan. 1992. *Impacts of industrialization upon the village's life in Northern Thailand*. Chiang Mai, Thailand: Faculty of Social Science, Chiang Mai University.

Markusen, Ann, Yong-Sook Lee, and Sean DiGiovanni, eds. 1999. *Second tier cities: Rapid growth beyond the metropolis*. Minneapolis: University of Minnesota Press.

Medhi, Krongkaew. 1996. *Thailand: Poverty assessment update*. Economic Research and Training Center research paper. Bangkok, Thailand: Faculty of Economics, Thammasat University.

Medhi, Krongkaew, Pranee Tinakorn, and Suphat Suphachalasai. 1992. Rural poverty in Thailand: Policy issues and responses. *Asian Development Review* 10 (1): 199-225.

Morell, David, and Samudavanija Chai-anan. 1981. *Political conflict in Thailand: Reform, reaction, revolution*. Cambridge, MA: Oelschlager, Gunn & Hain.

Nantawan, Polkwandee. 1998. Phoenix meeting lives up to its tradition of chaos. *Bangkok Post*, 30 April.

Nantiya, Tangwisutijit. 1994. Danger zone. *The Nation* (Bangkok), 27 February.

National Economic and Social Development Board of Thailand (NESDB). 1981-2000. *Gross regional product accounts*. Bangkok, Thailand: National Economic and Social Development Board of Thailand.

————. 1996. *Development planning report, volume I: Twin cities project for Chiang Mai and Lamphun* (in Thai). Bangkok: National Economic and Social Development Board of Thailand.

National Statistical Office of Thailand. 1978-1995. *Statistical yearbook*. Bangkok: National Statistical Office of Thailand.

————. 1983-1999. *Labor force survey*. February round. Bangkok: National Statistical Office of Thailand.

————. 1990. *Population and housing census*. Bangkok: National Statistical Office of Thailand.

————. 2000. *Population and housing census*. Bangkok: National Statistical Office of Thailand.

Northern Region Industrial Estate (NRIE). 1997. *Information on NRIE, details of land buyers in the NRIE, contact list of the industrial operators of the NRIE*. Lamphun, Thailand: Northern Region Industrial Estate.

OIC (Overseas Industrial Consultants), Ltd., Ballarpur & Straw Board Mills, Ltd., Agribusiness Consultants, Applied Scientific Research Corporation of Thailand, and Phoenix Pulp & Paper Co., Ltd. 1975. *A feasibility study for a 70,000 MT/year pulp mill*. Prepared for Phoenix Pulp & Paper Company Limited, Bangkok, Thailand.

Olpadwala, Porus, and William Goldsmith. 1992. The sustainability of privilege: Reflections on the environment, the Third World city, and poverty. *World Development* 20 (4): 627-40.

Parnwell, Michael. 1992. Confronting uneven development in Thailand: The potential role of rural industries. *Malaysian Journal of Tropical Geography* 22 (1): 51-62.

Parnwell, Michael, and Khamanarong Suranart. 1996. Rural industrialisation in Thailand: Village industries as a potential basis for rural development in the North-East. In *Uneven development in Thailand*, edited by M. Parnwell. Aldershot, UK: Avebury.

Pendakur, Setty. 1993. Congestion management and air quality: Lessons from Bangkok and Mexico City. *Asian Journal of Environmental Management* 1 (2): 53-65.

Phisit, Pakkasem. 1972. Thailand's Northeast economic development planning: A case study in regional planning. Ph.D. diss., University of Pittsburgh.

Phoenix hit by drop in pulp price. 2001. *Bangkok Post*, 28 July, p. 7.

Pugh, Cedric, ed. 2000. *Sustainable cities in developing countries: Theory and practice at the millennium*. London: Earthscan.

Rajesh, Noel. 1995. *Thailand country report on pollution*. Bangkok, Thailand: Project for Ecological Recovery.

Rigg, Jonathan. 2003. *Southeast Asia: The human landscape of modernization and development*. 2d ed. London: Routledge.

Rondinelli, Dennis. 1991. Asian urban development policies in the 1990s: From growth control to urban diffusion. *World Development* 19 (7): 791-803.

Ross, Helen. 1997. Bangkok's environmental problems: Stakeholders and avenues for change. In *Seeing forests for trees: Environment and environmentalism in Thailand*, edited by P. Hirsch. Chiang Mai, Thailand: Silkworm Books.

Ross, Helen, and Suwattana. 1995. The environmental costs of industrialization. In *Thailand's industrialization and its consequences*, edited by Medhi Krongkaew. London: St. Martin's.

Ruangdej Srivardhana. 1987. The Nam Pong case study: Some lessons to be learned. *International Journal of Water Resource Development* 3 (4): 238-46.

Satien, Sriboonruang. 1992. *Chiang Mai Province and its emerging development problems*. Chiang Mai, Thailand: Faculty of Economics, Chiang Mai University.

Satterthwaite, David. 1997. Sustainable cities or cities that contribute to sustainable development? *Urban Studies* 34 (10): 1667-91.

Sauwalak, Kittiprapas. 2001. The extended Bangkok Region: Globalization and sustainability. In *Globalization and the sustainability of cities in the Asia Pacific Region*, edited by F. Lo and P. Marcotullio. Tokyo: United Nations Press.

Sneddon, Chris. 2000. "Sustainability" in ecological economics, ecology and livelihoods: A review. *Progress in Human Geography* 24 (4): 521-49.

———. 2002. Altered rivers and scales of conflict: The case of Nam Phong Basin, Northeast Thailand. *Society and Natural Resources* 15 (8): 725-42.

Sombat, Raksakul. 1994a. Industrial waste poses a threat to Lamphun. *Bangkok Post*, 1 May.

———. 1994b. Mysterious deaths in Lamphun. *Bangkok Post*, 27 February.

Somrudee, Nicrowattanayingyong. 1991. Development planning, politics, and paradox: A study of Khon Kaen, a regional city in Northeast Thailand. Ph.D. thesis, Syracuse University.

Sternstein, Larry. 1977. Internal migration and regional development: The Khon Kaen Development Centre of Northeast Thailand. *Journal of Southeast Asian Studies* 8 (1): 32-53.

Suehiro, Akira. 1989. *Capital accumulation in Thailand, 1855-1985.* Tokyo: Center for East Asian Studies.

Theobald, Sally. 1995. Pressure points in industrial development: A gender analysis framework of the various stakeholders in the Northern Regional Industrial Estate, Thailand. Master's thesis, University of East Anglia.

Thongnoi, Keuakul. 1983. A study for planning of establishment of Northern Industrial Estate (Chiang Mai, Lamphun, Lampang) (in Thai). Master's thesis, Chulalongkorn University, Bangkok, Thailand.

Tuntuwanit, Nalinee, et al. 1996. A survey of Khoen Kaen municipality residents concerning water issues. Research and Development Institute report, Khon Kaen University, Khon Kaen, Thailand.

Turton, Andrew. 1987. Rural social movements: The Peasants' Federation of Thailand. In *Production, power, and participation in rural Thailand: Experiences of poor farmers' groups*, edited by A. Turton et al. Geneva: UN Research Institute for Social Development.

University study links paper mill to river pollution. 1993. *Bangkok Post*, 4 June, p. 6.

Walton, John. 1996. Problems of regional industrial development in North-East Thailand. In *Uneven development in Thailand*, edited by M. Parnwell. Aldershot, UK: Avebury.

World Bank. 1993. *The East Asian miracle: Economic growth and public policy.* New York: Oxford University Press.

Sustainable Development and Urban Growth in the Argentine Pampas Region

By
JORGE MORELLO,
SILVIA DIANA
MATTEUCCI,
and
ANDREA RODRÍGUEZ

This article describes the conflict between rural and urban development in the *Pampa Ondulada* (Rolling Pampas), the ecological region in which the city of Buenos Aires is located, which is one of the world's richest and most productive agricultural areas. It describes the ecological changes brought by urban growth in periurban and rural areas between 1869 and 1991. It also includes an analysis of the social and economical changes during the past decade (1991-2001) and their effect on ecological services. The article ends with a discussion of the lack of planning over the expansion process of the urban agglomeration, including the so-called suburbia settlements of the middle and upper classes and the speculative pricing of land in advance of its development.

Keywords: urban sprawl; regional sustainability; Buenos Aires; informal settlements; flooding

When unplanned urban sprawl encroaches on the most fertile agricultural lands of a country, the sustainability issue jumps to the

Jorge Morello is a plant ecologist specializing in Latin American ecosystems. He has worked in applied ecology, inventories, evaluations of development programs and development of ecosystems liable to flooding, and arid lands. He holds a Ph.D. in natural sciences from the University of La Plata, Argentina. He was appointed Robert F. Kennedy Visiting Professor of Latin American Studies at Harvard University. He has published more than 110 articles, including "Convergent Evolution in Warm Desert Ecosystems" (1977) and "Estilos de Desarrollo y Medio Ambiente" (1980). He has been an adviser to the Argentine government, a United Nations agency consultant, and a member of the Executive Committee of the International Association of Ecology. He is a professor emeritus at Buenos Aires University and the senior researcher of the National Research Council.

Silvia Diana Matteucci, a biologist, is a graduate of the University of Buenos Aires, Argentina, with a Ph.D. from Duke University. She has worked in landscape and regional ecology since the 1970s, both in Venezuela and in Argentina. Presently, she is a researcher of the National Research Council of Argentina and a teacher at the Faculty of Architecture, Design, and Urban Planning at the University of Buenos Aires.

Andrea Rodríguez holds two degrees from the Philosophy and Literature Faculty of Buenos Aires University:

DOI: 10.1177/0002716203256901

ANNALS, *AAPSS*, 590, November 2003

national level. This is the case in the Argentine Pampas region, where the main target cannot be to achieve a sustainable city in isolation from its spatial and functional relation to its rural surroundings. Neither can we think of a sustainable agriculture without considering the international socioeconomic environment, which puts pressure on production technologies and commercialization of grain and meat produce, changing the internal socioeconomic status (Morello and Matteucci 1997). In this prospect, it is not easy to work out indicators of sustainable development for the Pampean region. More difficult is to propose a feasible plan for sustainable management; however, it is possible to identify those activities that are not sustainable and those combinations of land use that are environmentally sound.

Argentina's Pampean region situation is hopeless judging from the table of indicators produced by the Commission for Sustainable Development of the United Nations (http://www.un.org/esa/sustdev/natlinfo/indicators/isdms2001/table_4.htm); during the past decade (from 1990), most of the indicators have changed for the worse, especially the percentage of the population living below the poverty line and the unemployment rate. All other relevant indicators, such as arable and permanent crop land area, area of urban formal and informal settlements, and percentage of total population living in coastal areas, depend on the poverty indicators, and even though the balance of trade in goods and services seems to be growing, poverty, unemployment, and urban migration will not decrease because the surplus has to be applied to canceling the foreign debt.

In spite of this situation, we believe that it is important to understand the relationships between urban growth and ecological changes in the fringe of cities in Argentina to be able to work out ameliorating actions to improve some of the social indicators at a local level. In this article, we describe some of the ecological changes brought by urban expansion of the metropolitan area[1] in periurban and rural areas between 1869 and 1991, the form that these have taken, the consequences of poverty increases during the 1990s on ecological services of the rural areas, and their bearing on other indicators of the Division for Sustainable Development of the United Nations Organization (1995), especially on the economic and human loss due to natural disasters. We discuss the lack of planning and control over the continued expansion of the urban agglomeration, including that caused by the residential settlements now favored by middle- and upper-income groups, and the speculative parceling of land in advance of its development.

geography teacher for secondary normal and special education and a licenciatura. She also obtained a postgraduate certificate in environmental sciences and environmental impact evaluation from Harvard University and Real Colegio Complutense, United States. She has been a member of the Landscape Ecology Group lead by Dr. J. Morello since 1993. She is currently a research and teaching assistant in the Faculty of Architecture, Design, and Urban Planning of Buenos Aires University. She is involved in research dealing with regional ecology in the metropolitan area of Buenos Aires. She is author or coauthor of twenty-four papers.

Fertile Lands of the Rolling Pampas

La Pampa Ondulada[2] (literally, the undulating or rolling Pampas) is one of the world's richest productive agricultural areas, and it occupies the central-eastern portion of the Province of Córdoba, north of Buenos Aires and southwest of Santa Fe (Secretariat of Agriculture, Livestock, and Fishery 1995). Its fertile soils, a low-energy relief, and widespread powerful aquifers (which have been intensively exploited to provide supplementary irrigation) have recently begun to provide an ideal medium for agricultural production. The region's climate is characterized by abundant annual precipitation (850-1,000 mm), which is distributed fairly uniformly throughout the year. The risk of frost is small; only for a short period of time do average monthly temperatures fall below 10 degrees Celsius. No snow falls in winter, so the same plot of land can be used to grow two or three crops each year. The ecoregion's agricultural wealth is attributable to its potential for alternate ranching with the cultivation of broadleaf (soy and sunflowers) and narrowleaf (wheat and maize) crops in space and time.

Average yields in this region show that this is the most richly endowed ecoregion of the Argentine Pampas in terms of cereal biomass per unit of area, and it accounts for the bulk of Argentina's export grain production (Scotta 1996). Slightly less than 400 kilometers of the rectangular Pampa Ondulada ecoregion (see Figure 1) border the Paraná River, where agroindustries and ports specializing in direct loading of grain, pellets, and oil onto transoceanic ships flourish. It also houses two of Argentina's major metropolitan areas, Buenos Aires and Rosario, which in 1991 had populations of 11.25 million and 1.09 million, respectively. These cities are part of the country's most important urban-industrial axis. In this moderately sized ecoregion of 44,000 square kilometers, competition between urban and rural land use is fierce. These two traditionally conflicting land uses assume uniquely dramatic proportions since the conflict is situated in Argentina's most important ecoregion for agricultural production in an agroexporting country and because the change from rural to urban use is a permanent one, as permanent as the extinction of a species.

The Buenos Aires metropolitan area (7,729 square km) is located on premium soil for agricultural production, with use capacities I through IV according to the classification of the U.S. Soil Conservation Service. The process of urban growth occurs at a biogeographic crossroads. This territory, whose geodesic center is the intersection of the 34°40' parallel and the 58°30' meridian, is home to interlocking ecosystems of biogeographic domains of wet tropical lineage, such as the Amazon, and seasonal tropical-subtropical ones, such as Chaqueño.

At this biogeographic crossroads, we find some woody species of tropical lineage, in the form of forests and savannas, with patches of landscape occupied by typical high-biodiversity jungle structures and low-diversity tropical riverside forests (Matteucci et al. 1999). Large areas of woody ecosystems, such as *Celtis spinosa* and *Prosopis alba*, and savannas of *Acacia caven* have disappeared where the land offered potential for agricultural use. Ever-shrinking patches of ecosys-

FIGURE 1
MAP OF THE PROVINCE OF BUENOS AIRES WITH THE LOCATION
OF THE PAMPA ONDULADA AND ITS REGIONS

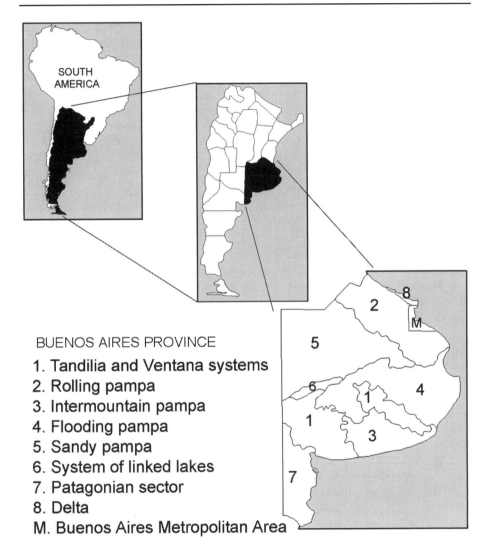

BUENOS AIRES PROVINCE

1. Tandilia and Ventana systems
2. Rolling pampa
3. Intermountain pampa
4. Flooding pampa
5. Sandy pampa
6. System of linked lakes
7. Patagonian sector
8. Delta
M. Buenos Aires Metropolitan Area

tems, such as monospecific riverside forests of *Salix humboldtiana*, *Tessaria integrifolia*, high-diversity jungles of the Paraná Delta, and ridges of fertile land known as *monte blanco* and *selva marginal*, respectively, survive and are subjected to wet periods and flooding (Matteucci et al. 1999).

Land Conversion in the
Rolling Pampas Ecoregion

Since the second half of the 1940s, the Pampa Ondulada has been Argentina's most important area for the conversion of very high-quality agricultural land into urban-industrial land in the broadest sense, that is, including the landscape impression or footprint that urban agglomeration makes on its environment, with the exploitation of low-cost, heavy-weight natural resources (topsoil, B and C horizons, grass, turf, wood), and where transportation accounts for a substantial share of the costs. Urban agglomeration will be defined as the conversion of open land into city-block-sized lots, whether or not they are built on.

A distinction is drawn between a city's landscape footprint and what William E. Rees defines as its ecological footprint (Rees 1992). A city's landscape footprint includes the ecologically productive land, water, and natural and seminatural landscapes that the city consumes, permanently changing its traditional uses and cover (Morello et al. 1998). It is the imprint of the appropriations and permanent changes of ownership of contiguous territory that the city requires to grow, obtain mineral resources, and dispose of waste materials. The landscape footprint is distinguished from the ecological footprint by contiguousness and border phenomena. The ecological footprint refers to the total area of productive land and bodies of water required on a permanent basis to produce all consumed resources and to absorb all waste materials produced by the agglomeration. Thus, a city has two types of hinterland. The ecological hinterland, which is fragmented and whose fragments are not necessarily contiguous to or near the city, is the area required to sustain present levels of consumption. The landscape hinterland is the near or contiguous territory that is being consumed by the growth of the agglomeration, the development of residential settlements, and mining production (parent rock limestone, expansive clay, and earth) and that, as a result, ceases to be agriculturally productive or to serve as soil-water support for natural and seminatural ecosystems with the relevant change of ownership and/or use.

Periurban can be defined as the area of urban and rural interaction where the landscape footprint is made. It is a space contiguous to the city that is affected favorably or unfavorably by that contiguousness (Gutman, Gutman, and Dascal 1987). The periurban system is neither rural nor urban. It is an interface (see Figure 2), where there is increasingly less provision for the various services provided within the urban agglomeration such as drinking water, electricity, storm sewers, pavement, and rubbish collection (Rodríguez 1997). When compared to the rural system, there is also increasingly less provision of ecological services such as the capacity to absorb carbon dioxide; to harness solar energy as chemical energy and convert it into food; to break down organic matter; to recycle nutrients; to control the animal and plant population balance; to prevent pest outbreaks; to regulate water flows; to absorb, store, and distribute short-term river flooding; and to form soils.

FIGURE 2
THE CHANGE IN ATTRIBUTES ALONG THE URBAN-RURAL GRADIENT

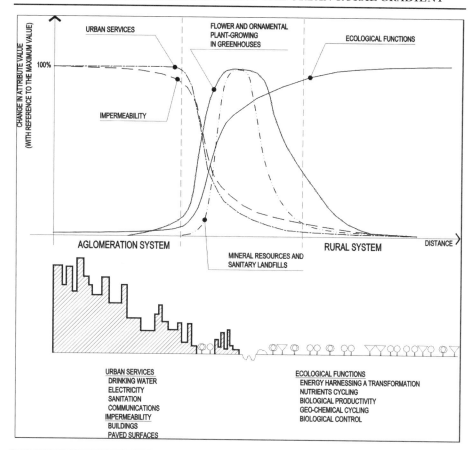

Buenos Aires periurban area's landscape footprints include the following:

- land parceling in city-block-sized lots;
- geophagy (Morello, Matteucci, and Buzai 2001), that is, the extraction of the soil (A, B, and C horizon) for building embankments, for brickworks, and for urban development landfills on land prone to flooding in order to raise the elevation;
- extraction of sections of turf for urban gardens;
- consumption of soil for nurseries and similar operations (another form of geophagy);
- legal and illegal disposal of refuse and industrial waste;
- urban wastelands;
- spontaneous settlements (including squatter settlements);
- country clubs, *barrios cerrados* (closed settlements), and *clubes campestres* (rustic clubs);
- industries;
- heavy infrastructure equipment;
- storage or dumping grounds;

- water purification facilities;
- automobile salvage yards and junkyards;
- clandestine pig farms and farm abattoirs and greenhouse and aviary complexes;
- road construction yards;
- graveyards for higher-income people;
- neoecosystems (brand new ecosystems), that is, seminatural landscapes where the dominant or most frequently occurring species are not native but accompanying and subordinated species; and
- brand new soils derived from landfills of domestic waste material or construction debris and decapitated soils for brick manufacturing.

After the classic description by Charles Darwin, the Argentine Pampas is considered a classic example of a highly vulnerable biogeographic unit in terms of the establishment of exotic species and the formation of ecosystems that are partially or totally stable. In the periurban area of the Buenos Aires metropolitan area, human activities such as selective tree felling, interference with the hydroperiodic pulse through infrastructure construction (dikes, highways), and water and soil contamination have stimulated the successful establishment of neoecosystems. Overexploited forests, deprived of flood pulses, have been replaced with *Ligustrum lucidum* and *L. sinensis* woods, both exotic species introduced as ornamental plants for streets and gardens. Land flooded episodically by water contaminated with heavy metals and hydrocarbons now harbors ecosystems in which the dominant cover species are *Rubus ulmifolius* and *Ricinus communis*, and the dominant species in damp soil borders of flat areas is now *Iris pseudacorus*, another species introduced into gardens for ornamental purposes (Matteucci et al. 1999). These three neoecosystems now occupy larger territories than the ones that they replaced or are in the process of replacing, as is the case with the iris.

Land parceling as indicator of urban growth

Land parceling is one of the indicators that can be used to assess the conversion of rural landscapes into urban ones and is one of the easiest to quantify, as it can be viewed on old cadastral maps, aerial photographs, and satellite images. Available census and cartographic information were used to study the advancement of parceling. The study area includes the federal capital and the twenty-three administrative sections surrounding it, with an area of 3,880 square kilometers, 60 percent of which corresponded to agglomeration in 1991. The information came from a variety of sources, including the eight national population and housing censuses conducted in Argentina between 1869 and 1991, historical cartography for the first four censuses, official agency cartography for the period 1970 through 1980, and satellite images for 1991 (Buzai 1993).

Eight thematic maps were produced using the Geographic Information System (OSU Map for the PC, version 4.0). These maps show the size and location of the parceled areas at each point in time (1869, 1895, 1914, 1947, 1960, 1970, 1980, and 1991). The maps are like snapshots, and pairs of them can be compared to identify the advancement of the agglomeration.

The soil map of the area was prepared by the Soil Institute of National Institute of Agricultural Technology–Castelar (Instituto de Suelos, Instituto Nacional de Tecnología Agropecuaria-Castelar), with extrapolation of information from systematic soil surveys by National Institute of Agricultural Technology in the areas surrounding the Buenos Aires conurbation and in the patches of native vegetation and unoccupied spaces that perforate the urban matrix. The ninth thematic layer is soil units, with seven soil association categories (Godagnone and Casas 1996; Palacio 1996). A relief map with four altitude categories was also used.

The Geographic Information System was used to overlay thematic layers to obtain agglomeration maps for each cartographic soil and relief unit and to calculate the areas occupied by each category on each map (Buzai 1993).

Urban growth of Buenos Aires metropolitan region from 1869 to 1991

In 1869, the Pampa Ondulada appeared to be perforated[3] with eleven plots of parceled land (Morello el al. 2000). The largest agglomeration was in the center of the city of Buenos Aires, which had developed as a port settlement on the estuary of the Rio de la Plata. Corridors of perforations could already be observed along the path of railroads to the west and to the south. Between 1869 and 1895, most growth occurred in the central agglomeration, although it did not combine with the neighboring perforations. During this period, three new perforations began later on, joined by a new railroad, which was built along the coast at the beginning of the twentieth century. Nine lines of dissection[4] were already visible in 1960, the last two of which (highway routes) appeared between 1947 and 1960. New perforations continued to appear until 1991 all along transportation corridors, although the number of agglomerations started to decrease substantially beginning in 1960, when the existing ones began to grow and combine. The Buenos Aires city center grew steadily, and the agglomerations on its border combined to produce a dissection of the grasslands, savannas, pampas, and riverside copses in primitive river valleys, along diverging radii from the city center. Fragmentation, however, is not perceived at the scale of the study. The divergent radii, rather, continued to widen and combine, and by 1970, they all appeared to be forming continuous corridors. The process in general can be described as a creeping fungal growth of agglomeration into grasslands, savannas, and elongated patches of copses. Between 1970 and 1991, no appreciable expansion occurred; the radii widened and combined, and a few new perforations appeared.

Surprisingly, during the last period, the growth in land parceling decelerated, with an initial phase of slow growth between 1869 and 1947 (approximately 7 square km per year), a phase of rapid linear growth from 1947 until 1970 (61 square km per year), and a decrease in the growth rate during the period 1970 through 1991 (16 square km per year). The widening of the radii indicates that the agglomeration was advancing into virtually isolated land between areas that had already been parceled.

Given the low energy and scope of relief, there is no evident association between hypsometry and the growth in parceling; in other words, no clear preference for any particular relief has affected expansion in a particular cartographic unit of relief at the scale of study. At the first three points in time, agglomeration had moved into land situated 10 to 20 meters above sea level, probably as the result of this cartographic unit's proximity to the coast. Substantial amounts of land below 10 meters (such as the present sites of the Palermo Hippodrome, the airport, and the promenade) were later reclaimed from the river and were therefore not available during the initial stages of growth in the city center. From 1960 onward, most of the growth occurred at the 20- to 30-meter level. Land above 30 meters occupies a small fraction of the area studied and is situated far from the coast, with the exception of one peninsula over 30 meters altitude, which leads to the bank of the estuary. Accordingly, this area might be expected to include the smallest proportion of parceled land at all points in time. Of course, the risk of flooding has consistently been the key determinant in space occupied by the elite and low-income populations. The social map of the city prepared by Torres (1992), using indicators such as the number of persons employed or holding university degrees by census area, shows a clear socioenvironmental segregation with relation to flooding. In 1960, the Matanza river valley appeared to be totally parceled along the middle and coastal sections, and the Reconquista River Valley[5] seemed to be fragmented by parceling in sections along its path. In 1991, most of the land between 0 and 20 meters was already occupied. One might expect all subsequent growth to move into land in the 20- to 30-meter range, corresponding to higher areas' being more valuable for agricultural production.

Despite the importance of agricultural production to the national economy and the soil's suitability for this activity, since the beginning of Argentina's urban history, the rolling relief cut by ravines, streams, and tributaries of the Parana-Plata System and a predominance of soils suitable for agricultural activities typical of the Pampa Ondulada (land use capacity [LUC] II) have made the Pampa Ondulada a preferred expansion area for the agglomeration. In 1869, 37 percent of the 3,321 parceled hectares were situated on this land type, and 10 percent in another section of the Pampa Ondulada endowed with deep, rich soil (also LUC II). Forty-nine percent of the parceled land was on the terraces of the River Plate (LUC IV), and only 4 percent was in the depressed coastal fringe (LUC VII) and other units less suited to agricultural production (LUC III). The soil type was clearly not a factor in planning growth in agglomeration. The larger land units, which are of most interest as they have the greatest LUC, register low occupation levels, implying that all future growth in agglomeration will occur on agricultural land.

Sustainability changes during the past decade (1992-2002) in the Rolling Pampas cities

A similar study performed in the city of Rosario, located on the Río Paraná coast, to analyze urban growth from 1931 to 2000 (Buzai and Baxendale 2002) shows tendencies comparable to those of Buenos Aires. Rosario agglomeration grew from 52.2 to 199 square kilometers in sixty-one years. Between 70 and 75 percent of the best agricultural soils (LUC III) of the study are covered by the agglomeration at all times. This is probably the tendency in the thirty-one agglomerations with more than 100,000 inhabitants of Argentina, most of which are coastal cities.

During the past decade (1991-2001), Argentina's social conditions worsened significantly. The unemployment rate increased steadily from 5.3 percent in October 1991 to 18 percent in October 2001 for the whole country. The figures for the urban agglomerations are 7 percent in 1991 and 14.7 percent in 2001 (Instituto Nacional de Estadística y Censos de la República Argentina 2003a, 2003b). In 1991, 19.7 percent of Buenos Aires citizens lacked access to primary health care facilities; in 2001, the figure increased to 26.2 percent (Instituto Nacional de Estadística y Censos de la República Argentina 2003a, 2003b). Within urban populations in cities with more than 100,000 inhabitants, the percentage of people living below the poverty line increased from 21 percent in 1991 to 57.5 percent in 2002, of which 27.5 percent are below the line of absolute poverty. Even though there are no figures to assess the urban population in informal settlements, we hypothesize that these populations have expanded and increased due to the migration of impoverished farmers, cotton pickers, and so forth to big cities, first to the municipal capital, later to the province's capital, and if possible, to the few cities of more than 0.5 million inhabitants in the Rolling Pampas. Residential urban settlements for the high-income population has also increased in number and extension as a response to insecurity in downtown areas.

The ecological consequences of the expansion of both formal and informal urban settlements on stream banks and riverbanks are changes in the natural drainage system and decreases in the water infiltration rate of soils due to construction. This increase in vulnerability to flooding is aggravated by water diversion devices upstream; excess water that would be absorbed by the hinterland is redirected to the river, reducing the hinterland's buffer capacity and causing floods downstream, in the city's outskirts, and even in the downtown area.

The floods affect both the settlers and the agricultural lands; for example, the extraordinary flood event of 1940 affected eight cities in the Rolling Pampas, covering 465,000 hectares (Etulain and López 2000). In 1940, 1958, 1989, and 1993, significant human and economic losses occurred in the southeast coastal fringe of the metropolitan area (Nussbaum, cited by Etulain and López 2000). In the flood event that lasted from November 1982 to July 1983 on the Chaco-Pampean Plain, 2,350,000 hectares were inundated and 70,000 persons had to be removed; direct and indirect losses amounted to $1,650 million and $3,753 million, respectively (Fundación para la Educación, la Ciencia y la Cultura 1988; Bertonati and Corcuera 2000). In the last events, extensive economical losses resulted from damages to crops, which lower living standards even more. As there are more people inhabiting lowlands, economic and human losses due to natural disasters also increase. Thus, Argentineans seem to be riding a vicious circle of poverty, causing ecological deterioration, causing further poverty.

The role of policy on urban growth

The urban-rural conflict in the Buenos Aires metropolitan area must be understood as a parasitic association by which the city encroaches on the rural surroundings, through both parceling and construction on former agricultural land and through resource extraction for use in the newly built areas. Thus, it is not a case of a rich city and poor surroundings but one in which the surroundings are important for the nation's economy.

The conflict goes back a long way, probably since the post–World War II years, when the United States, emerging from the war a powerful nation, set off the European Recovery Plan, which resulted in the exclusion of Argentina from both the international food market and the international transportation network. The

---

*During the past decade (1991-2001),
Argentina's social conditions
worsened significantly.*

---

response was a substitute industry that stimulated urbanization and the growth of a periurban population. The conflict peaked during the 1990s, however—a culmination of more than twenty-six years of the neoliberal economic model, which dates back to 1976 with the beginning of the military dictatorship. The military's economic policy reversed decades of protectionist policies aimed at industrialization and developing the internal market. The main contributions of the military government to neoliberalism were the partial opening of goods markets to trade, which caused many local enterprises to go bankrupt, and the opening of capital markets, which gave rise to the prominence of international financial speculation in Argentina. The standard bearers of neoliberalism, however, were Ex-President Menem and his Ministry of Economy who, under the banner of demonopolization of public services by the state to gain in efficiency and social benefits, conducted the privatization of the country's major industries, opened the capital markets to unrestricted foreign capital inflows, and established a currency board system that pegged the Argentine peso to the U.S. dollar on a one-to-one exchange rate.

There is no simplistic explanation for the results of this experience. A combination of factors, such as global economy, transnational cultural and social trends, corruption on the part of local elite, and a long succession of misguided economic and political measures took the foreign debt from $7.5 billion in 1976 to $243 billion in 2001 and caused the loss of the country's industrial capacity, the closing of hundreds of domestic businesses, and extreme inequality in income distribution leading to the disappearance of much of Argentina's middle class (in 1983, the gap between the top 10 percent and lowest 10 percent was fourteen to one; in 2000, the gap grew to twenty-five to one).

The economic stagnation brought about by the successive crises caused the proliferation of squatter settlements in the periurban area in the 1970s; the squatters were low-income groups that could not gain access to land due to the decline of the real salary. Living standards worsened: there was little access to adequate water, sanitation, or refuse collection. In these conditions, both environmental quality and human health were at risk.

The second cycle of land occupation in the periurban area during the 1990s had very different characteristics. Degradation of living conditions in the city pushed the upper middle class to the suburbs. At the beginning, people moved on a permanent basis to their weekend estates; later, increasing numbers of settlements appeared. Since the period from 1985 through 1990, highways have been the preferred axes for the advancing urban frontiers, and with the necessary expressways, they have defined new forms of occupation, with various types of barrios cerrados (closed settlements), which by April 1990, covered more than 20,000 hectares and housed 250,000 persons at a very high living standard (Tella and Aguilar 1999). More remote, closed, urban developments have produced perforations in the matrix of agricultural and natural ecosystems, many of which reconcile accessibility with sparse or concentrated occupation of the surrounding area and have eliminated patches of native vegetation, including ecosystems vital to the country's natural heritage, such as jungles on the banks of the Plata River estuary. With liberation of restrictions brought about by neoliberalism, the new suburban developments are accompanied by consumerism: megacenters such as shopping malls, movie theater centers, and various leisure and sports centers; high-technology hospitals; and private university campuses (Tella 2000). These megacenters are not within public spaces and can be reached only by car. Two percent of the population of greater Buenos Aires lives in the various types of suburban closed settlements whose total area equals half the area of the federal capital. Furthermore, this involves individual development efforts that are not coordinated, and there are no direct plans to connect these settlements to the sewer and drinking water systems. Unfortunately, there is no direct relationship between the advancement of parceling and direct need. This is attributable primarily to real estate speculation, as a lead time of as much as five years is required for an area to be ready for acquisition for a business venture (Campanario 1998).

Concluding Remarks

This study has shown the process of the spread of urbanization to agricultural land in a pilot area, with an analysis based on one of many possible indicators, namely, agglomeration. Other landscape footprints could be better indicators, since signs of deterioration appear well in advance of parceling in the periurban fringe.

In the 1990s, the urban frontier ceased to advance as a stretching out of the existing urban area, but it is now moving forward in perforations well within the countryside. Each new settlement causes landform modification and the loss of ecosystem services, multiplying the adverse impact and synergistic loss of sustainability.

At present, two different realities coexist within the same space: the squatter settlements and the closed settlements of country houses. Both are equally unplanned and unsustainable.

A national sustainable development strategy is badly needed. It should be accompanied by a reinforcement of public awareness of the role of prime farmland and unique ecosystem patches in both city and rural ecological and economical sustainability. This requirement cannot be fulfilled under the present economic model, with middle-class incomes continually declining and the poorest concerned only about surviving.

Notes

1. The metropolitan area, also called Great Buenos Aires, is Argentina's largest agglomeration: the third in population and first in area of Latin America.

2. The Rolling Pampas, with 44,000 square kilometers, is a subregion of the Pampean ecoregion, which covers 2,179,303 square kilometers. Argentina ranks eighth in the world in cultivated area and third in cultivated area per capita. The Pampas and a portion of the Chaco region have 100,000 square kilometers under double cropping per year without irrigation, based on five main crops—soybeans, wheat, corn, sunflowers, and sorghum—and its main degradation problem since the 1950s is soil erosion. Soil erosion by running water, loss of fertility, and soil compaction at a 25-centimeter-deep layer reduce corn production by 40 to 50 percent, soybean production by 30 to 40 percent, and the land's price by 20 percent. The critical environmental problems of the Pampean ecoregion are regional flooding with an increasing trend; high erosion rates in the subregion with a larger urban population (Rolling Pampas), also with an increasing trend; and the fragmentation and disappearance of the few remaining patches of natural ecosystems.

3. Perforation is the process of making holes in an object, such as a habitat or land type (Forman 1995). Of the identified spatial processes, it is probably the most common way of beginning land transformation.

4. Dissection is the process of subdividing a homogeneous habitat or land type with equal-width lines (Forman 1995), such as happens with roads, railways, ducts, and so forth. It is an alternative way to begin land transformation.

5. The Matanza and Reconquista Rivers are two of the three main tributaries in the metropolitan area.

References

Bertonati, C., and J. Corcuera. 2000. *Situación ambiental Argentina 2000*. Buenos Aires, Argentina: Fundación Vida Silvestre.

Buzai, G. D. 1993. Buenos Aires 1869-1991: Análisis SIG de su evolución espacial. In *Annals, Fourth Latin American Conference on Geographic Information Systems, and Second Brazilian Symposium on Geoprocessing*, 333-51. São Paulo, Brazil: Escola Politécnica, Universidad de Sao Pablo.

Buzai, G. D., and C. Baxendale. 2002. *El crecimiento de la aglomeración de Rosario (1931-2000) y su relación con las unidades cartográficas de suelo, capacidad de uso e índices de productividad. Informe técnico*. Buenos Aires, Argentina: Centro de Estudios Avanzados, Universidad de Buenos Aires.

Campanario, S. 1998. El Nuevo Mapa del Boom Inmobiliario. *Clarín*, Suplemento Económico, 9 August.

Division for Sustainable Development of the United Nations Organization. 1995. Indicators of sustainable development: Guidelines and methodology. Available from http://www.un.org/esa/sustdev/natlinfo/indicators/isdms2001/isd-ms2001isd.htm#environment.

Etulain, J. C., and I. López. 2000. *Crecimiento y forma urbana. Directrices para una gestión territorial integrada de la franja ribereña de la Región Metropolitana de Buenos Aires. Segundas Jornadas Platenses de Geografía: Resignificando una Geografía para todos.* La Plata, Argentina: Departamento de Geografía, Universidad Nacional de la Plata.

Forman, R. T. T. 1995. *Land mosaics: The ecology of landscapes and regions.* Cambridge, UK: Cambridge University Press.

Fundación para la Educación, la Ciencia y la Cultura. 1988. *El deterioro del ambiente en la Argentina.* Buenos Aires, Argentina: Centro para la Promoción de la Conservación del suelo y del Agua.

Godagnone, R. E., and R. R. Casas. 1996. Los suelos del conurbano bonaerense. Research report. Castelar, Argentina: Soil Institute, Centre for Natural Resource Research, National Institute of Agricultural Technology.

Gutman, P., G. Gutman, and A. Dascal. 1987. *El campo en la ciudad: La producción agrícola en el Gran Buenos Aires.* Buenos Aires, Argentina: Centre for Urban and Regional Studies.

Instituto Nacional de Estadística y Censos de la República Argentina. 2003a. Censo Nacional de Población y Vivienda 1991. Available from http://www.indec.mecon.ar/.

———. 2003b. Censo Nacional de Población y Vivienda 2001; resultados provisionales. Available from http://www.indec.mecon.ar/.

Matteucci, S. D., J. Morello, A. Rodríguez, G. Buzai, and C. Baxendale. 1999. El crecimiento de las Metrópolis y los cambios de biodiversidad. In *Biodiversidad y uso de la tierra: Conceptos y ejemplos de lationamérica*, edited by S. D. Matteucci, O. T. Solbrig, J. Morello, and G. Halffter, 549-80. Buenos Aires, Argentina: UNESCO-EUDEBA.

Morello, J., G. D. Buzai, C. Baxendale, A. Rodríguez, S. D. Matteucci, R. E. Godagnone, and R. R. Casas. 2000. Urbanization and the consumption of fertile land and other ecological changes: The case of Buenos Aires. *Environment and Urbanization* 12 (2): 119-49.

Morello, J., and S. D. Matteucci. 1997. El modelo agrícola del Nucleo Maicero como sistema complejo. In *Argentina granero del mundo: Hasta cuando?* edited by J. Morello and O. T. Solbrig, 201-31. Buenos Aires, Argentina: Orientación Gráfica Editora, SRL.

Morello, J., S. D. Matteucci, and G. Buzai. 2001. Urban sprawl and landscape perturbation in high quality farmland ecosystems: The case of the Buenos Aires Metropilitan region. In *Globalization and the rural environment*, edited by O. T. Solbrig, R. Paarlberg, and F. di Castri, 447-81. Cambridge, MA: Harvard University Press.

Morello, J., S. D. Matteucci, G. D. Buzai, C. Baxendale, and A. F. Rodríguez. 1998. Aplicación de la tecnología SIG para el análisis del soporte biofísico en áreas metropolitanas como herramienta de planificación: El caso de Buenos Aires. In *Sistemas ambientales complejos: Herramientas de análisis espacial*, edited by S. D. Matteucci and G. D. Buzai, 409-24. Buenos Aires, Argentina: University of Buenos Aires Press.

Palacio, M. I. 1996. *Cartas a color del conurbano bonaerense: Suelos, capacidad de uso, índice de productividad.* Castelar, Argentina: Soil Institute, Centre for Natural Resource Research, National Institute of Agricultural Technology.

Rees, W. 1992. Ecological footprints and appropriated carrying capacity: What urban economics leaves out. *Environment and Urbanization* 4 (2): 121-30.

Rodríguez, A. F. 1997. Cambios de uso de suelos en el entorno periurbano del Gran Buenos Aires: Estudio de usos de neoecosistemas y ecosistemas residuales en al área no urbana del partido de Berazategui. Licenciatura Thesis, School of Philosophy and Literature, University of Buenos Aires.

Scotta, E. S. 1996. Estimación del valor económico de la erosión hídrica en la agricultura de Entre Ríos. Research paper. Paraná, Brazil: Experimental Agricultural Station, National Institute of Agricultural Technology.

Secretariat of Agriculture, Livestock, and Fishery, and Federal Agricultural Council. 1995. *El deterioro de las tierras en la República Argentina: Alerta Amarillo*. Buenos Aires, Argentina: Secretariat of Agriculture, Livestock, and Fishery, and Federal Agricultural Council.

Tella, G. 2000. Efectos de una modernización tardía en la región metropolitana de Buenos Aires: Area N7, Facultad de Arquitectura, Diseño y Urbanismo. Buenos Aires, Argentina: Buenos Aires University.

Tella, G., and F. Aguilar. 1999. Barrios cerrados. In *Estudio de la ciudad de Buenos Aires en el Sistema Metropolitano*, edited by M. Aguilar and A. Pusiol. Buenos Aires, Argentina: Faculty of Architecture, Design, and Urbanism, UBA-Secretariat of Urban Planning of the City of Buenos Aires.

Torres, H. A. 1992. Cambios en la estructura socioespacial de Buenos Aires a partir de la década de 1940. In *Después de Germani: Exploraciones de la estructura social en Argentina*, compiled by J. Jorrat and R. Sautu, 158-75. Buenos Aires, Argentina: Paidos.

Poverty, Sustainability, and the Culture of Despair: Can Sustainable Development Strategies Support Poverty Alleviation in America's Most Environmentally Challenged Communities?

By
AMY K. GLASMEIER
and
TRACEY L. FARRIGAN

Appalachia is considered one of the nation's poorest areas. Many communities live in isolation. The material use of the natural landscape has affected citizens' views of the viability of and potential for sustainable resource practices. In many resource dependent communities, land is externally owned and controlled. Despite living and working in areas with enormous natural resource wealth, residents have only limited access to these resources. Recognizing the inability of conventional practice to resolve many of the development problems confronting communities in distress, a series of new policy initiatives are focusing on building sustainable community capacity from the ground up. Can notions of sustainability be used as a means of redistributing power and access to natural resources, or does the peculiar fate of a region, tied to massive natural resource extraction, eliminate such potential?

Keywords: poverty; sustainable development; natural resources; Appalachia

Poor communities and sustainable development at first blush seem incompatible and unattainable. Poor communities usually have few resources under their control, and thus the possibility of in situ resource exploitation is often an issue of survival. The valuation of resources by poor residents of a community is made more complex by the fact that in many

Amy K. Glasmeier is a professor of geography and regional planning in the geography department at Pennsylvania State University. Her first coauthored book on high-technology industries ushered in a decade of policy discourse and programming to encourage the growth of technology industries. In her second and third books, she turned her attention to the special development problems of rural areas and worked closely with academics and policy makers around the country to fashion programs designed to assist in the formulating of sustainable development in rural areas. Her recently published book Manufacturing Time *is a historical account of the development of the world watch industry. She has worked all over the world, including Japan, Hong Kong, Latin America, and Europe. She currently works with the Organization for Economic Cooperation and Development, numerous federal agencies, and international development organizations in constructing development*

DOI: 10.1177/0002716203257072

instances, poor communities are sites of resource exploitation by extralocal interests. Thus, they inconveniently find themselves sitting on top of high-value resources of which they have little to no ownership yet by whose disturbance they will find themselves heavily affected. Also, based on past economic development experience, poor communities end up occupying locations where noxious economic activities find acceptable homes, due to economic forces that regulate land markets (Fox 2002; Solitare and Greenberg 2002; Morello-Frosch et al. 2002). Local land use policies in the United States often mandate such outcomes. Poor communities and examples of sustainable development often coexist in the global South, where right of access to resources is an overwhelming necessity in light of depravation-based problems of resource overutilization. Less thoroughly explored are similar instances in which resource exploitation intersects with the struggle among class interests in a developed world context. Specifically, sustainable development finds some of its greatest challenges in its own backyard, in communities where choices between resource utilization and livelihood creation are highly contested. In these situations, resource exploitation yields wealth for some and environmental hazards for others.

Sustainable development is increasingly proffered as a development mantra for practices that seek to be ecologically sensitive and economically sound. The Brundtland Commission Report of 1992, *Our Common Future*, attempted to reconcile and join economic and environmental goals, defining *sustainable development* as "development that meets the needs of the present without compromising the ability of future generations to meet their own needs" (Graham 2000). This momentous document has led to discussions of how to achieve sustainable development. As one author noted,

> The concept affirms that it is possible to reconcile environmental and economic objectives by changing our accounting to emphasize intergenerational equity, the passing on of not only a viable ecological base to the next generation; and the "needs" implies a menu of

policies to alleviate poverty and uneven economic opportunity. Her primary projects include the formulation of an international network of researchers and policy makers working to integrate concerns about uneven economic development with the need for sustainable development practices. She continues to work in Appalachia's troubled communities to assist citizens in defining a life and livelihood of which they can be proud. In 1996, she was appointed the John D. Whisman Appalachian Scholar and worked closely with the Appalachian Regional Commission, a federal agency responsible for economic development efforts in one of the nation's most challenged regions.

Tracey L. Farrigan is a Ph.D. student in the geography department at Pennsylvania State University. She is the author or coauthor of several research reports and manuals on rural community development issues. Her areas of expertise include regional and resource economics with an emphasis on planning and evaluation. Her research has focused on community and economic development in historically natural resource–based regions of the United States and the incorporation of social dimensions in the analyses of economic phenomena. Her current projects include socioeconomic impact analyses of transitioning economies in areas with persistently poor populations, particularly in relation to community asset building and perceptions of well-being. She was the 2002 recipient of the Society of Woman Geographers Fellowship.

human wants that goes beyond mere resources sufficient for survival to include a need for nature's spaces and vistas and textures, even for sustainable hunting and fishing. (Graham 2000)

Thus, at least according to some proponents' perspectives, sustainable development can lead to a world of greater ecological awareness and sensitivity on one hand and higher levels of human well-being on the other hand. Perhaps because the Brundtland Commission was articulated within a rhetorical context in which Western standards were implied as the benchmark of development, critics have challenged the original meaning given to the term *sustainable development*. Specifically, the original discussion has been disparaged because it ignores underlying problems of existing patterns of development, including inequality, poverty, and environmental degradation. Although more inclusive and optimistic interpretations of sustainable development have been put forth, including perspectives that give much greater attention to environmental and other "externalities" excluded from neoclassical accounts, "nonetheless, what is to be sustained is largely the capacity for autonomous increases in productive capability and, thus, per capita GDP" (Donnelly 1999).

Democratic institutions and unfettered political access are seen as key prerequisites to the pursuit of alternative forms of development.

In light of the aforementioned critiques of the term *sustainable development*, can they be applied specifically to practices within poor communities that are sites of resource exploitation and uneven development? How do discussions of sustainable development intersect with preexisting communities where social relations and economic context are inextricably intertwined? This article begins within a framework in which current economic development policy loosely focuses on attempts to use natural resources as a basis for sustainable livelihood development. It then explores socioeconomic relationships in the region of Appalachia and probes the extent to which past economic practices can be reconciled with sustainable development goals. The article emphasizes the challenges facing efforts to pursue ecologically sound forms of development in contexts with highly unequal access to resources and an absence of consistent livelihood-generating activities. Democratic institutions and unfettered political access are seen as key prerequisites to the pursuit of alternative forms of development.

In considering the efficacy of natural asset–based sustainable development programs, this article examines the historical development of one of the nation's wealthiest resource regions, Appalachia. Despite the abundance of natural resources, Appalachia, a sprawling region that straddles the major mountain belt of the Eastern United States, has for the past 100 years been considered one of the nation's poorest areas. Today, while the urban reaches of the region look increasingly like the nation as a whole in terms of levels of income, employment, and other measures of economic well-being, the rural portions of Appalachia appear surprisingly untouched by the economic development of the postwar period. At present, the peculiar fate of the region, tied as it has been to massive natural resource extraction, reflects a landscape of uneven development. Many communities live in isolation, locked out of the nation's growing prosperity.

Appalachia's history is inextricably tied to the economic development of the United States and its insatiable appetite for natural resources. For more than a century, the removal of natural resources from the region has occurred at exceptional levels. Ambiguity about land ownership has contributed to feelings of impermanence and vulnerability among the region's citizens. Lacking public-sector services and denied a sense of personal efficacy, citizens have few avenues for using the natural environment in support of sustainable development.

The poverty so evident in Appalachia today arises from a complex history of regional economic and political exploitation. Despite thirty years of active policy intervention and billions of dollars in federal and state funds allocated to encourage economic development in the region, the heart of Appalachia remains stagnant and distinct from economic trends experienced both nationally and within the more immediate urban areas of the region.

Historically, how has material use of the natural landscape affected citizens' views of the viability of and potential for sustainable resource practices? In many resource-dependent communities, land is externally owned and controlled. In such instances, the exploitation of local resources occurs with little or no citizen consultation. The maintenance of the environment is by default decided nonlocally, often by fiat. Despite living and working in areas with enormous natural resource wealth, residents often have only limited access to these resources. Adding insult to injury, they find themselves living in environments despoiled by past eras of economic development. In many of these communities, resource exploitation also has been a focal point of significant social struggle, often with citizens' concerns subordinated to other economic interests. Long-standing feelings of powerlessness over one's own life and livelihood and the use of the surrounding natural environment have led over time to a culture of despair.

This sense of powerlessness presents important challenges to citizen involvement in efforts to alleviate poverty by promoting sustainable community development. Like several other articles in this collection, using the case of a resource-dependent region, this article examines how sustainable development concepts might be applied to questions of poverty alleviation and the construction of social well-being in Appalachia. First, we offer a thumbnail sketch of some of the persistent environmental problems in the region. To understand how such troubled environmental circumstances can exist, we present a historical context for resource development in the region. With resource history as a backdrop, we then examine the meaning of powerlessness in the context of Appalachian development. Drawing on John Gaventa's (1980) award-winning book, *Power and Powerlessness: Quiescence and Rebellion in an Appalachian Valley*, we explore how powerlessness can lead to a culture of despair. Amid many perspectives on the effect of the region's economic legacy, our focus is on how a sense of powerlessness can help shape citizens' responses to environmental challenges. We then examine how one county in central Appalachia is struggling to address long-standing problems of environmental degradation and economic decline, in some instances by building unconventional local assets. The article concludes with some thoughts on the interaction between asset building and the development of civic capacity.

The Central Appalachian Landscape: A Drive through the Valleys

Driving along narrow valley bottoms, which parallel constantly shifting dendritic streambeds, you are immediately struck by the unexpected sight of voluminous amounts of waste material hanging in the trees and encasing the low-lying brush. It appears as if a great flood upstream scoured a landfill site and then scattered humanity's waste in every direction. Every waterway is thick with black or dark brown silt, and the smell of decaying organic material is pungently evident. All along the highway are heaps of human residue, plastic bottles, old tires, household appliances, broken toys, and abandoned cars. Sometimes the piles seem almost deliberately stacked to look their best, given the circumstances.

Unexpectedly, around another narrow corner, a coal tipple juts up from the ground. Here, coal trucks, streaming out of the mountains, converge to consolidate their hauls for later removal. Leaving the tipple, for 200 yards in either direction, the highway is sooty with coal dust, the vegetation dulled by a relentless spray of black carbon residue.

As you rise up out of the valley bottom, the sky lightens, and a smooth, bare, yellow-gray, humped-back vista appears. It stands distinct from its craggy neighbors, which are otherwise covered by pine trees and oaks and dotted with an occasional graveyard. On closer inspection, the mountain no longer maintains the profile of its surrounding neighbors because it has been beheaded. This is mountaintop mining at its most garish. As the price of Western and Eastern coal has become more closely competitive, companies extracting coal out of Appalachia argue that the only way to make money is by mining using the cheapest method possible, which is to remove the top of mountains and strip out the underlying coal. The resulting process, known as mountaintop strip mining and accompanying valley fill, scrapes away the surface material, pouring it into adjacent stream valleys. No trees, no brush, and no color remain—just a flat surface whose pallor stands out against the deep blue skyline.

Not much farther down the highway, the landscape changes once again. Against the deep green of the pine forest emerges a red, rivulet-scoured scab where a stand of trees, once tall, has been literally pulled down off the steep mountainside. Vegetative residue sits in a heap at the bottom of the adjacent gully, which is now choked with the silt from the hillside above.

In Appalachia, ground and surface water pollution is not always so visible. The Environmental Protection Agency and state environmental boards record dangerously high levels of fecal colloform and other human waste–related contaminants in most of the region's streams. Despite millions of dollars of federal and state funds expended during the past thirty years for water and sewer provision, an unacceptable number of Appalachian communities still lack sanitary water and sewer services. In eastern Kentucky coalfield counties, an average of only 20 percent of all households have access to public sewers. Public water service is only slightly more available. On average, 40 percent of homes are connected to some form of municipal water service.

This sense of powerlessness presents important challenges to citizen involvement in efforts to alleviate poverty by promoting sustainable community development.

As for the other 80 percent of households lacking access to sewers, septic systems and other nonstandard forms of waste removal process their effluent. In many central Appalachian counties, the underlying soils cannot support septic tanks, and therefore the rate of failed septic systems is extremely high. Given low incomes and haphazard land occupancy, many homes therefore do not even have septic tanks. Instead, they run a "straight pipe" out of the house and into an adjacent creek. In Letcher County, Kentucky, alone, an estimated 3,000 straight pipes are serving as many as 12,000 of the county's 30,000 residents (County may require some homes 1999). Community service organizations indicate this is a likely underestimate of the problem. And Letcher is actually in better shape than many other smaller surrounding central Appalachia counties. One of its nearest neighbors, Martin County, has a decrepit public sewer system that serves only 15 percent of the population, often on an intermittent basis. It regularly fails, spilling semiprocessed sewage into the creek. The local water system also is a marginal operation that loses hundreds of thousands of gallons of water a month due to old pipes and faulty installations. Citizens are often told to boil their water before drinking it.

The refuse that lines the waterways and clutters the roadsides is a harsh reminder of the deep poverty that plagues the region. In many of the poorer counties, there are virtually no municipal or county-level services. The lack of services such as municipal waste disposal is tied to inadequacies in the local tax base. Land values have historically been underassessed, particularly coal lands. In addition, the hilly terrain and the high degree of external land ownership restrict the land available for other taxable business activities. Although coal companies are required to pay taxes on in situ coal deposits, rampant tax evasion further reduces revenues available to support local services. Another major source of potential revenue, the coal severance tax, is only partially returned to the affected counties. And even this source of revenue has limited utility as it is used primarily for the construction of roads in support of the coal industry. Horror stories also abound of how corrupt political officials siphon off millions from the severance tax funds for their own personal use (Gary Lafferty, personal interview, 1999). Thus, these counties, despite their considerable resource wealth, have almost no revenue-generation capacity and hence can provide only the minimum level of service. If citizens want trash removal, they must gather it up and deposit it at collection points such as the county dump. Yet many counties do not operate sanitary landfills.

This brief but accurate depiction of the central Appalachian landscape begs the question of how and why the environment has become so degraded. Furthermore, why have the region's citizens not struggled to improve their circumstances? To understand the origin of such serious environmental poverty, it is necessary to examine the links in the region's long history of natural resource extraction, coupled with the social and political fallout that has accompanied a century of dependent development.

The Enduring Effects of External Ownership and Environmental Degradation

From its earliest settlement, much of the land in Appalachia has been owned by outside interests. External ownership patterns date back in some instances to the Revolutionary War. In parts of the region, returning soldiers were given tracts of land as compensation for their participation in the war effort.

More important than these deeded land transactions was the rampant speculation that accompanied the nation's settlement, whereby representatives of Eastern capitalists traveled the region in search of large tracts of unsettled land. In a detailed accounting of absentee ownership in Appalachia from 1790 through 1810, using tax lists, Wilma Dunaway (1995) showed that by the beginning of the nineteenth century, the majority of lands in many states in Appalachia were almost completely owned by outside interests. In West Virginia alone, almost all of the state's lands were owned by outside interests. In Kentucky, Tennessee, and Virginia, more than 50 percent of each state's lands were owned by outside interests. From its earliest settlement, nonlocal interests owned the region's natural resources.

This long-established land ownership pattern has had grave implications for later periods of resource exploitation. As the American frontier closed at the end of the nineteenth century, the stage was set for rampant exploitation of Appalachian resources. Proximity to Eastern, Southern, and later, Midwestern markets made the region's resources ripe for the taking once railroads were established to bring the resources out of the mountains.

Dating back to the past century, parts of central Appalachia have been important coal and timber reservoirs, mined in support of the development of the country. It was timber that first found its way to markets outside of Appalachia. Prior to the arrival of trains, the availability and location of streams and rivers strongly influenced the exploitation of timber. Harvesting adjacent to streams and larger waterways made it simple to raft logs together and float them downstream during spring runoff. When the railroad began penetrating the interiors of more remote counties, logging moved to an industrial scale. Early coal production also took place alongside streams where coal seams were laid bare by runoff, down-cutting the stream banks.

The amount of timber and coal removed from Appalachia's interior counties in the first thirty years of the past century is mind boggling by any standard. By all accounts, West Virginia's forest was gigantic. Timber harvesting in the state began in earnest around the Civil War and reached its height by 1880. According to Lewis (1995), although timber had been cut for more than twenty years, in 1880, more than two-thirds of the state still "remained under a canopy of virgin forest" (p. 297). Unbelievable as it might seem, by 1920, the state had been virtually cut over. Before the timbermen were through, West Virginia had given up an estimated 30 billion board feet of lumber during the forty-year period. Other parts of Central Appalachia were similarly denuded of timber, particularly those places also enjoying the expansion in coal mining from the late nineteenth century until the 1930s.

Railroads, initially established to relieve the region of its timber resources, also made it possible to exploit the region's coal reserves. It was not until the turn of the twentieth century that coal became truly economical to exploit. As the nation turned toward modernization and industrial development, Appalachian coal became a valuable, abundant, and accessible energy source to fuel the nation's growing factory economy.

According to estimates, at the turn of the century, Appalachia contained 80 percent of the nation's coal reserves. From the turn of the century until after the Great Depression, Appalachia supplied the majority of the nation's coal for steel production and industrial energy supply. Coal production placed additional pressure on the remaining timber reserves since timbers were needed for railroads, outbuildings, and as supports in the mines.

Coal production reached its initial height in the late 1920s but began to falter with the onset of the Depression. Severe economic decline followed as the price of

coal dropped dramatically and as previously war-torn European mines came back
on line. The coal industry did not fully recover until World War II; however, by that
time, both mining technology and mine ownership had changed dramatically.
While the volume of coal removed from the region accelerated, the number of jobs
for miners began a slow but steady decline. A short burst of demand for timber
associated with the mining of coal precipitated a brief renewal of employment in
the industry. Wartime production and the need for new construction also fueled
demand for timber proximate to the nation's population centers. The rapid buildup
of demand saw tens of thousands of acres of additional timbered hillsides stripped
naked in less than a decade.

Just as rapidly as the buildup in coal and timber in support of the war effort
occurred, its abrupt ending brought renewed recession to the region. Many counties lost 30 to 40 percent of their wartime population after 1950. The region lost
more than 2 million residents between 1940 and 1960. The end of the war not only
brought population decline but also exposed for the first time the severity of the
region's lack of economic diversity. After the war, the absence of jobs outside of the
mines pushed many of the more mobile residents out of the region in search of
work elsewhere.

By the 1960s, the national economy had moved significantly beyond a reliance
on commodity-based manufacturing, toward more complex goods based on chemicals and other new technologies. Coal, the most important resource base of Appalachia in the early twentieth century, soon found itself competing against oil and
natural gas as feedstocks for power generation and other industrial markets. During the oil crisis of the 1970s, the region once again experienced a rise in the
demand for coal. By then, the simmering poverty of the region boiled over. The
coal-dependent economies of the interior counties fell into a long cycle of despair.
Government support of one form or another became the most important source of
residents' livelihoods, with the few remaining coal jobs being meted out to workers
who complied with coal company practices, no matter how harsh.

Power and Powerlessness in Appalachia

The historical legacy of resource extraction in the region, coupled with the
effects of outside ownership, produced an economy heavily dependent on a few
sectors and a citizenry deeply suspicious of outside interests and fearful of the local
power structure. Attempts at political organization by local residents were met
with harsh treatment by local elites (Duncan 1998). Cross a mine owner and you
were out of a job. Fail to show up to vote for a crony and a member of your extended
family could lose his or her house. Unions were grudgingly accepted, but only after
terrible battles in which people died and families were impoverished. Even when
unions were finally accepted, they too were ultimately corrupted by big business.
The United Steel Workers fell in behind the large mines in opposition to smaller,
more locally based operations.

In a stunning portrayal of the economic and political subjugation of rural poor and working-class citizens living in Central Appalachia, political theorist and activist John Gaventa (1980) asked,

Why in a social relationship involving the domination of a non-elite by an elite, does challenge to that domination not occur? What is there in certain situations of social deprivation that prevents issues from arising, grievances from being voiced, or interests from being recognized? Why in an oppressed community where one might intuitively expect upheaval, does one instead find, or appear to find, quiescence? Under what conditions and against what obstacles does rebellion begin to emerge? (P. 3)

Answers to these questions form the core of Gaventa's book, in which he concluded that the multifaceted nature of power and its application to those who are powerless maintains and even reinforces the status quo, even in the face of obvious injustice and cruelty.

In trying to understand the challenges faced by the citizens of the region in order to bring about a better way of life, it is necessary to explore the many ways in which power manifests and can be utilized to thwart community change.

Gaventa (1980) identified three dimensions of power that serve to repress actions in the face of inequality. The first is the mechanisms of power, which are exercised as forces of control. These include political resources such as votes, jobs, and other manifestations of influence. Politics in Appalachian coal counties have a long history of cronyism and nepotism. The second dimension of power is the "rules of the game" used to privilege one group over another. In many instances, the mobilization of bias takes the form of nondecisions. Many Appalachian communities are played off one another by withholding decisions through the failure to consult residents about issues of concern. The third dimension of power is the "social myths, language, and symbols," which are constructed to shape or control public opinions of situations or conditions. Examples of each dimension of power are easily found in the everyday lives of Central Appalachians.

Recent editions of the *Mountain Eagle*, a progressive weekly newspaper published in Letcher County, provide invaluable insights into the continuing abuse of power in the region and its likely influence on programmatic efforts to support sustainable forms of development. The democratic governor, wishing to have a sports arena built in Pike County, his home county, recently threatened the county's Republican chief executive officer with the revocation of state funds for water lines if she did not buy private land in downtown Pikeville for an arena. In most parts of the country, a democratic governor would be presumed to support public service extension in opposition to more boosterist economic development schemes. But in the coalfields, the Democratic Party has long been the status quo, strongly backed by coal industry interests and often in opposition to local citizens' concerns. Even though the judge executive went on record as stating she wanted to put the arena on hold until the rural areas of the county had clean water, the governor said he intended to make decisions on how coal severance money would be spent. He went on record as saying as long as he was the governor, he would decide how public funds were spent in support of economic development in Pike (*Mountain Eagle* 1999).

In an example of the second dimension of power, a recent legal finding by West Virginia District Judge Charles Haden would have stopped mountaintop mining and the filling in of adjacent valleys with the removed material; this finding generated considerable local fear among coal miners. The coal companies issued collective statements to the effect that they would have to close down. Several companies immediately laid off workers on hearing of the judge's decision, even though they were not strip mine operators and were not in danger of losing contracts immediately. To add fuel to residents' fears, the governor of West Virginia laid off 10 percent of the state's employees as a warning to environmentalists of what will happen if the judge's ruling prevails. Scare tactics are a common feature of the coal region (Letcher's recycling successes 1999).

The historical legacy of resource extraction in the region, coupled with the effects of outside ownership, produced an economy heavily dependent on a few sectors and a citizenry deeply suspicious of outside interests and fearful of the local power structure.

The third dimension of power is clearly seen in the attempt by the bottling lobby to stop the passage of a bottle bill currently working its way through the Kentucky legislature. To incite fear of outside interests, citizens were given incorrect information on the meaning and possible implementation of the bill. In Letcher County, ads placed by bottle lobbyists in the local newspaper stated that food would be taxed if the bill passed and that outside interests were behind the bill and trying to tell local residents what to do. Petitions against the bill were circulated in local grocery stores. County residents lined up to sign the petition on the advice of local business interests, who did not provide citizens with a copy of the proposed bill. Despite strong local efforts to improve the environment by reducing public litter, and a 75 percent support rating for the bill by voters in the state, its unquestioned opposition in the coal fields verified the power of the myth of "outside interests" as a means of social control (Bottle bill support grows 1999).

Almost two decades after the publication of Gaventa's (1980) book, the political context and power relations have changed little in Appalachia. Jobs are still meted out based on whom you know. Failure to respect the status quo can still result in job loss and sometimes eviction from land owned by outside interests. While some things have changed in the region, it is striking how much has stayed the same. What role has the public sector played in relieving or reinforcing these patterns of development?

The Links between
Environmental and Economic Poverty

Gaventa's book, written in 1980, coincided with the creation of the Appalachian Regional Commission's (ARC's) program on distressed counties. The commission, charged with bringing jobs and highways to the mountains, stemmed from the war on poverty and represents one of the enduring legacies of the Kennedy administration. At the time of its creation, contemporary solutions to poverty were increasingly falling out of favor at the federal level. The commission was seen as embracing a new form of development that emphasized building the region's assets in the form of infrastructure and roads as a means of attracting and retaining economic development activities. The efficacy of this program is instructive in considering the effect of place- versus people-based asset policies.

In 1960, on the eve of his presidential campaign, Senator John Kennedy journeyed into the inner reaches of Appalachia (Branscome 1977; President's Appalachian Regional Commission 1964). He found families living in shacks with no running water or indoor toilets, minimal dirt roads, and a landscape left wasted, filthy, and poisoned by years of opportunistic coal mining and timber cutting. Jobs were scarce, and the powerful meted out jobs in return for obedience. One hundred years of exploitation and external control created an economically dependent and democratically stunted society.

In the early 1960s, on being elected president, Kennedy kept his promise and set up the President's Appalachian Regional Commission to study the fate of the region. Governors of the then eleven affected states proposed creating a federal agency to help resolve the enduring economic problems of the region. Kennedy died before he could secure funding for the agency, but in 1964, Johnson pushed legislation through a divided Congress and brought to life ARC, a state-federal agency with responsibility for bringing economic development to the region. The commission's broad mandate was to provide support for health, education, child development, community development, water, sewers, and road construction. The broad focus of the program was abruptly changed in the early 1970s when the governors overturned the code and abolished categorical spending. For the next ten years, the commission turned away from human development needs and emphasized infrastructure. As the decade wore on, there was less and less congressional resolve to support a federal role in overcoming poverty and development problems, which eventually led to a hostile attempt by Congress to eliminate all federal funding for development initiatives, including the commission.

On 31 December 1981, the eve of the new year, the thirteen governors of ARC filed with Congress *A Report to Congress from the Appalachian Governors*, which gave birth to the concept of a Distressed County Initiative (Decker 1994). At the time of the issuance of the Finish-Up Program, the administration, the Congress, and the public had come to focus on the need for a less costly national government and thus sought to reduce the size and number of domestic development agencies, including ARC. Like many federal "development agencies," during the 1980s, ARC began to feel pressure to articulate a "finish-up" strategy designed to identify within limits a plan to bring the agency's mission to completion.

Yet the defining moment for the creation of the distressed county designation cannot be understood outside the pressures the agency felt as it stared down its possible demise. Creation of the designation can be understood as a final effort to secure some level of support for those counties in the thirteen-state region that had not benefited from the early days of the program due to their small, rural, and remote conditions (ARC 1982).

At the time of its creation, the Distressed Counties Program explicitly cited as an area of greatest need the provision of clean water and adequate sewers. Hence, the program's emphasis has been and continues to be primarily on support for water and sewer systems. The initiative set aside a share of existing funds but did not step outside of the broad institutional mandates that had come to characterize the program after 1975.

With the acceptance of the 1981 report, the Finish-Up Program, which was planned around a five-year cycle, gave the commission time. More important, it established the cycle of program development for a series of new initiatives, one of which was to provide special assistance to areas deemed of greatest need. The set-aside's mandate coincided with a drastic decline in overall program funds. Any hope of coupling substantial development funding with water and sewer funding was never realized.

Unfortunately, implementation of the program did not emphasize the complex and multifaceted needs of residents in counties with the most severe problems, nor were the program targets able to counter or reduce the deeper underlying problems facing these areas. Distressed program funds have largely emphasized the provision of basic infrastructure. Relatively few of the set-aside resources have been targeted to the social needs of these communities. In addition, these funds were not of a type or magnitude to confront the deeper underlying problems that precipitated distressed counties' social needs.

Twenty Years Later: The Legacy of Domination and the Persistence of Distress Lives On

Work conducted by Lawrence Wood for ARC identified distressed counties in Appalachia between 1960 and 1990 (Wood 1999; Whitson et al. 2000). Since the early 1980s, ARC has mandated that states allocate a certain level of ARC funds to

TABLE 1
DISTRESSED COUNTIES BY STATE

State	Total Appalachian Regional Commission Counties	1960	1970	1980	1990	Distressed 1960 and 1990	Distressed 1960, Not 1990
Alabama	35	24	13	2	1	1	23
Georgia	35	14	3	1	0	0	14
Kentucky	49	44	41	34	38	38	6
Maryland	3	1	1	0	0	0	1
Mississippi	21	20	19	7	10	10	10
North Carolina	29	15	13	3	2	2	13
New York	14	0	0	0	0	0	0
Ohio	29	7	6	2	11	7	0
Pennsylvania	52	2	0	0	2	1	1
South Carolina	6	0	0	0	0	0	0
Tennessee	50	37	27	17	7	7	30
Virginia	21	14	8	1	5	5	9
West Virginia	55	36	30	11	30	27	9
Total	399	214	161	78	106	98	116

what the commission defines as "distressed counties." ARC annually determines distressed status: to be considered distressed, a county must meet the following criteria: poverty rates of at least 150 percent of the U.S. average, unemployment rates of at least 150 percent of the U.S. average, and per-capita market income (income less transfer payments) not more than two-thirds of the U.S. average. However, if a county has poverty rates that are at least 200 percent of the national average, then it only needs to match one of the two remaining criteria to be considered distressed. ARC believes that its distress measure is a sufficiently objective and reasonable basis for policy and appropriations (ARC 1989). The analysis included 399 counties.

There was a notable decline in the number of distressed counties in Appalachia between 1960 and 1980; the number of distressed counties fell from 214 in 1960, to 161 in 1970, to 78 in 1980. This trend, however, ended during the 1980s, and the number of distressed counties rose to 106 by 1990. Table 1 shows the number of distressed counties by state.

In addition to identifying underlying changes in the number of distressed counties over time, we also modeled the characteristics of these special places as a first step in considering future possibilities for asset-based development (Glasmeier and Fuellhart 1999). In this additional work for ARC, we carried the analysis a step further by suggesting that the socioeconomic condition of an individual in a distressed county carries with it special burdens that encumber his or her ability to secure a satisfying, fulfilling, and self-determined life experience. First and foremost, as the county index of economic health deteriorates, residents in distressed

counties display special circumstances. Distressed counties have a larger dependent population compared with more prosperous counties in the region; this population consists of single female–headed households with dependent children younger than 17 and the percentage of the population older than 65. We know from
national studies that single mothers tend to have very low incomes, live in or near
poverty levels, and require access to support programs such as child care services
and health care to work effectively in the wage-earning economy. We also know
that single female–headed households face special difficulty in securing employment, given the needs of children for parental support and oversight. Similarly,
national studies suggest the elderly tend to experience low levels of income, have
problems with mobility, and must rely on public programs, particularly for health
care.

Neither home ownership nor membership
organizations were correlated with positive
differences in county economic health. In
contrast, we did find a weak positive
association between noncorporate-owned
forests and positive economic health.

Human capital resources are scarce in distressed counties. Low numbers of the
population with greater than a high school education are thought to signify a lack of
local capacity as represented by technically trained individuals capable of under-
taking complex, skill-based jobs. Of considerable importance are the institutional
implications behind these results. Distressed counties lack college-educated citizens. This deficit has implications for both the supply of and the demand for education. From the supply side, individuals need supportive institutions to encourage
them to pursue higher education. Thus, the extent to which distressed counties
lack effective secondary educational institutions contributes to the reduced number of citizens able to attend and interested in attending college. On the demand
side, diminished interest in college is in part the result of a lack of role models who
by example demonstrate an ability to achieve and to benefit from a college education. The complexity of this problem is well-known. Special efforts are required to
bring the two sides of the issue effectively together.

Serious labor force issues may be found in the region's aging population. Appalachia is facing a serious future labor shortage as the populations in distressed

counties age in place while younger and more mobile residents seek opportunities elsewhere. The implications of this development are quite significant. Any attempt at job attraction requires a community to have an adequate labor supply. Thus, changing demographics will place a premium on employer retention efforts through job training and skills upgrading as well as export promotion. More problematic and costly is the fact that an aging population is going to generate more demand for medical and social services, which will only further strain the local health care financing system. A growing elderly population will be least able to financially support the need for more social services and therefore is going to further burden the region's tax base.

The economy of distressed counties illustrates additional distinct attributes not usually associated with conditions of growth and development. These results suggest that comparatively speaking, the sources of income relied on by residents are not dynamic but in fact reflect dependency. Distressed counties have not benefited equally from growth in manufacturing in the region during the past thirty years. They lack manufacturing jobs, a quality seen as important in the success of other counties that have left the distressed category, as well as those rural counties that have more generally experienced significant progress during the past eighteen years. Others have interpreted the strong association between distressed status and income from the government sector as signifying the absence of other sources of income. In many of the ARC distressed counties, government has become the employer of last resort.

As part of our research on the role of assets in the economic development of troubled places, we went an additional step and examined the importance of conventional assets such as home ownership, membership organizations, and education and their links to differences in county-level economic health (Whitson 1999). In many cases, the results were quite surprising. We found that neither home ownership nor membership organizations were correlated with positive differences in county economic health. In contrast, we did find a weak positive association between noncorporate-owned forests and positive economic health. For the most part, we found that assets at a local level are very difficult to measure and that there are significant intervening relationships, which diminish the importance of assets such as home ownership. Communities in Appalachia have high levels of home ownership, but housing values are so low that a home cannot be considered a viable tradable asset.

Conditions in Central Appalachia are by any measure bleak. There are few jobs, the environment has been significantly degraded, and despite thirty years of government involvement, very little has changed. Citizens still live in a state of permanent impermanence, land ownership is continually contested, the natural resource–based economy is in a persistent state of decline, and political cronyism is still the major means by which decisions are made. Asset-based development is not new to the region. Indeed, the widely copied policy program promoted by ARC, which emphasizes collective assets in the form of infrastructure, is the centerpiece of the program. The lack of deep-seated change raises questions about the efficacy

of programs that emphasize place over people, particularly in the context of enduring poverty.

What Are the Alternatives?

This article closes with a final story from Letcher County, a coal county of about
30,000 residents in Eastern Kentucky. After years of steady decline, Letcher
County has begun to stabilize. The election of a new judge executive has led a small
turnaround in the local environment. Carroll Smith, a former miner, has been
working with state financial resources and citizen groups to establish a recycling
program for household metal goods. The county has sponsored two buy-back programs and is formulating a plastics recycling program to reduce surface waste. The
county still does not have solid waste disposal service throughout the region, but
citizens are working together to try to establish regular trash pickup. It is recognized by many of the county's residents that basic public services, water, sewer, and
trash are prerequisites for more substantial programs that link environmental
sustainability and economic security. Carroll Smith, a Republican, struggles to
maintain concern at the state level for the county's problems. But his political affili-
ation makes his job particularly hard, and there are times when the denial of funds
for water service, for example, is rooted in Democratic Party politics.

Smith has commented that people want better lives, better living conditions,
more jobs, and a better circumstance for their children. Citizens know that many of
the actions required to bring about a better life are in their own hands. But the high
level of external ownership of land, combined with ruthless coal operators, breeds
extreme caution when it comes to change.

Using Assets to Build Community Capacity

Admittedly, Appalachia presents remarkably complex and politically charged
problems that have resisted resolution for more than thirty years. People have
been oppressed a long time and are filled with fear. Formulating goals, such as
cleaning up the streambeds and roadways, seems simple, yet such actions are the
first signs of community respectability and self-respect. Does the successful implementation of natural asset strategies have certain necessary prerequisites? We
believe it does.

From the long history of research on the region, it seems obvious that the basic
set of social relationships and institutional trust that must be formulated to ensure
some possibility of success are not yet developed. There is no intrinsic reason why
citizens of the region, deeply tied to the land, should find a sustainable development program anything but desirable. But as the previous anecdotes suggest, citizens in this poor region have been let down many times in the past and have been
threatened at a deeply personal level with the revocation of jobs and other means of

livelihood if they fail to follow the status quo. Thus, for the truly poor to commit to a program of development based around principles of sustainability may be out of reach of their daily lives.

Several programmatic options are embedded in the notion of assets-based development. To be effective, the region needs more community-based development strategies that broaden the local base of participants and include new groups, citizens, nongovernmental organizations, churches, and private funders in planning for development. Assets in this context are not those that just focus on the individual but must also transcend to the level of the community, where civic capacity is still underdeveloped.

While it might be disconcerting to consider conventional approaches to economic development as viable prescriptions for the region, nonetheless, the high share of small establishments that are emblematic of the economic base of poor counties needs technical support. The most challenged entrepreneurs, those with limited incomes and in isolated areas, require considerable support services in addition to the more typical small-firm support activities.

In many parts of the region, the lack of skills, education, and previous work experience limits economic options for the area's residents. Unlike parts of the region, which are more metropolitan and therefore attractive to external investment, deeply distressed counties are remote and distant from markets. A grassroots job development program, building on the needs of residents in the region for quality housing, public facilities, and infrastructure, could help establish the base of skills needed to be successful in the future. Such programs also could help build trust and experience, which is needed for more complex endeavors.

There is no question that access to natural resources in this resource-rich region is critical. Citizens already collect, trade, and exchange natural herbs, wild plants, and ginseng as part of the informal economy. Illegal dog mines are a source of coal that is exploited to meet the heating needs of many of the region's poorest citizens. Firewood harvesting also is a common practice. But beyond this, how can the resources of such a rich region be used to form sustainable development efforts?

This article has tried to suggest the importance of understanding the complexity of the local context when considering efforts to utilize natural assets in the alleviation of poverty in Appalachia. The peculiar fate of Appalachia may represent the extreme case of a region wracked by deep-seated poverty. Clearly, efforts to use asset-based approaches to development must be informed by the historical legacy of the region in question. Appalachia's poorest citizens have a long and tragic history of intervention, most of which has fostered little change in extant circumstances. Such basic factors as civil rights, democratic institutions, and an effective public sector are in this case necessary prerequisites for the construction of sustainable development.

References

Appalachian Regional Commission (ARC). 1982. Transcript from the May 4th commission meeting. ACE Federal Reports. Washington, DC: Government Printing Office.

————. 1989. Appalachian Regional Commission distressed counties program. Internal memo. Washington, DC: Appalachian Regional Commission.

Bottle bill support grows. 1999. *Mountain Eagle*, 8 December, p. 2.

Branscome, James. 1977. *The federal government in Appalachia*. New York: Field Foundation.

County may require some homes to get public sewer. 1999. *Mountain Eagle*, 13 October, p. 1.

Decker, Robert. 1994. *Internal memorandum: Distressed counties*. Washington, DC: Appalachian Regional Commission.

Donnelly, Jack. 1999. Human rights, democracy, and development. *Human Rights Quarterly* 21 (3): 608-32.

Dunaway, Wilma A. 1995. Speculators and settler capitalists: Unthinking the mythology about Appalachian landholding, 1790-1860. In *Appalachia in the making*, edited by Mary Beth Pudup, Dwight B. Billings, and Altina L. Waller, 50-75. Chapel Hill: University of North Carolina Press.

Duncan, Cynthia. 1998. *Worlds apart: Why rural poverty still exists*. New Haven, CT: Yale University Press.

Fox, Mary A. 2002. Evaluating cumulative risk assessment for environmental justice: A community case study. *Environmental Health Perspectives* 110 (Suppl. 2): 203-9.

Gaventa, John. 1980. *Power and powerlessness: Quiescence and rebellion in an Appalachian Valley*. Chicago: University of Illinois Press.

Glasmeier, Amy, and Kurtis Fuellhart. 1999. *Building on past experiences: Creating a new future for distressed counties*. Washington, DC: Appalachian Regional Commission.

Graham, Otis L. 2000. Epilogue: A look ahead. *Journal of Policy History* 12:1.

Letcher's recycling successes draw attention of state officials. 1999. *Mountain Eagle*, 17 November, p. 1.

Lewis, Ronald L. 1995. Railroads, deforestation, and the transformation of agriculture in the West Virginia back counties, 1880-1920. In *Appalachia in the making: The mountain South in the nineteenth century*, edited by Mary Beth Pudup, Dwight B. Billings, and Alice Waller, 297-320. Chapel Hill: University of North Carolina Press.

Morello-Frosch, Rachel, Manuel Pastor Jr., Carlos Porras, and James Sadd. 2002. Environmental justice and regional inequality in Southern California: Implications for future research. *Environmental Health Perspectives* 110 (Suppl. 2): 149-54.

Mountain Eagle. 1999. 15 December.

President's Appalachian Regional Commission. 1964. *Appalachia: A report by the President's Appalachian Regional Commission*. Washington, DC: Government Printing Office.

Solitare, Laura, and Michael Greenberg. 2002. Is the U.S. Environmental Protection Agency Brownfields Assessment Pilot Program environmentally just? *Environmental Health Perspectives* 110 (Suppl. 2): 249-57.

Whitson, Risa. 1999. Regional economic development: An assets perspective. Master's thesis, Pennsylvania State University.

Whitson, Risa, Larry Wood, Kurt Fuellhart, and Amy Glasmeier. 2000. Appalachia: Rich in natural resource wealth, poor in human opportunity. A geographic view of Pittsburgh and the Alleghenies: Precambrian to post-industrial. Paper prepared for the 96th annual meeting of the Association of American Geographers, Pittsburgh, PA, 4-8 April.

Wood, Lawrence. 1999. *Staying in and moving out of distress: Distressed counties in Appalachia 1960-1990*. Final report to the Appalachian Regional Commission. Washington, DC, Appalachian Regional Commission.

Environmental Activism and Social Networks: Campaigning for Bicycles and Alternative Transport in West London

By
SIMON BATTERBURY

A key element of sustainable development in cities is the implementation of more effective, less polluting, and equitable transportation policy. This article examines the role of activist organizations promoting transport alternatives in London, Britain's capital city and its largest metropolitan area. Major national, citywide, and local policy changes have permitted citizens' groups to work more actively with progressive elements in government planning, breaking down citizen-expert divides. In West London, the most congested sector of the metropolis, an environmentally based social network, the Ealing Cycling Campaign, promotes cycling as a sustainable transport alternative. Its strategies require active cooperation with the local state rather than radical opposition to it, raising questions about the oppositional stance more commonly found among urban social movements. Environmental citizenship needs to be founded on social realities and conduced in mainstream political systems if it is to be effective in complex urban environments.

Keywords: bicycle planning; London; Ealing; social networks; environmental citizenship; transport

Sustainable development requires significant changes in our transportation system to increase economic efficiency, equity, and environmental security. This cannot be achieved simply by changing vehicle designs or improving traffic flow. It requires changing the way

Simon Batterbury is an assistant professor in the Department of Geography and Regional Development at the University of Arizona and a visiting research fellow at the London School of Economics, United Kingdom.

NOTE: The ideas presented in this article have emerged from my own participation in action and research in Ealing from 1994 to 2000. I would like to thank my friends in the Ealing Cycling Campaign for their solidarity, several Ealing Council employees, Louise Every for research assistance, and former colleagues at Brunel University who permitted me to combine the duties of academia with activism on and off a bicycle. Funding for the Thames Valley University study came from the U.K. Department of Transport's Cycle Challenge fund (1996-1997).

DOI: 10.1177/0002716203256903

transportation professionals approach problems, and how individuals behave as citizens and consumers.

Litman (1999)

I wouldn't call it a reducing of the standard of living, but a simplifying of our way of living. And I think it would be good for us . . . be good for us to do more walking, or to ride bicycles to school instead of driving a car.

Edward Abbey (1982)

Urban Sustainability and Transport

This article offers some evidence to show urban environmental movements based on a sense of environmental "citizenship" have responded to injustices and deficiencies in urban transport networks and infrastructure. As a contributor to this special issue on current themes in sustainable development (Fernando 2003), I focus specifically on the opportunities opened up by active cooperation between different citizen groups and the state—particularly the local government—in a period when new forms of metropolitan governance and political decentralization are widespread. In certain cases, this opens up new possibilities for citizen involvement in formal planning and, more generally, in the policy process. The empirical material for the article is drawn from the global city of London, United Kingdom, where a transportation crisis has existed for many years.

A sustainable transportation system is integral to almost all aspects of city life—work, leisure, emergency planning—and to the ways in which the city is nested within the region and the national political economy. Urban environments require sustainable forms of transportation and overcoming automobile dominance and congestion. Unsustainable transport systems have tended to persist for many reasons. Previous rounds of infrastructure investment, conceived and built when attitudes toward energy use and design in the transport sector were different, have a lasting imprint in cities.[1] In North America, the most frequent response to rising vehicle ownership and roadway congestion in the twentieth century was simply to expand the road network, thus generating more road use. Robert Moses's (1888-1981) decision to carve up New York's neighborhoods with massive freeway construction in the 1930s, 1940s, and 1950s transformed the urban landscape of New York City and was considered a dark moment by many urban planning and community activists (Merrifield 2002). Major public investments in alternative transportation modes, including light rail and efficient buses and trains, have been confined to just a few cities, for example, Portland and Seattle. The overarching problem in the United States, and elsewhere, is that the growth in private vehicle numbers in cities and high levels of consumption and hypermobility have appeared as consequences of modernity. While public transportation, especially for commuting to work, has in some cases offered realistic alternatives to the car, it requires an extremely strong planning system to function well, combined with an adequate capital investment program and willing customers. It is extremely difficult for public transport to keep pace with a growing population and workforce, and (as all readers of this journal will be aware) it is often difficult to pry urban residents from their private vehicles, even for simple urban journeys for which alternatives exist.

My focus will be on the conditions under which small and sustainable changes to transportation systems can be produced. Lasting change to the urban streetscape and transport modes will involve major commitments by urban and transportation managers, rather than the piecemeal implementation of stopgap measures like road-widening schemes or new restrictions on car parking. But certain of these commitments, for example, investment in light rail networks or the imposition of some form of ecotaxation to de-emphasize private vehicle use, have always been a political battleground. Roads and railways are public spaces, and the design and use of public space is contested in the modern city (Staeheli and Thompson 1997;

Partnerships and coalitions between the state and movements can occur, alongside and parallel to, acts of resistance.

Mitchell 2000). Transport policy divides political parties, social classes, and neighborhoods, and any attacks on the ease of vehicle use tend to antagonize voters. The lessons from some of the best transportation systems in Western cities, for example, Copenhagen in Denmark (where 34 percent cycle to work and bike lanes have been carved out of the major roads, car ownership is low, and public transport has received huge investment), is that political conflicts over funding and maintaining the transport system are almost inevitable.

London is an interesting case not only because its transport system is currently overloaded and car use is so high but also because of its strong planning system and the wide range of actors involved in decision making, from planners to private developers and lobbyists (from local residents who are car commuters, to conservationists and Green anarchists). Urban social moments can, and frequently do, arise around urban transportation issues. In *The City and the Grassroots*, Manuel Castells (1983) argued that inequalities in access to collective consumption facilities (e.g., leisure, shopping, and health facilities) help to create the frustrations and sense of injustice that actually create the major targets of some new types of urban social movements (p. 319). An active engagement in politics (which involves struggling for local democracy and for decentralization of territorial control) seems to mark out those movements, along with the formation of new cultural identities (Dryzek et al. 2003). For Castells, new social movements are largely oppositional in nature. Yet if we shift the gaze to nonprofits and movements fighting for more sustainable urban transportation, a rather different picture emerges: loose coalitions and small groups that move between opposition to local and city government and active collusion with it. We see multiple actors struggling to control and influence transportation discourses. Partnerships and coalitions between the state and movements can occur, alongside and parallel to, acts of resistance. Urban transportation infrastructure and transportation behavior in London result from a constellation of competing actors that struggle over technological choices, financing, the planning process, and public space. Urban transportation therefore has a distinctive environmental politics, the playing out of which is etched into the landscape.

Lessons from Britain and London

London is Britain's capital city and one of a handful of global cities linked into truly international networks of finance, capital, and movement. The administrative unit called Greater London had 7.1 million people in 2001, although its hinterland is much larger than this. The city's transport authority, Transport *for* London, estimates that 27.3 million journeys are made in Greater London every day, with 8.5 million on public transport (4.5 million by bus, 3 million by subway, and 1 million by rail). Some 11 million journeys are made by car or motorcycle, 7 million on foot, and only 0.3 million by bicycle.[2] The volume of flights from London's five passenger airports is also high. London experiences the most intense and widespread road congestion in the country; vehicles in inner London averaged less than 10 miles per hour in the years 1998 through 2000 and only 3 miles per hour in the central business district, the slowest average in the postwar period. It is generally believed—by central government officials as well as by local planners—that much of the road network is stretched to capacity, particularly during the working week. Air quality monitoring shows frequent breaches of national pollution guidelines for nitrogen dioxide and other compounds (even carcinogens such as benzene), caused predominantly by fossil fuel emissions. In addition, the railroads and the subway (the Tube) are expensive and consistently overcrowded during peak periods, exacerbated by even a minor accident, a breakdown, or adverse weather. These networks have suffered a lack of investment during many decades, resulting in frequent service interruptions and delays. These and other frustrations have become a part of everyday life for all Londoners, and while some of them have endured for decades (Collins and Pharoah 1974), it was in the 1990s that public concerns saw a marked increase. These concerns were driven in part by a series of rail accidents caused by poor track maintenance and errors made during a period of rail privatization.[3] A cascade of high-level resignations; acrimony between the government, private rail companies, and the aggrieved public; and a massive overhaul of the rail network followed these incidents.

Transport policy rose to the top of the national political agenda in the late 1990s when Deputy Prime Minister John Prescott took over the government's transport portfolio and called for substantial investment in a new British transportation system, with government backing (Tempest 2002). He pronounced boldly in 1998 that "Labour's aim is simple and indeed ambitious. It is to transform our transport's infrastructure over the next ten years, and to make Britain's transport the rival of any in Europe" (Panorama 2003). But other factions within the Labour government felt Prescott's sweeping transport proposals, which included ecotaxation and a national congestion reduction target of 6 percent over a relatively short period (Department for Transport 1998), would be interpreted by the voting public as anti-car in their sentiment and detail. Five years later, Prescott's vision does indeed seem unrealistic—road use is rising rather than falling, partly in response to continuing safety fears about rail transport. Train delays have increased. As a result of political jockeying, the binding legislation that followed the 1998 report, the Transport Act (Department for Transport 2000), was a watered-down strategic document, a sop to the "middle England car owning traveling public" (Panorama 2003) that promoted buses and cycling but effectively passed the buck for any moderately anti-car measures back down to local governments. Local governments were not provided with substantial funding for major new initiatives and still have little control over the mass transportation systems that serve their areas. They were permitted to close roads temporarily if pollution reached danger levels and to be more innovative in tackling congestion and road safety. In December 2002, the new transport secretary unveiled a £5.5 billion package of transport improvements nationally, of which more than £3 billion is to be spent on road building and road expansion (Panorama 2003). In sum, national policy has seen a U-turn on Prescott's desire to promote low fossil fuel emission transport, and a return to business as usual on road building.

While the national picture has given environmentalists much cause for concern in recent years, London has developed its own transport debate. A rise in traffic volume can be traced back to the 1840s and was the subject of a Royal Commission enquiry at that time. Suburban rail and Underground (Tube) routes expanded in the late 1800s, permitting the gradual extension of the metropolis around these major transport networks. The real escalation in London car ownership occurred from the early 1950s, when postwar fuel restrictions were lifted, but policies on vehicle use and parking in London at that time were laissez faire (Collins and Pharoah 1974, 24). It took some time for the growth in motor vehicle use and problems in public transport management to be addressed by the planning system. Some quite innovative ideas, such as a short-lived major reduction in Tube fares to increase demand, were introduced by the Greater London Council, but this body was disbanded in 1986 by the Thatcher government amid a storm of political controversy. During the period from 1986 through 2000, there was, effectively, no London government, so policy and funding delivered from central government was amended and administered and delivered through the elected local government system, the thirty-three London Borough Councils. These institutions date back to the year 1000 and are elected bodies.[4] However, the new Labour government of 1997 committed to reinstating a democratically elected metropolitan government, which was restored in 2000 and named the Greater London Authority (GLA). Strategic planning functions are today split between the thirty-three boroughs (themselves with restructured governance mechanisms as set out under two

Local Government Acts, 1999 and 2000); GLA, which has an $8 billion budget; and central government. Central government has been reluctant to devolve all its powers to GLA, making it an unusual institution with piecemeal powers (Travers 2002). The GLA makes strategic decisions on transport but does not control private transport firms; it provides funds to local government for road improvements and other transport schemes. The 2000 Local Government Act empowers the boroughs to get involved in transport issues a little more, for instance, by permitting congestion-management schemes.

Tempting skeptical Londoners onto bikes requires sticks (e.g., ecotaxes and other market-based instruments, a much less car-friendly streetscape) and carrots (e.g., integration of public transport and bikes/pedestrians, secure bike parking and cycle routes, employer incentive schemes, and employer mileage allowances for bike use).

It is hard to escape the conclusion that governance in London has been a political football and that successive administrations have moved the goalposts. Three levels—national, metropolitan, and local (borough)—now operate, but for fourteen years, there was no metropolitan government. The GLA is now headed by the populist "true Londoner," Ken Livingstone, as mayor. The irony of Mayor Livingstone's appointment has not been lost on the British public; he was also the person who headed the Greater London Council in the 1980s when it attracted Thatcher's ire. His reappointment was seen in some quarters as a posthumous dagger in the side of Thatcherite Conservatism, but he is highly unpopular with New Labour too. Livingstone won the election as an independent after being expelled from the Labour Party for standing against its official candidate.

In 2000, Livingstone said that "the single biggest problem for London and Londoners is the gridlock of our transport system. Remedying this will be my first priority" (see http://www.london.gov.uk/mayor/state/soltrans.jsp). Indeed, some major policy shifts have occurred in the city since 2000, and these mark this administration out from central government, which as I have shown is retreating to a pro-motorist stance (Mayor of London Office 2001). Livingstone has, as of February

2003, instituted an $8 congestion charge for almost all motorized vehicles wishing to enter inner London during the daytime in midweek. No other Western city of this size has ever tried this form of ecotaxation (there are some schemes in Norway and in Singapore), and Londoners are split as to its desirability since it requires a huge surveillance apparatus and is perceived as a tax on car use and legitimate small business activity. The London bus service has been significantly enhanced across the capital, with changes to ticketing and the installation of more dedicated bus lanes (which have, of course, reduced the width of the carriageway for other vehicles). The management of the London Underground has been a serious battle over which the government and the mayor have serious disagreements, most of them caused by the government's enthusiasm for public-private partnerships. A watered-down partnership for the Tube has finally been pushed through, against strenuous GLA (and public) opposition.

If we now look at local government, we find an equally numerous set of policy changes. In the London boroughs, local transportation issues are handled in slightly different ways by each borough. For example, the borough of Ealing is an outer West London borough that contains a mix of residential areas, industrial districts, urban parkland, several major commercial centers including Ealing town center, and Southall, a suburb dominated by people of South Asian descent. Although once christened "Queen of the Suburbs" for its affluent, well-manicured housing tracts, there is also significant urban deprivation. Ten of the borough's twenty-five wards (administrative subunits) rank among the most deprived in the country. The U.K. national census in 2001 revealed that 41.3 percent of Ealing residents are from an ethnic minority (9.1 percent nationally, and 28.8 percent across London as a whole). Some 38.9 percent travel to work by car compared to 33.5 percent across London; 23.4 percent of sixteen- to seventy-four-year-olds in the borough travel to work by Tube (greater than the London average of 18.9 percent); and 10.7 percent use a bus. The use of bikes for commuting is low at 2.2 percent (about 3,150 people daily).

In Ealing, transport matters were for many years handled by a team of career planners and engineers, employed by the borough, with specialist knowledge in this area. There was only limited public consultation on transport schemes such as pedestrianization of shopping areas or traffic calming since very little was required. Nonetheless, some of the major proposals had to be taken for approval to a borough transport committee consisting of elected local councilors to be debated and voted through. Planners received money for transport works from central government by submitting a grant proposal called the Transport Policies and Proposals document. When the money was received, council workers would labor to repair roadways, improve sidewalks, and so on before the next funding deadline. Under a now-defunct Thatcherite experiment called Compulsory Competitive Tendering, these latter services were forced by law to be subcontracted out to the lowest-bidding private contracting firms (Patterson and Theobald 1996). This resulted in an extra layer of complication and frequent arguments between the council and the contractors. In an effort to save costs, the contractor firm could, and often did, engage low-paid and frequently poorly trained staff.[5] Since 2000, when the Local Government Act came into force, Ealing Council has received greater autonomy over the budget for transport planning and has reorganized its structure of committees and decision-making mechanisms. It now receives its budget from GLA, bidding for money to support Local Transport Plans (the new process is similar in many respects to the Transport Policies and Proposals).

Ealing has, like several other London boroughs, developed a coherent policy toward environmental issues. Aside from making some effort to "green" its own activities as a major employer generating environmental impacts, its various departments are involved in anything from pollution monitoring to the management of parks and open space, and it employs a full-time sustainability coordinator, who has worked hard to bring community and local authority elements together. His team organizes research on environmental issues, has been involved in setting up a Green Travel Plan for council employees, hosts annual environmental events, and liaises with local organizations and groups. In addition, under the banner of Local Agenda 21 (LA21) (a worldwide planning and policy framework widely adopted following its launch at the UN Environment Conference in 1992), a small group of citizens, planners, and businesspersons meet regularly to discuss key areas of local sustainability and council policy. Ealing's LA21 (see www.la21.org) works in an advisory and voluntary role only, so whether these ideas become policy and get implemented is primarily dependent on the availability of council funding and the political process. Several high-profile councilors have embraced environmental causes, and Ealing is regarded as one of the more progressive London boroughs in this regard.

Environmental Social Networks and Citizenship

There are many citizens' and nonprofit groups in London who clearly believe that better urban transportation systems are a pressing concern and that they are achievable. Citizens' involvement takes several forms. Frustration and complaints are fueled daily by delays and gridlock; evidence of incompetence; safety breaches; frequent strikes by unionized Tube, rail, and bus workers; and even high fuel prices (peaking in September 2000 when fuel depots were actually blockaded by the public, almost paralyzing public services for a week). Such sentiments can also drive specific interest groups and movements to form around issues such as neighborhood safety, commuting, and organizations to promote walking, cycling, rail use, driving, and other transport modes. Some community members who are concerned about Green issues or the lack of attention to urban sustainability policies more generally also participate in networks of groups concerned with urban transportation.

In Britain, environmental groups have gathered sufficient momentum to be able to influence formal politics. In the middle 1990s, examples included the actions of radical so-called Green warriors who had some success at halting some new road-building schemes through direct action (road building is an issue that has always exercised environmental activists much more than in the United States).

The highly controversial This Land is Ours campaign occupied a vacant commercial development site in central London and turned it into an urban ecovillage for several weeks as a protest against land speculation and housing shortages. Reclaim the Streets staged several street parties that blocked freeways and major roads through the 1990s. At the national level, environmental organizations frequently berate the government for selling out on its pre-election promises and failing to prioritize sustainability and environmental reform. As Dryzek et al. (2003) showed, Britain's major environmental organizations (such as Friends of the Earth and

Small social networks . . . can only provide
carrots—only regulatory bodies and the
state itself can provide the sticks.

Greenpeace) have consistently adapted to a changing regulatory and political environment through professionalizing their activities away from gung-ho radicalism, and the membership of environmental organizations is believed to be higher than the membership of political parties (Pepper 1996). Some, such as Friends of the Earth (and the London Cycle Campaign, discussed below), operate efficiently through local cells that work on issues relevant to each London borough.

Environmental groups, I believe, often function as social networks. While members of such networks may exercise their citizenship rights by voicing opinions about governance and participating in the democratic process, they also operate with shared values and form networks of trust (Staeheli and Thompson 1997; Pepper 1996). This sense of shared values is important since it distinguishes such groups from labor unions or neighborhood-based organizations, where the ties between members are very different. Evans (1995) suggested that with increasing mobility, affluence, and ethnic and class diversity in suburbs like those of West London, social networks of like-minded individuals come together for specific goals and projects. There are parallels here with Castells's (1983) "new social movements," but the tasks they perform are rather different and perhaps more mundane. Participants often use e-mail, listservers, newsletters, websites, and the telephone more often than face-to-face meetings, but they also operate with some level of consensus on the values that guide their participation and any activities that the network performs. They agree to share tasks and responsibilities, such as lobbying and community service (Campfens 1997). Values guiding the social network, if they are formalized at all, might coalesce around a form of environmental citizenship, but individuals within the network may have differing visions of what this means and different reasons for participating.

The presence of such networks in West London is made easier by the high population density, relatively high incomes, and wider range of issues around which people of different social classes and ethnic backgrounds have chosen to organize and agitate. These networks include organic gardening clubs, local economic trading groups using alternative currencies, "time banks" for volunteers, cycling organizations, and the local cells of national and international nonprofits. Their presence has coincided with a greater degree of public participation in planning matters and local government policy making since the 1990s. In the case of transport campaigning in West London, active social networks have coincided with greater transparency in the local planning process, and more inventive solutions to congestion and road pollution, such as Safe Routes to School for children, an ambitious plan to create a London cycle network of relatively safe and well-connected cycle tracks designed for both commuting and leisure use (now more than 500 miles long across London), and traffic calming measures. Community consultation, rather than hasty and secretive council spending, is now the norm (Elster 2000). Even Mayor Livingstone's new interest in cycling (which may itself be the effect of several years of tireless lobbying by cyclists!) has provided new opportunities across London—GLA funded a series of free publications available at Tube stations and information points, together with nineteen detailed cycle maps covering London (Andrews, Cavell, and Wall 2003). GLA is now funding a Cycling Centre of Excellence (under the leadership of a tireless advocate, Rose Ades), and bike stations at some major commuter nodes are planned.

All of these initiatives have received impetus from nonprofit groups and local organizations of various types. I will demonstrate how the experience of one particular new social network, a local branch of the London Cycling Campaign (LCC), forged alliances and had a productive involvement in the formal planning of urban sustainability.

Campaigning Locally on Transport Issues

Campaigning by social networks, or individuals, does not always require a political position that is wholly outside the existing bureaucracy of city governance—some groups tend to work best when they engage actively with formal state institutions since these are the gatekeepers of the metropolitan streetscape. In doing so, they risk "cooption [*sic*]" (Dryzek et al. 2003) of their key agenda, as well as being "used" by state institutions that may operate with much more bureaucratic constraint and fewer fresh ideas. There are, therefore, dangers to partnerships and cooperation.

The promotion of urban bicycle use is a case in point. Collins and Pharaoh (1974) devoted only half a page to bicycles in their 700-page assessment of London's transport needs, noting vaguely that there was "even less information about cyclists than pedestrians, even though it is known that cycle traffic has declined sharply over the post-war period" (p. 516). Bicycle use was seemingly out of synch with the modernism, new technologies, and higher speeds of Londoners in the fashionable 1960s and early 1970s. Yet as I have noted, cycling rose again in public consciousness in the 1990s despite its much-diminished contribution to urban transportation. The reasons were numerous but linked to personal mode choice: road congestion and pollution in the city and the rising costs of car use, propelling at least 300,000 Londoners to keep cycling daily by the end of the decade despite the same indifferent weather and poor road conditions as before.[6] Cycling five miles to work is not uncommon; many travel much longer distances.[7] Some commuters combine biking with public transport or use bikes as a matter of necessity to cut through stationary traffic and heavy road congestion. Cycling is a missing link in London's transport infrastructure. It delivers exercise and therefore health (Hillman 1992); it uses no fossil fuels; it is quiet; and it takes up little road or parking space—in other words, it is sustainable and inexpensive (Andrews, Cavell, and Wall 2003).[8] It cannot, of course, be the mode of choice for those with very long urban journeys unless many more bikes may be carried on public transport; it is not an option for people in all types of occupations by any means, or for those with physical disabilities, or for the very young or very old. It is good for distributing people, rather than heavy goods, efficiently. But raising the proportion of cycling journeys in London made by millions of adult commuters would have immeasurable benefits for Londoners and for the quality of streetscapes and air quality—even if the very high percentages of cycling journeys attained in Amsterdam, Copenhagen, and other European and Asian cities are unlikely. Tempting skeptical Londoners onto bikes requires sticks (e.g., ecotaxes and other market-based instruments, a much less car-friendly streetscape) and carrots (e.g., integration of public transport and bikes/pedestrians, secure bike parking and cycle routes, employer incentive schemes, and employer mileage allowances for bike use) (McClintock 2002).

The Ealing Cycling Campaign (ECC) is a branch of the LCC (see www.ealingcycling.org.uk). The LCC is a citywide nonprofit organization operating from a small central office, which campaigns for cyclists' rights in the capital city and thereby for improvements to health and safety through cleaner air, better bike facilities, and lower accident rates on London's roads (see www.lcc.org.uk). It is a member organization founded in 1978.[9] An early LCC success was the lobbying of the Greater London Council to build a bike-friendly scheme at Albert Gate in Central London. Membership services, publicity and campaigns, a bimonthly magazine, and a "name and shame" campaign to highlight poor road maintenance (the Buckled Wheel of the Year Award, given to the worst London Borough) soon developed their own momentum. Close links were established with the Greater London Council by the 1980s, but following the Greater London Council's demise, the LCC was particularly successful at spawning local cells of members in most London boroughs, who concerned themselves exclusively with the promotion of cycling and campaigning in that local area. Today, most London boroughs have local LCC groups, and these are heavily engaged in public outreach and organized leisure rides, lobbying, planning matters, and other campaigns that could broadly be identified with pro-cycling concerns. The borough groups, linked to the head office via e-mail listservers, have no official anti-car stance, although this can be the politics of many active members.

Ealing's group, the ECC, dates to the 1990s and became particularly active after 1995 when it was reconstituted by five individuals, most of whom had no prior experience at group organizing but a strong commitment to bicycle travel. An agreement to hold monthly meetings was made, which has continued to this day. The group has been run with a core team of five to twelve activists at any one time, who represent about 300 members in Ealing who subscribe to the LCC publications and hold a membership card. While the social makeup of the membership is diverse and varies over time, there is a preponderance of male members (66 percent male, in a small sample survey) (ECC 2002), although a variety of professions are represented. Motivations for participation in the group range from anger (e.g., "Let us *do* something!") to safeguarding a leisure activity (e.g., "I like cycling with the kids on weekends and want to reserve that right"). The group is maintained by a mutual, altruistic effort by the core group to pitch in and assist at certain events or with certain tasks, according to time, ability, and skills; there is no hierarchy nor any exhortations to participate, and the budget is about $700 annually. Members may remain dormant for months, to become reactivated when pressures of outside work subside or when an issue seizes them.

An early realization of the group was that local Councils—including Ealing— have to act on sustainable transport issues; a changing national planning system gave them no choice. The Transport Policies and Proposals submission to central government had to contain up-to-date road planning and environmental proposals, as does the new system of GLA-funded Local Transport Plans that has replaced it. Faced with this, some persistence from 1995 to 1996 resulted in the small team of Ealing Council transport planners' being prepared to draw ECC members into consultations and, finally, into planning some proposed road projects such as new bike lanes and cycle parking schemes. For ECC, this required the establishment of personal contacts with key council officials and exploiting political opportunities within the local government bureaucracy. Aggressive complaining against new road schemes that ignored cyclists was combined with blatant flattery when such schemes were successfully revised. Letters addressed to junior council staff were copied to senior managers to force a reply. Yet progress was sometimes slow. Transport planners, all with professional qualifications and socialization into their own expert culture, were sometimes hesitant to draw in members of ECC who were perceived as part-time nonprofessionals. To overcome this, ECC members had to demonstrate their competence as amateur planners and report writers, producing several widely read documents and conducting street surveys (Batterbury 1996, 1997; Ealing Friends of the Earth and Ealing Cycling Campaign 1999). ECC also counted at least two professional engineers among its membership, and by 2003, at least four activists had held jobs in the council, one working with the sustainability coordinator himself and another running cycling training programs and serving as cycling officer. ECC also aligned strongly with other pro-environmentalist camps within the council to gain support for its campaigns.

One way ECC could demonstrate its competence was by applying for and winning external funding. Working with the LA21 Transport Group and Thames Valley University, a research proposal was submitted late in 1995 to a government funding pool set up by Sir George Young, the Conservative Secretary of State for Transport. The successful application was one of only eight funded in London.[10] The project attracted incredulity when it was first suggested, but it was then heartily supported by the council. This project tried to improve environmental and transport awareness at a key Ealing employer. Thames Valley University is based from an urban campus in central Ealing and employs several thousand people in addition to having a large student population, many drawn from Ealing's less-advantaged wards. It had no well-developed environmental strategy and almost no provision for bicycles. The project funded $20,000 of new cycle racks on campus as well as providing workshop sessions on attitudes toward cycling, classroom activities, a competition to win fifteen free bikes, training workshops for nervous cyclists, and fix-it sessions to get rusty old bikes out of the garage, repaired, and back on the road. ECC refined these initiatives through initial user surveys that revealed generally positive attitudes toward cycling and cyclists and made specific suggestions for improvements including better bike security and more education about transport issues (Batterbury 1997).

The project concluded with a large meeting hosted by Thames Valley University, at which local residents, students, and staff heard talks by several key individuals and held a debate. The project, although not wholly successful, raised important issues and provided a small legacy of local improvements to cycle access and bike use. Projects like these are hard to get off the ground and tend to run against a prevailing indifference unless significant benefits can be realized. In this case, mutual benefit for the university, the council, and cyclists were consistently juggled to maintain momentum.

To gain trust from the community, from other community groups, and from the council, the ECC core group also participated in a number of local public events. The key aim of these meetings is to connect official politics (those who hold power) with local residents, and they attract a wide range of participants as well as significant publicity opportunities and press coverage (Dobson 1995). These have included participation in several national events such as the Don't Choke Britain campaign (with local programs in Ealing annually since 1996), National Bike Week (annually since 1996), and several town meetings on local transport issues. National Bike Week activities have included leading a leisure bike ride for families (often with key local politicians participating), a day of free bicycle maintenance called Doctor Bike where passersby could receive basic repairs and information, and in 1997, a larger event in a local park, cohosted with an organization that showcased adapted bikes for the disabled. Again, this event was attended by a local member of Parliament who posed for the press, thus reinforcing the link to formal politics. In 1996, the group co-organized a meeting called Taming Local Traffic with Friends of the Earth and the Council for the Protection of Rural England. At the meeting, a local council official framed the problem nicely when he said that "the wheels of local government often grind too slowly for impatient activists." But the council (and the local member of Parliament) explained their policies and responded to criticisms from the public, and the audience at least pinned them down to verbal commitments to improving local transport.

Although participation in these public events and meetings may seem to be a logical extension of the activities of a small lobbying network such as ECC, preparing for them takes up considerable time, and all group members work on a voluntary basis in their spare hours. It was noticeable that ECC was asked to participate in them by the same council staff that had for several weeks been studiously ignoring their submissions on road design or other community issues. Thus, while it was

---

Planning is too important to be left to planners—especially those who do not ride bikes. The microgeography of the urban streetscape is best managed, and made more friendly and sustainable, by a coalition of citizens and professionals.

---

expedient for the council to demonstrate that community groups were working with them (and, indeed, putting in many hours of service), there was a great difference between this rather mild form of citizen "participation" and the much stronger form—real inclusion in formal planning—that ECC was seeking. The payoff in terms of public exposure and debate, however, was very valuable from all of these activities.

A further avenue to inclusion, however, was provided by the LA21 process. LA21 groups are far less common in the United States than in Britain, where even there, they would never have been permitted by the gray bureaucratic structures of previous decades of local government. Their guiding philosophy is that everybody with a stake in a locale or region may assert their right to participate in semistructured forums for debating and planning the future of that area. Citizens and local councils can benefit from lively and informed discussion in committees and working groups. In Ealing, a network of individuals, in which cyclist campaigners became involved, formed the LA21 Transport Group in 1995 and have produced a number of papers looking at the future design of Ealing's transport systems. These included a detailed and comprehensive document outlining the need for innovative traffic engineering measures and high-profile traffic management projects (Batterbury 1996). Other LA21 groups have looked at air pollution, waste management, biodiversity, and design of urban spaces, and by the late 1990s, Ealing's LA21 process had produced several ideas that became incorporated in the council's own master plans and policies. This demonstrated a clear link between formal and citizen planning. The LA21 Transport Group supported reductions in car use and the promotion of sustainable forms of moving about West London, and the council gave it a space to hold meetings and totally free rein to come up with new ideas. Although the work of LA21 arguably peaked in the late 1990s when its main documents were completed, it has been sustained ever since, despite occasionally dissolving into partisan discussions of relatively minor issues.

In the pursuit of a safe and pollution-free road network, ECC and the LA21 group proposed the notion of investing time to develop a few high-impact schemes that send a message about sustainable transport. David Pepper (1996) called such symbolic actions "prefiguring" the future—creating enduring small examples of good practice. ECC assisted in drawing up a proposal for a centrally located, but rather risky and difficult to engineer, scheme to supply the main railway station in Ealing with a direct, dedicated cycle lane that ran counter to the traffic direction on a one-way street. The idea behind this plan was to send a clear message to motorists about road priorities, reclaiming some road space from cars and linking this to better bike parking facilities outside the station. Although the bid was rejected for funding by the Department for Transport in 1996, it has remained on the agenda of certain council officials and has appeared in several planning documents, suggesting it may receive future funding. Being a controversial scheme, it reached the front pages of the local newspaper and provoked a mixture of angry and supportive responses from local residents. Its significance is that it was initially proposed by a local ECC member and only later taken up and supported by the council's transport contractor. It is extraordinary that the scheme proceeded as far as it did if one considers the generally low level of public involvement in transport planning in the United Kingdom at that time.

As one of Britain's premier environmental intellects, George Monbiot, has noted, effective and honest publicity is vital for environmental campaigners of all hues (www.monbiot.com). ECC contacts its own local membership through exploiting the LCC's own mail shots and sending them a regular *Ealing Newsletter*. As the Internet has grown in significance, the group transferred its archive to a frequently updated and public website that is now linked to other sites, including the council's own. It has also reported its activities in the local newspapers and gotten the council to pay for handbills and posters for National Bike Week and other events. It has successfully participated in staged commuter races between bikes and motorists and public transport users—always a hit with the local media since the bike invariably wins. From 1997 until 2001, an LA21 member who is decidedly pro-car claimed to represent the "voice of the people" in Ealing. By exposing the anti-car policies of the LA21 group to the local newspaper and prompting an editorial, a debate was set up that echoed through the letters page for weeks and led to good coverage of other transport-related events. This public debate has been continued during the past three years in relation to the borough's major east-west thoroughfare, the Uxbridge Road. Long targeted by ECC for major upgrades and a dedicated cycle lane (Ealing Friends of the Earth and Ealing Cycling Campaign 1999), safe and speedy travel on this strategic road had proven impossible. Transport *for* London now plan to run a new urban tramway along a significant stretch of this road, which has added a new angle to the debate; in brief, trams and bikes can mix, but should cars be diverted to surrounding streets to make room for the tramway? It has not been built as of 2003, but public protest for and against the scheme suggests this bold initiative is forming opinion on alternative solutions to local transport congestion.

Conclusion

The activities described above required a good understanding of the politically possible and a combination of skills. What are the limitations of such a strategy of cooperation and partnership by a small social network? Perhaps the greatest is that the activities of ECC and similar groups do not make significant challenges to other aspects of human behavior in cities. They are concentrated around single issues, constrained spatially, and by their very nature will be exclusive to certain individuals and groups. They appeal to a constituency of citizens who are already cyclists or who are seriously considering cycling and alternative transport modes due to delays, road accidents, or even for heath reasons. As Andrews, Cavell, and Wall (2003) said,

> when you cycle in London you become part of a community, a diverse kinship of couriers, racers, tourers, commuters, students and professionals who all get the same buzz and benefits from travel on two wheels, as well as a mutual awareness of London's unique cycling environment. (P. 8)

Andrews, Cavell, and Wall are really referring to joining a social network rather than a community. Groups like ECC are not explicitly about developing social capital or Castells's (1983) new identity politics—they are really trying to reach out more widely to people and planners. But such groups clearly form part of the alternative approach to transport that is supported by GLA and by certain elements in the national government. Yet the latter's hands are tied by questions of electability and anti-car accusations from voters, and we should recognize that for the majority of Britons who are trapped in patterns of overconsumption, or who have real need for vehicular travel (the disabled, the elderly, small businesses owners), the actions of these and similar lobbying groups are no more than an irrelevance. The key point here is that lobbying by social networks, for all their benefits, cannot *enforce* sustainable patterns of travel behavior among urban citizens. It can only probe, suggest, and help provide modifications to the road network and urban streetscape. To actually promote a move away from fossil fuel–powered vehicles in London, comprehensive urban planning must be combined with more radical actions that promote, legislate, and enforce sustainable systems. This is why influencing policy makers in local and regional government is absolutely essential.

The ultimate aim of networks like ECC is to generate sufficient groundswell opinion to overcome the major financial, bureaucratic, and behavioral barriers that constrain the adoption of a real new transport agenda—something that has so far eluded planners and politicians since the 1970s. Such an agenda must go much further than the half-hearted measures currently being considered: it would have streets and public transportation that have space for us all, key employers and public institutions that take responsibility for the journeys made by their workforce,

---

[W]here the local government is steering a course more accommodating to social justice and sustainability, and retains a modicum of honesty and efficiency in its actions despite its bureaucratic procedures, a strategy of cooperation can open up significant and lasting political spaces as well as contribute something to friendlier urban streetscapes.

---

and children who can walk and cycle in safety as they grow up in a pluralistic, multimode transport culture that de-emphasizes car reliance, all enforced by a variety of legal and economic instruments. Small social networks such as ECC can only provide carrots—only regulatory bodies and the state itself can provide the sticks. The effort of ECC to nudge urban planners toward doing this in Ealing is an early, partially successful example of partnership.

The argument in this article has been that today's urban realities call for a different form of organizing and lobbying, namely, social networks of concerned citizens and, in West London, partnerships with the local authorities that are entrusted with the bulk of transport and environmental planning. Planning is too important to be left to planners—especially those who do not ride bikes. The microgeography of the urban streetscape is best managed, and made more friendly and sustainable, by a coalition of citizens and professionals. This does not necessarily require social movements that are largely oppositional and free of influence from the state, as Escobar (1995) and Esteva (1992) have famously supported in the context of rural Third World development. But it does require that the new breed of social networks such as ECC invest considerable energies in fostering, and maintaining, a working relationship with elements of the local government while retaining their own political space for action and debate. ECC has gone beyond agitation and uniquely aggressive lobbying. It and similar groups are not trying to drive the juggernaut of public policy but attempting to steer it in new directions. While our understanding of new social movements and the politics of resistance highlights the necessity of strong opposition and resistance (Agyeman, Bullard, and Evans 2003; Peet and Watts 1996; Dryzek et al. 2003), it is important to remember that the actions of such movements always try to fit the social and political context in which they arose and in which they were sustained. For Escobar and Esteva, a corrupt, duplicitous, and Westernized state in Latin America lacks credibility and was invariably hostile to community autonomy. The evasive and anti-environmental actions of some governments and corporations certainly require an aggressive posture and strong counter-movements. Yet where the local government is steering a course more accommodating to social justice and sustainability, and retains a modicum of honesty and efficiency in its actions despite its bureaucratic procedures, a strategy of cooperation can open up significant and lasting political spaces as well as contribute something to friendlier urban streetscapes. Although some activists will disagree, London is now in a position to benefit from such efforts.

Edward Abbey, the curmudgeonly American writer and environmentalist who provided my opening quotation, died in Arizona in 1989, before too many of his neighbors took to walking or riding the bus to work and before he would have seen too many children cycling safely to school in his small town of Oracle (Abbey 1982). Yet such things are everyday sights in many European cities. In London prior to the 1960s, they were relatively common too. They may well be so in future, but only if multilevel politics, the planning process, and citizens' groups work together to make it so.

Notes

1. In the newly emerging urban centers of the global South, airborne particulates and NOx levels frequently rise as developing cities adopt more fossil fuel–powered vehicles and are slow to pave roadways. Transport safety often worsens as passenger growth occurs before adequate safety measures are installed.

2. Cycle trips in London stood at 3.76 million in 1952 and fell to 0.61 million in 1968 (Collins and Pharoah 1974, 516).

3. A crash at Southall, West London, killed 7 and injured 150 in September 1997. In October 1999, a second head-on crash killed 31 and injured 400 commuters just outside Paddington in Central London. A further incident at Hatfield outside London killed 4 and injured 35 due to a broken rail, and again in May 2002, 7 people died and more than 70 were injured after a derailment close by at Potters Bar. In January 2003, a Tube train derailed in a central London tunnel after a motor came loose, injuring 32 people and closing the Central Line for safety upgrades for months.

4. The city of London is not actually a borough; it comprises the original business district and has a very small number of voting residents.

5. Since 1999, Labour has instituted a much more rational system called Best Value, under which councils are able to choose how best to deliver services through their own employees or through specialist contractors as long as there is "continuous improvement of local authority functions, [and they] have regard to a combination of economy, efficiency and effectiveness." These arrangements are closely monitored by central government, although in 2003, there are plans to allow some well-performing councils much more autonomy in how they conduct their affairs.

6. Protest has accompanied this rising profile. Most notably, Critical Mass—massed, slow cycling in the peak evening commuter hours in central London by up to 2,500 cyclists traveling together—is a leaderless and spontaneous protest against car cultures and pollution. Critical Mass is a worldwide phenomenon and originated in California.

7. The average weekly distance cycled by sixty-four Ealing Cycle Campaign members in 2002 was forty-seven miles (Ealing Cycling Campaign 2002).

8. Nor is it patriarchal, although as the theorist Ann Oakley (2002) noted, aggressive male car drivers are a primary road hazard in London.

9. The London Cycling Campaign was preceded by a small number of local affinity groups and by a national campaign to promote cycling that was first initiated by the large nonprofit Friends of the Earth.

10. "Green Commuting: Promoting Bicycle Use at the Urban University." Awarded as part of the Cycle Challenge Initiative, Department for Transport. Funded under a governmental initiative to promote cycling as a sustainable transport option: April 1996 through April 1997.

References

Abbey, E. 1982. Edward Abbey interviewed by Eric Temple. Available from http://www.abbeyweb.net/articles/etemple/index.html.

Agyeman, J., R. D. Bullard, and Bob Evans, eds. 2003. *Just sustainabilities: Development in an unequal world*. Boston: MIT Press.

Andrews, G., P. Cavell, and J. Wall. 2003. *The rough guide to cycling in London*. London: Rough Guides.

Batterbury, S. P. J. 1997. TVU Cycle Challenge Project cycling and travel survey: Ealing Cycling Campaign. Available from www.ealingcycling.org.uk.

Batterbury, S. P. J., with R. Gurd, Ol, and P. Mynors. 1996. Report & recommendations of Cycling Sub-Committee, Local Agenda 21 Transport Group, Ealing: Ealing Cycling Campaign. Available from www.ealingcycling.org.uk.

Campfens, H., ed. 1997. *Community development around the world*. Toronto, Canada: Toronto University Press.

Castells, M. 1983. *The city and the grassroots: A cross-cultural theory of urban social movements*. Berkeley: University of California Press.

Collins, M. F., and T. M. Pharoah. 1974. *Transport organisation in a great city: The case of London*. London: Allen and Unwin.

Department for Transport. 1998. A new deal for transport—Better for everyone. Available from http://www.dft.gov.uk/itwp/paper/.

———. 2000. Transport Act. Available from http://www.dft.gov.uk.

———. 2001. Transport 2010: The 10-year plan. Available from http://www.dft.gov.uk/.

Dobson, A. 1995. No environmentalisation without democratization. *Town & Country Planning* 64 (12): 322-23.

Dryzek, J. S., D. Downes, C. Hunold, and D. Schlosberg. 2003. *Green states and social movements: Environmentalism in the United States, United Kingdom, Germany, and Norway*. Oxford, UK: Oxford University Press.

Ealing Cycling Campaign (ECC). 2002. Cycle survey 2002: Ealing Cycling Campaign. Available from www.ealingcycling.org.uk.

Ealing Friends of the Earth and Ealing Cycling Campaign. 1999. *Uxbridge Road cycle route*. Ealing, UK: Ealing Cycling Campaign and Ealing Friends of the Earth. Available from www.ealingcycling.org.uk.

Elster J. 2000. *Cycling and social inclusion: CASE report 8*. London: Centre for Analysis of Social Exclusion, London School of Economics. Available from http://sticerd.lse.ac.uk/case/publications/casereports.asp.

Escobar, A. 1995. *Encountering development: The making and unmaking of the Third World*. Princeton, NJ: Princeton University Press.

Esteva, G. 1992. Development. In *The development dictionary—A guide to knowledge as power*, edited by W. Sachs. London: Zed Books.

Evans, B. 1995. Planning, sustainability & the chimera of community. *Town & Country Planning* 64 (4): 106-8.

Fernando, J. 2003. Preface: The Power of Unsustainable Development: What Is to Be Done?. *Annals of the American Academy of Political and Social Science* 590:6-34.

Hillman, M. 1992. Cycling and health. *British Medical Journal* 304 (6832): 986-87.

Litman, T. 1999. *Reinventing transportation: Exploring the paradigm shift needed to reconcile transportation and sustainability objectives*. Victoria: Victoria Transport Policy Institute, Canada. Available from http://www.vtpi.org/reinvent.pdf.

Mayor of London Office. 2001. *The mayor's transport strategy*. London: Greater London Authority.

McClintock, H., ed. 2002. *Planning for cycling: Principles, practice and solutions for urban planners*. Cambridge, UK: Woodhead.

Merrifield, A. 2002. *Metromarxism: A Marxist tale of the city*. New York: Routledge.

Mitchell, D. 2000. *Cultural geography: A critical introduction*. Oxford, UK: Blackwell.

Oakley, A. 2002. On the problem of women and bicycles. In *Gender on planet earth*, edited by A. Oakley, 13-27. Cambridge, UK: Polity.

Panorama. 2003. *Promises promises*. Transcript from TV transmission, 16 February 2003. London: BBC.

Patterson, A., and K. Theobald. 1996. Local Agenda 21, compulsory competitive tendering and local environmental practices. *Local Environment* 1 (1): 7-19.

Peet, R., and M. J. Watts, eds. 1996. *Liberation ecologies: Environment, development, social movements*. London: Routledge.

Pepper, D. 1996. *Modern environmentalism*. London: Routledge.

Staeheli, L., and A. Thompson. 1997. Citizenship, community, and struggles for public space. *Professional Geographer* 49 (1): 28-38.

Tempest, M. 2002. Timeline: Labour's transport policy. *Guardian*, 13 December 2002. Available from http://politics.guardian.co.uk.

Travers, T. 2002. Decentralization London-style: The GLA and London governance. *Regional Studies* 36 (7): 779-88.

Urbanization and the Politics of Land in the Manila Region

By
PHILIP F. KELLY

Land ownership has long been a source and outcome of political power in the Philippines. This article shows how in the 1990s land and politics continued to be closely entwined, but the disposal of agricultural land for urban uses, rather than its ownership, was sought by the powerful. By examining the process of land use conversion in Manila's extended metropolitan region, two dimensions of the politics of land are examined: policy choices relating to the uses of land that reflect a particular set of developmental priorities and the facilitation of conversion through the use of political power relations to circumvent regulations. These points are made at three interconnected scales: the national scale of policy formulation, the local scale of policy implementation and regulation, and the personal scale of everyday power relations in rural areas. The article draws on fieldwork in the rapidly urbanizing province of Cavite, south of Manila.

Keywords: Philippines; Manila; land; politics

T his article examines some of the developmental priorities and political processes involved in land conversion in the Philippines and the region around Manila in particular (see Figures 1 and 2). It is in the agricultural provinces of Manila's extended metropolitan region that some of the country's most productive farmlands form the core region of an industrializing and globalizing national economy. The result has been a process of regionalized urbanization in which urban land uses and employment

Philip F. Kelly is an associate professor of geography at York University in Toronto and was previously an assistant professor of Southeast Asian studies at the National University of Singapore. He is the author of Landscapes of Globalization: Human Geographies of Economic Change in the Philippines *(2000, Routledge).*

NOTE: This is a revised and updated version of an article originally published as "The Politics of Urban-Rural Relations: Land-Use Conversion in the Philippines" in *Environment and Urbanization.* In conducting research for the revised version, I am very grateful to Ony Martinez for her assistance, to Carolyn King for cartographic services, and to the Social Sciences and Humanities Research Council of Canada for funding.

DOI: 10.1177/0002716203256729

FIGURE 1
MANILA AND ITS EXTENDED METROPOLITAN REGION

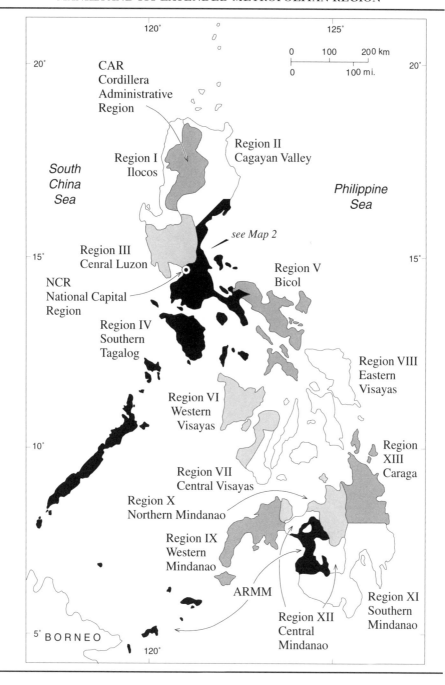

FIGURE 2
ADMINISTRATIVE REGIONS OF THE PHILIPPINES

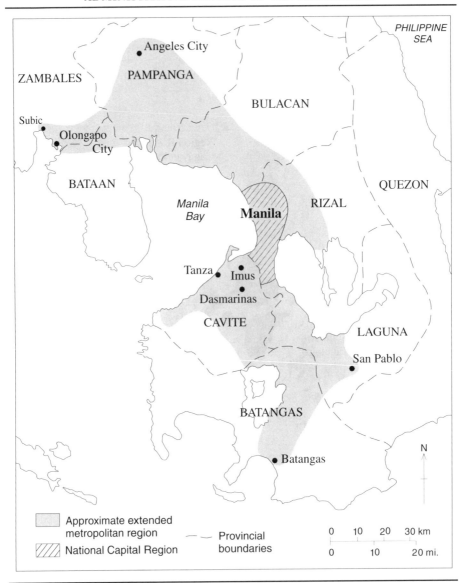

encroach into rural settings. Large swathes of irrigated agricultural land in the so-called rice bowl provinces of Central Luzon and Southern Tagalog have been converted into a variety of urban and industrial uses: export processing zones and industrial estates; institutions such as hospitals and universities; leisure landscapes including golf courses, resorts, and theme parks; and most significant in terms of the area involved, residential subdivisions. The result is a reworking of the social and economic, as well as the physical, landscape of formerly rural areas, such that even within the same household, the urban-industrial economy might coexist with agricultural production (Kelly 2000).

This blurring of boundaries is, however, a process that is deeply embedded in political power relationships at multiple scales. In the Southern Tagalog region in particular, the process of land conversion from agricultural to urban uses has been an issue of contentious public debate in recent years. It precipitates emotive issues of national food security, the priority given to industrial versus agricultural development, and the rights of tenant farmers and agricultural laborers. It is, therefore, an inherently political process in which decisions are made and options are exercised concerning land use and developmental priorities.

In this article, I examine the political contestation and negotiation of the land conversion process and suggest that rural-urban relations in Manila's mega-urban region must be seen as politicized at three interconnected scales of social relations—the national, the local, and the personal. At a national level, specific policy frameworks exist that regulate the land conversion process, but they are frequently circumvented and undermined by developmental strategies geared toward industrialization rather than agricultural modernization. At the level of local municipal governments, legislation allows considerable flexibility in interpreting zoning bylaws and therefore determining land uses. More important, this flexibility is applied in a context where the boundaries between public and private roles, and between regulatory responsibilities and vested interests, are frequently blurred. Finally, the everyday politics of relations between landlords, tenants, and other local powerbrokers creates a context in which tenant farmers find it difficult even to assert their legal rights to adequate compensation or land redistribution through agrarian reform programs.

The article is structured in the following way. The first section outlines the dimensions of land conversion in the Philippines and then focuses on the province of Cavite on Manila's southern flank in particular. Using unpublished government data, I will suggest that while they are, in themselves, dramatic, official figures may actually underestimate the extent of land conversion. The second section will highlight some of the social, economic, and environmental issues that are associated with land conversion and that form the basis for opposition to the process. The subsequent three sections of the article then describe the political processes, negotiations, and resistance that have emerged around the issue of land conversion at multiple scales. The article draws on a total of nine months of fieldwork in 1994-1995, both in Manila and in the adjacent province of Cavite to the south, along with subsequent research in 1998, 1999, and 2002.

The Dimensions of Land Conversion

In the 1990s, growing political concern and protest over land conversion in the Philippines reflected the intensification of the process itself. Sluggish economic

TABLE 1

PHILIPPINE AGRICULTURAL LAND AREA CONVERTED, 1987 TO 2001 (in hectares)

Region	Approved	Disapproved	Total
CAR—Cordillera	171	11	182
I—Ilocos	780	44	824
II—Cagayan Valley	404	15	419
III—Central Luzon	7,707	742	8,449
IV—Southern Tagalog	14,501	954	15,455
V—Bicol	1,625	405	2,030
VI—Western Visayas	2,337	495	2,832
VII—Central Visayas	519	233	752
VIII—Eastern Visayas	355	97	452
IX—Western Mindanao	326	0	326
X—Northern Mindanao	1,566	257	1,823
XI—Southern Mindanao	4,396	1529	5,925
XII—Central Mindanao	526	21	547
XIII—Caraga (NE Mindanao)	99	16	115
Philippines	35,314	4,818	40,132

SOURCE: Unpublished data, Department of Agrarian Reform, Quezon City (2002).

growth and centralized land use planning in the final years of the Marcos dictatorship and in the early years of the Aquino presidency meant that land conversion was slow until around 1990 (Magno-Ballesteros 2000). The Department of Agrarian Reform (DAR), the government agency responsible for recording and regulating the land conversion process, started systematically recording conversions in March 1988. Table 1 provides DAR figures between 1987 and 2001. Figure 1 indicates the parts of the country that correspond to each region.

The table shows that according to DAR records at least, during a fifteen-year period, a total of 35,314 hectares of agricultural land were legally converted to other uses. It is also apparent that the process of land conversion has a distinctive geographical pattern within the Philippines. Taking the approved conversions alone, more than half of the national total was accounted for by region IV (Southern Tagalog) and region III (Central Luzon). This pattern reflects the mega-urbanization of Manila into its surrounding agricultural provinces—particularly Cavite and Laguna to the south.

The importance of mega-urbanization in these figures can be illustrated by taking the province of Cavite as an example. There, the process of conversion has been driven by the development of large industrial estates and new residential subdivisions in the 1990s. Over the course of the decade, more than 150,000 industrial jobs were created in the province. By 2002, registered industrial establishments outside of export processing zones accounted for 62,893 jobs, while firms inside economic zones employed 96,894. When associated employment in service sectors is added, this represents a phenomenal level of economic growth and one that

TABLE 2

LAND CONVERSIONS IN CAVITE APPROVED BY
THE DEPARTMENT OF AGRARIAN REFORM, 1988 TO 2001

Year	Residential	Industrial	Mixed or Other Uses[a]	Total
1988	7.0	0	21	28
1989	17.4	25.0	0	42.4
1990	137.6	161.5	15.2	314.3
1991	68.1	34.9	148.9	251.9
1992	204.6	218.5	139.1	562.2
1993	99.1	24.8	22.0	145.9
1994	73.3	7.9	52.2	133.4
1995	225.2	0	322.3	547.5
1996	79.5	55.0	155.2	289.7
1997	58.8	78.9	392.1	529.8
1998	165.2	163.4	871.6	1,200.2
1999	17.4	0	33.5	50.9
2000	73.2	0	107.9	181.1
2001	45.7	5	9.5	60.2
Total	1272.1	774.9	2,290.5	4,337.5

SOURCE: Unpublished Data, Department of Agrarian Reform, Quezon City (2002).

a. Including mixed residential-commercial, industrial-commercial, and industrial-residential developments and other categories such as memorial parks, tourist sites, institutions, commercial sites, and dump sites.

was paralleled by a provincial population expansion from 1.15 million in 1990 to 2.06 million in 2000.

To house these workers, and to accommodate commuters employed in Manila, housing estates started to proliferate across the province in the 1990s. Table 2 indicates the conversions that were approved by DAR between 1988 and 2001 and illustrates the importance of residential, and to a lesser extent industrial, activities in the process of land conversion. Alongside these data, it is also significant to note that the mean wet season hectarage of rice in Cavite declined from 30,795 in the period from 1970 through 1979, to 18,573 in the 1980s, and finally to 11,727 hectares from 1990 through 1999 (see http://dirp.pids.gov.ph/~sspn). Some of this decline can be attributed to farmers' switching to other crops, especially in the 1970s and 1980s. In the 1990s, however, the harvested area declined from a peak of 14,120 in 1991 to a low of 10,105 hectares in 1998—a trend that appears to be closely correlated with the process of conversion shown in the table.

There are, however, reasons to suspect that figures on land conversion from DAR represent only a fraction of the land actually taken out of agricultural production. It is important to note that they represent only those lands approved for conversion rather than those exempted from DAR's jurisdiction because they were zoned for nonagricultural uses before 1988 (an issue I will return to later). The figures also exclude land that is lying idle because its owners have removed the tenant farmers and are waiting for a more profitable moment at which to seek conversion approval. In addition, many lands have simply been converted without the knowledge of DAR.

An indication of the extent to which land conversion goes unrecorded can be gleaned from data recorded at the municipal level using Tanza in Cavite as an example. Records at the municipal offices showed 248 hectares of agricultural land as being approved, or exempted from approval, for conversion between 1989 and 1994 and a further 119 hectares as having been forwarded to the provincial DAR office for processing. These figures indicated a significantly higher rate of conversion than data held by the national DAR office, which recorded just 214 hectares of land converted during the same period and none being processed. Furthermore, local figures also record 222 hectares of land as having been converted without permission, the vast majority being for residential subdivisions. These conversions do not feature anywhere in national DAR records. Separate data on rice lands in Tanza, gathered by local Department of Agriculture extension workers, suggest that more than 400 hectares of irrigated rice land were lost to other uses between 1989 and 1995. Putting these figures together suggests that official national figures for a town such as Tanza must be almost doubled to match locally collected data on legal and illegal conversions. Furthermore, it would seem that irrigated rice lands account for almost all of the total conversion. This is corroborated by data from the municipality of Imus, one of the province's most important agricultural territories. The town saw its agricultural land base decline from 2,536 hectares in 1990 to 1,744 hectares in 1995. Its ten-year municipal development plan prepared in 1995 designated just 1,226 hectares of cropland for protection from development, thereby acknowledging a 50 percent reduction in agricultural land between 1990 and 2005.

Contested Territory:
The Politics of Land Conversion

The landscape of rural towns such as Tanza and Imus is characterized by a patchwork of urban development and continuing agricultural production. In more remote villages, agricultural land is still farmed, although water supply for irrigation and labor supply at harvesting and planting times represents a perennial problem for farmers (Kelly 1999). In more accessible areas, however, large swathes of land have been converted to industrial uses or residential subdivisions. Alternatively, land may simply lie idle, with cattle grazing on grassed-over rice fields whose owners await either development permits or more propitious market conditions. When subdivisions are created, individual house lots remain empty until a buyer is found or until the new owner decides to construct a house on the lot. The result is often a bleak landscape of occupied houses interspersed with vacant units or empty lots strewn with garbage.

The incursion of the urban into the rural in this way has implications at multiple scales. At the village level, socioeconomic and environmental changes are experienced that have, on several occasions, led to outright resistance against land conversion. At a national level, the politics of resistance to land conversion are motivated by broader issues of food security and developmental priorities. In this section, I will outline each of these issues in turn.

The residents of new subdivisions tend to be a mixture of young families related to long-standing villagers and migrants from outside the barrio, most of whom have arrived to work in the emerging local industrial sector. In one such subdivision in Cavite, a survey conducted in 1995 of 301 residents revealed that approximately two-thirds were born outside the municipality in which the subdivision is located. Inevitably, significant social changes have resulted from this influx of migrants to expanding villages in Cavite. During interviews in one village in 1995, those who were born in the barrio spoke of the breakdown of formerly tight social networks and a growing feeling of anomie and urbanness:

> Question: Are there big differences from when you were growing up in Mulawin?
> Answer: Big ones! Of course, it's not the same as before; the camaraderie is different. Those who are really from here are different. Everybody was like a relative. Unlike now, when the trend is for those people from other provinces [to come here], it's as if it's every man for himself. Not like before, when if someone was sick you would visit them because they are relatives and friends. It's like Manila now. Manila lifestyle. (author's interview, Cavite villager, 1995, translated from Tagalog)

The sheer number of new people in the village means that they cannot be absorbed into existing social networks. A personalized system, through which relationships ranging from personal disputes to business arrangements were structured, has been broken down by the influx of newcomers. Inevitably, tensions and suspicions result: "When subdivisions were constructed, it became disordered, with lots of different kinds of people here. It's difficult to get along with different people, and that's why it's become very difficult since we've had these subdivisions" (author's interview, Cavite villager, 1995, translated from Tagalog).

The social consequences of land conversion also include issues of equity and justice. As will be described later, conversion is frequently used as a means of circumventing agrarian reform, so an opportunity for redistribution of rural income is lost (Canlas 1991). But displaced tenant farmers will, at least, receive disturbance compensation. The biggest losers in the process of land conversion are landless agricultural laborers who do not have tenancy rights that must be compensated, who are dependent on agricultural work for their livelihoods, and who have little formal education or experience that might open opportunities in the urban-industrial economy. For this group, already the most marginal in rural society, land conversion represents a profound dislocation. Many in the farm lobby point out that the agricultural sector has the ability to absorb such labor in a way that the manufacturing industry is incapable of doing on a similar scale (Philippine Peasant Institute 1993).

The environmental consequences of land conversion have been widely criticized (Zoleta-Nantes 1992). Vicente Ladlad (1993), for example, highlighted the impact of land use conversion in Laguna on the biological productivity of Laguna de Bay, a freshwater lake to the southeast of Manila. Elsewhere, urban and industrial development conflicts directly with agricultural activities. In Cavite, farmers complain that irrigation canals have become silted up with eroded material from local building sites, thus impeding water supply. In other cases, water supply is also constricted by household refuse as new residents respond to inadequate service provision by simply discarding their waste in nearby canals. Farmers also complain that crop pests have become an increasing problem with the development of residential areas in the midst of farmland.

The biggest losers in the process of land conversion are landless agricultural laborers, who do not have tenancy rights that must be compensated, who are dependent on agricultural work for their livelihoods, and who have little formal education or experience that might open opportunities in the urban-industrial economy.

The conversion of land in some of the country's most productive agricultural areas has raised issues of national food security. Total rice production in the Philippines continues to fall short of domestic demand. After importing minimal quantities of rice in the early 1990s, the latter half of the decade saw massive increases in shipments. In some years, this has represented a response to climatic factors reducing yearly domestic yields—in 1998, for example, more than 2 million metric tons were imported to compensate for a smaller than usual harvest. But in 1999, with production at record levels, more than 800,000 tons were still imported. Every decision to purchase rice has been met with condemnation from opposition politicians and agrarian advocacy groups. Official figures indicating approximately 35,000 hectares of land converted since 1988 would seem to represent only a fractional impact on the country's total rice land area in excess of 2 million hectares. But many believe that the concentration of conversions in the most productive rice-growing regions of Southern Tagalog and Central Luzon has compromised national food security and necessitated imports.

A broader theme, incorporating many of the issues already described, concerns the relative importance given to agricultural development versus industrialization. The administration of President Fidel Ramos (1992-1998) was explicitly committed to rapid industrial development, and incentives packages were established to attract foreign direct investment in export-oriented industries. While plans called for agro-industrialization, with linkages to be established between industry and local agricultural producers, the mechanisms for creating these linkages were seldom spelled out. Indeed, the sectoral focus of the plan left little space for such linkages. Agro-industrialization, it seemed, had come to mean industrial development located in agricultural areas rather than the formation of functional linkages between the two sectors. The administration of Joseph Estrada (1999-2001) was ostensibly pro-farmer, but there was little change in the pace of land conversion. Nongovernmental organizations have been outspoken in criticizing these developmental priorities.

Land conversion has, then, been a contested issue at both local and national scales in the Philippines (McAndrew 1994; Kelly 1997). Yet the process has continued and accelerated in recent years. To understand why this is so, it is necessary to explore not just the political issues involved in land conversion but also the political process, constituted at multiple scales. This question will be addressed in the subsequent three sections, which focus on the national, local, and everyday politics of land conversion.

Laws of the Land: The National Politics of Land Conversion

The formal legal context for the conversion of land uses in the Philippines was established by a complex series of laws, administrative orders, memoranda, and legal precedents in the late 1980s and 1990s. While most have ostensibly sought to protect agricultural land, and farmers, from land conversion, they have done little to prevent a decade of urbanization, particularly in the Manila region.

The single most important piece of legislation governing the process has been the Comprehensive Agrarian Reform Law (CARL) of 1988 (Republic Act 6657), which protects from conversion those rice and corn lands eligible for redistribution from landlord to tenant farmer. In addition, CARL gave authority to DAR to regulate the conversion of any agricultural land, regardless of tenure arrangements and crop types.

CARL, however, far from limiting land conversion, has in many cases accelerated the process. Under the law, landlords keen to avoid seeing their lands distributed to tenants can do so by converting them to other crops or to nonagricultural uses. Tenant farmers have often been removed, and the land has been left idle. This might seem an irrational use of a productive asset, but the institutional and legal framework established by CARL renders it an attractive option for landowners. Leaving a farmer to cultivate rice would present difficulties in obtaining a nonagricultural zoning from the local government. Moreover, the longer a tenant is allowed to farm while land prices increase, the higher compensation packages are inflated. This extra compensation would likely far outweigh any rental payments the owner might receive from the tenant if cultivation continued for a few extra years. There are then both legal and economic rationales as to why landowners are keen to remove their tenant farmers as soon as possible and that explain the common sight in Manila's hinterland of former rice land sitting idle, occupied only by grazing cattle.

The tension between agrarian reform and land conversion first came to a head in 1990. In a widely publicized case, farmers in the village of Langkaan in Dasmarinas, Cavite, came into conflict with the developers of an industrial estate over the fate of 232 hectares of rice land. The land was owned by a governmental agency, the National Development Corporation, which planned to develop the First Cavite Industrial Estate on the site in collaboration with the Marubeni Corporation of Japan. In October 1989, the partners applied to DAR for permission to convert the land. By that time, however, DAR had identified the property as eligible for redistribution under CARL, with 180 potential farmer-beneficiaries. DAR denied permission for the conversion on the grounds that the land was irrigated and productive, that tenant farmers could be clearly identified, and because the process of acquisition for redistribution had started prior to the application for conversion (Sermeno 1994; McAndrew 1994).

The dispute came down to a simple choice. Would the property be retained as productive agricultural land and redistributed to tenant farmers under CARL, or would the owners of the land be allowed to develop it as an industrial estate? The dispute pitched the Department of Trade and Industry against DAR, with the Department of Trade and Industry finally prevailing after seeking and obtaining a legal opinion from the Department of Justice (opinion number 44, series of 1990) that the authority of DAR to rule on conversions applied only to those land classification changes made after 15 June 1988 (when CARL or R.A. 6657 became effective). In other words, where a municipal or city development plan prior to that date zoned land as nonagricultural, then it takes precedence even if the land is, in fact, still being cultivated. The outcome of the Langkaan controversy was, therefore, less a technical legal decision and more a political decision to prioritize industrial development over the agricultural sector. The consequences of the decision were far reaching: in the five years following the ruling, 14,739 hectares nationally were approved for conversion by DAR, but a further 17,348 were converted with exemptions from DAR jurisdiction under opinion 44.

The following year, 1991, saw the scope of land use management by local governments substantially enhanced through the Local Government Code (Republic Act 7160). The Local Government Code is a broad piece of legislation that devolves significant administrative and revenue-raising powers to local government units with the intention of enhancing service provision, accountability, and local democracy (Tapales 1992). Section 20 of the code gives municipalities the power to reclassify up to 15 percent of agricultural land not covered by CARL to nonagricultural uses if it is deemed by the local council (*Sanggunian*) to be either no longer sound for agriculture or of substantially greater value if used for residential, commercial, or industrial purposes. These remarkably loose conditions effectively gave power over land use conversion to local municipalities—an issue that will be examined further in the next section.

By the end of 1992, public concern over the extent to which agricultural lands were being converted prompted presidential involvement. In November, President Fidel Ramos issued administrative order number 20, directing that all irrigated and irrigable land covered by existing irrigation projects should be immune from conversion. The purpose of the order was to protect prime agricultural lands from conversion, but the one-page directive lacked any implementing regulations or punitive measures to deter transgressors.

> *The result of these loopholes and avoidance strategies is that relatively few land conversions are technically illegal, but many clearly contravene the spirit and intent of the laws regulating conversion.*

While such legislative support for preserving agricultural land lacked mechanisms for enforcement, the political process of undermining protective regulations continued. In September 1993, executive order 124 outlined guidelines for prioritizing agricultural land conversion in areas designated as regional agri-industrial centers, regional industrial centers, tourism development areas, and "socialized" housing sites. The order did not supersede the president's previous directive to protect irrigated lands, but it did provide a mechanism for presidential approval if such lands were needed. Once again, however, no sanctions were stipulated for noncompliance. On a national scale, the areas involved in the provisions of executive order 124 are relatively small, but perhaps more than any other piece of legislation, executive order 124 highlights the political decisions being made at a national level about the priority given to urban-industrial development over the agricultural sector.

Through the 1990s, DAR continued to promulgate administrative orders addressing the issue of land conversion, but significant loopholes remained in each—in particular, a great deal rested on the certification of the Department of Agriculture and/or the National Irrigation Administration. Under these circumstances, several steps can be taken by landowners to enable land conversion (and avoid agrarian reform measures). First, national and regional officials in various government agencies are frequently found to be open to persuasion. Reports circulate of officials in the National Irrigation Authority certifying land as unirrigated or of DAR failing to recognize legitimate tenants eligible for agrarian reform. One land developer in Cavite talked openly to me about using high-level government contacts in Manila to secure a land conversion clearance from DAR. Second, landlords may simply pay disturbance compensation to tenants, removing them from land that will then sit idle. After a few years in such a state, the owner can claim that the land is nonproductive and therefore eligible for conversion. Third, cases have been reported of irrigation canals being destroyed and filled so that regulations such as administrative order 20 do not apply. Finally, local officials have the authority to redefine some land as zoned for nonagricultural use even when it is still being cultivated. The result of these loopholes and avoidance strategies is that relatively few land conversions are technically illegal, but many clearly contravene the spirit and intent of the laws regulating conversion.

For more than a decade, the Philippine government has acknowledged the need for a national land use plan that would rationalize the various land conversion laws into an integrated set of regulations with appropriate sanctions to punish noncompliance. As of 2003, a bill to enact a National Land Use Policy is still under consideration by the Philippine Senate (Senate bill 1944). This ongoing saga gives some indication of the political sensitivity of the issue, particularly among legislators with extensive business interests in farming and real estate. More important, it is possible that the lengthy passage of the legislation has accelerated the conversion of lands as landowners seek to preempt any tightening of restrictions that might come into effect with a new policy.

At the national level, then, a pattern of administrative and legislative action exists that has produced regulations with numerous paths for circumvention. At the same time, industrial development has been aggressively promoted, creating a political environment in which urban-industrial land uses have taken priority over agriculture. Examining legislation, however, shows only the policy directions and frameworks that are provided. It is at a local level that key decisions are made and the politics of land conversion are enacted.

The Local Politics of Land Conversion

National legislation on land conversion provides flexibility in implementation and, in many cases, opportunities for noncompliance with little threat of punishment. It is, however, largely at the level of municipal and provincial politics that regulations and procedures become open to interpretation, avoidance, and selective enforcement.

In a formal sense, this local-level control is mandated by the Local Government Code of 1991 described earlier. But the Local Government Code assumes the existence of an independent and efficient bureaucratic system at a local level and a clear division between regulators and developers. In many instances, neither of these conditions apply. Many towns do not even have precisely defined or publicly available zoning maps—in 1998, for example, 51 of the Southern Tagalog region's 223 cities and municipalities were without approved land use plans (Magno-Ballesteros 2000). The result is that decisions about the reclassification of land often fall to local officials, particularly mayors. Numerous reports and personal interviews suggest that such rezoning decisions often involve bribery and kickbacks (Bankoff 1996; Sidel 1999). Moreover, as the process of DAR conversion clearance starts with the municipal agrarian reform officer, that process too can be open to abuse by local officials who may certify that the land has "ceased to be economically feasible and sound for agricultural purposes" and that farmers on the land have been properly compensated, when the opposite is true. Farmers' rights as agrarian reform beneficiaries have also been compromised where redistribution has been prevented or withdrawn, often with pressure being applied to local agrarian reform officials. It should also be said, however, that many farmers have been only too happy to sell their tenancy rights given the marginal profitability of rice cultivation and the often generous compensation packages that are negotiated.

In addition to their regulatory roles, municipal mayors are also frequently powerful political bosses in a more informal sense, with considerable coercive resources in the form of law enforcement officers and private retainers (the Local Government Code also placed local police detachments under the jurisdiction of municipal officials). Numerous documented examples exist of pressure being brought to bear on farmers in Cavite who have resisted the decision to convert farmland. As a result, municipal politicians have been able to exert considerable control over the land conversion process. When asked why irrigated land has been converted even though the law states that it is protected, one village official told me, "With our current system [of government] it passes through." Another Caviteno, this time a relatively wealthy banker, elaborated on this sentiment:

> In fact, they're the ones selling all the lands. No lands here move without the mayor knowing it. People will not buy agricultural lands, and therefore they will only buy land if there is a chance of having it converted. And therefore, you'd have to go to the mayor because he's the only one empowered to certify that this land is part of a zone converted to industrial use. (author's interview, Cavite resident, 1995)

The heavy involvement of local politicians in the land conversion process relates partly to a desire to foster residential and industrial growth within their jurisdictions—land uses that provide far greater revenue-raising potential than agricultural production. But mayors and councilors are also usually significant players in the local economy in their own right and in many cases have vested interests in the land conversion process. These interests might involve ownership of land that will increase in value as other parcels of land are urbanized or simply kickbacks from developers wishing to smooth the process of obtaining permission for land conversion and development permits. Interviewed in 1995, one farmer in Cavite commented,

> I don't know why [it happens], but I really don't like it. We cannot do anything about it. It's our leaders who let it happen. They [developers] pay them so that it will be built. There's nothing that can be done. (author's interview, Cavite farmer, 1995, translated from Tagalog)

Another villager echoed that sense of powerlessness: "even if you protest, the person to whom you take your grievance will have something to do with the project." Moreover, the involvement of local politicians was evident in more than just the hearsay of villagers. Land developers too described encounters with mayors who demanded kickbacks in exchange for granting certification that the land could be converted. In one case, this demand, made behind closed doors, was for two lots in the planned subdivision and a substantial cash payment (Magno-Ballesteros 2000 provides similar examples).

Resistance has not . . . proven to be effective in curbing the accelerating process of conversion during the last decade.

Provincial authorities technically have little power to influence land conversion decisions, but in Cavite, accusations were widespread in the early 1990s that Governor Juanito Remulla (1979-1995) was complicit in coercing conversion in several instances (Sidel 1999; Kelly 2000). The principal ways in which this influence was exercised was through the persuasion or coercion of uncooperative municipal officials and tenant farmers. Such persuasion took the form of money to add a further incentive for compliance or the provision of manpower for forced evictions (McAndrew 1994; Coronel 1995; Sidel 1999).

The local politics of individual enrichment and bureaucratic corruption cannot, however, be divorced from the wider politics of development that lie behind the changes occurring in Cavite. In broad terms, this refers to the political agenda described earlier that focuses on industrialization through globalized development. Two sets of forces, then, work against the proper regulation of the land conversion process. One is in the priorities set by the national government in terms of development strategies, particularly the relative importance given to agricultural versus industrial development. Appeals against land conversion fall on deaf ears at both provincial and national scales. The other is the power given to local-level political leaders and their overlapping regulatory and business interests.

The Everyday Politics of Land Conversion

The institutional politics of land conversion at national and local levels provide only a partial picture of the process of land conversion as it is actually experienced by individual tenant farmers. To complete the picture, a less formal set of everyday power politics must be explored in the form of personal relationships between landlords and tenants (see also Kerkvliet 1990). Such relationships carry with them substantial weight in propelling the conversion process.

The start of the land conversion process from the farmer's point of view comes when the landowner approaches him or her with the suggestion that he or she might wish to sell the land and tries to evaluate the tenant's likely demands for compensation:

> What they will do is they will approach us. Naturally, we first talk about farming. [Then they say,] "If perhaps I were to sell this land, would you be agreeable to my suggestion?" And the tenant says, "If you can grant our rights, we could reach an agreement." Two or three times, they'll approach you. Of course, he is the one who is more eager to sell. In our case, since what we want is to avoid a dispute, then we agree. That is how the system works. (author's interview, ex-farmer in Cavite, 1995, translated from Tagalog)

Negotiations inevitably vary according to the individuals involved, but the social relationship between landlord and tenant, going beyond their economic arrangements, means that farmers often feel ashamed or embarrassed to negotiate as strongly as they might. Farmers feel unable to go beyond certain culturally prescribed bounds:

> It is inappropriate for you to act superior to the owner of the land. (author's interview, Cavite farmer, 1995, translated from Tagalog)

> For us, we just go along with the agreement because it's theirs, and it's inappropriate for us to say we don't want to. It will appear that we are becoming greedy over it. (author's interview, Cavite farmer, 1995, translated from Tagalog)

A farmer's association with the owner is thus more than just a legalistic, landlord-tenant relationship. The bond between the two families may date back several generations. Consequently, tenants are reluctant to try forcing their legal rights and souring personal relationships:

> That's it, that's their proposal. Of course, you're ashamed because we've been together for a long time. We don't want them to say we were greedy when the law [agrarian reform] came, doing everything by the letter of the law. We don't want that, so I just accepted it. Even though what is happening is painful, there's nothing we can do about the situation. (author's interview, ex-farmer in Cavite, 1995, translated from Tagalog)

The result is that landowners are able to persuade tenants to relinquish their tenancy rights, even where farmers might have legal rights to the land or legal means to block a conversion. In any case, the system of verbal agreements and unwritten understandings on which agrarian life is based is inconsistent with a legal system of documentation and regulation. In such circumstances, it is invariably the educated landlord, with high social status, sufficient resources to bribe officials, and access to legal counsel whom the situation will favor. But once again, it should also be added that there are farmers (and potential agrarian reform beneficiaries) who would rather enjoy a lucrative cash settlement than continue farming with marginal profits or take on the added burden of amortization payments under agrarian reform. Thus, all land is effectively negotiable if the two parties can reach an agreement. As one village official noted, "With every law, there is an exception if two persons agree with each other."

The settlement that is eventually reached between landlord and tenant will usually provide both a cash payment and a small parcel of land on which the tenants can build houses for themselves and for their children. Cash payments have escalated in recent years, but individual settlements vary according to the location of the land involved and the negotiating skills of the tenant. While land conversion laws stipulate compensation of at least five times the annual gross harvest of the land, in practice, the amounts paid have usually far exceeded this. In 1995, a typical compensation package amounted to approximately 500,000 pesos (around U.S.$20,000 at 1995 exchange rates) for each hectare of farmland (or 50 pesos per square meter) and a house lot of 1,000 to 2,000 square meters. The selling price of land to a developer, meanwhile, might be many times higher. One price being quoted by a landowner in Tanza in 1995 was 350 pesos per square meter (3.5 million pesos per hectare).

Conclusion: Politics at the Rural-Urban Interface

For at least a century, land has been the key source of power and conflict in the Philippines. In the past, the struggle has been focused on the control of agricultural land as the basis for wealth, patronage, and political dominance. This article has shown that land continues to be a highly politicized asset but that it is now the potential of agricultural land for urban-industrial uses that motivates the will to control it, rather than the need to dominate the agricultural economy and workforce. Nowhere is this more apparent than in struggles over land conversion in the hinterland of Manila.

Land conversion has, however, been a contested process. For reasons of social dislocation and injustice, and environmental conflicts between urban and rural sectors, the conversion of land for urban-industrial uses has been resisted at a local level. At the same time, issues of food security and the relative merits of a globalized industrialization strategy for development have motivated political opposition at broader scales. Such resistance has not, however, proven to be effective in curbing the accelerating process of conversion during the past decade.

This article has described the political processes that have facilitated land conversion at three different levels of analysis. At the national scale, a complex web of legislation has created numerous loopholes and opportunities for evasion without adequate deterrents. At the same time, a national development strategy has aggressively promoted industrial development while the agricultural sector has been implicitly neglected. At the local level, power over land use decisions has been decentralized into contexts where boundaries between public-sector regulation and private economic interests are blurred. This has, in turn, created a political framework conducive to conversion. Finally, at the level of personal relationships between landlords and tenants, the everyday politics of conversion is played out in a cultural context of patron-client ties that preclude farmers from asserting their legal rights.

References

Bankoff, G. 1996. Legacy of the past, promise of the future: Land reform, land grabbing, and land conversion in the Calabarzon. *Bulletin of Concerned Asian Scholars* 28 (1): 39-51.

Canlas, C. 1991. *Calabarzon project: The peasants' scourge*. Saliksik: PPI research papers. Manila: Philippine Peasant Institute.

Coronel, S. 1995. The killing fields of commerce. In *Boss: Five case studies of local politics in the Philippines*, edited by J. F. Lacaba. Manila: Philippine Centre for Investigative Journalism.

Kelly, P. 1997. Globalization, power and the politics of scale in the Philippines. *Geoforum* 28 (2): 151-71.

———. 1998. The politics of urban-rural relations: Land-use conversion in the Philippines. *Environment and Urbanization* 10 (1): 35-54.

———. 1999. Everyday urbanization: The social dynamics of development in Manila's extended metropolitan region. *International Journal of Urban and Regional Research* 23 (2): 283-303.

———. 2000. *Landscapes of globalization: Human geographies of economic change in the Philippines*. London: Routledge.

Kerkvliet, B. 1990. *Everyday politics in the Philippines: Class and status relations in a Central Luzon village.* Berkeley: University of California Press.

Ladlad, V. 1993. *Land use problems in urbanizing regions: The case of Laguna Lake Basin*. Manila: Philippine Peasant Institute.

Magno-Ballesteros, M. 2000. *Land use planning in metro Manila and the urban fringe: Implications on land and real estate market*. Philippine Institute of Development Studies discussion paper 2000-20. Makati City: Philippine Institute of Development Studies.

McAndrew, J. 1994. *Urban usurpation: From friar estates to industrial estates in a Philippine hinterland*. Manila, Philippines: Ateneo de Manila University Press.

Philippine Peasant Institute. 1993. Philippine NIChood: Stunting agriculture for fast-track growth. *PPI Briefing Paper* 2 (3): 2-12.

Sermeno, D. 1994. *Circumventing agrarian reform: Cases of land conversion*. PULSO monograph no. 14. Manila, Philippines: Institute on Church and Social Issues.

Sidel, J. 1999. *Capital, coercion and crime: Bossism in the Philippines*. Stanford, CA: Stanford University Press.

Tapales, P. 1992. Devolution and empowerment: LGC 1991 and local autonomy in the Philippines. *Philippine Journal of Public Administration* 36 (2): 101-14.

Zoleta-Nantes, D. 1992. Changes in land use of irrigated paddies: A study of land conversions in Plaridel, Bulacan. *Philippine Social Sciences Review* 50 (1-4): 129-58.

Neoliberalism and Nature: The Case of the WTO

By
ELAINE HARTWICK
and
RICHARD PEET

Political pressures exerted by environmental movements have forced governments otherwise committed to neoliberal policies to find reconciliatory policy positions between two contradictory political imperatives—economic growth and environmental protection. This article explores some ideological means of reconciliation, as with notions of sustainable development, which appear to bridge the impassable divide, and some of the institutional means for dealing with contradiction, as with the displacement of political power upward, away from elected national governments and toward international agreements and nonelected global governance institutions. Through these two strategic maneuvers, the authors argue, environmental concern has been ideologically and institutionally incorporated into the global neoliberal hegemony of the late twentieth century. The global capitalist economy can grow, if not with clear environmental conscience, then with one effectively assuaged. This process of neoliberal deflection is illustrated using the case of the General Agreement on Tariffs and Trade and the World Trade Organization.

Keywords: environmental agreements; growth; ideology; neoliberalism; WTO

Neoliberalism is grounded in a system of economic, social, and political ideals that are right-wing versions of the modern, post-Enlightenment themes of rationality, democracy, and individual freedom. In the late eighteenth and early nineteenth centuries, classical economics, developed on behalf of the progressive, liberal, industrial bourgeoisie, outlined a theory of the optimizing efforts of self-interested entrepreneurs, efficiently coordinated by self-regulating markets, to produce the economic growth underlying the dominance of the European peoples. Neoclassical economics

Elaine Hartwick teaches geography at Framingham State University and is interested in commodity chains and the global economy.

Richard Peet teaches geography at Clark University and is interested in global governance and critiques of neoliberal economic policy and neoconservative foreign policy. His book Unholy Trinity was published by Zed Press in August 2003.

DOI: 10.1177/0002716203256721

rethought these principles of economic modernism in terms of a set of terms— *price*, *cost*, *margins*, and *equilibrium*— that proved amenable to mathematization, making neoclassical economics the nearest social scientific equivalent to physics and thereby lending truth effects to even the most casual statement made by professional economists. But equilibrium statements proved easier to compile in the economic imagination than to construct in economic reality. So for a while, economics reluctantly abandoned pure market determination for limited state regulation of still privately owned production during the Keynesian interlude of the postwar period. Then, in the 1970s, widespread problems of stagflation were deemed beyond the reach of Keynesian fiscal policy, and in the early 1980s (with the elections of Margaret Thatcher in Britain and Ronald Reagan in the United States), nineteenth-century liberalism was revived in a right-wing version of neoliberalism. As with earlier liberal positions in classical and neoclassical economics, neoliberalism sees markets as optimally efficient means of organizing economies. State intervention, especially in social-democratic forms, disturbs the natural tendency for competition, specialization, and trade to generate economic growth. So neoliberal economic policies favor an outward-oriented, export economy, organized entirely through markets, along with privatization, trade liberalization, and limited state budget deficits. This set of policies became the standard recipe, the "Washington Consensus," applied by global governance institutions to supplicant countries, regardless of national or cultural circumstance (Peet 2002).

Yet popular concern mounted concerning the efficacy of neoliberal growth in solving the development problems of Third World countries. And at the same time, concern continued to be expressed about the disastrous effects of unlimited, unregulated economic growth on global and regional natural environments. Green parties received modest electoral support in some of the former social democracies of Western Europe, environmental protests merged with movements for social justice, and distress over the destruction of endangered species and the disappearance of tropical rain forests became conventional public opinion in many, if not most, advanced capitalist countries. The political pressures exerted by widespread environmental movements forced governments to find reconciliatory policy positions between two contradictory political imperatives—economic growth and environmental protection. In this article, we explore some ideological means of reconciliation, as with the notions of sustainable development, which appear to bridge the impassable divide, and some of the institutional means for dealing with contradiction, as with the displacement of political power upward away from elected national governments and toward international agreements and nonelected global governance institutions. Through these two strategic maneuvers, we argue, environmental concern has been ideologically and institutionally incorporated into the global neoliberal hegemony of the late twentieth century. The global capitalist economy can grow, if not with clear environmental conscience, then with one effectively assuaged. We illustrate this process of neoliberal deflection by using the case of the General Agreement on Tariffs and Trade (GATT) and the World Trade Organization (WTO).

GATT/WTO

At the end of World War II, several new global organizations were formed by international agreement among nation-states. The imperative behind these agreements was exclusively a concern about economic and political stability in the aftermath of the depression of the 1930s. Little attention was paid to the natural environment at the time, although questions of natural resources were sometimes raised, usually as the material bases for sustaining postwar economic growth. In the economic realm, the idea initially was to establish three main international institutions: an International Monetary Fund, an International Bank for Reconstruction and Development (later called the World Bank), and an International Trade Organization that would regulate trade as a necessary complement to the other two organizations. The United States wanted a trade organization to be formed that

---

The global capitalist economy can grow,
if not with clear environmental conscience,
then with one effectively assuaged.

---

would free up interchanges in the specific interest of large, exporting corporations, but with a market-oriented, deregulated international economy more generally in mind. "The world that was imagined was the kind of world Americans wanted" (Wilcox 1949, 24). As the main source of funds for the reconstruction of Europe in the post–World War II period, and as the world's most powerful economy, an emergent United States exerted considerable political pressure charting the eventual course of trade agreements (Hoekman and Kostecki 1995, 2-3). Four preliminary conferences on trade were convened under United Nations auspices: a "Preparatory Committee" meeting in London in 1946; a "Drafting Committee" meeting at Lake Success, New York, in 1947; a Geneva Conference later in 1947; and a Havana Conference between November 1947 and March 1948. The Geneva Conference produced an interim measure, known as the General Agreement on Tariffs and Trade, that became the main international basis for managing trade in the postwar period when proposals in Havana to found a regulatory organization, the International Trade Organization, foundered in the U.S. Congress (Loree 1950, 2).

GATT regulated trade in goods (i.e., physical commodities) using agreed-on, liberal principles of trade liberalization, equal market access, reciprocity, nondiscrimination, and transparency. The basic idea behind GATT was to eliminate pro-

TABLE 1

ARTICLE XX OF THE GENERAL AGREEMENT ON TARIFFS AND TRADE

Subject to the requirement that such measures are not applied in a manner that would constitute a means of arbitrary or unjustifiable discrimination between countries where the same conditions prevail, or a disguised restriction on international trade, nothing in this agreement shall be construed to prevent the adoption or enforcement by any contracting party of measures
  1. necessary to protect public morals;
  2. necessary to protect human, animal, or plant life or health;
  3. necessary to secure compliance with laws or regulations that are not inconsistent with the provisions of this agreement, including the protection of patents, trademarks, and copyrights, and the prevention of deceptive practices;
  4. relating to the products of prison labor;
  5. imposed for protecting national treasures of artistic, historic, or archaeological value; or
  6. relating to the conservation of exhaustible natural resources if such measures are made effective in conjunction with restrictions on domestic production or consumption.

SOURCE: Multilaterals Project of the Fletcher School of Law and Diplomacy, Tufts University (see http://fletcher.tufts.edu/multi/texts/BH209.txt).

tectionism and discrimination, allowing the trade in goods (but not yet services) to flow smoothly from one country to another, without disruption or distortion, supposedly permitting all countries to achieve larger output levels and ultimately increasing the level of economic growth everywhere. GATT, in other words, attempted to resurrect the classically liberal free trade principles of the nineteenth century, but with an appeal to the twentieth century, Keynesian-social-democratic notion that growth was universally beneficial in terms of producing better standards of living for the general populace. Thus, the basic purpose of GATT was stated as raising living standards, ensuring full employment, increasing real income and effective demand, and assuring the full use of the resources of the world by expanding the production and exchange of goods through reducing tariffs and other barriers to trade. To this end, GATT laid out thirty-eight articles of agreement regulating the conditions of trade among member countries. Under article XX, it provided exceptions to what otherwise amounted to a set of free trade principles for governmental measures necessary to protect human, animal, or plant life or health or were related to the conservation of exhaustible natural resources (if such measures were made in conjunction with restrictions on domestic production or consumption) (see Table 1). However, issues of human rights, cultural integrity, human and animal health, and the conservation of natural resources, covered by article XX, were generally ignored by GATT until recently.

The penultimate GATT trade negotiations, the Uruguay Round, lasting from 1986 to 1994, signified a new phase in world trading history within a new era of neoliberal globalization. This last round attempted to eliminate export subsidies on agricultural goods and textiles and dealt with nontariff barriers, technical aspects of trade, and trade-related investment and intellectual property rights issues. The

Uruguay Round also established the WTO as the enforcing organization. The agreement finalizing the Uruguay Round was signed in the Moroccan city of Marrakesh in 1994 and was, for the most part, approved routinely by the legislatures of most member countries. Under the WTO, ministerial meetings have subsequently been held at Singapore in 1996, Geneva in 1998, Seattle in 1999, and Doha, Qatar, in 2001 (Dunkley 1997).

The WTO structure is headed by a Ministerial Conference meeting at least once every two years. Below this is the General Council, normally made up of trade ambassadors and heads of delegations, but sometimes with officials sent by member counties to meetings held several times a year at the Geneva headquarters of the WTO. Some member countries participate in an Appellate Body, various Dispute Settlement panels, the Textiles Monitoring Body, and several plurilateral committees. Numerous specialized committees, working groups, and working parties deal with individual agreements and other areas, such as the environment, development, membership application, and regional trade agreements. Other working groups deal with the relations between trade and investment, the interaction between trade and competition policy, and transparency in government procurement. The WTO Secretariat, based in Geneva, has around five hundred staff members and is headed by a director-general and a deputy director-general. The current director of the WTO is Mike Moore, formerly a member of the New Zealand Labour Government, which came to power in 1984 (Kelsey 1995). That government, led by Prime Minister David Lange and Finance Minister Roger Douglas, introduced a radical program of neoliberal restructuring that devastated the New Zealand welfare state system, previously the finest in the world (tax-supported free health care, education, etc.). The 144 members of the WTO, as of early 2002, account for 90 percent of world trade. Thirty other countries are negotiating membership. Two-thirds of WTO members are developing nations, although the descriptions "developed" and "developing" are self-designations. The WTO's annual budget of about U.S.$78 million comes from dues paid by member nations. As with voting, dues are based on a country's share of world trade, with the United States contributing the largest amount.

Trade and the Environment: Arguments from the WTO

The WTO exists for the purpose of liberalizing trade across national boundaries. "Liberalizing" means removing governmental restrictions on the free movement of goods and services. "Restrictions on trade" may include national or international regulations that protect the environment, ensure food quality, and safeguard public health. What happens when the WTO's imperative for freeing trade comes into conflict with the need to regulate the economy for reasons of environmental protection, in an age of burgeoning production, massive consumption, and the prevalence of powerful technologies?

The WTO insists that it is not an antienvironmental organization. It points to "several references to the environment" in the organization's provisions as with article XX outlined above, dealing with "General Exceptions." Then too, the preamble to the Marrakesh Agreement says that the purpose of the WTO is to expand member countries' production and trade in goods and services while "allowing for the optimal use of the world's resources in accordance with the objective of sustainable development, seeking to both protect and preserve the environment and to enhance the means for doing so in a manner consistent with their respective needs and concerns at different levels of economic development." The WTO also refers to the Agreement on Technical Barriers to Trade and the Agreement on Sanitary and Phytosanitary Measures, two closely linked health and safety agreements emerging from the Uruguay Round, as evidence of its environmental concern.

In addition, the WTO says that it has long-established special committees dealing with trade and environmental issues. In 1971, the GATT Council of Representatives agreed to set up a Group on Environmental Measures and International Trade that would meet at the request of GATT members. However, no country asked for it to convene until 1991. A somewhat more active group, the Committee on Trade and Environment, came into existence along with the WTO in 1995. Its mandate is

> to identify the relationship between trade measures and environmental measures in order to promote sustainable development; to make appropriate recommendations on whether any modifications of the provisions of the multilateral trading system are required, compatible with the open, equitable and non-discriminatory nature of the system.

In its statement of the basic principles guiding its work, the Committee on Trade and Environment points out that the WTO is not an environmental protection agency and that its competency for coordinating policy in this area is limited to aspects of environmental policies related to trade. However, this competency does include looking at how trade policy can "benefit the environment." The committee says that the WTO is interested in building a "constructive relationship" between trade and environmental concerns to promote sustainable development. The WTO Secretariat has organized a series of regional seminars on trade and environment for government officials, the objective being "to raise awareness on the linkages between trade, environment and sustainable development, and to enhance the dialogue among policy-makers from different ministries in WTO member governments." The WTO also holds symposia on trade, environment, and sustainable development in Geneva, which involve senior trade and environment officials together with representatives of selected nongovernmental organizations.

The basic argument propagated by GATT and the WTO is that increased trade benefits the environment. As expressed by the GATT Secretariat, expanding trade and increasing market access has led to larger per capita incomes that, in turn, provided more resources to "contain environmental damage." If the average citizen could also be convinced of the need to devote more material and human resources to achieving a better environment as incomes rise, the growth of per capita income ultimately leads to increased expenditures on the environment. A country with a stagnant economy, by contrast, tends to spend less on improving the environment. Furthermore, new technologies often first appear in countries at the frontier of environmental regulation, and products embodying these technologies have to be exported if other countries are to catch up. Similarly, trade can help consumers make environmentally beneficial choices—for instance, imports of low-sulphur coal could discourage the use of domestic high-sulphur coal. Trade in recycled

---

The basic argument propagated by GATT and the WTO is that . . . expanding trade and increasing market access has led to larger per capita incomes that, in turn, provided more resources to "contain environmental damage."

---

inputs could help countries economize on resource use. Even so, GATT/WTO admits, trade liberalization could worsen particular environmental problems in the absence of appropriate domestic environmental policies. Indeed, conceivably, an expansion of trade could produce negative environmental effects that outweigh the conventional benefits from open markets (increased specialization, more competition, and so forth), resulting in an overall decline in national welfare. However, this is possible only if a country lacks a domestic environmental policy that reflected its environmental values and priorities. If such proves to be the case, the most effective action is to concentrate on introducing appropriate environmental policies, rather than forgoing trade liberalization or attempting to fine-tune interventionist trade policies. Manipulating trade policies is not only costly, in terms of a less efficient international division of labor, but also ineffective in dealing with the absence of appropriate environmental policies (GATT Secretariat 1992).

Mainstreaming Environmentalism

In March 1999, anticipating the Seattle Ministerial meetings later in the year, and realizing that environmental opposition was on the rise, the WTO sponsored a high-level symposium on trade and environment. By this time, the WTO was speaking in terms of the "synergies between trade liberalization, environmental protection, sustained economic growth and sustainable development," with communication and interaction between the trade and environmental "communities." Renato Ruggiero, outgoing director-general, said that the WTO was an ally of sustainable development and that the trade and environmental communities had common objectives—strong, rule-based trading regimes and strong and effective environmental regimes. These common objectives, he said, could not be attained through unilateralism, discriminatory actions, or protectionism but had to be reached through global consensus on all environmental issues and giving this consensus a stronger institutional voice. The Rt. Hon. Sir Leon Brittan QC, vice president of the European Commission, who had suggested the idea of a high-level meeting on trade and environment, bringing together top-level policy makers to "push the Trade and Environment debate forward," said that the debate on the relationship between trade and environment had become "bogged down in technicalities" but that underlying the genuine complexities were a limited number of issues that could be resolved by elevating the level of debate and opening it up. While there were extremists on both sides of the argument, a broad consensus and a balanced approach could be achieved between traditional free-traders, such as himself, who nonetheless saw the importance in today's world of accommodating environmental concerns in trade policy, and environmentalists who saw that their objectives could best be achieved by incorporating them in that system in a reasonable way rather than pursuing protectionist policies. He advocated following the European Union's approach through commitment to the concept of sustainable development highlighted by the Earth Summit in Rio in 1992, where 178 states had committed themselves to sustainable development. In particular, he advocated using Multilateral Environmental Agreements (MEAs) as the common base, agreed to by as many states as possible, for tackling particular environmental problems, including the protection of global resources and, of course, animal welfare. MEAs were clearly preferable to unilateral action, which would often rightly fall foul of WTO rules. It was infinitely better, he said, to have an internationally agreed-on approach on accommodating legitimate environmental concerns in the multilateral trading system than to allow these concerns to be reflected in inconsistent, unilateral measures. Also, to have legitimacy, the trading system had to have the support and understanding of all, experts and nonexperts. The Seattle meetings of the WTO should set an overall guideline: that the objective of the New Millennium Round, the set of negotiations that was supposed to follow, was to produce a sustainable outcome. Ministers should, in the jargon, he said, "mainstream sustainability." Finally, a statement sent to the symposium by Bill Clinton, then president of the United States, expressed hope for an international consensus behind policies that promoted free trade and open markets while protecting the global environment. He said that more must be done to ensure that spirited economic competition among nations never became a race to the bottom. We should be leveling environmental protections up, not down, he said. International trade rules had to be supportive of national policies that provided high levels of environmental protection and effective enforcement (WTO 1999).

Toward a Win-Win Solution

A new WTO Secretariat report on trade and environment, the longest and most sophisticated of all, was released in 1999, again just before the Seattle meetings. The report argued that there was no basis for the "sweeping generalizations" often heard in the public debate, arguing that trade was either good or bad for the environment. Instead, the environmental repercussions of trade were "theoretically ambiguous" because they depended on three interacting factors: (1) trade-induced changes in industrial composition, and hence the pollution intensity of national output, (2) changes in the overall scale of economic activity, and (3) changes in production technology. The net outcome was, therefore, a priori undeterminable. The real-world linkages between trade and environment were a little of both. However, the report continued, "win-win"outcomes could be assured through well-designed policies in both the trade and the environmental fields. Most environmental problems resulted from polluting production processes, certain kinds of consumption, and the disposal of waste products—trade as such was rarely the root cause of environmental degradation, except for pollution associated with the transportation of goods.

The key question addressed by the 1999 report on trade and environment was this: is economic growth, driven by trade, part of the environmental problem or part of the solution? The WTO Secretariat report gave a complicated answer. On the whole, it argued that low incomes were one reason that environmental protection lagged in many countries. Countries living on the margin might not be able to set aside resources for pollution abatement, nor did many think they should sacrifice their growth prospects to help solve global pollution problems caused in large part by the consuming lifestyles of richer countries. So if poverty were at the core of the pollution problem, economic growth would be part of the solution—this was because growth allowed countries to shift gears from immediate concerns to long-run sustainability issues. Here the report referred to the notion of an Environmental Kuznets Curve (EKC)—the idea of an inverted-U-shaped pollution path taken by countries undergoing economic growth, so pollution increased at early stages but decreased after a certain income level had been reached. Trade entered into this debate for several reasons: trade was one cylinder that propelled the engine of growth; trade might affect the shape and relevance of the EKC; competitive pressures might prevent environmental standards from being upgraded; and growth driven by liberalization of the world economy might then prevent the onset of mechanisms that could generate an EKC. So economic growth might be part of the solution, but primarily for local pollution problems, as with urban air pollution or some types of freshwater pollutants, but not for other important indicators, as with pollutants of a more global nature, notably emissions of carbon dioxide. In other words, economic growth, while perhaps necessary, was not sufficient to reverse environmental degradation. National accountability, good governance, and a democratic political process could be underestimated in this regard—governments that were not held accountable for their actions, or rather inactions in this case, might fail to upgrade environmental polices. Good governance was also needed at the international level—the Montreal Protocol and the Kyoto Agreement were cited as examples. The growing number of MEAs (currently 216 in number) might be a further indication of a trend in that direction. Initiative might have to shift from the national to the supranational level, as with the shift to the central level in federal states in the 1970s to overcome environmental policy foot-dragging at the local level. The cooperative model of the WTO, based on legal rights and obligations, could potentially serve as a model for a new global architecture of environmental cooperation. Meanwhile, even within its current mandate, the report concluded, the WTO could do a few important things for the environment. The most obvious contribution would be to address remaining trade barriers on environmental goods and services to reduce the costs of investing in clean production technologies and environmental management systems. Another contribution would be to seek reductions in government subsidies that harm the environment, including energy, agriculture, and fishing subsidies. In short, trade was really not the issue, nor was economic growth. The issue was how to reinvent environmental polices in an ever more integrated world economy so as to ensure that we live within ecological limits. The way forward, it seemed, was to strengthen the mechanisms and institutions for multilateral environmental cooperation, just as countries, fifty years ago, had decided that it was to their benefit to cooperate on trade matters by forming GATT (Nordström and Vaughan 1992).

Trade and the Environment: Arguments against the WTO

This last report, effectively summarizing the current WTO position on trade, environment, and sustainable development, will be the immediate object of our critique. As we have seen, GATT was founded on the claim that liberalizing trade leads to higher growth, larger incomes, and more consumption. Indeed, "change in the scale of economic activity" in an upward direction is the main benefit the WTO claims that its activities bring to the broad mass of the world's population. But this creates a dilemma for the WTO when it comes to the effects of production on the environment. For if, indeed, the GATT/WTO trading system generates growth, and growth is accompanied by pollution, then the system championed by the WTO generates pollution. That is, the trade and growth policies of the WTO can be held accountable for the environmental degradation. This is particularly the case when the increased international competitiveness favored by a neoliberalized WTO trading system reduces the political and economic ability of member countries to environmentally regulate production. The argument is so compelling that the WTO, through its 1999 report, for instance, has to address the relations between trade, growth, and environmental degradation previously so neglected that its committee on trade and environment had never met!

On one side, the WTO argues that trade-induced growth provides resources for addressing environmental problems (or, rather, environmental "challenges" in the jargon of neoliberal optimism—the word "problem" being systematically avoided). On the other side, when it comes to environmental degradation, neither trade nor growth is a root cause. Instead, the root cause of environmental degradation is pollution. Most environmental problems result from polluting production processes

---

The WTO makes the audacious claim that the GATT/WTO agreements on trade, together with the WTO dispute settlement system, provide an effective model for enforceable international environmental regulation.

---

that can be effectively regulated, even in the face of increased competitiveness, by national environmental policy and, with globalization, through MEAs—the 1999 report uses as examples the Montreal Protocol and the Kyoto Accords on greenhouse gas emissions and global warming, and it is often mentioned that GATT and the WTO were supporters of the Rio Declaration on environmentally sustainable development. Notice here the logical ellipses underlying the very structure of the argument and the attempt to turn potential critiques of the WTO into supportive claims for the organization.

In the first ellipse, the WTO denies that trade-induced economic growth is the basic causal condition for the increased pollution that causes dangerous levels of environmental degradation; yet the WTO claims that trade-induced growth is definitely part of the solution. This is a case of denying you caused that bite-shaped hole in the cake but enjoying its taste all the more! The WTO relies on the dubious notion of an EKC, in which pollution decreases after a certain (high) level of income is achieved in growing economies. But this finding has been hotly contested. For example, one study used data on ambient air pollution in cities worldwide to examine the relationship between national income and pollution. It concludes that there is little empirical support for an inverted-U-shaped relationship between several important air pollutants and national incomes (Harbaugh, Levinson, and Wilson 2000). Another study on sulfur emissions, using a larger and more globally representative sample than previous sulfur EKC studies, found that sulfur emissions per capita are a monotonic function of income per capita when a global sample of countries is used but an inverted-U-shaped function of income when a sample of only high-income countries is used—that is, the U-shaped find-ings occur only when a certain set of already developed countries is carefully cho-sen (Stern and Common 2001). And even a casual glance at the data demonstrates one undeniable fact about environmental pollution: the main cause of pollution is not population pressure, as claimed by Malthusian organizations such as the World Resources Institute (itself in desperate need of deconstructive critique), nor is it the poverty cited by the WTO. Instead, the advanced countries spend more on environmental programs exactly because their affluence is the basic cause of envi-ronmental problems. Take one key indicator in an area of pollution—carbon diox-ide emissions—mentioned prominently by the WTO. The high income countries, with 15 percent of the world's population, generate (within their borders) 47 per-cent of global emissions because, for each person, twelve tons of carbon dioxide are emitted annually; however, the low-income countries of the world, with 40 percent of the world's population, generate 11 percent of emissions because, for each per-son, one ton of carbon dioxide is emitted. And furthermore, countries following an export-oriented industrialization model of growth like that advocated by the WTO (i.e., producing exports destined for the markets of the rich countries) show rapidly increasing levels of carbon dioxide emissions—so the "upper middle income coun-tries," with 9.6 percent of the world's people, generate 12 percent of emissions because, for each person, five tons of carbon are released (World Bank 2001, 278-79, 292-93). In brief, the single, most prominent cause of global pollution is the same process of trade-oriented, global industrialization that the WTO wants fur-ther to deregulate through liberalization.

In the second ellipse, the WTO claims that despite the increased international competitiveness brought on by the liberalization of trade, governments can, through multilateral agreement, implement effective environmental regulations. This shunts responsibility for environmental destruction away from liberalized trade and places the onus squarely on governmental and intergovernmental policy. (Notice also that these are always clean-up policies rather than the preventative policies that would contravene neoliberal deregulation.) It also substitutes vague wishful thinking for concrete political action. In this regard, the WTO favors the version of "sustainable development" proclaimed by the Declaration on Environ-ment and Development at the United Nations Conference on Environment and Development in Rio de Janeiro in 1992, a conference in which GATT actively par-ticipated. The key position established by the Rio Declaration, summarized by principle number 7, says, "States shall cooperate in a spirit of global partnership to conserve, protect and restore the health and integrity of the Earth's ecosystem." The declaration goes on to suggest that to achieve sustainable development and a higher quality of life for all people, "states should reduce and eliminate unsustain-able patterns of production and consumption and promote appropriate demo-graphic policies." Under principle 12, the Rio Declaration follows the direct lead of GATT by adding that

> States should cooperate to promote a supportive and open international economic system
> that would lead to economic growth and sustainable development in all countries, to

better address the problems of environmental degradation. Trade policy measures for environmental purposes should not constitute a means of arbitrary or unjustifiable discrimination or a disguised restriction on international trade. Unilateral actions to deal with environmental challenges outside the jurisdiction of the importing country should be avoided. Environmental measures addressing transboundary or global environmental problems should, as far as possible, be based on an international consensus. (Consortium for International Earth Science Information Network 1992)

Thus, the Rio Declaration sets up a fine ideal in the form of a loose, malleable objective defined by that term for all reasons, "sustainable development." Yet the declaration advocates "cooperation in good faith and in a spirit of partnership" with the means for carrying this out left for "the further development of international law in the field of sustainable development"—that is, means of implementation are to be worked out some time in the future. In the declaration, population growth features prominently as the basic cause of environmental pollution rather than economic growth or overconsumption. And further still, GATT managed to insert its own position into the declaration in one of its few more exact statements, the notion that unilateral trade action should not be used to address environmental problems, but instead, measures must be based on "international consensus"—should that, one day, maybe, if we all work together, perhaps occur!

In terms of reducing pollution through MEAs, the WTO mentions the Montreal Protocol and the Kyoto Accords. The Montreal Protocol on Substances that Deplete the Ozone Layer, agreed on in 1987 after "rigorous negotiations," sets the "elimination" of ozone-depleting substances as its "final objective" and was ratified by countries accounting for 82 percent of world consumption. The Kyoto treaty, signed by 100 countries in 1997, mandating that the United States and other industrialized nations "find a way" by the year 2012 to reduce greenhouse gas emissions by between 5 percent and 7 percent of 1990 levels, is often described as "the only practical measure we have to tackle climate change." In November 2001, 160 countries signed an accord requiring emissions of carbon dioxide to be reduced by an average of 5.2 percent of the 1990 level by 2012. Yet the accords were specifically rejected by the G. W. Bush administration in March 2001 on the grounds that they damaged the American economy, excusing developing countries from decreasing emissions, while the scientific evidence on global warming remained unclear. (The United States, with 4.6 percent of the world's population, accounts for 23 percent of global carbon dioxide emissions.) Instead, in early 2002, the Bush administration announced a set of voluntary measures and tax incentives aimed at reducing carbon dioxide and other greenhouse gas emissions based on the "common-sense idea that sustainable economic growth is the key to environmental progress because it is growth that provides the resources for investment in clean technologies." Under a cap-and-trade approach, the U.S. government will set mandatory limits on emissions of three pollutants while establishing a new market in which major polluters can purchase credits from nonpolluting companies toward meeting their pollution targets. The idea is to allow pollution to increase, but at a slower rate than economic growth. And all this is so despite the fact that Americans see global warming as a serious problem, believing three to one that carbon dioxide emissions help account for global warming, with two-thirds wanting the president to find a way to reduce such emissions. In brief, the WTO places responsibility for environmental action on vague MEAs that, when specified in terms of objectives such as limiting emissions to the already dangerous levels reached in 1990, are rejected by trade- and growth-oriented administrations that instead use neoliberal notions of trading the right to pollute and voluntary compliance by industries. In other words, the WTO is a global growth machine, with international environmental policy as its conscientious disguise.

The WTO Dispute Settlement System

But we have saved the best for last. The WTO makes the audacious claim that the GATT/WTO agreements on trade, together with the WTO dispute settlement system, provide an effective model for enforceable international environmental regulation. From this, the WTO miraculously emerges as a potential model of an environmental savior. Such a claim can be examined only through the practice of an institution—in the sense that deeds speak more truthfully than claims. The WTO's practice in this area occurs mainly through the settlement of disputes among member governments about issues of trade and the environment. Briefly, the dispute settlement system is set in motion when member governments bring conflicts over trade, largely different interpretations of the GATT/WTO Articles of Agreement, to the WTO. Should consultation not result in a settlement, the WTO's Dispute Settlement Understanding requires the establishment of an investigative panel, normally consisting of three persons of "appropriate background and experience" proposed by the WTO Secretariat or the director-general, from countries not party to the dispute. Panel reports are adopted by the WTO Dispute Settlement Body (DSB) unless the DSB decides by consensus not to adopt the report or one of the parties notifies the DSB of its intention to appeal. Appeals are handled by a WTO Appellate Board made up of three of the seven (semipermanent) members of the WTO Appellate Body. Appeals are limited to issues of law covered in the panel report and legal interpretations developed by the panel. The resulting report is then adopted by the DSB and has to be unconditionally accepted by the disputing parties unless the DSB decides by consensus against its adoption. Once the panel or Appellate Body report is adopted, the government found against has to notify the WTO of its intentions for implementing the adopted recommendations. The DSB keeps the implementation under regular surveillance until the issue is resolved, with rules being set for compensation or the suspension of trade concessions in the event of nonimplementation.

In DSB cases concerning trade and the environment, intergovernmental disputes have focused on article XX of the 1947 GATT agreement but have included references to other articles (mainly articles III and XI [1] and [2]). These allow exceptions from the other articles of the agreement dealing with the rules governing trade, for measures necessary to protect human, animal, or plant life or health (subsection b) and relating to the conservation of exhaustible natural resources (subsection g), subject to the requirement that these measures not be applied in a manner that would constitute a means of arbitrary or unjustifiable discrimination between countries where the same conditions prevail or a disguised restriction on international trade. Table 2 summarizes seven cases from the records of the DSB dealing with environmental issues in the period 1982 through 2001.

When issues essentially of free trade, on one hand, and environmental regulation, on the other, have come into conflict, the GATT/WTO dispute system has always found in favor of trade and against environmental regulation. Consistently, the principle of freeing trade from regulations and restrictions has been found more important than restricting trade in the interests of environmental regulation. And this is the system the WTO proposes for settling the interminable controversies that necessarily arise from the tensions inherent in the principle of sustainable development! Trade and growth win every time—a "win-win" solution.

> *When issues essentially of free trade, on one hand, and environmental regulation, on the other, have come into conflict, the GATT/WTO dispute system has always found in favor of trade and against environmental regulation.*

There might be a partial exception. In an eighth environmental case, the Shrimp-Turtle case, summarized in Table 3, the WTO dispute settlement system again found several times in favor of trade. But in this case, the government requesting an exception under article XX, the United States, made extensive efforts to comply with a series of findings by the WTO's panel and Appellate Body that would be difficult to replicate, especially under more conservative administrations. For example, a regional agreement between twenty-four countries was tentatively agreed on in Kuantan, Malaysia, in July 2000, dealing with the conservation of sea turtles, with the United States actively participating. More significantly, the panel's finding came after massive environmental criticism, in part by demonstrators dressed as turtles, at the Seattle Ministerial meeting of the WTO in late 1999. Even so, this was a most tentative finding for article XX: in its summation, the panel noted that should any one of its conditions cease to be met in the future, the recommendations of the DSB might no longer be complied with. In other words, in the history of GATT/WTO disputes, the WTO has tentatively allowed a single exception that conserves environmental resources under article XX, in this

TABLE 2

SEVEN ENVIRONMENTAL DISPUTES IN THE GENERAL AGREEMENT
ON TARIFFS AND TRADE (GATT) AND THE WORLD TRADE
ORGANIZATION, 1982 THROUGH 2001

1. United States—Prohibition of Imports of Tuna and Tuna Products from Canada, adopted on 22 February 1982, BISD 29S/91

    An import prohibition was introduced by the United States after Canada seized nineteen fishing vessels and arrested U.S. fishermen fishing for albacore tuna, without authorization from the Canadian government, in waters considered by Canada to be under its jurisdiction. The United States did not recognize this jurisdiction and introduced an import prohibition as a retaliation under the Fishery Conservation and Management Act. The panel found that the import prohibition was contrary to article XI:1 and not justified under either article XI:2 or article XX(g) of the General Agreement.

2. Canada—Measures Affecting Exports of Unprocessed Herring and Salmon, adopted on 22 March 1988, BISD 35S/98

    Under the 1976 Canadian Fisheries Act, Canada maintained regulations prohibiting the exportation or sale for export of certain unprocessed herring and salmon. The United States complained that these measures were inconsistent with General Agreement on Tariffs and Trade article XI. Canada argued that the export restrictions were part of a system of fishery resource management aimed at preserving fish stocks and were therefore justified under article XX(g). The panel found that the measures maintained by Canada were contrary to GATT article XI:1 and not justified under either article XI:2(b) or article XX(g).

3. Thailand—Restrictions on Importation of, and Internal Taxes on, Cigarettes, adopted on 7 November 1990, BISD 37S/200

    Under its 1966 Tobacco Act, Thailand prohibited the importation of cigarettes and other tobacco preparations but authorized the sale of domestic cigarettes; moreover, cigarettes were subject to an excise tax, a business tax, and a municipal tax. The United States complained that the import restrictions were inconsistent with GATT article XI:1 and were not justified by article XI:2(c) or by article XX(b). The United States also requested the panel to find that the internal taxes were inconsistent with GATT article III:2. Thailand argued, inter alia, that the import restrictions were justified under article XX(b) because the government had adopted measures that could only be effective if cigarette imports were prohibited and because chemicals and other additives contained in U.S. cigarettes might make them more harmful than Thai cigarettes. The panel found that the import restrictions were inconsistent with article XI:1 and not justified under article X1:2(c). It further concluded that the import restrictions were not necessary within the meaning of article XX(b). The internal taxes were found to be consistent with article III:2.

4. United States—Restrictions on Imports of Tuna, not adopted, circulated on 3 September 1991, BISD 39S/155

    The Marine Mammal Protection Act required a general prohibition of "taking" (harassment, hunting, capture, killing, or attempt thereof) and importation into the United States of marine mammals, except with explicit authorization. It governed in particular the taking of marine mammals incidental to harvesting yellowfin tuna in the Eastern Tropical Pacific Ocean, an area where dolphins are known to swim above schools of tuna. Under the Marine Mammal Protection Act, the importation of commercial fish or products from fish caught with commercial fishing technology that results in the incidental killing or incidental serious injury of ocean mammals in excess of U.S. standards was prohibited. In particular, the importation of yellowfin tuna harvested with purse-seine nets in the Eastern Tropical Pacific Ocean was prohibited (primary nation embargo)

(continued)

TABLE 2 (continued)

unless the competent U.S. authorities established that (1) the government of the harvesting country has a program regulating taking of marine mammals that is comparable to that of the United States, and (2) the average rate of incidental taking of marine mammals by vessels of the harvesting nation is comparable to the average rate of such taking by U.S. vessels. The average incidental taking rate (in terms of dolphins killed each time the purse-seine nets are set) for that country's tuna fleet must not exceed 1.25 times the average taking rate of U.S. vessels in the same period. Imports of tuna from countries purchasing tuna from a country subject to the primary nation embargo are also prohibited (intermediary nation embargo).

Mexico claimed that the import prohibition on yellowfin tuna and tuna products was inconsistent with articles XI, XIII, and III of GATT. The United States requested the panel to find that the direct embargo was consistent with article III or, in the alternative, was covered by articles XX(b) and XX(g). The United States also argued that the intermediary nation embargo was consistent with article III or, in the alternative, was justified by article XX, paragraphs (b), (d), and (g). The panel found that the import prohibition under the direct and the intermediary embargoes did not constitute internal regulations within the meaning of article III, was inconsistent with article XI:1, and was not justified by article XX, paragraphs (b) and (g). Moreover, the intermediary embargo was not justified under article XX(d).

5. United States—Restrictions on Imports of Tuna (Son of Tuna-Dolphin), not adopted, circulated on 16 June 1994, DS29/R

The European Communities and the Netherlands complained that both the primary and the intermediary nation embargoes, enforced pursuant to the Marine Mammal Protection Act, did not fall under article III, were inconsistent with article XI:1 and were not covered by any exceptions under article XX. The United States considered that the intermediary nation embargo was consistent with GATT since it was covered by article XX, paragraphs (g), (b), and (d) and that the primary nation embargo did not nullify or impair any benefits accruing to the European Communities or the Netherlands since it did not apply to these countries. The panel found that neither the primary nor the intermediary nation embargo was covered under article III, that both were contrary to article XI:1 and not covered by the exceptions in article XX (b), (g), or (d) of GATT.

6. United States—Taxes on Automobiles, not adopted, circulated on 11 October 1994, DS31/R

Three U.S. measures on automobiles were under examination: the luxury tax on automobiles, the gas guzzler tax on automobiles, and the Corporate Average Fuel Economy regulation (CAFE). The Environmental Export Council complained that these measures were inconsistent with GATT article III and could not be justified under article XX(g) or (d). The United States considered that these measures were consistent with the General Agreement. The panel found that both the luxury tax—applied to cars sold for more than $30,000—and the gas guzzler tax—applied to the sale of automobiles attaining less than 22.5 miles per gallon—were consistent with article III:2 of GATT. The CAFE regulation required the average fuel economy for passenger cars manufactured in the United States or sold by any importer not to fall below 27.5 miles per gallon. Companies that are both importers and domestic manufacturers must calculate average fuel economy separately for imported passenger automobiles and for those manufactured domestically. The panel found the CAFE regulation to be inconsistent with GATT article III:4 because the separate foreign fleet accounting discriminated against foreign cars, and the fleet averaging differentiated between imported and domestic cars on the basis of factors relating to control or ownership of producers or importers rather than on the basis of factors directly related to the products as such. Similarly, the panel found that the separate

(continued)

TABLE 2 (continued)

foreign fleet accounting was not justified under article XX(g); it did not make a finding on the consistency of the fleet averaging method with article XX(g). The panel found that the CAFE regulation could not be justified under article XX(d).

7. United States—Standards for Reformulated and Conventional Gasoline, adopted on 20 May 1996, WT/DS2/9 (Appellate Body and panel reports)

Following a 1990 amendment to the Clean Air Act, the Environmental Protection Agency promulgated the Gasoline Rule on the composition and emissions effects of gasoline to reduce air pollution in the United States. From 1 January 1995, the Gasoline Rule permitted only gasoline of a specified cleanliness (reformulated gasoline) to be sold to consumers in the most polluted areas of the country. In the rest of the country, only gasoline no dirtier than that sold in the base year of 1990 (conventional gasoline) could be sold. The Gasoline Rule applied to all U.S. refiners, blenders, and importers of gasoline. It required any domestic refiner in operation for at least six months in 1990 to establish an individual refinery baseline, which represented the quality of gasoline produced by that refiner in 1990. The Environmental Protection Agency also established a statutory baseline intended to reflect average U.S. 1990 gasoline quality. The statutory baseline was assigned to those refiners who were not in operation for at least six months in 1990 and to importers and blenders of gasoline. Compliance with the baselines was measured on an average annual basis. Venezuela and Brazil claimed that the Gasoline Rule was inconsistent, inter alia, with GATT article III and was not covered by article XX. The United States argued that the Gasoline Rule was consistent with article III and, in any event, was justified under the exceptions contained in GATT article XX, paragraphs (b), (g), and (d). The panel found that the Gasoline Rule was inconsistent with article III and could not be justified under article XX, paragraphs (b), (d), or (g). On appeal of the panel's findings on article XX(g), the Appellate Body found that the baseline establishment rules contained in the Gasoline Rule fell within the terms of article XX(g) but failed to meet the requirements of the chapeau of article XX.

SOURCE: Nordström and Vaughan (1992, 81-84).

case conservation of an endangered species, under the condition that its own trade-oriented rules be strictly followed. As important as these findings may be for evaluating the WTO's claim that its dispute settlement system is a model worthy of following in settling environmental issues, we might also look at the method used to conduct inquiries. Under the GATT/WTO Dispute Settlement Understanding, panel proceedings are confidential. People who are neither parties nor third parties to the dispute are not permitted to attend panel proceedings, nor are transcripts made available. Only the panel's final report, or the Appellate Body report, together with some nonconfidential summaries, are publicly released, after the case is over. Moreover, the panelists are selected essentially from Geneva-based officials, ambassadors to the WTO, trade advisers to government trade ministries, or academic specialists in trade law and policy, but never environmentalists, usually from an "indicative list" maintained by the WTO Secretariat. For example, several key decisions on trade and the environment were made by panels chaired by Michael D. Cartland, formerly financial services and economic analysis secretary to the Hong Kong Government and its trade representative to GATT, a person with no environmental background or knowledge. The Appellate Body is staffed by semipermanent members each serving for four years, with the possibility of one reappointment, a process that ensures Geneva insider representation. Access to the dispute settlement system is limited to WTO member governments. Nongovernmental organizations have a limited ability to participate through amici curiae briefs, although panels often refuse to consider the contents. Panels may ask for expert opinions on scientific and technical matters on an ad hoc basis and have broad discretion on whether they follow the advice they get or whether to mention this advice (Stewart and Karpel 2000). In one assessment (Ragosta 2000, 9), there is a "lack of serious democratic controls on the DSB" because the views of ad hoc panelists and Appellate Body members becomes international "law" without effective means for legislative intervention, while in addition, open hearings, open decisions, rights of affected parties to be heard, and many other democratic procedures are absent. Finally, the panel reports on disputed cases are lengthy legal dossiers of several hundreds of pages with long summations of each party's arguments, third party arguments, and expert opinions. Sometimes 20,000 to 40,000 pages of records are involved. The panel findings are similarly lengthy—100 single-spaced pages in the Shrimp-Turtle case. They are phrased in legal and technical language accessible only to lawyers and experts, making public discussion difficult. And this antidemocratic, legalistic, expert-dominated, closed system, the WTO suggests, is ideal for enforcing international environmental agreements!

Conclusion

We might now outline the relationship between two central, yet contradictory, positions in contemporary neoliberalism: trade-led, unregulated economic growth and state regulation of pollution and other environmental impacts of economic growth. Economic growth produces the profits and jobs that in turn provide incomes and consumption for all classes of economic actors. Hence, the forces behind growth are integral to the neoliberal economic process. But growth is also integral to the political process, particularly in the following way: multinational and large national corporations increasingly pay the mounting expenses of media-led political campaigns that elect the leadership of the democratic states of all the advanced capitalist countries. Thus, contemporary neoliberalism is structured by an alliance between the multinational corporations and business, trade, and growth-oriented political parties, whether these be of the Left or Right, and that considerable part of the popular interest concerned about growth and employment. All agree that the Keynesian regulatory policies of post–World War II extended since the 1960s to include environmental regulation, retard the central growth imperative of the capitalist system. Yet the environmental contradictions of unregulated growth have also been produced by powerful environmental movements and concerned public opinion. We propose, therefore, that the political and economic tensions between growth and environmental degradation are relieved through a number of "strategies," a term we use to imply both conscious institutional intention and a less conscious process of searching for a workable answer by

TABLE 3

WORLD TRADE ORGANIZATION (WTO)—THE SHRIMP-TURTLE CASE

United States—Import Prohibition of Certain Shrimp and Shrimp Products, adopted on 6
November 1998, WT/DS58/AB/R (Appellate Body) and WT/DS58/R and RW (panel
reports)

Seven species of sea turtles are currently recognized. Living in subtropical and tropical
areas, they migrate between foraging and nesting grounds. Sea turtles have been
adversely affected by human activity, directly (exploitation of their meat, shells, and
eggs) or indirectly (incidental capture in fisheries, destruction of their habitats, pollution
of the oceans). The U.S. Endangered Species Act of 1973 lists as endangered or threatened five species of sea turtles living in U.S. waters and prohibits their take within the
United States, within the U.S. territorial sea, and in the high seas. Pursuant to the
Endangered Species Act, the United States requires that U.S. shrimp trawlers use turtle
excluder devices in their nets when fishing in areas where there is a significant likelihood
of encountering sea turtles. Section 609 of public law 101-102, enacted in 1989 by the
United States, provides, inter alia, that shrimp harvested with technology that may
adversely affect certain sea turtles may not be imported into the United States unless the
harvesting nation is certified to have a regulatory program and an incidental take rate
comparable to that of the United States or that the particular fishing environment of the
harvesting nation does not pose a threat to sea turtles. In practice, countries having any
of the five species of sea turtles within their jurisdiction, and harvesting shrimp with
mechanical means, must impose on their fishermen requirements comparable to those
borne by U.S. shrimpers, essentially the use of turtle excluder devices at all times, if they
want to be certified and export shrimp products to the United States.

India, Malaysia, Pakistan, and Thailand complained that the prohibition imposed by
the United States on the importation of certain shrimp and shrimp products was contrary to articles I, III, and XI of The General Agreement on Tariffs and Trade (GATT).
In April 1998, a panel set up to examine this claim found that the U.S. measure at stake
was inconsistent with GATT article XI (general elimination of quantitative restrictions)
and could not be justified under GATT article XX (general exceptions) because it constituted "unjustifiable discrimination between countries where the same conditions pre-
vailed." The United States had maintained that section 609 fell within the exception
under article XX(g) of GATT permitting import restrictions relating to the conservation
of an exhaustible natural resources. The United States appealed the panel findings to the
WTO Appellate Body.

In October 1998, the Appellate Body found that the measure at stake qualified for
provisional justification under article XX(g) but failed to meet the requirements of the
chapeau (introductory paragraph) of article XX and therefore was not justified under
article XX of GATT 1994. However, the Appellate Body added that GATT and all other
WTO agreements must be read in light of the preamble to the WTO Agreement, which
endorses sustainable development and environmental protection. In November 1998,
the United States announced that it would comply with the Appellate Body report in a
manner consistent with its firm commitment to the protection of endangered sea turtles.
The United States and the other parties to the dispute reached agreement on a thirteen-
month compliance period, which ended in December 1999.

At the Dispute Settlement Body meeting on 27 January 2000, the United States stated
that it had implemented the Dispute Settlement Body's rulings and recommendations.
The United States noted that it had issued revised guidelines implementing its Shrimp/
Turtle law, which were intended to (1) introduce greater flexibility in considering the
comparability of foreign programs and the U.S. program and (2) elaborate a timetable
and procedures for certification decisions. The United States also noted that it had

(continued)

TABLE 3 (continued)

undertaken and continued to undertake efforts to initiate negotiations with the governments of the Indian Ocean region on the protection of sea turtles in that region. Finally, the United States stated that it offered and continued to offer technical training in the design, construction, installation, and operation of turtle excluder devices to any government that requested this training.

On 12 October 2000, Malaysia (but not the other, original complainants) requested the re-establishment of the original panel to examine whether the United States had in fact complied with the Appellate Body findings, considering that by not lifting the import prohibition and not taking the necessary measures to allow the importation of certain shrimp and shrimp products in an unrestrictive manner, the United States had failed to comply with the recommendations and rulings of the Dispute Settlement Body. The original panel remet to consider these issues. As part of its consideration, the panel received two submissions from nongovernmental organizations: the Earth Justice Legal Defense Fund and the National Wildlife Federation. Malaysia contended that the panel did not have the right to accept, or consider, unsolicited briefs; the United States argued that the panel had the discretion to consider either or both of the submissions from nongovernmental organizations and that the panel should exercise its discretion to consider the National Wildlife Federation submission. At the same time, however, the United States decided to attach the National Wildlife Federation brief to its own submission in this case. The panel concluded that the National Wildlife Federation submission was part of the submissions of the United States in this case and, as a result, was already part of the record.

The United States also argued that the Appellate Body had earlier confirmed that its effective import prohibition was provisionally justified under GATT article XX(g) as a measure relating to the conservation of an exhaustible natural resource but that the Appellate Body report also found that certain specifically identified aspects of the application of the U.S. measure amounted to unjustifiable or arbitrary discrimination under the chapeau of article XX. The United States claimed that the steps it had taken to comply in applying section 609 included revised guidelines that provide more flexibility in decision making, enhanced due process protections for exporting countries, efforts to negotiate a sea turtle conservation agreement in the Indian Ocean region, and enhanced offers of technical assistance. Malaysia argued that the import prohibition contained in section 609, although provisionally justified under GATT article XX(g), was not justified under article XX because it fails to meet the requirements of the chapeau and that it should be removed for the United States to bring the measure into conformity with its obligations under that agreement.

The panel considered that the prohibition fell within the "prohibitions or restrictions, other than duties, taxes or other charges" maintained by a member on the importation of a product from another member and violated article XI:1 of the GATT 1994 but that section 609 of public law 101-162, as implemented by the Revised Guidelines of 8 July 1999, and as applied so far by the U.S. authorities, was justified under article XX of the GATT 1994 as long as conditions, such as ongoing serious good faith efforts to reach a multilateral agreement, remained satisfied. The panel concluded that "the United States has made a prima facie case that Section 609 is now applied in a manner that no longer constitutes a means of unjustifiable and arbitrary discrimination, as identified by the Appellate Body in its Report."

Malaysia may appeal the panel's report to the WTO Appellate Body.

SOURCE: WTO Secretariat Overview of the State-of-play of WTO Disputes (2 May 2001) (see http://docsonline.wto.org/gen); WTO United States—Import Prohibition of Certain Shrimp and Shrimp Products WT/DS58/RW, WT/DS58/23 2001 (see http://www.wto.org/english/ news_e/news01_e/dsb_21nov01_e.htm).

genuinely concerned groups and individuals. The first strategy is the production of conceptual devices employing appealing terms that appear to bridge the impassable divide between growth and environment, as with the notion of "sustainable development." In this term, we suggest, "development" essentially means the economic growth that fuels ever-increasing consumption, the main marker of mass happiness and contentment in neoliberal societies. "Sustainable," we think, has now to be understood ideologically, as the effects that the majority of people can be persuaded to find tolerable, as the necessary environmental consequences of an even more necessary growth process. Sustainability in this sense has a number of meanings that range from keeping growth going using state intervention, through swapping pollution rights in the market, to minimizing pollution effects so that public concern does not result in organized political action (unorganized action can be dismissed as deranged anarchism). The second strategy involves a displacement of regulatory power upward to unelected and only partially responsible global governance institutions. These relieve pressure on nation-states and provide the thin regulatory context for the smooth operation of global capitalism. This regulatory context has to pretend reconciliation between global economic growth and global environmental destruction. Yet all global institutions are now dominated by neoliberal, trade-oriented, growth-based policy regimes. All have therefore learned to turn a sympathetic eye on environmentalism: as Bill Clinton said, "We should be leveling environmental protections up, not down." Here the key phrases are coined by the Rt. Hon. Sir Leon Brittan QC, vice president of the European Commission: broad consensus, a balanced approach, a reasonable way, that places legitimate environmental concerns within trade policy, through an internationally agreed-on approach, with the use of MEAs; or in the single, summarizing term that he revealingly used, "mainstreaming sustainability."

In this mainstreaming process, global governance institutions like the WTO play increasingly significant roles. These involve the production, but more important the enforcement, of a global ideological framework, for membership in the WTO has now become essential for nation-states wishing to participate in the global community. Our examination of the GATT/WTO ideological apparatus reveals a fundamental commitment to trade-induced growth that denies the environmental consequences of growth. This denial is achieved through two main means: by reversing the real position, so that trade-based growth solves, rather than causes, pollution and by appeal to environmental policy regimes established at the national or increasingly the multilateral level (MEAs). We suggest that the "trade solves pollution" position may be undercut by the more compelling argument that trade-induced growth is the main cause of pollution. And we suggest that the appeal to multilateral environmentalism is wishful thinking in that MEAs lack agreement and enforcement governance institutions with anything like the power exerted by the WTO. At this point, we examined the WTO's most audacious strategic gambit, the claim that its dispute settlement system, mainly used to adjudicate internation quarreling over trade matters, provides exactly the required enforcement mechanism for deciding international differences over issues of global environmental regulation. We found the WTO dispute settlement system to be a secretive practice that finds consistently against environmental restrictions on the freedom of trade. Yet again, however, we also suggest that massive opposition to the WTO, particularly at the Seattle ministerial meeting in 1999, may have resulted in the one partial finding for the environment by the WTO's dispute settlement system. On this note, we make the following political conclusion. The contradictions embedded in terms such as "sustainable development" can be employed in the interests of environmental protection through a combination of radical political interpretation and mass political action. In terms of interpretation, the meaning of "sustainable" can be directed through critique of its use by organizations like the WTO toward its radical extreme—zero environmental damage. Likewise, the meaning of "development" can be turned from consumptive growth to the satisfaction of basic human needs. And political action, as we have seen especially since 1999, has to be directed at the new global centers of institutional power, the World Bank, the International Monetary Fund, the WTO, and the World Economic Forum, in massive efforts to make them recognize the more radical meanings of sustainability and to draw public attention to their limited, dangerous usage of terms like this. In such a radical political action, therefore, we need to combine two types of counterforce: the thousands of protestors willing to face systematic violence by the police and military protecting the existing global order and the hundreds of research institutions and nongovernmental organizations dedicated to uncovering the sophisticated lies that global governance organizations persist in telling us.

References

Consortium for International Earth Science Information Network, Environmental Treaties and Resource Indicators, 1992. *The Rio declaration on environment and development*. New York: Consortium for International Earth Science Information Network.

Dunkley, G. 1997. *The free trade adventure: The WTO, the Uruguay Round and globalism*. London: Zed Books.

GATT Secretariat. 1992. Trade and the environment. In *International trade 1990-1991*. Vol. 1. Geneva: General Agreement on Tariffs and Trade.

Harbaugh, W., A. Levinson, and D. Wilson. 2000. Reexamining the empirical evidence for an environmental Kuznetz curve. Working paper no. w7711, NBER, Washington, DC.

Hoekman, B., and M. Kostecki. 1995. *The political economy of the world trading system: From GATT to WTO*. Oxford, UK: Oxford University Press.

Kelsey, J. 1995. *Economic fundamentalism: The New Zealand experiment—A world model for structural adjustment?* London: Pluto.

Loree, Robert F. 1950. *Position of the National Foreign Trade Council with respect to the Havana Charter for an International Trade Organization*. New York: National Foreign Trade Council.

Nordström, Håkan, and Scott Vaughan. 1992. *Trade and environment*. WTO special studies trade and environment number 4. Geneva: World Trade Organization.

Peet, R. 2002. Ideology, discourse and the geography of hegemony: From socialist to neoliberal development in post-apartheid South Africa. *Antipode* 31:1.

Ragosta, J. A. 2000. Unmasking the WTO: Access to the DSB system. Paper presented at the First Fifty Years of the WTO Conference, Georgetown University Law Center, Washington, DC, 20-21 January.

Stern, D. I., and M. S. Common. 2001. Is there an environmental Kuznetz curve for sulfur? *Journal of Environmental Economics and Management* 41:162-78.

Stewart, T. P., and A. A. Karpel. 2000. Review of the dispute settlement understanding: Operation of panels. Paper presented at the First Fifty Years of the WTO Conference, Georgetown University Law Center, Washington, DC, 20-21 January.

Wilcox, C. 1949. *A charter for world trade*. New York: Macmillan.

World Bank. 2001. *World development report*. Washington, DC: World Bank.

World Trade Organization (WTO). 1999. International Institute for Sustainable Development report on the WTO's high-level symposium on trade and environment, Geneva, 15-16 March 1999. Available from http://wto.org/english/tratop_e/envir_e/sumhlenv.htm.

NGOs, Organizational Culture, and Institutional Sustainability

By
DAVID LEWIS

This paper draws on ongoing qualitative research on a sericulture project in Bangladesh to explore the ways in which the concept of organizational culture—which is rarely considered within the analysis of development interventions—can help reveal the complex roots of sustainability problems within multiagency rural development projects. The approach focuses both on local organizational realities and on power in the relationships that link project actors and process with wider systems and structures. It was observed that many of the initial project meanings have gradually fragmented over time, despite the earlier coherence expressed through the formal project culture expressed through documents and other artifacts.

Keywords: sustainability; Bangladesh; development projects; organizational culture; development anthropology

This article draws on data collected within the Bangladesh component of a recent three-country research project on organizational culture and empowerment within multiagency rural development projects, which is currently being written up. The overall objective of the research is to explore the potential relevance of organizational culture in development projects seeking poverty reduction through income generation and empowerment of so-called organizations of the poor.[1] The Bangladesh study has focused on the World Bank's Silk Development Project (hereafter referred to as the silk project), which is a multiagency project comprising a partnership between nongovernmental organizations (NGOs), grassroots organizations, and a not-for-profit foundation designed to provide

David Lewis teaches in the Department of Social Policy at the London School of Economics. He is the author of The Management of Non-Governmental Organizations: An Introduction (2001) and Anthropology, Development and the Post-Modern Challenge (with K. Gardner, 1996).

NOTE: The author wishes to acknowledge and thank M. Shameem Siddiqi for his assistance with the main research project on which much of this article is based.

DOI: 10.1177/0002716203256904

support to the sericulture sector in Bangladesh. The research undertaken was primarily qualitative, based on semistructured interviews, document analysis, and focus group discussions with a wide range of project participants.

The argument presented in this article is that the concept of organizational culture—a frequently neglected aspect of international development projects—can form a useful entry point to the analysis of the workings of development projects. The focus here is on the relationship between organizational culture and sustainability, particularly in relation to the roles of NGOs and grassroots groups within such projects.

The silk project has been successful in many respects, but in recent evaluations, critics have drawn attention to, among other things, problems of sustainability. This article argues that the roots of these sustainability problems can be usefully analyzed through the lens of organizational culture, that they have international as well as local dimensions, and that we should in this analysis be concerned with both material and nonmaterial aspects of sustainability. The organization and activities of the silk project are linked into international markets through the attempt to export silk products by the project actors and into the international aid system through the funding arrangements of involved organizations, which help drive the project itself. At the same time, all such projects need to sustain a level of shared meaning about values and purposes if they are to remain coherent. The focus on organizational culture allows us to explore the ways in which meanings are constructed and contested within development projects and also draws attention to the local and international relationships that form part of these processes.

The article aims to contribute to debates on the general concept of sustainability, which, it is argued, needs to be situated within a wider context and wider processes. Development projects are time-bound interventions with a stated intention of providing lasting benefits for the poor beyond the life of the project. Institutional sustainability in the project setting can usually be seen as having three interrelated levels (Cannon 2002). Financial sustainability refers to a project's ability to generate resources from a variety of sources, which will, over time, reduce its dependency on development assistance funds. Organizational sustainability refers to the capacity of organizational arrangements to continue to provide a framework through which benefits to the poor can be delivered over time. Finally, benefit sustainability refers to the continuing availability or otherwise of benefits such as services beyond the life of the project, even if these are provided from other sources such as the state or the private sector.[2] Each of these levels of sustainability has cultural dimensions, and the idea of sustainability is itself a site of contested meaning among project actors. This approach also aims to serve as a counterweight to continuing tendencies within critical development research—particularly by anthropologists—to conceive of a single dominant development discourse in which developers act on objects of development (see, e.g., Grillo and Stirrat's 1997 critique of Escobar 1995) and to present an overparticularized conception of the relationship between the global as a homogenizing force and the local as a site of resistance (Sivakrishnan and Agrawal 1998).

The discussion presented here draws primarily on material relating to two of the local NGOs involved in the silk project as well as their project relationships. Although NGOs are often conceived as a unitary group of organizations with similar characteristics, in practice, there may be important differences in ideology, scale, approach, and culture.

For example, each of these two NGOs has a contrasting operating style (see note 2). Organization 1 is a local NGO dedicated to the welfare and empowerment of women, run by a charismatic founder who still retains a strong level of control over the organization's decision making and public image. Organization 1 can be characterized as an NGO influenced by a charitable and rather top-down approach. Organization 2, on the other hand, is an organization with its origins in a more political, Freire-influenced analysis of poverty, and organization 2 has no charismatic founder to represent the organization to the outside world. These two NGOs were selected for case studies during the research because they can be seen, at least in general terms, to represent quite well the two different strands of motivation espoused within the Bangladesh NGO sector—the charitable tradition of welfare and "helping the poor" on one hand and the more radical language of the politics of inequality and empowerment on the other (Hulme 1994; Lewis 1997).

Organizational Culture

While organizational culture has been widely discussed within organizational theory and management, it has received far less attention within nongovernmental sector research and wider development studies (Lewis 2002). Simple definitions of organizational culture often refer to "the way we do things around here," "the way we think about things round here," or "the commonly held values and beliefs held within an organization" (Hudson 1999), while Handy (1988) offers a general definition of organizational culture as "the overall 'character' of an organization." At the other, more complex end of the definitional spectrum, the work of Edgar Schein (1985), influenced by social psychology, focuses on the construction and negotiation of values and meanings as expressed through organizational artifacts, motivations, and behaviors. Schein's work shows, for example, how cultural incompatibilities may be at the root of problems experienced when companies attempt to diversify product lines or expand into new markets. Alongside the definitional complexity, organizational culture can also be seen as a particularly difficult subject of research since it cannot easily be isolated as a theme in itself and needs instead to be observed in relation to ongoing events and processes.

A useful starting point for any discussion of organizational culture is Handy's (1988) outline of four general types that can be found to exist, each corresponding loosely with an overall organizational style. First is club culture—in which a charismatic leader sits in the center of an organization, surrounded by a group of like-minded people who work on behalf of the leader, a form arguably common within the NGO sector. This is contrasted with role culture, in which a machinelike structure divides an organization into a collection of clearly defined roles, emphasizing rules and order, such as a Weberian bureaucracy. The third variation is task culture, in which teams of people with combinations of skills are used to address different tasks as necessary, emphasizing plans rather than procedures. The task culture is increasingly found in areas of the private sector where flexible restructuring has been prioritized. Finally, a person culture exists in organizations in which people themselves are seen as the main resource of the organization but serviced only by a minimal structure. An academic department is often cited as an example of the person culture.

The cultural diversity found among NGOs is a fact that often goes unappreciated by policy makers—both governments and donors.

This framework provides the means to analyze organizational culture in general terms, but more detail is needed to capture the cultural dynamics and difference that may exist within and between organizations. Hudson (1999), drawing on Schein's (1985) work, referred to three levels of organizational culture. First are the visible representations, which include buildings, structures, language, and images, such as the NGO with a smart, well-equipped office as compared to the NGO with the broken-down, untidy one. Second is group behavior (which includes the ways people act and react under different circumstances, such as making decisions, dealing with a crisis, or the ways they treat users) or the ways senior managers treat junior managers. Third are the underlying beliefs, which include the values that influence people's behavior, such as a belief in radical empowerment or a belief in more charitable welfare ideas.

For some management writers, the concept of organizational culture has come to be seen simply as a crucial variable, which, if gotten right, can contribute to improved organizational performance. The work of Peters and Waterman (1982), which drew attention to the role of values as the single most important key to management excellence, exemplifies such a view, and the authors identified eight qualities they found to exist in what they considered the best-run companies in the United States. However, many anthropologists—also known of course for their strong interest in the idea of culture—have been critical of the work of management writers in this area. Anthropologists have been wary of a tendency among management writers to oversimplify the idea of culture and posit a straightforward causal relationship between culture and various organizational effects. Instead, anthropological approaches emphasize the negotiated and conflictive manner in which culture is constructed by behaviors within organizations as an ongoing process, not as a set of outcomes. Cultures shift and change, and a range of subcultures may exist, both reflecting and exercising power relations within an organization. As Wright (1994) observed, organizations do not have cultures that can be identified and isolated from other aspects of an organization—instead, organizational cultures *are* and are constantly enacted and recreated as part of an organization's ongoing everyday existence.

First, despite these different approaches to organizational culture, it is clear that both versions of the concept can draw useful attention to the fact that organizations are best seen as sociocultural systems that are embedded in wider social and political environments, a fact that is often neglected in the technocratic worldview often expressed by development planners. Second, the organizational culture concept also suggests that significant events within organizations are often ambiguous and uncertain and that the same events may mean different things to different people. In this sense, organizations are filled with internal contradictions and conflicts and cannot be regarded as either unitary or predictable structures.

The Silk Project

Sericulture is a well-established sector in Bangladesh, but it has long been characterized by top-down bureaucratic interference and has remained relatively uncompetitive in international markets compared with other production centers in China and Thailand (Van Schendel 1995). The sericulture sector in Bangladesh has two separate subsectors: a traditional subsector in which households have been active as silk producers for many generations and a nontraditional subsector—which forms the concern of this article—in which development organizations such as NGOs have promoted sericulture through extension and training to low-income households as a new supplementary income source. For many of Bangladesh's NGOs, sericulture has featured as a particularly attractive element of the portfolio of possible rural, nonfarm, income-generation activities for the poor since it is a high-value commodity that lends itself to small-scale, household-based production. In a society where women's subordinate position in the labor market is widespread, it is also an activity that is relatively gender neutral and that creates a range of employment opportunities for women at different stages of the silk production cycle, from silkworm rearing to silk thread spinning.[3] Part of the attraction for NGOs is that many of Bangladesh's NGOs are themselves currently seeking sources of improved sustainability for their operations as they become less dependent on foreign aid—either by choice or necessity. One option for these organizations is to turn to the market for income, and the sale of locally produced handicrafts and other products has become one possible route to improved NGO financial viability (Stiles 2002).

The silk project was approved with U.S.$11.35 million International Development Assistance (IDA) credit by the World Bank in November 1997 as a five-year project designed to revitalize silk production in Bangladesh. The total cost of the project was U.S.$13 million, with the difference made up by contributions from the government and participating NGOs. The first objective of the project is to assist in increasing the incomes of small-scale silk producers, most of whom are poor women, through introducing improved technology and creating institutional and policy improvements designed to encourage sustainable development of the silk sector. This aim has both an income generation component at the household level and an empowerment element at both an individual and a grassroots group level.

The second objective of the project is to address the institutional, economic, and technical constraints that are affecting silk development in Bangladesh. To shift the silk sector away from a traditional dependence on government-owned parastatal production and marketing agencies, the project created a new autonomous organization, called the Silk Foundation, to provide technical assistance to private-sector and nongovernmental work in the sericulture sector. The Silk Foundation works with nine NGOs that view sericulture as an employment-generation activity for low-income rural people. The target group has been mostly poor women, and these tend to be organized by the NGOs into their own semiautonomous grassroots groups.

The structure of the silk project is set out in simplified form in Figure 1. It is not the purpose of this article to review the structure and performance of the project in detail (further aspects of which can be found in Lewis and Siddiqi 2003); instead, the aim is to discuss issues related to organizational culture that may have wider relevance. The important issue to note for the present argument is that project evaluation reports undertaken in 2001 stated that the project had proved relatively successful in two main areas. First, it has increased silkworm-rearing productivity and provided useful additional income for female producers (see note 3). Second, the evaluation found evidence that the status of women had improved in terms of greater knowledge levels about sericulture, increased local mobility, and improved access to financial resources (Lewis and Siddiqi 2003).

A main area of weakness that was identified by the report related to the government's continuing resistance to the wider restructuring of the silk sector, such that the Silk Foundation was given insufficient access to government-controlled hatcheries to produce high-quality silkworm eggs. Another problem related to the differences in attitudes and practices among the NGOs in relation to certain aspects of the project's strategy. For example, there was found to be a high level of continuing dependence by the grassroots groups on "their" NGOs, which supplied sericulture inputs and then bought back what was produced from the group members, often at fixed, below-market prices. Related to this dependence was a perceived reluctance on the part of the NGOs to follow up on World Bank and Silk Foundation ideas about encouraging group members to form more autonomous business-focused producer associations, which could then increase silk productivity by producing for the wider market. My own fieldwork raised some critical questions about the foundation itself, which was struggling to find sources of funding that could make it sustainable beyond the life of the project, which was to end in 2002. There were also some NGOs that questioned the capacity and effectiveness of the foundation itself in providing relevant support to sericulture producers in the field.

FIGURE 1
A SIMPLIFIED OUTLINE OF THE SILK PROJECT

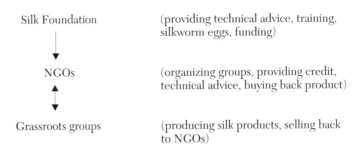

Silk Foundation   (providing technical advice, training,
                                silkworm eggs, funding)

NGOs   (organizing groups, providing credit,
                                technical advice, buying back product)

Grassroots groups   (producing silk products, selling back
                                to NGOs)

The project is one of the current end points of a long history of sericulture policies in both the Indian state of West Bengal and Bangladesh, which Van Schendel (1995) has characterized in terms of "authoritarian developmentalism." This has left production in the region lagging far behind production in other parts of India (such as Karnataka), Thailand, and China in terms of productivity and quality.[4] Various international donors and agencies of different kinds have had a long history of involvement with the promotion of sericulture, from the Salvation Army in the early part of the twentieth century to the Swiss government from the late 1970s. The evolution of a group of so-called silk bureaucrats within the Bangladesh Silk Board combined with the ideas of the international agency experts contributed to the definition of the problem of sericulture and poverty chiefly in technical terms, in need of ever more scientific research and administrative intervention and driven primarily by the availability of external resources and little attention given to "the view from below" (Van Schendel 1995, 181).[5]

Cultural Perspectives on the Project

At the heart of the project's problems as outlined in recent evaluations is the problem of the financial sustainability of the Silk Foundation beyond the life of the project, on one hand, and the unwillingness of the participating NGOs to embrace wholeheartedly the World Bank's vision of the reformulation of NGO grassroots groups into dedicated single-purpose producer groups, on the other hand. Using the analytical lens of organizational culture and drawing on some of the ethnographic data collected during the research, it is possible to explore in more detail how these differences between project actors emerged and why it has proved difficult to build and sustain shared meanings around key project purposes among these actors. These are revealed through the documentation of a range of different narratives constructed by different actors about what is going on.

The project itself is founded on one of the key ideas that remains strong within development discourse: the idea that NGOs have significant inherent advantages over other types of development organizations, which is often expressed in terms of their high level of flexibility and closeness to the community.[6] In this project, silk producers tended to support a view that NGOs presented a different culture than did government. Both NGOs were viewed by group members as having a more accessible culture than local public-sector institutions, such as the Union Parishads, which are the smallest local government units. Such a perception fits into the commonly held view that NGOs tend to be closer to the people than government agencies in Bangladesh, with less rigid bureaucratic structures and fewer status barriers. Group members tended to see NGOs as far more accessible than government:

> There is no comparison. If we want to go to the union, we need to get a middleman first [to bribe]. Here we can just walk in. But of course we still need the union when disputes need to be settled.

But the unitary view of NGOs does not hold for very long. Beyond some very broad generalizations, all NGOs do not share a common culture but display important differences in the ways they work. In this project, there were differences of organizational culture in relation to their overall approaches to decision making and management. These became apparent during discussions with junior staff about the roles of individuals within administrative systems. Organization 2 was found to possess some of the characteristics of a role culture, which allowed systems to operate relatively independently of individuals:

> It is not that we are led by a leader—rather, our systems drive people so even if the managers change, there will be others to implement the systems.

On the other hand, staff within organization 1 seemed reluctant to step outside of clearly circumscribed roles that were linked with particular individuals:

> For policies, we have different people in the administration—they know about policy, so you should talk to them. We do sericulture and if you want to know about that, you will get all the information from us.

There were also different narratives in the project about community development, with some setting it within a notion of market-based sustainability while others placed a stronger emphasis on public social responsibility and welfare. These differences emerged in discussions about the possibility of creating sericulture producer groups. As discussed above, there is a key area of tension within the project concerning the future of the grassroots groups that have been built and supported by the NGOs. In keeping with the market-based or business philosophy espoused by dominant groups at the World Bank, and to a large extent reproduced within the new Silk Foundation, there was an intention to encourage the grassroots groups to evolve over time into autonomous sericulture producer groups or cooperatives.

One of the reasons the NGOs were reluctant to encourage such autonomous, market-based activity by the grassroots groups was that the groups, many of which predate the project, are perceived by the NGOs as multipurpose and developmentally focused rather than merely vehicles for business:

> Our groups are not sericulture groups or apiculture groups or fishing groups or anything else; they are formed for the development of the members as people.

Two of the project actors, the World Bank and the Silk Foundation, are engaged in a struggle to build—impose would perhaps be too strong a word—a single coherent logic of market-based sustainability among the different project actors. This

---

Organizations are filled with internal contradictions and conflicts and cannot be regarded as either unitary or predictable structures.

---

view of the potential of the NGO groups as future producer cooperatives conflicts with the very different set of values brought to the groups formed by the NGOs with a different purpose. But the conflict of views here is not straightforward or clear cut in that some grassroots groups are interested in the idea and some NGO staff themselves at the local level have ideas that run counter to the view of senior NGO staff. Some staff in organization 2 are giving support to a local grassroots group that wishes to explore this option:

> It [the producer association] . . . is seven months old. Now they have twenty-five members, and the savings rate is Tk20 minimum per month. They meet monthly to discuss problems and possible solutions. They set up the association because they think they can do some collective buying of mulberry inputs like fertilizer and other equipment through loans from the association.

A more nuanced view of organizations—often presented in development literature simply as "black boxes"—is therefore needed to reflect different sets of values and cultures that coexist within such organizations.

This is also true within the grassroots groups themselves, which display variations within and between each other. The perceptions of the group members of the organizations of the poor revealed changes in the balance of power within the household, which might be equated with the project's overall aim of empowerment:

> Since we came to the group, we do not have to ask our husbands for money in our hands, and we have something to spend.

Yet within the groups associated with organization 1, there were signs that an authoritarian leadership culture was sometimes present, which ran counter to the norms of democratic decision making (implied by the NGOs' presentation of group dynamics), and this was often resented by other members:

> Look, I am the leader and I have to be responsible for any nonrepayment. . . . If necessary, I apply force to get the money paid back. For example, I say that organization 1 will be forced to take the roof off the house or take away some utensils. People get scared and then they make the repayment any way they can.

At the same time, there was a strong view of the NGO as protector or patron and a reluctance in most cases to see an autonomous future for the groups, either as producer cooperatives or otherwise freestanding entities:

> If the people from the organization are not there, having only money will not be enough. The root of a tree is very important. If organization 1 is not there, it will be hopeless.

This was also reported from organization 2 group members, one of whom remarked, "Organization 2 has looked after us like children, so we cannot leave them."

When the group members were ready to sell their produce, they were heavily circumscribed in terms of their market choices since they were effectively locked into a relationship with the NGO. There were frequently cited criticisms of the style in which these transactions were conducted, with both a lack of transparency and an apparent arbitrariness in relation to calculations and prices:

> Because we take the eggs from organization 1, the condition is that we must give them what we produce. Even if another organization gives a higher price, we cannot sell our gutis to them.

> My husband was offered less than Tk100 by one staff member. Then another staff member said, "Let's not give him so little, let's make it Tk100." Organization 1 don't weigh the produce in front of us; they just give us a lump sum.

Moving from the NGOs and "their" groups to other aspects of the project, it was found that there were aspects of organizational culture that affected the performance of the project. From discussions among NGO staff, it was found that there was a widely held perception that the Silk Foundation was a remote body out of touch with both the NGOs and the grass roots. One staff member commented,

> We appreciate the foundation because we need it to play a coordination role in sericulture. But we'd like it to sit regularly with producers and discuss problems with them.

The foundation is based in Dhaka, in a tower block in one of the city's wealthier neighborhoods, where formal office attire and air-conditioned work spaces contrast starkly with the conditions under which silk producers and NGO field staff normally work. Another NGO staff member reported,

> The foundation people don't know anything about ordinary peoples' culture and conditions. They are educated people, but they don't know anything about the poor.

There were also criticisms made by group members about the attitudes of some of the trainers brought by the Silk Foundation from outside the country to assist local producers in the field, some of whom, it was suggested, did not know how to behave in culturally appropriate ways.

Organizational Culture and the Life of the Project

Returning first to Handy's (1988) framework, it is possible to see the ways in which different NGOs experience a range of organizational cultures within and between them. While role culture is strong in both, it is combined with elements of a club culture within Organization 1 and with a task culture within Organization 2. The cultural diversity found among NGOs is a fact that often goes unappreciated by policy makers—both governments and donors—who may generalize in functional terms about the strengths and weaknesses of NGOs. These organizational, culture-based insights can also draw attention to the ways in which meanings and values are constructed, negotiated, and contested within and between project actors. Organizational culture can be seen as expressed through the visible representation of project buildings and other artifacts, through the group behaviors taking place within and between the different organizational actors involved in the project, and in the different values and beliefs expressed among individual project employees, staff, and clients.

The process of cultural negotiation can be observed in the ways that, while some areas of the project can be seen to agree on common aims and approaches, other areas are characterized by sites of culture-based conflict. One example is the tension around the future of the grassroots groups/producer associations. This partly reflects differences between the market-based development values espoused by the World Bank, which views development success in terms of autonomy judged as market choice as opposed to values that stress broader nonmonetary elements of social solidarity and political relationships that NGOs may themselves favor. Another area of tension is between a culture of patron-clientelism that is evident within some NGO structures and relationships—such as decision-making and leadership norms—and between NGOs and grassroots groups, in the form of a dependent relationship based on services and security. This patron-clientelism is partly reproduced within organizations as part of wider societal norms, and as

Wood (1997) showed, such vertical social relationships are a dominant feature of rural Bangladesh.

These cultural tensions or incompatibilities have profound implications for the sustainability of the project. At the level of financial sustainability, differences in relation to a profit-maximizing versus a social benefit approach to business activities have created a situation in which the financial viability of the Silk Foundation is in doubt once the project period is completed. From the point of view of organizational sustainability, the differences of opinion that exist in relation to the formation of producer cooperatives as opposed to multipurpose, community-based organizations cast doubts on the project's ability to contribute to self-sustaining organizations of the poor, which can continue as a framework for poverty reduction activities and secure income generation through silk production. Finally, in considering the sustainability of project benefits, tensions in relation to cultures of professionalism in relation to the provision of technical assistance to poor silk producers who have tended to stress top-down, hierarchical relationships may have restricted the impact of training in improving technical practices at the grassroots level. These norms of organizational culture cannot be read off as fixed aspects of social interaction but instead are negotiated and reshaped, or even abolished, within certain situations. The focus on organizational culture therefore highlights the interactions between power, agency, and structure. Areas of culture clash are constantly being negotiated, and the fact that one producer association did emerge through the efforts of certain IIRD field staff and group members who shared certain ideas and values that ran against the dominant culture is significant because it shows how outcomes from such interactions are not always predictable. Indeed, these atypicalities may turn out to be sites of potential innovation and creativity as well as tension and fragmentation.

Conclusion

This brief review of organizational culture issues within the silk project in Bangladesh has attempted to show the ways problems of sustainability require an analysis that can take account of both local organizational realities and the relationships that link local relationships into wider systems and structures. A focus on organizational culture, when combined with other areas of organizational analysis into structures and resources, can help to reveal the complex roots of sustainability problems. In the case of the silk project, these can be linked to the project's inability to build a sufficiently coherent and sustained set of meanings among the different individual and organizational actors involved.

The focus on organizational culture is not simply a way of highlighting intraorganizational or interagency structures and processes. It can also provide insights into the link between the micro and macro dimensions of the operation of a development project and the actors who are involved. The tensions within the silk project, which have been briefly explored here, inevitably reflect a number of wider factors—the reproduction of vertical social relationships between people and groups within organizations (such as patron-client ties), the efforts of the World Bank and other international development agencies to reduce the role of the state in the silk sector in line with neoliberal ideologies of privatization, and the efforts of local NGOs to seek ways of reducing their dependence on foreign aid through the generation of income from new sources, such as through efforts at for-profit participation in international export markets.

The tensions around organizational culture and values within the silk project may also provide insights into the ways in which sericulture problems and project solutions are constructed. As in the case of the livestock project in Lesotho (Ferguson 1990) and, closer to home, the aquaculture sector in Bangladesh (Lewis 1998b), the potential of nontraditional sericulture in Bangladesh is presented as a problem that can be solved by a technically conceived project intervention and a process of administrative restructuring. In this case, the construction is not merely one of a technical scientific problem that requires solution by research and bureaucratic intervention, as has traditionally been the case within the "developmentalist" silk sector discussed by Van Schendel (1995). The sector is now also subject to a market ideology that is expected to unlock the potential of sericulture for the benefit of the poor as part of the wider global discourses of neoliberalism. Such ideas of course sit somewhat uneasily among the bureaucratic traditions of many of the individual and organizational actors within the silk project, which are shaped by the earlier top-down traditions, as well as by newer participatory paradigms that have been in vogue among NGOs and that may sometimes bring their own less than flexible orthodoxies. While there are several different approaches to sericulture evident among different participating agencies, the prevailing atmosphere in the project and the nontraditional sericulture sector more widely is mainly one of periodic optimism punctuated by long periods of frustration and disappointment. This can be observed within the project in which initial project meanings have gradually merged or fragmented over time, despite the earlier coherence expressed through the formal project culture expressed through its documents and other artifacts.

Notes

1. The research was commissioned by the World Bank and funded by the Netherlands Ministry for Foreign Affairs. In related publications from this research project (Lewis and Siddiqi 2003; Lewis et al. 2003), the organizational culture of a wider set of agencies within projects located across three study countries (Bangladesh, Ecuador, and Burkina Faso) is considered, as is the organizational culture of the World Bank itself. Long (2001) documented a recognition during the 1990s within the World Bank that its prevailing "approval culture" (i.e., a system of incentives and rewards to staff based primarily on being successful at "moving the money") needed to change in line with its growing stated emphasis on participation but that staff promotion still remained closely linked to financial criteria. My research also bears this out.

2. To preserve anonymity, the actual names of these two local nongovernmental organizations have been changed. This article is concerned with the relationship between organizational culture and forms of institutional sustainability and does not engage with related debates about the issue of environmental sustainability.

3. Silk production involves a complex chain of seven interlinked stages: (1) mulberry sapling preparation at nurseries, (2) mulberry plantation (in land "blocks" or by the roadside), (3) silkworm rearing, (4) cocoon production, (5) silk yarn reeling, (6) weaving silk thread into fabric, and (7) producing garments. Because they

are difficult to produce, eggs (*dim*) are not available on the market but only from the Bangladash Silk Board hatcheries and now also from the Bangladesh Silk Foundation. The nongovernmental organizations buy a quantity of eggs and then pass them on to their producers as part of an overall credit and training package. The eggs cannot be bought by producers individually due to economies of scale involved in production. Once the silkworms hatch, they are fed on mulberry leaves.

4. Recent cooperative sericulture initiatives driven "from below" in West Bengal and showing benefits in terms of increasing the power and visibility of *adhivasi* women (Webster 2002) may constitute an alternative—and potentially more sustainable—trajectory within the ongoing struggle to make sericulture a tool for poverty reduction.

5. There is a striking parallel here with the case of aquaculture in Bangladesh, which has been constructed as a problem in technical terms at the expense of social and economic concerns, and where projects and agencies have operated to construct what Ferguson famously termed an "anti-politics machine" (Lewis 1998b).

6. While it would not be accurate to describe this simply as a myth, there is plenty of evidence to suggest that such advantages are not inherent in any nongovernmental organization and cannot be taken for granted.

References

Cannon, L. 2002. Defining sustainability. In *The Earthscan reader on NGO management*, edited by M. Edwards and A. Fowler. London: Earthscan.

Escobar, A. 1995. *Encountering development: The making and unmaking of the Third World*. Princeton, NJ: Princeton University Press.

Ferguson, J. 1990. *The anti-politics machine: Development, depoliticization and bureaucratic power in Lesotho*. Minneapolis, MN: University of Minnesota Press.

Grillo, R. D., and R. L. Stirrat, eds. 1997. *Discourses of development: Anthropological perspectives*. Oxford, UK: Berg.

Handy, C. 1988. *Understanding voluntary organizations*. Harmondsworth, UK: Penguin.

Hudson, M. 1999. *Managing without profit: The art of managing non-profit organizations*. Harmondsworth, UK: Penguin.

Hulme, D. 1994. NGOs and social development research. In *Rethinking social development: Theory, research and practice*, edited by D. Booth. London: Longman.

Lewis, D. 1997. NGOs and the state in Bangladesh: Donors, development and the discourse of partnership. *The Annals of the American Academy of Political and Social Science* 554:33-45.

———. 1998a. Nonprofit organizations, business and the management of ambiguity: Case studies of "fair trade" from Nepal and Bangladesh. *Nonprofit Management and Leadership* 9 (2): 135-52.

———. 1998b. Partnership as process: Building an institutional ethnography of an inter-agency aquaculture project in Bangladesh. In *Development as process: Concepts and methods for working with complexity*, edited by D. Mosse, J. Farrington, and A. Rew, 99-114. London: Routledge.

———. 2001. *The management of non-governmental development organizations: An introduction*. London: Routledge.

———. 2002. Organization and management in the third sector: Towards a cross-cultural research agenda. *Nonprofit Management and Leadership* 12:4.

Lewis, D., A. J. Bebbington, S. Batterbury, A. Shah, E. Olson, M. S. Siddiqi, and S. Duvall. 2003. Practice, power and meaning: Frameworks for studying organizational culture in multi-agency rural development projects. *Journal of International Development*, 15:1-17.

Lewis, D., and M. S. Siddiqi. 2003. Empowerment, income generation and organizational culture: Making sense of a silk development project in Bangladesh. In *Practical theory, reflective action: Social capital, empowerment strategies and development projects at the World Bank*, edited by A. Bebbington, M. Woolcock, and S. Guggenhiem.

Long, C. 2001. *Participation of the poor in development initiatives: Taking their rightful place*. London: Earthscan.

Peters, T., and R. Waterman. 1982. *In search of excellence: Lessons from America's best-run companies*. New York: Harper and Row.

Schein, E. 1985. *Organizational culture and leadership.* San Francisco: Jossey-Bass.

Sivakrishnan, K., and A. Agrawal. 1998. Regional modernities in stories and practices of development. Conference paper presented at Global and Local Knowledges in Development, Ford Foundation Crossing Borders Initiative, Yale University, New Haven, CT, February.

Stiles, K. 2002. International support for NGOs in Bangladesh: Some unintended consequences. *World Development* 30 (5): 835-46.

Van Schendel, W. 1995. *Reviving a rural industry: Silk producers and officials in India and Bangladesh 1880s to 1980s.* Dhaka, Bangladesh: University Press Limited.

Webster, N. 2002. Local organizations and political space in the forests of West Bengal. In *In the name of the poor: Contesting political space for poverty reduction,* edited by N. Webster and L. Engberg-Pedersen, 233-54. London: Zed Books.

Wood, G. 1997. States without citizens. In *Too close for comfort? NGOs, states and donors,* edited by D. Hulme and M. Edwards. London: Macmillan.

Wright, S., ed. 1994. *Anthropology of organizations.* London: Routledge.

The Paradox of Sustainability: Reflections on NGOs in Bangladesh

By
JOSEPH DEVINE

Drawing on research from Bangladesh, this article questions the dominance of a narrow view of sustainability that rests predominantly on financial considerations. The push for financial sustainability has produced ambiguous results and, more important, has also introduced a degree of uncertainty into the relationship nongovernmental organizations maintain with their members. This article will argue that in the context of Bangladesh, an accurate notion of sustainability rests more on social and political considerations than on economic ones. Fundamental tensions exist between social/political and economic considerations, and paradoxically, the relentless pursuit of one may undermine efforts to establish the other. The article therefore seeks to subject the logic and validity of efforts to promote sustainability among nongovernmental organizations in Bangladesh to theoretical and empirical scrutiny.

Keywords: sustainable development; NGOs; Bangladesh; foreign aid; micro finance; poverty

For more than a decade now, the issue of sustainability has been a subject of fascination for policy makers, social scientists, and development practitioners alike. Not only has sustainability been described as the dominant development challenge of the 1990s (Dichter 1997); it has also been used (albeit cautiously) as a synonym for *development success* (Uphoff, Esman, and Krishna 1998). At the heart of the concern for sustainability lie two quite basic ideas. First, the principle of sustainability repre-

Joseph Devine is a lecturer in international development at the University of Bath, United Kingdom. His main research interest is policy processes in developing countries and their impact on poor communities. He has worked and researched in Bangladesh since 1989 and has also carried out research in India. In his research, he has engaged with a number of substantive policy fields including land, human rights, HIV/AIDS, and coastal management. He is currently the Bangladesh country coordinator for the ESRC Research Group on Wellbeing in Developing Countries (WeD).

NOTE: I am grateful to Dr. Allister McGregor and Mark Ireland at the University of Bath for comments and suggestions that have helped improve this article.

DOI: 10.1177/0002716203257067

sents a certain *rite de passage* for development organizations, a sign that they are serious about breaking out of a charity or welfarist cocoon to embrace a more effective and professional approach to development (Dichter 1997). Second, sustainability is seen as an important ingredient in the attempt to build on and "scale up" development successes (Hulme and Edwards 1997). In development circles, therefore, sustainability is an important issue that carries very high stakes, and its pursuit has left an indelible mark on a host of development organizations, in particular on nongovernmental organizations (NGOs). In the words of one author, NGOs have had to shift from a position where "sustainability was never before a value" (Dichter 1997, 132) to one in which the drive for sustainability overshadows their energies and in some instances displaces their original missions and activities.

This article seeks to provide a critical analysis of the current preoccupation with sustainability. It is based on ongoing research into NGOs in Bangladesh. Specifically, it draws on research from two distinct moments: first, a one-year period of village-based research conducted in 1997 that focused primarily on an NGO working in the northwest of Bangladesh (Devine 1999) and, second, a commissioned review of the role of big NGOs in Bangladesh that was carried out between February and April of 2000 and in which the author was a member of the core research team (Thornton et al. 2000).

In the article, I first offer a brief overview of the NGO sector in Bangladesh, highlighting aspects of its growth and expansion. Then I argue that the quest for sustainability has set in motion a process that has affected NGOs at their organizational and operational levels. I will show that the changes have allowed some NGOs to decrease their level of financial dependence on donors but have forced them to rely much more on resources derived from their members. Following this, the article will move to a micro-level analysis to show, contra Dichter (1997), that NGOs and their members have always valued the notion of sustainability—albeit under a different name. Case studies in the final section will explore how organizational and operational changes affect the quality of the relationship between NGOs and their members.

NGOs in Bangladesh

NGOs in Bangladesh have a particularly high public profile and occupy center stage in the development landscape of the country. Their growth over the years has been exponential in terms of numbers, size, membership, and finances. This growth has occurred in a particular context in which levels of skepticism and mistrust in the public sector have remained stubbornly high and funding levels for government spending have been in decline. NGOs therefore attract public attention and are an obvious focus of discussion in Bangladesh. The reasons they have come to occupy their current position are complex and rooted in the relatively short history of the country (Devine 1999; Davis and McGregor 2000). However, it is possible to identify two interrelated factors that have played a continuous role in determining the development of the NGO sector: first, the persistent influence of

SAGE Publications • 2455 Teller Road, Thousand Oaks, CA 91320 U.S.A. • Telephone: (800) 818-7243 (U.S.) / (805) 499-9774 (Outside of U.S.)
FAX: (800) 583-2665 (U.S.) / (805) 499-0871 (Outside of U.S.) • E-mail: order@sagepub.com • Website: www.sagepub.com

CALL: 800-818-7243   FAX: 800-583-2665   E-MAIL: order@sagepub.com   WEBSITE: sagepub.com

H00786

THE ANNALS OF THE AMERICAN ACADEMY OF POLITICAL AND SOCIAL SCIENCE – PAPERBOUND   *Frequency: 6 Times/Year*

☐ Please start my subscription to The ANNALS of the American Academy of Political and Social Science – Paperbound (J295)

ISSN: 0002-7162

Prices	U.S.A.	Int'l / Canada*
Individuals	☐ $71	☐ $95
Institutions	☐ $454	☐ $478

PAYMENT

☐ Check enclosed. (Payable to SAGE)   ☐ Bill me.

☐ Charge my: ☐ MasterCard ☐ VISA ☐ AmEx ☐ Discover (Phone number required)

Card # _____   Expiration Date _____

Signature _____

Name _____

Address _____

City/State/Zip Code/Country _____

Phone _____   E-mail _____

☐ **Sign me up for SAGE CONTENTS ALERT (please include your e-mail address).**

SAGE Publications • 2455 Teller Road, Thousand Oaks, CA 91320 U.S.A. • Telephone: (800) 818-7243 (U.S.) / (805) 499-9774 (Outside of U.S.)
FAX: (800) 583-2665 (U.S.) / (805) 499-0871 (Outside of U.S.) • E-mail: order@sagepub.com • Website: www.sagepub.com

BUSINESS REPLY MAIL

FIRST-CLASS MAIL   PERMIT NO. 90   THOUSAND OAKS, CA

POSTAGE WILL BE PAID BY ADDRESSEE

SAGE PUBLICATIONS
PO BOX 5084
THOUSAND OAKS CA 91359-9707

NO POSTAGE
NECESSARY
IF MAILED
IN THE
UNITED STATES

foreign aid in the form of resources, ideas, and personnel and, second, the changing nature of state-society relations and specifically the (in)ability of the state to provide sufficient services to a growing population.

The 1990s proved to be a decade in which the growth of the NGO sector in Bangladesh intensified. A number of reasons facilitated this growth. First, there was a marked increase in the level of direct foreign assistance to NGOs. While NGOs received 6 percent of total aid disbursed to Bangladesh in 1990, five years later, this had risen to 17.9 percent and has remained around the 17 percent mark ever since (Thornton et al. 2000). Second, donors have established specific funds with the

For most of the 1990s, NGO funding decisions were heavily influenced by criteria such as efficiency, value added, effectiveness, and output/performance orientations.

sole aim of supporting particular NGO operations. The most significant of these is the Palli Karma Shahayak Foundation, a revolving loan fund that supports micro credit operations. More recent initiatives such as the Social Development Fund and a Human Rights and Governance Fund also offer NGOs new opportunities to secure funding. Finally, NGOs themselves have diversified their resource mobilization strategies by engaging in a wide range of profit-seeking activities. These range from traditional activities such as fisheries projects, fertilizer supply, animal husbandry services, and handicrafts to more recent initiatives in banking, garment manufacturing, retail outlets, telecommunications, and so forth.

The NGO sector in Bangladesh is one of the most sophisticated national development networks in the world. There are in the region of 22,000 NGOs operating in the country, and of these, approximately 1,250 receive foreign assistance. While the overall number of NGOs continues to rise, it is the increase in national NGOs that is particularly striking (see Table 1). To many, 1,000 NGOs may still seem a relatively small number of organizations given the prevalence of poverty and the number of poor people in Bangladesh. However, the number fails to reveal how NGOs have managed to extend their presence throughout the country. Thus, NGOs operate in more than 78 percent of rural villages in Bangladesh (World Bank 1996, 5), and their activities directly benefit 35 percent of the entire population (Thornton et al. 2000). NGOs offer a wide range of services that are fundamental to people's daily struggle to survive. These include credit,[1] education, health, agricultural extension, sanitation, and so forth.

TABLE 1

NONGOVERNMENTAL ORGANIZATIONS (NGOS)
REGISTERED WITH THE NGO AFFAIRS BUREAU

| Year | Number of Development NGOs Registered with NGO Affairs Bureau | | |
	National	International	Total
1990-1991	395	99	494
1991-1992	523	111	634
1992-1993	600	125	725
1993-1994	683	124	807
1994-1995	790	129	919
1995-1996	882	132	1,014
1996-1997	997	135	1,132
1997-1998	1,096	143	1,239
1998-1999	1,215	146	1,361
1999-2000	1,223	147	1,370

SOURCE: NGO Affairs Bureau, Government of Bangladesh.

NGOs and Sustainability—A Macro Analysis

The overview of NGO growth and expansion, however, conceals what is arguably the most defining aspect of the NGO sector in Bangladesh today. With the introduction of large-scale donor support at the start of the 1990s, an elite group of NGOs have moved into a league of their own in terms of size, budgets, and staffing. Of the 1,250 NGOs receiving foreign assistance in 1999-2000, eleven of the biggest organizations[2] received 85 percent of donor assistance to all NGOs. Even within this group of big NGOs, however, there were important disparities. Thus, while the top three NGOs[3] accounted for 85 percent of the total share allocated to the eleven big NGOs, the bottom five of the same group shared slightly less than 5 percent. In other words, the three biggest NGOs controlled more than 72 percent of the total funds available to all NGOs in Bangladesh. The pattern of favoring bigger NGOs intensified throughout the 1990s,[4] and this has had far-reaching consequences for the entire NGO sector. Disparities among NGOs are increasing, with smaller organizations being forced to compete for a diminishing slice of donor funds by acting as subcontractors (not always on favorable terms) to the bigger NGOs.

The role of donors[5] has been crucial in the whole process of encouraging NGO expansion and engineering the growth of a very small number of elite NGOs. These outcomes respond to a number of demands placed on donors, including the desire to scale up successful development operations, reduce burdensome transaction costs, decrease NGO reliance on donor money, and initiate a process that would secure financial sustainability. In pursuing these goals, however, donors have wanted to retain maximum influence over NGO outputs and performance. Thus, for most of the 1990s, NGO funding decisions were heavily influenced by

criteria such as efficiency, value added, effectiveness, and output/performance orientations. At the same time, continued donor support was premised partly on the
ability of an NGO to offer a credible story on how it intends to secure longer-term
survival. In the vast majority of cases, NGOs in Bangladesh have responded to the
donor demand for sustainability by introducing strict micro credit programs.

At one level, then, the issue of sustainability can be perceived simply as a donor-
driven, rational exercise to promote greater organizational maturity and efficiency.
In Bangladesh, however, the issue of sustainability has also acquired a more politicized, almost nationalist character because NGOs have used it to rebut the emo-
tionally charged criticism that they are puppets of the donor (Western) community.
The search for sustainability therefore assumes a particular form in Bangladesh, a
form in which honor and pride also come into play. Competition over the issue of
sustainability has intensified among NGOs. As one donor representative put it,

> NGOs are very vain organizations. They always want to be the first or the best, and that
> means downplaying the achievements of others. The new competition is all about
> sustainability. If one NGO claims to be sustainable, other NGOs will soon be disputing the
> claim. Usually this means showing that NGO is simply making up the claim, telling only
> part of the truth or stealing from its members to become autonomous.

There is, however, another level of analysis at which the logic of sustainability has to
be explored. The concern here, not in any way peculiar to Bangladesh, is whether
the quest for sustainability forces NGOs to radically alter their missions and values.
Thus, in Bangladesh, commentators such as Feldman (cited in Stiles 2002, 838)
have argued that NGOs have undergone a profound transformation in which their
original objectives of mobilizing and empowering the poor have been replaced by a
much narrower concern with securing funds that enable organizational growth.
The drive for sustainability, therefore, has inverted priorities, with the result that
NGOs have become inward looking and anxious more about their own survival
than about the long-term security of their members.

A useful starting point for exploring Feldman's (cited in Stiles 2002) statement is
to look at NGO income-expenditure flows. Table 2 provides an overview of the
combined expenditure of the eleven big NGOs from 1989 to 1999. What is immediately apparent is that the overall combined expenditure has increased during the
ten years, and this resonates quite considerably with statements made earlier
regarding NGO expansion. While in 1989-1990, the big NGOs spent TK1,097 million,[6] by 1998-1999, that figure had risen tenfold to TK11,287 million. If we then
consider the different activities, we see that the most significant single expenditure
increase has occurred with economic programs (mostly the provision of micro
financial services and related technical assistance, training, and so forth). This is
again consistent with earlier statements that most NGOs have introduced micro
credit regimes to generate the local funds required to sustain their operations.
However, what the table also clearly shows is that the total expenditure on social
programs (mostly mobilization and social services) remained high during the ten
years, increasing by a factor of slightly less than seven. This is surprising and runs

TABLE 2
COMBINED EXPENDITURE OF ELEVEN
BIG NONGOVERNMENTAL ORGANIZATIONS

	1989-1990		1994-1995		1998-1999	
Expenditure	Taka (millions)	%	Taka (millions)	%	Taka (millions)	%
Social mobilization	122	11	321	8	696	6
Social services	360	33	1,051	27	2,486	22
Economic: micro finance and loans	317	29	1,200	31	4,279	38
Economic: technical support	298	27	1,326	34	3,826	34
Total	1,097	100	3,898	100	11,287	100

SOURCE: Thornton et al. (2000).

counter to Feldman's argument. Indeed, since NGOs have managed to increase their spending across the whole range of services they offer, it may be argued that they have not fundamentally altered their development priorities but simply strengthened those activities where they were less experienced (i.e., micro credit).

This general overview of aggregate figures, however, begins to sharpen considerably when we look at individual expenditures as a proportion of total expenditures. Thus, in 1989, social programs accounted for 44 percent of all NGO expenditure, while in 1999, the same activities accounted for only 28 percent. This represents a significant decrease and implies an equally significant shift in policy direction and programs. In contrast, the proportion of expenditure on economic programs rose from 56 percent to 72 percent during the same period of time. Thus, Feldman's (cited in Stiles 2002) suggestion of a change in programmatic choices seems to have some credence, and the indications are that the direction of the change is one in which the emphasis on social programs has been replaced by an emphasis on economic programs.

Table 3 provides data on the income sources of the same NGOs during the same period. The first point to notice is that overall donor funds for the big NGOs increased almost fourfold during the ten years, and again, this is in line with the strategy of supporting the expansion of the NGO sector. However, donor funding has not been the primary source for the total increase in NGO expenditure. Thus, in 1989, donor funds accounted for 94 percent of all NGO funding sources, but by 1999, that figure had decreased to 35 percent. The additional funds required to keep the organizations in operation were generated locally via a combination of capital funds from loans, member savings, and service charges. In 1999, locally generated revenue constituted 65 percent of total NGO incomes, while in 1989, they constituted a mere 6 percent. Of all the local income sources, the most significant increase has been the contribution from service charges that moved from 5 percent in 1989 to 31 percent in 1999. Service charges refer mostly to revenue attached to micro credit operations. Not only do NGOs spend more on economic programs, as Feldman (cited in Stiles 2002) argued, but they are also more

TABLE 3
COMBINED INCOME SOURCES OF
ELEVEN BIG NONGOVERNMENTAL ORGANIZATIONS

	1989-1990		1994-1995		1998-1999	
Income Source	Taka (millions)	%	Taka (millions)	%	Taka (millions)	%
Donor grants	1,032	94	2,853	73	3,903	35
Service charges, bank interests, own resources	48	5	640	16	3,510	31
Members savings	5	0	111	3	1,328	12
Bank and other borrowings	12	1	294	8	2,546	22
Total	1,097	100	3,898	100	11,287	100

SOURCE: Thornton et al. (2000).

dependent on these same programs to secure a sufficient flow of funds for their own survival.

Based on the discussion thus far, two interrelated conclusions can be tentatively drawn. First, the issues of sustainability and self-reliance have affected NGO programmatic priorities. During the past decade, economic programs (micro finance) have been prioritized over and above other traditional NGO activities such as social programs. The institutional implications of this shift in emphasis are far reaching. Stiles (2002), for example, has argued that micro credit activities not only absorb the vast proportion of NGO staff time, efforts, and energies but also require the recruitment of more qualified, technically competent, and professional staff. At the field level too, NGO employees and members have assimilated the change in priorities. In 2000, when visiting *samities*[7] of an NGO, both members and local staff routinely referred to their weekly meetings as "collection meetings." Interestingly, I had spent some time with these samities in 1997, and then they used to mock the weekly meetings of another big NGO for being interested only in giving and taking loans while championing their own meetings as dealing with issues that really matter to the poor.

Second, there is evidence that some of the organizational revenue objectives of the economic programs have been met. Revenue from micro credit operations has allowed some of the big NGOs to reduce their level of dependence on donor funds. The irony, however, is that to facilitate their autonomy, NGOs have had to depend more on contributions from their members. Service charges and member savings together constitute 43 percent of income sources for the big NGOs, that is, 7 percent more than the amount received via donor grants. The economic programs of NGOs therefore play an ambiguous role: on one hand, they help NGOs address the challenge of becoming self-reliant and less dependent on donors, and on the other hand, they put the onus of organizational sustainability on those who are meant to benefit most from the same organizations. This would not be such a bad outcome if it (1) meant that the poor gained fuller ownership of the NGOs and (2) produced greater and more sustainable gains for the poor. The jury, however, is still very much out on both counts.

Sustainability and the Poor—A Micro Analysis

The renaming of samity meetings as "collection meetings" not only reflects a shift in NGO operational emphasis but indicates a more profound change in the type and quality of relationship between NGOs and their members.

The notion of relationships is fundamental to understanding the complex dynamics of poverty and its reproduction in Bangladesh. For poor people, the ability to access and make use of effective relationships constitutes an important social resource in their struggle to maintain or improve their livelihoods. These relationships are embedded in various connections and networks that include household members (Cain 1979), kinship (Indra and Buchignani 1997), community members (Bertocci 1970), mafia-style gangs (Khan 2000), and more distant elite or influential actors (Wood 1994). In resource-scarce contexts such as Bangladesh, competition to access goods and services is fierce (Jansen 1987). Relationships, alliances, and networks are the most common (and often only) mechanisms through which poor people can stake a credible claim on resources. The obverse of what has been stated is also true. Thus, poor people with weak, dysfunctional, or ineffective relationships find themselves in a particularly vulnerable position. This general statement is what is inferred in the distinction people in Bangladesh make between *amar keu ache* (I have someone) and *amar keu ney* (I have no one), with the latter being used to denote a more profound sense of helplessness, risk, and vulnerability (Devine 1999).

Historically in Bangladesh, the patron-client linkage—a system of organization where vertical relations across class lines are forged between elite patrons and clients—has been the most effective mechanism in the competition for resources (Wood 1994). The patron-client linkage functions around the satisfaction of demands and expectations of those involved in the relationship. Normally, this takes the form of patrons offering material aid, protection, and advice in return for political allegiance, support, and loyalty. The relation has been described as a moral or benevolent one because of the perceived advantages and the ensuing obligations and commitments it imposes.

In Bangladesh, the welfare credentials of the patron-client relation, however, are ambiguous and contradictory. If patrons and clients are tied in some so-called moral social order (Maloney 1988, 7), it is ultimately an order in which the superior rank and status of the patron is assumed and reinforced. If the relationship implies loyalty and reciprocity, it does so in such a way that clients have to do what is necessary to maintain the goodwill and grace of patrons. Thus, while clients use loyalty to appeal to their patrons' favor, relatively privileged patrons use their clients' loyalty to demonstrate and strengthen their political clout. Finally, if the relationship is intended to benefit all those involved, it does so on very unequal terms. For patrons, a strong and loyal client base offers an opportunity to increase personal wealth and social standing; for clients, the best that can be hoped for is that some of their patrons' success trickles down to them in the form of privileged access to resources or goods. A great deal therefore hinges on the type and quality of relationship forged between patrons and clients. An effective relationship can help alleviate poverty; an ineffective one can lead to worsening poverty and oppression. The relation between patron-client linkages and the dynamics of poverty in Bangladesh is captured nicely by Maloney (1988), who, while reflecting on the definition of poverty, noted that

> [What] a Bangladeshi means by the word is to set up a *relationship* of inequality between himself and the person addressed in anticipation of possible patronage, or at least in a statement of the moral social order which he needs to make *his relationships function*. (P. 7, emphasis added)

Making relationships function, therefore, becomes a condition for survival and security, the antithesis of amar keu ney (I have no one).

Early studies (Bertocci 1970; Wood 1994; Jahangir 1979; Jansen 1987) into rural poverty in Bangladesh identified a range of key actors who operated as patrons to the poor. These included moneylenders, landlords, employers, political leaders, and local bureaucrats. The same studies acknowledged that a significant part of the "development predicament" of the poor was that their relationships to key patrons were overexploitative and represented a form of class domination in which the opportunities for mass movement among the poor were stifled. Studies like these had a huge influence on the early formation of NGOs.

To combat the politics of class domination embedded in the patron-client linkage, many of the first NGOs began with radical agendas of pursuing a more open politics of class struggle. Conscientization, solidarity, and mobilization were the principles chosen to drive this agenda. In elaborating their goals, NGOs followed a dual strategy. First, they contributed to ongoing analyses into the significance of patronage in reproducing rural poverty and dominating the poor (Bangladesh Rural Advancement Committee 1983). Second, they presented themselves as poor-friendly organizations capable of freeing the poor from their oppressive relationships. What was less clear in this strategy was how this change would occur. Initially, there was some hope (and some evidence) that with the arrival of organizations such as NGOs, a class-based revolution of sorts was imminent (Jahangir 1979). However, this proved to be an overoptimistic analysis. Another approach explored the idea that the patron-client relation was far more resistant to change (McGregor 1994) and indeed was more likely to accommodate and adjust to the arrival of new organizations such as development NGOs (Devine 1999). Rather than herald the disappearance of patron-client relations, NGOs came to be seen in this perspective as new patrons, and the hope was that they would also turn out to be better patrons offering a quality of relationship that was a real improvement on the traditional patron-client linkage.

Sustainability and Loyalty

Success for the first NGOs in Bangladesh implied having a strong membership base, and this in turn presumed that they could convince enough poor people to shift their loyalty and allegiance from traditional patrons to the organization. Two main factors helped NGOs secure a strong membership base. First, they had increasing access to material goods, services, and resources and were able to ensure the delivery of these to poor people. Second, they were able to demonstrate that they could function as reliable and trustworthy patrons. This second factor is as important as the first because the risk entailed in changing patrons is very serious and the decision to become an NGO member is far more complex than simply signing up and attending meetings (Devine 1999, 2002). Anyone contemplating a shift in patron allegiance becomes exposed to a number of scenarios including the possibility that the new patron might be ineffective, the old patron may take revenge, or they may end up being patronless. Each of these scenarios implies considerable risk and uncertainty for poor people seeking to establish reliable livelihood options. In their early years, then, NGOs' success depended on their ability to convince poor people that it was in their interest to shift their loyalties to the organization and that by doing so, their livelihood options would be strengthened rather than jeopardized.

Dichter's (1997) statement that for NGOs, "sustainability was never before a value" (p. 132) seems, therefore, to be inaccurate. Indeed, one may argue that sustainability was not only a value for NGOs but the sine qua non of their very success. Even before the term *sustainability* was in vogue, NGOs had already understood that their long-term success was intrinsically tied up with their ability to establish sustainable relations with their members. Loyalty and solidarity (in place of sustainability) were paramount to this endeavor. This meant that NGOs and their members were committed to a relation of continued interdependence and solidarity that could be relied on during a long period of time. Sustainability in this perspective is different from current ideas that underpin the drive for sustainability. It is a broader notion that rests more on social and political considerations (articulated in loyalty and allegiance) than financial ones. Also, its focus is more outward looking emphasizing reciprocity and the relation between NGOs and members. This contrasts with the current notion of sustainability that focuses almost exclusively on the fortunes of only one party of the relation.

Throughout the period when NGOs have looked to reinforce their expansion and growth via the introduction of strict credit regimes, a number of disconcerting observations about the relationship between NGOs and their members have come to the fore. These include statements about NGOs engaged in turf wars (Devine 1999), NGOs purging members with poor repayment records (McGregor 1998), NGOs applying extreme pressure on loanees and threatening to take assets such as roofing materials as security on loans (Thornton et al. 2000), and NGOs pressuring staff to establish specified numbers of new credit groups within a given time frame (Fernando 1997). That these incidents have occurred as NGOs have changed the focus of their operations is no coincidence. Instead, they can be seen as surface-level signs of deeper changes occurring to the type and quality of relationship between NGOs and their members.

In an important piece of research, Fernando (1997) offered crucial insights into how the shift in NGO operations unfolds at the village level. The NGOs he was observing had all changed the focus of their activities, with micro credit programs prioritized at the expense of other social development activities. The pressure on local staff to establish new groups and impose credit discipline on older ones was such that they were forced to seek the support and protection of village local elites. Choosing to establish samities in this way is a shrewd decision for it shortcuts the

Not only do NGOs spend more on economic programs, . . . but they are also more dependent on these same programs to secure a sufficient flow of funds for their own survival.

lengthy and staff-intensive process of nurturing loyalty and solidarity among prospective samity members. More significantly, it is also a rational and justified decision because loyalty and solidarity are not considered as important for savings and credit programs as they might have been for traditional NGO samities. Successful credit regimes emphasize self and group discipline rather than loyalty and focus more on the individual borrower as opposed to the group as a single solidarity. It is not surprising, then, to discover that NGOs now set up new samities in a matter of days and that local elites help fast track the whole process. The significance of local elites should not be underestimated. First, they act as intermediaries brokering NGO access to village or community members. Second, they help identify reliable and trustworthy new members. Finally, their support is important in seeking to impose credit discipline especially in cases where members default on payments. There are risks involved in this process (and these will not surprise anyone!), namely, that elites take local control over the new samities[5] and gradually over other NGO activities and decisions.

The potential convergence of elite and NGO interests is, however, not the only consequence that needs to be considered. When comparing the credit provision of NGOs and other traditional sources such as moneylenders, Fernando (1997) discovered that although NGOs offered comparatively small amounts of credit, the discipline they demanded was much greater and far stricter. This was found to be a cause of major concern for NGO members. While they prioritized "the flexibility of [the] loan repayment and the additional benefits that accrue from various sources of borrowing" (Fernando 1997, 172), NGOs were more interested in imposing a discipline that would render the credit program more efficient and profitable. Ironically, Fernando found that villagers considered moneylenders (traditionally cast by NGOs in the role of cruel oppressors of the poor) "to be *more flexible* with respect to negotiating the terms and conditions of loans, and *they are more responsive to the needs of the people*" (p. 172, emphasis added). For years, NGOs have built up reputations as credible organizations that, unlike traditional patrons, would stand by the poor in times of need. Fernando's observations, however, suggest a dramatic role reversal, with traditional patrons now being considered more flexible and responsive to the needs of the poor. This goes to the very heart of the NGO-member relationship and reminds us that in terms of livelihoods, what is uppermost in poor people's considerations is not money, goods, or services per se but the quality of the relationship they can establish with the source of these goods and services (McGregor 1999). This is the essence of the moral order that is so vital to poor people in their struggle against poverty and uncertainty.

The growing tension in NGO-member relationships is most evident in contestations over the obligations, rights, and responsibilities that each party perceives to be important. In the following case, the actions of a particular NGO lead members to question the moral order that links them.

In 1997, while carrying out fieldwork, I heard of a particular incident involving one of the country's most prominent NGOs. The incident can be summarily reconstructed in these terms:

> The NGO in question had provided loans to some of its samities and sought repayment on these. While most of the samities repaid their loans on time, the majority of members in a particular samity failed to repay in full. Initially, NGO staff sought to redress the situation by encouraging the other samities to apply peer pressure on the defaulting members. When this failed, the NGO decided to initiate legal proceedings against the defaulting members. As a result of this, the local police were called in, and some of the defaulters were arrested. Unfortunately, on the way to the police station, the vehicle carrying the police and the defaulters was involved in a road accident, and some of the members died in the accident. This provoked the anger of local people including other samity members. A group gathered around the scene of the accident and marched from there toward the NGO office shouting anti-NGO slogans and inciting more and more people to join them. By the time they arrived at the office, the protesting group had grown considerably. In their anger, they targeted the NGO office and completely destroyed the building. The NGO staff had already fled, and no one (including the samity members) tried to either stop the procession or protect the property of the NGO.

Given that the incident had received widespread coverage in the national press, I used it in various discussions to explore the dynamics of NGO-member relations. In discussions with NGO and donor leaders, two forms of explanation were emphasized. First, the procession had been provoked by a number of local elites who used the accident to settle old scores with the NGO. Second, in seeking repayment on a loan, the NGO had acted justly and legitimately. Indeed, if the NGO had not taken action, there was a risk that other samities would follow the example of the defaulters and try to avoid repaying. One NGO leader put it this way: "our country is full of loan defaulters, and this only encourages corruption, nepotism, and indiscipline. We NGOs believe in a different system." In both explanations, the NGO is acquitted of any serious responsibility, and its actions represented as reasonable and legitimate.

The poor . . . have been the primary benefactors in the initiative to secure NGO sustainability. It is not clear whether they have been the primary beneficiaries.

These explanations contrast significantly with discussions I had with NGO members in the village where I was carrying out my fieldwork. When asked to comment on the incident, one of the NGO members replied,

> Of course the poor were wrong (*bhul koreche*) in destroying property in that way, and of course the local touts have taken advantage of the situation to tell the poor that the NGO worked against rather than in favor of their well-being. But even if the poor were wrong or if they were wrongly influenced, they did not act unjustly (*onnay koren ni*). If our NGO here tried to put that kind of pressure on us to repay loans, I am sure many of us would do the same. NGOs are not supposed to be banks or touts, and yet most of them are only interested in collecting money and giving out loans. They are becoming worse than banks or touts. When that happens, poor people won't care about the NGO and will start leaving the samities because they are looking for something else besides loans.

This second explanation helps clarify and summarizes some of the points raised in this article. The distinction between acting wrongly (bhul) and unjustly (onnay) reinforces the significance of the perceived moral content of the NGO-member relationship. The understanding that between NGOs and members there exists some form of moral order enables the NGO member to accuse the NGO of reneging on their side of the bargain. In contrast, the NGO leader who considered the actions of the NGO legitimate speaks from within a different order where the link between successfully managed credit programs and organizational sustainability is stressed.

The most important source of tension in the NGO-member relation is not that credit programs have come to occupy the center of the relationship but that the social and moral contents of the same relationship have been squeezed out. A reliable supply of credit has always been an integral part of poor people's attempts to secure a better livelihood and quality of life. While NGOs are a vital source of credit in Bangladesh, other traditional sources offer more money and at more favorable terms.[9] There is no shortage, therefore, of credit sources for the poor (although most remain highly exploitative), but there is a continued need for the type of relationship that poor people can rely on and turn to when in need. The current development obsession with a very limited notion of financial sustainability constitutes a major threat to the NGO-member relationship because it encourages NGOs to introduce new terms of reference to the relationship with their members. Indications are that these new terms of reference fall far short of what poor people expect from and value in NGOs. If this is the case, there is very little reason why members should not look for alternative solidarities where they can expect more relevant returns on their loyalty.

Conclusion

As is the case with many development initiatives, the promotion of NGO sustainability has been presented as a rational and unproblematic exercise. However, when one examines in detail the context in which the drive for sustainability occurs, the story that emerges is more complex. In Bangladesh, the current quest for NGO sustainability follows a very narrow route that focuses almost exclusively on financial considerations. The consequence of this has been that almost all NGOs have introduced strict micro credit regimes with a view to generating the resources required to attain self-sufficiency.

The analysis presented in this article indicates that the current preoccupation with NGO sustainability is limited and ambiguous in a number of respects. First, to manage the credit programs that generate local revenue, NGOs have had to introduce a number of organizational and operational changes. The most important of these is that economic programs have been prioritized over and above social programs. Within the NGO sector, these changes in policy emphasis have been as radical as they have been pervasive. The question that has not been explored is whether these changes help NGOs tackle poverty in a better way. Given what is known about the dynamics of poverty in Bangladesh, the deprioritization of social programs has to be initially seen as a deeply worrying development.

Second, the pursuit of sustainability appears to have been partially successful as some NGOs (those privileged with significant donor support) have managed to reach a position where (1) they are less reliant on donor funds and (2) they have developed diverse resource-mobilization strategies. However, to attain this relatively successful position, NGOs have had to secure and extract local revenue. The main source of this local revenue has been NGO members. The poor therefore have been the primary benefactors in the initiative to secure NGO sustainability. It is not clear whether they have been the primary beneficiaries.

Finally, the emphasis on sustainability has meant that attention has focused almost entirely on NGOs and their longer-term security. This article has argued instead that there is an alternative way of thinking about sustainability in which poor people are placed more at the center of attention. For poor people in Bangladesh, sustainability is ultimately about securing a stable livelihood. NGOs have successfully entered this equation as an important resource or ally of the poor. The relationship between NGOs and members was built not only on expectations around materialistic exchanges but also on an ethic that stressed a sense of belonging, solidarity, and loyalty. These normative or moral dimensions of the relationship were and continue to be considered important in the daily struggle against poverty. However, the introduction of strict credit regimes that derive directly from the logic of sustainability has undermined the moral content of the NGO-member relationship. The ultimate paradox of this is that the mechanisms (micro credit operations) around which NGOs are constructing their longer-term survival and expansion demand a type and quality of relationship that actually limits poor people's room to maneuver.

The limits and ambiguities identified here are not as yet foregone conclusions in Bangladesh. However, there are already signs that the outcome of the attempt to secure organizational sustainability will have profound implications for the overall fight against poverty and inequality. One central lesson can be drawn from this article: it is crucial that the endeavor to secure organizational sustainability be built more around the needs of the poor than the organizations themselves. To have any chance of achieving this, it will be necessary at a minimum to pay far more attention to how general strategies and principles are played out in local, specific contexts. Right now in Bangladesh, this requires a closer assessment of whether the current direction of NGO growth and expansion is helping NGOs play a role as friends and allies of the poor.

Notes

1. By 1995, the amount of rural credit disbursed by nongovernmental organizations (NGOs) accounted for approximately 65 percent of the total formal rural credit (including government and national banks) disbursed in Bangladesh (World Bank 1996, 12).

2. The use of the word *biggest* is taken from the title of the research carried out by Thornton et al. (2000). Eleven NGOs were selected for the study on the basis of their membership base, number of staff, and significance in national policy debate. All the organizations were national NGOs.

3. Bangladesh Rural Advancement Committee, PROSHIKA, and Association for Social Advancement.

4. For example, in 1992, thirty of the largest NGOs received 80 percent of total funds to NGOs, 60 percent of which was controlled by the largest eight of those NGOs (World Bank 1996, 45).

5. There is significant heterogeneity among donors, and I use the term here to refer mostly to official donors.

6. Taka is the local currency in Bangladesh. TK40 = U.S.$1.

7. *Samity* is the common term used to describe small NGO member groups.

8. For example, seven of twelve NGO leaders in Fernando's (1997) study came from families who were known moneylenders (p. 169). The term *local control* is deliberate as it may be the case that what happens locally may be unknown to staff and leaders centrally.

9. Fernando (1997) claimed that households received only 10 percent of their credit from NGOs (p. 170). This is broadly consistent with McGregor's (1994) statement that "as much as 70 percent of informal lending is reported as being between friends, neighbours and relations" (pp. 269-70).

References

Bangladesh Rural Advancement Committee. 1983. *The net: Power structure in ten villages*. Dhaka: Bangladesh Rural Advancement Committee.

Bertocci, P. J. 1970. Elusive villages: Social structure and community organization in rural East Pakistan. Ph.D. thesis, Michigan State University.

Cain, M. 1979. The economic activities of children in a village in Bangladesh. *Population and Development Review* 3:201-27.

Davis, P., and J. A. McGregor. 2000. Civil society, international donors and poverty in Bangladesh. *Commonwealth & Comparative Politics* 38 (1): 47-646.

Devine, J. 1999. One foot in each boat: The macro politics and micro sociology of NGOs in Bangladesh. Ph.D. thesis, University of Bath, UK.

———. 2002. Ethnography of a policy process: A case study of land redistribution in Bangladesh. *Public Administration and Development* 22:403-22.

Dichter, T. 1997. Appeasing the gods of sustainability: The future of international NGOs in microfinance. In *NGOs, states and donors: Too close for comfort*, edited by D. Hulme and M. Edwards, 128-39. Hampshire, UK: Macmillan.

Fernando, J. L. 1997. Nongovernmental organizations, micro-credit, and empowerment of women. *Annals of the American Academy of Political and Social Science* 554:150-77.

Hulme, D., and M. Edwards. 1997. NGOs, states and donors: An overview. In *NGOs, states and donors: Too close for comfort*, edited by D. Hulme and M. Edwards, 3-22. Hampshire, UK: Macmillan.

Indra, D. M., and N. Buchignani. 1997. Rural landlessness, extended entitlements and inter-household relations in South Asia: A Bangladesh case. *Journal of Peasant Studies* 24:25-64.

Jahangir, B. K. 1979. *Differentiation, polarisation and confrontation in rural Bangladesh*. Dhaka, Bangladesh: CSS.

Jansen, E. G. 1987. *Rural Bangladesh: Competition for scarce resources*. Dhaka, Bangladesh: University Press Limited.

Khan, I. 2000. Struggle for survival: Networks and relationships in a Bangladesh slum. Ph.D. thesis, University of Bath, UK.

Maloney, C. 1988. *Behaviour and poverty in Bangladesh*. Dhaka, Bangladesh: University Press Limited.

McGregor, J. A. 1994. Village credit and the reproduction of poverty in contemporary rural Bangladesh. In *Anthropology and institutional economics*, edited by J. Acheson, 261-82. London: University Press of America.

———. 1998. *Evaluation of BRAC rural development II and III*. DFID evaluation study EV606. London: DFID.

———. 1999. Growing NGOs: The relationship between donors and NGOs in microfinance. Paper presented at the DSA Conference, Bath, UK, 12-14 September.

Stiles, K. 2002. International support for NGOs in Bangladesh: Some unintended consequences. *World Development* 30 (5): 835-46.

Thornton, P., J. Devine, P. Houtzager, and D. Wright. 2000. Partners in development: A review of big NGOs in Bangladesh. Unpublished report commissioned by DFID-Bangladesh.

Uphoff, N., Milton Esman, and A. Krishna. 1998. *Reasons for success: Learning from instructive experiences in rural development*. West Hartford, CT: Kumarian Press.

Wood, G. D. 1994. *Bangladesh: Whose ideas, whose interests?* Dhaka, Bangladesh: UPL, Intermediate Technology.

World Bank. 1996. *Pursuing common goals: Strengthening relations between government and development NGOs*. Dhaka, Bangladesh: University Press.

An Innovative Combination of Neoliberalism and State Corporatism: The Case of a Locally Based NGO in Mexico City

By
ROGER MAGAZINE

Nongovernmental organizations are frequently represented as the agents of international organizations, slaves to a singular neoliberal development paradigm imposed from above. In this article, the author describes a locally based nongovernmental organization in Mexico City that eludes such critiques by innovatively combining aspects of neoliberalism with elements of state corporatism. In its effort to improve the lives of street children and impoverished families, the organization borrows from neoliberalism its distrust of government and other potentially paternalistic institutions. Meanwhile, it rejects neoliberalism's reliance on the market and attempts to empower families and communities to act as intermediaries between individuals and the ravages of global capitalism.

Keywords: NGOs; street children; Mexico; neoliberalism; corporatism

Generally speaking, researchers have portrayed nongovernmental organizations (NGOs) in one of two manners. According to some, NGOs are heroic representatives of the civil society's interests in an ongoing battle against corrupt and abusive governments. According to

Roger Magazine is a professor and researcher in the Graduate Program in Social Anthropology, Department of Social and Political Sciences of the Universidad Iberoamericana in Mexico City, Mexico. He received his Ph.D. in anthropology from the Johns Hopkins University in 2000. He is the author of a number of articles and book chapters on soccer fan clubs and gangs of street children in Mexico City and is in the process of completing a book manuscript on the latter. Currently, he is conducting research on the effects of urban expansion in a village outside Mexico City.

NOTE: An early version of this article was presented at the 2001 Congress of the Latin American Studies Association, Washington D.C., 6-8 September, thanks to a LASA Congress Travel Fund grant. I am indebted to John Gledhill, the discussant, and the other participants for their valuable comments. I take full responsibility, however, for all shortcomings in the final version. I also wish to acknowledge the generous financial support provided by the Wenner-Gren Foundation for Anthropological Research, the Fulbright Foundation, and the Universidad Iberoamericana.

DOI: 10.1177/0002716203257103

others, NGOs are in cahoots with the international leaders who are imposing neoliberal policies on the weak states of underdeveloped nations: NGOs play the good cop role, easing the suffering caused by the bad cops' economic restructuring. While the categories "civil society" and "state" blind those who take the first approach to the common "governmentality" (Foucault 1991)[1] of actors working for governments and NGOs, the second overlooks the variation in local responses to global projects (Mintz 1977).

Logical contradictions between global and national projects do not inevitably result in conflict or cultural schizophrenia. . . . On the contrary, the juxtaposition of contradictory ideologies is a necessary, although not sufficient, condition for innovation.

In this article, I describe the practices of an NGO providing services for street children in Mexico City that does not fit either of these portrayals. The organization, although not part of the government and supposedly a representative of the interests of a small segment of the population, attempts to put into practice a new narrative for development: an undoubtedly state-like practice. Meanwhile, even though it receives funding from international private donors and employs aspects of the neoliberal narrative in its practices, it adds these aspects to segments of nationalist narratives in such a way as to create an innovative scheme irreducible to the sum of its parts.

This latter characteristic of the NGO carries a pair of implications. First, logical contradictions between global and national projects do not inevitably result in conflict or cultural schizophrenia among local leaders. On the contrary, the juxtaposition of contradictory ideologies is a necessary, although not sufficient, condition for innovation. Second, this innovation can only succeed under particular organizational circumstances. That is, the NGO I discuss here, because it is locally based, enjoys greater success in its attempts at innovation than organizations that are local branches of international NGOs and thus find their attempts at innovation hindered by responsibilities to a central authority. After describing the NGO's practices and situating them in the context of twentieth-century Mexican governmental strategies, I will further discuss these implications of its innovative capacity.

NGOs and Street Children in Mexico City

My interest in this and other NGOs emerged out of field research on gangs of so-called street children in Mexico City. Many of the street children I knew spoke of their past or ongoing experiences with governmental and nongovernmental service-providing organizations. I began to visit the organizations that the street children most frequently mentioned and to interview one or more of the workers. One NGO in particular, known as Educación de Niños Callejeros (EDNICA), caught my interest, and I decided to study it more closely using in-depth interviews and participant observation.

When I asked workers at other organizations for a recommendation of the NGOs I should include in my research, without fail, they all put EDNICA at the top of their list and described it as doing the best and most innovative work in the city. EDNICA is not typical of NGOs working with street children in Mexico City, but it does exemplify an ideal for most workers at other organizations. In fact, a group of young women and men with experience working at other organizations, but dissatisfied with their objectives and methods, founded the NGO in 1989 as an alternative. When I told EDNICA's workers in September of 1996 of my wish to conduct an in-depth study of the organization, they invited me to join them as a volunteer. For the following nine months, I spent one day a week at the NGO as a volunteer and researcher.

The NGO Workers' Ideal: EDNICA

Workers at other organizations mention two factors when praising EDNICA. First, they state that the organization's programs are set up to "help the street children help themselves" rather than provide for all their needs. Second, they say that EDNICA gives priority to the family, attempting to reintegrate street children into their families and doing preventive work to stop other children from leaving their homes.

EDNICA workers themselves employ comparisons to government agencies to explain their objectives. They state that most government agencies' and some NGOs' practices are *asistencialistas*, meaning that instead of assisting street children, they give them everything they need, which makes them complacent and dependent. EDNICA workers also describe the resulting relation as paternalistic since the street children come to depend on the agency like a child depends on his or her parents. In contrast, they explain, their objective is to demand (*exigir*) that the street children be active participants in changing their own lives and leaving behind life in the street. This aspect of the organization's project recalls the bottom-up strategies integral to theories of sustainable development (see below). Furthermore, they posit that the government's capitulation to neoliberalism has led to the elimination of state protection, thereby individualizing people already on the economic margins and exposing them to the ravages of global capitalism.[2] In response, their efforts to strengthen familial as well as community bonds are aimed at creating intermediaries between individuals and global capitalism and a collective basis for political action. This second side of EDNICA's project resonates with Durkheim's (1992) call for secondary groups to mediate between state power and newly individualized persons in the context of late-nineteenth-century liberalism (Cladis 1992).

EDNICA's distinctive organizational structure reflects and resonates with these two goals. Most NGOs are organized around a *casa hogar* (group home). They send workers out to convince street children to come and live in the casa hogar. If they agree to come live there, the street children are subjected to a rigid schedule meant to resocialize them. Once the children are considered resocialized, the NGO helps them to begin an independent existence or to rejoin their families. Compared to the typical NGO, EDNICA is decentralized. It consists of an administrative office, a small casa hogar[3] in another part of the city, and most important, *los clubes de calle* (the street clubs)—an organizational structure conceived of specifically to prevent the paternalism resulting from *asistencialismo* (overassistance) and the individual vulnerability caused by neoliberalism.

EDNICA approaches community leaders in areas of the city where street children live and where a significant population of impoverished families is at risk of having children leave home for the street and proposes the establishment of a street club as a joint venture between EDNICA and the community. The street club is a space where both the street children and neighborhood at-risk children can get an inexpensive healthy meal, basic medical treatment, family or individual psychological therapy, or help with homework. At the club, they can also participate in recreational activities, learn work skills such as carpentry or hairstyling, learn to solve community and other problems through collective organization, or just hang out in a safe, drug-free environment. EDNICA provides training for community volunteers and employees. The NGO—with funding from national and international private sources—and the community share the costs of establishing the space and paying the staff for the first few years; then the community takes over the club completely and EDNICA moves on to do the same in another area. Thus, the overall organizational structure of the club is meant to prevent overassistance by involving community members and individual vulnerability by fomenting familial and community bonds.

When I first learned of EDNICA, it was getting ready to leave the first street club, in a working-class neighborhood surrounding the Observatorio metro stop, in the hands of the community. The local parish had provided land to build the street club beside the church, and the priest was an active participant in the project. The club counted eight employees, half paid by the NGO and half paid by the parish. EDNICA was waiting for the community (the parish or otherwise) to provide enough funding or volunteers to take over the project, after which EDNICA would move its employees on to another club. Twenty-five street children and more than three hundred at-risk children were participating in the club's activities at the time.

The street club occupies a new three-story building beside the church. The first floor contains showers for the street children and rooms for group activities. The second floor consists of a kitchen and a large room used as a dining hall or a meeting place. The third floor includes an area where neighborhood children can get help with their homework, a living room with a TV and ping-pong table where the street children can pass the daytime hours, and offices used for staff meetings and therapy sessions. Finally, there is a small room on the building's roof where a couple of the street children had asked to sleep as part of their effort to leave the street.

EDNICA's workers talk about working toward *fortalecimiento* (empowerment) or *ayudándolos a ayudarse* (helping them to help themselves). My own observations suggest that their efforts at empowerment are focused at three different levels: the family, the community, and the individual.

Familial Empowerment

The fact that EDNICA's first priority is familial empowerment makes sense if we consider its concept of what constitutes a street child. According to workers at EDNICA, street children are people who have left their parents' home and have cut off relations with their parents or other familial guardians. This separation is seen as a problem because they consider the family to be the only source of genuine emotional support as well as an important source of economic support. The street child is imagined as vulnerable to the sufferings of rejection, loneliness, and poverty without the family. Whether or not they are legally children (younger than eighteen) matters little to the boundaries of the category. EDNICA workers state that young adults can be considered street children because they find themselves in the same predicament of vulnerability without familial support.

How EDNICA goes about solving this problem through familial integration must be understood in the context of how they imagine the process of separation. EDNICA's therapists explain that the process of leaving home begins when neoliberal economic policies bring about a lowering of wages. The wage earner, imagined as a man, has no outlet for his frustrations, so he takes them out on his family. Other family members, also with no outlet, take out their frustration at being treated badly by the father on weaker family members. EDNICA therapists posit that one child, with a particular personality type, usually takes most of the blame. This is the child most likely to leave home both to escape abuse and to help the family since he or she feels he or she has caused the family's problems.

EDNICA's workers claim that this misplaced blame and guilt is the biggest problem to be overcome to achieve reintegration or to prevent separation in the case of at-risk children. When working with street children, the therapists begin with individual therapy to help the person realize that he or she is not the cause of the family's problems but also that his or her abusers cannot ultimately be blamed for their actions. At this point in the reintegration process, the therapists expect that the street child will have realized his or her true desire to return to his or her family. EDNICA's workers state they are careful not to rush the process, forcing the street children to face too much psychological trauma too quickly, which would lead them to reject help, nor to go too slowly and not push the child, which is like asistencialismo and would lead to a stagnant relation of dependency.

When the street child demonstrates a desire for reintegration, the therapists and the street child visit his or her home to see if his or her family members are willing to participate in family therapy. If the family is unwilling, EDNICA may try again later to convince them or may just settle for helping the street child through individual and group empowerment. If the family is willing, they come to the street club for regular family therapy sessions until the therapists consider the misplaced

> *The organization's programs are set up to "help the street children help themselves" rather than provide for all their needs. . . . EDNICA gives priority to the family, attempting to reintegrate street children into their families and doing preventive work to stop other children from leaving their homes.*

blame and guilt to be gone and feel that the street child is ready to go live with the family. They conduct follow-up visits to check how the reintegrated family is doing. Overall, the NGO workers conceive of the problem in a way that puts the blame on neoliberal policy, but that involves the actions of family members. Thus, even though they cannot bring about large-scale economic change, they feel that they can still do something to resolve the problem in an immediate sense.

They are careful to point out that rather than imposing their own interests on the family through therapy, they do "exactly what the family wants." In doing so, they see themselves as avoiding the unequal exchanges of a paternalistic relation wherein a street child receives benefits in exchange for doing what the organization wants. Yet avoiding paternalism also involves limiting access to services offered. For example, workers visit the homes of at-risk families to evaluate the family's precise needs. Depending on those needs, EDNICA offers each family a particular combination of services, such as low-cost afternoon meals, basic medical services, help with homework, or family therapy. According to EDNICA workers, maintaining the provision of services contingent on need is necessary to avoid asistencialismo and dependence and to encourage families to resolve their own problems.

Empowering Community

EDNICA hopes to achieve the empowerment of the residents in the area around the street club through community members' participation in the club itself. In addition, the NGO attempts to foment group consciousness among the street children and the at-risk children with the intention of encouraging them to come up with their own solutions to problems—an alternative to the dependency of asistencialismo—and to make collective demands—as a response to the increased individual vulnerability brought about by neoliberalism. To achieve these goals, EDNICA organizes the street and neighborhood children into seven different groups. The street children constitute one group, while the neighborhood children are divided up into six different groups depending on age and income levels. One of the staff members explained to me that these divisions were necessary because children at different ages and with different income levels experience different problems. She added that each group elects a leader through a democratic process and that the leaders of the groups meet regularly to discuss common problems. The neighborhood children's parents also meet every month to try to resolve problems in a collective manner.

Individual Empowerment

The third objective, individual labor skills acquisition and empowerment, is seen as a last resort when family reintegration is not an option. It is somewhat problematic for the EDNICA workers since individual skill acquisition and empowerment, although formidable barriers to asistencialismo, do nothing to counter the individualizing effects of neoliberalism. According to EDNICA's therapists, after they help street children to stop feeling guilt over leaving home and thus help them to realize that they can stop punishing themselves by living in the street, they encourage them to enter a group home if younger than eighteen or live independently if eighteen or older. To help the street children confront this novel situation, EDNICA teaches job skills such as carpentry and hairstyling as well as money management and other abilities deemed necessary for living alone. It also organizes a carpentry cooperative at the club that some of the older street children work for and help to run.

Although they sometimes perceive their own failure to achieve their goal of simultaneously impeding the effects of both asistencialismo and neoliberalism, in general, EDNICA's workers are confident that their primary strategies of empowering families and communities can prevent the formation of relations of dependency while counteracting the vulnerability of individuals without state protection. In the next section, I discuss the dominant narratives for national betterment and principal governmental strategies in twentieth-century Mexico in an attempt to place EDNICA workers' concerns in a broader social and historical context.

Governmental Strategies and Narratives
for the Nation in Twentieth-Century Mexico

EDNICA workers' preoccupation with asistencialismo must be understood in the context of what political scientists refer to as state corporatism and historians know as the narrative of revolutionary nationalism. The origins of this governmental form are generally linked to the presidency of Lázaro Cárdenas in the 1930s. The Cárdenas administration, in the name of the Mexican Revolution, expropriated land from large estates and redistributed it to peasants in the form of plots known as *ejidos*. Imitating indigenous communalism, the ejidos could not be bought or sold, but the national government retained control of this communalism through direct administration of the ejidos. In addition, Cárdenas expropriated foreign interests in certain sectors such as the oil industry and established a number of state-owned enterprises in which not only the management but also the workers' unions were administered by the government. These actions paved the way for the implementation of broader import substitution policies in the years following his administration. While Cárdenas' "great political achievement was to bring popular movements under state control by incorporating local peasant and worker organizations into national confederations" (Gledhill 1994, 106), his great historical achievement was to establish as a narrative for national prosperity the struggle to prioritize national interests over those of global capitalism.

This political strategy of incorporation led to the formation of what participants and analysts alike describe as a combined political and social structure in the form of a pyramid, with the president at the apex, peasants and industrial workers constituting the base, and administrators and regional and local political leaders in between (Lomnitz 1982). A series of exchanges between patrons and clients hold the pyramid together. Services, jobs, and in general, protection from the ravages of international capitalism are exchanged downward in return for loyalty, which is passed from the bottom up. The problem of asistencialismo arises out of this context. While the pyramid provides people like street children with services, its stability and very existence depends on their continued positioning at the base of the pyramid as clients of government institutions.

Meanwhile, EDNICA's concerns with neoliberalism must be understood in the context of the national government's adoption in the 1980s of a narrative for national prosperity diametrically opposed to Cárdenas's. In response to the debt crisis of 1982, international and national leaders blamed the country's economic problems on state control over the economy and argued that only global capitalism could bring prosperity (see Cornelius 1996; Cornelius, Craig, and Fox 1994; González de la Rocha and Escobar Latapí 1991; Otero 1996). EDNICA's workers and other critics claim that the privatization of national industries and the end of import substitution policies, rather than bringing prosperity to Mexicans, have made them the victims of global capitalism's need for cheap and flexible labor. They are also aware that neoliberal policy shifts include a reduction of government spending on social welfare, but they are less critical of this change. They realize that this situation forces the government to accept and even to require their services. Plus, they see that it has lessened and weakened, although not eliminated, government agencies' *asistencialista* practices, freeing more street children from the grips of paternalism and giving them an opportunity to change their lives.

The process of leaving home begins when neoliberal economic policies bring about a lowering of wages.

But while EDNICA bases its work on a critique of these two prosperity narratives, revolutionary nationalism and neoliberalism, it draws on these same two narratives or at least on the broader symbolic orders or metanarratives from which they emerge for its solutions. EDNICA's strategy of prioritizing and empowering the family and the community and Cárdenas's attempt to create a corporate unit at the national level to shield individual citizens from global capitalism both resonate with intellectuals' representations of indigenous social institutions. Meanwhile, EDNICA's idea of helping the family, community, or individual to help himself in an effort to prevent the formation of a harmful relation of dependence between the welfare agency and the beneficiary draws on aspects of liberalism. More specifically, it reflects the liberal notion that there are cases in which problems of governance should be solved not by improving or augmenting government action but by reducing it since governmental action itself may constitute a chief cause of the problem. While EDNICA opposes the application of liberal strategies to certain aspects of governance such as the regulation of the national economy, it supports their application in the context of the prevision of social welfare services by the government or NGOs.

Political scientists note that the "popular social movements" of the late 1980s, in particular *neocardenismo* (the movement surrounding the 1988 presidential campaign of Lázaro Cárdenas's son Cuauhtémoc Cárdenas), combine in a similar manner aspects of revolutionary nationalism and neoliberalism. Jaime Tamayo (1990), for example, posited,

> *Neocardenismo* reversed the tendency of social movements to sectorialize their demands by permitting their insertion into a national project that aggregated all criticisms of the economic and social policy of the regime and arguments for the defense of national sovereignty and the rejection of the state party and corporatism. (P. 131)

Joe Foweraker (1990) noted that this combination, at first sight, appears contradictory: "but is there not some contradiction in talking of popular movements that defend the corporatist state, with its institutional charisma and discretional use of law, while struggling simultaneously for an *estado de derecho*?" (p. 16). He answered in the negative: "the popular movements clearly defend corporatism for the social pact it enshrines, and not for the clientelistic lines of control it contains and organizes" (p. 16).

Thus, participants in social movements as well as, I would add, NGO workers can and do integrate certain aspects of metanarratives or ideologies into their practices while rejecting others. In fact, one could argue that the formulation of a novel governmental strategy—on the part of a social movement, an NGO, or a government—must combine elements of two or more previously existent and contradictory strategies. If the strategies were not contradictory, nothing new would be produced through their combination. Claudio Lomnitz (1996) has stated otherwise. He posited that contradictions between national and global narratives in contemporary Mexico obviate the possibility of innovation.

Fissures in Mexican Nationalism?

Lomnitz (1996) argued that the recent shift in favored modernizing formulas at the global level from one based on national protectionism to one based on integration into the flows of global capitalism has thwarted attempts to come up with a new narrative for the Mexican nation. He suggested that in the age of revolutionary nationalism, what was good for the nation was good for achieving global standards of modernity and vice versa but that in the age of neoliberalism, a fissure has opened between the two projects: some view the open economy of neoliberalism as a threat to things Mexican, including the nation, while others view things Mexican as impediments to achieving global standards of modernity. Because of the separation of the two projects, attempts to gain ground in either direction are doomed to imperfection and only partial success since modernizers can never shed their so-called dismodern Mexicanness, and nationalists, with their hopes for national betterment measured on an international scale, are closet modernizers. Lomnitz stated that Mexicans, or at least Mexico City residents, consider the impure results of these incomplete efforts a vulgar kind of kitsch and have adopted the derogatory term *naco* (originally, "country bumpkin") to describe their agents.

According to Lomnitz's (1996) formulation, EDNICA would be a naco organization. Yet workers at other organizations do not criticize EDNICA in this manner. On the contrary, I heard nothing but praise for its work. I propose that Lomnitz's understanding of the production of narratives for the nation in contemporary Mexico cannot account for the case of EDNICA and that a slight reformulation of Lomnitz's thinking is called for. We need a conceptual framework that can account not only for failed instances of cultural borrowing but for successful ones as well.

Impersonation: A Framework for Understanding Cultural Borrowing

Roy Wagner (1972) conceptualized impersonation as "simply another form of metaphorization, representing people or objects in the form of other known cultural elements to extend the given, literal forms of culture into meaningful relations" (p. 9). Thus, "one 'becomes' a father, friend, or a good host by 'acting like' one, hence by impersonating the role" (p. 170). Among the Daribi of New Guinea, possession by a ghost is an example of impersonation. This act of impersonation extends the abilities and characteristics of the medium into the realm of the dead—the medium can communicate with the spirits of other dead people—and extends the abilities and characteristics of the dead into the realm of the living—the ghost gains physical form, making him imaginable and accessible to the living. The medium "becomes the embodiment of an innovative relation, a sort of human metaphor, for he is animated simultaneously by two identities and wills" (p. 132). Not reducible to either a dead or a live being, he is an innovative extension of both.

I suggest that it is helpful to think of what EDNICA's workers do as impersonation. When they give priority to the family and community over the individual, they are impersonating Mexico's corporatist leaders such as Lázaro Cárdenas. When they help street children to help themselves, they are impersonating the protagonists of neoliberalism. By empowering families and communities, they perform a double impersonation, extending their abilities to include those of both national and global leaders.

But what of the apparent paradox implied by a neoliberal corporatist? Wagner (1972) responded,

> These contradictions only assume the form of paradoxes when we think of them as simultaneously "valid" corollaries of a consistent "belief-system," and thus ignore their dialectical relationship. And this, in turn, suggests that the conceptual basis of a culture can never be adequately summed up as a logical ordering or a closed system of internally consistent propositions. (P. 10)

Not primarily concerned with upholding the consistency of belief systems, the NGO workers in Mexico City readily accept EDNICA's double impersonation.

Yet impersonation does not preclude the possibility of *naquismo*. Not all are successful:

> The efficacy of such undertakings is directly dependent on the degree to which the participants are able to assume their roles. . . . If the roles are maintained, the dual and mediating significance of the performance is realized; if not, the performance becomes a parody. (Wagner 1972, 172).

Thus, an impersonation appears vulgar not, as Lomnitz (1996) suggested, when it is incomplete in the sense of remaining partially what it was originally. Rather, it becomes a parody only when it is incomplete in the sense of failing to combine what it was originally with something else. The difference between innovation and naquismo lies not in the disparity among the elements involved but in the performance of the act of appropriation.

To understand what makes EDNICA's performance a success in the eyes of workers at other organizations, we must take into account two factors: first, the homogeneity of local workers at these organizations and, second, EDNICA's unique history and structure. The majority of the workers at these organizations are women from the Mexico City area, between twenty and thirty-five years old, and trained in social work, psychology, pedagogy, or sociology at the National Autonomous University, the traditional training ground for government workers and politicians at the national level. The fact that almost all of them place EDNICA at the top of their lists is understandable if we consider that this category of persons conceived of, founded, and continues to run EDNICA, while most of the other NGOs are local branches of international organizations. In other words, local workers enjoy greater autonomy at EDNICA than they do at other organizations where local workers must conform to objectives shaped outside the country.

For example, most of these organizations revolve around large group homes. While local workers have been able to implement projects aimed at reuniting street children with their families, the group homes, with their asistencialista implications, dominate the efforts of these organizations. With large group homes overshadowing the locally implemented projects of familial integration, these organizations come across to local workers as foreign actors imitating local trends. Thus, while not simply handmaidens to a central authority, local workers at these organizations are unable to pull off a convincing innovation.

EDNICA and Sustainable Development

Even though EDNICA does not concern itself directly with environmental problems, its project clearly resonates with and has potential to contribute to thinking about sustainable development. Proponents of sustainable development have proposed transferring responsibility for development planning and implementation from organizations to the beneficiaries themselves (see Barkin 1998). They argue that the beneficiaries are more likely to achieve sustainability since they, unlike many organizations, will not lose sight of their best long-term interests. Similarly, EDNICA's plans derive from distrust of the government and certain NGOs, arguing that these organizations often end up more concerned with their own need of maintaining clients than with the well-being of street children and at-risk families. EDNICA's effort to bypass these organizations and place projects in the hands of families, communities, and individuals is aimed at achieving real and lasting improvement in people's lives and avoiding the temporary fixes that bind clients to paternalistic organizations.

The case of EDNICA suggests that plans for sustainable development or even the discourses underlying these plans do not necessarily originate among "Western scientists," "the fathers of the World Bank," or the "few cosmopolitan Third Worlders who made it to the World Commission" like the versions Arturo Escobar (1995, 193) critiqued. EDNICA's project is based on the innovative combination of contradictory discourses by young women and a few men in Mexico City. Furthermore, EDNICA demonstrates that such plans need not derive from a market-based economics (Escobar 1995, 197): the organization's focus on family and community as intermediary institutions is deliberately opposed to the effects of a free

---

EDNICA's plans derive from distrust of the government and certain NGOs, arguing that these organizations often end up more concerned with their own need of maintaining clients than with the well-being of street children and at-risk families.

---

market. Of course, Escobar's (1995) critique could be applied on a different scale since the innovation I have described comes from the NGO and not from the street children, the at-risk families, or the community. While my research provides data to comment on the EDNICA's plan and the initial stages of implementation, further investigation is needed to measure the success of the project, to see how much room it leaves for innovation at other levels once the organization pulls out, and the extent to which power remains in the hands of a few at the community level, reproducing the top-down problem at still another level. Despite the fact that EDNICA is undoubtedly not above the kind of critique posed by Escobar, it does offer a concrete example of a plan for sustainable development that is not determined by a singular development paradigm imposed from above.

Conclusion

An analysis that focuses on the conflict between the logical premises of neoliberalism versus state corporatism will unfailingly conclude that the NGO workers face a paradox or a choice between the better of two evils. Perhaps our tendency as researchers to abstract, define, and categorize requires that we abstract elements that our informants have combined in successful impersonations and thus leads to this kind of analysis, that is, an analysis that examines ideologies, narratives, or discourses without taking into account the practices that constantly place them in dialectical relationships. The case of EDNICA demonstrates that although the terms *global* and *national* may be useful for describing contradictory narratives, we must be prepared to follow our informants when they move beyond these categories in favor of innovative combinations irreducible to their parts.

Notes

1. Foucault (1991) used this term to describe the modern preoccupation with the welfare or prosperity of a population. It includes a preoccupation over the extent of state responsibility. Thus, "governmentality" encompasses the state rather than the other way around.

2. It is important to note that the common notion of preneoliberal state protection in Mexico is perhaps more myth than reality. That is, many Mexicans were exposed to the ravages of global capitalism all along.

3. Educación de Niños Callejeros's *casa hogar* has fewer than twenty residents. Many of the group homes in Mexico City have more than twenty-five, and a couple count more than one hundred.

References

Barkin, David. 1998. *Wealth, poverty and sustainable development*. México, DF: Centro de Ecología y Desarrollo/Editorial Jus.

Cladis, Mark. 1992. *A communitarian defense of liberalism: Emile Durkheim and contemporary social theory*. Stanford, CA: Stanford University Press.

Cornelius, Wayne A. 1996. *Mexican politics in transition: The breakdown of a one-party-dominant regime*. San Diego: Center for U.S.-Mexican Studies, University of California, San Diego.

Cornelius, Wayne A., Ann L. Craig, and Jonathan Fox, eds. 1994. *Transforming state-society relations in Mexico: The national solidarity strategy*. San Diego, CA: Center for U.S.-Mexican Studies, University of California, San Diego.

Durkheim, Emile. 1992. *Professional ethics and civic morals*. London: Routledge.

Escobar, Arturo. 1995. *Encountering development: The making and unmaking of the Third World*. Princeton, NJ: Princeton University Press.

Foucault, Michel. 1991. Governmentality. In *The Foucault effect: Studies in governmentality*, edited by G. Burchell, C. Gordon, and P. Miller, 87-104. London: Harvester Wheatsheaf.

Foweraker, Joe. 1990. Popular movements and political change in Mexico. In *Popular movements and political change in Mexico*, edited by J. Foweraker and A. L. Craig, 3-20. Boulder, CO: Lynne Rienner.

Gledhill, John. 1994. *Power and its disguises: Anthropological perspectives on politics*. London: Pluto.

González de la Rocha, Mercedes, and Agustín Escobar Latapí, eds. 1991. *Social responses to Mexico's economic crisis of the 1980's*. San Diego: Center for U.S.-Mexican Studies, University of California, San Diego.

Lomnitz, Claudio. 1996. Fissures in contemporary Mexican nationalism. *Public Culture* 9:55-68.

Lomnitz, Larissa Adler. 1982. Horizontal and vertical relations and the social structure of urban Mexico. *Latin American Research Review* 17:51-74.

Mintz, Sidney W. 1977. The so-called world system: Local initiative and local response. *Dialectical Anthropology* 2 (4): 253-70.

Otero, Gerardo, ed. 1996. *Neoliberalism revisited: Economic restructuring and Mexico's political future*. Boulder, CO: Westview.

Tamayo, Jaime. 1990. Neoliberalism encounters *neocardenismo*. In *Popular movements and political change in Mexico*, edited by J. Foweraker and A. L. Craig, 121-36. Boulder, CO: Lynne Rienner.

Wagner, Roy. 1972. *Habu: The innovation of meaning in Daribi religion*. Chicago: University of Chicago Press.

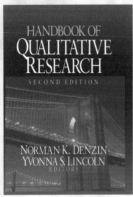
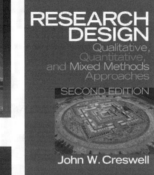

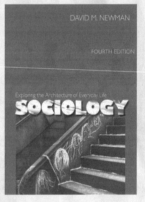

STATEMENT OF OWNERSHIP, MANAGEMENT, AND CIRCULATION
P.S. Form 3526 Facsimile

1. TITLE: THE ANNALS OF THE AMERICAN ACADEMY OF POLITICAL AND SOCIAL SCIENCE
2. USPS PUB. #: 026-060

3. DATE OF FILING: October 1, 2003

4. FREQUENCY OF ISSUE: Bi-Monthly
5. NO. OF ISSUES ANNUALLY: 6
6. ANNUAL SUBSCRIPTION PRICE: Paper-Bound Institution $454; Cloth-Bound Institution $513; Paper-Bound Individual $71; Cloth-Bound Individual $108

7. PUBLISHER ADDRESS: 2455 Teller Road, Thousand Oaks, CA 91320
   CONTACT PERSON: Mary Nugent, Circulation Manager
   TELEPHONE: (805) 499-0721

8. HEADQUARTERS ADDRESS: 2455 Teller Road, Thousand Oaks, CA 91320

9. PUBLISHER: Sage Publications Inc., 2455 Teller Road, Thousand Oaks, CA 91320
   EDITORS: Dr. Alan W. Heston, The American Academy of Political and Social Science, 113 Laurel Street, Fairhayen, MA 02719
   MANAGING EDITOR: Julie Odland

10. OWNER: The American Academy of Political and Social Science, 3814 Walnut Street, Philadelphia, PA 19104-6197

11. KNOWN BONDHOLDERS, ETC.
    None

12. NONPROFIT PURPOSE, FUNCTION, STATUS:
    Has Not Changed During Preceding 12 Months

13. PUBLICATION NAME: THE ANNALS OF THE AMERICAN ACADEMY OF POLITICAL AND SOCIAL SCIENCE

14. ISSUE FOR CIRCULATION DATA BELOW: JULY 2003

15. EXTENT & NATURE OF CIRCULATION:

		AVG. NO. COPIES EACH ISSUE DURING PRECEDING 12 MONTHS	ACT. NO. COPIES OF SINGLE ISSUE PUB. NEAREST TO FILING DATE
A.	TOTAL NO. COPIES	2958	3075
B.	PAID CIRCULATION		
	1. PAID/REQUESTED OUTSIDE-CO, ETC	1861	1954
	2. PAID IN-COUNTY SUBSCRIPTIONS	0	0
	3. SALES THROUGH DEALERS, ETC.	403	400
	4. OTHER CLASSES MAILED USPS	118	128
C.	TOTAL PAID CIRCULATION	2382	2482
D.	FREE DISTRIBUTION BY MAIL		
	1. OUTSIDE-COUNTY AS ON 3541	75	79
	2. IN-COUNTY AS STATED ON 3541	0	0
	3. OTHER CLASSES MAILED USPS	0	0
E.	FREE DISTRIBUTION OTHER	0	0
F.	TOTAL FREE DISTRIBUTION	75	79
G.	TOTAL DISTRIBUTION	2457	2561
H.	COPIES NOT DISTRIBUTED		
	1. OFFICE USE, ETC.	501	514
	2. RETURN FROM NEWS AGENTS	0	0
I.	TOTAL	2958	3075
	PERCENT PAID CIRCULATION	97%	97%

16. NOT REQUIRED TO PUBLISH.

17. I CERTIFY THAT ALL INFORMATION FURNISHED ON THIS FORM IS TRUE AND COMPLETE. I UNDERSTAND THAT ANYONE WHO FURNISHES FALSE OR MISLEADING INFORMATION ON THIS FORM OR WHO OMITS MATERIAL OR INFORMATION REQUESTED ON THE FORM MAY BE SUBJECT TO CRIMINAL SANCTIONS (INCLUDING FINES AND IMPRISONMENT) AND/OR CIVIL SANCTIONS (INCLUDING MULTIPLE DAMAGES AND CIVIL PENALTIES).

8/30/2003
Michael Rafter   Date
Director of Circulation
Sage Publications, Inc.